William Mason Grosvenor

Does Protection Protect?

An Examination of the Effect of Different Forms of Tariff upon American Industry

William Mason Grosvenor

Does Protection Protect?
An Examination of the Effect of Different Forms of Tariff upon American Industry

ISBN/EAN: 9783337811310

Printed in Europe, USA, Canada, Australia, Japan

Cover: Foto ©Suzi / pixelio.de

More available books at **www.hansebooks.com**

DOES PROTECTION PROTECT?

AN EXAMINATION

OF THE

EFFECT OF DIFFERENT FORMS OF TARIFF UPON AMERICAN INDUSTRY.

BY

W. M. GROSVENOR,

EDITOR OF THE ST. LOUIS DEMOCRAT.

NEW YORK:

D. APPLETON AND COMPANY,

90, 92 & 94 GRAND STREET.

1871.

To the American Free Trade League,

Whose earnest efforts to diffuse information have awakened multitudes to examine the results of the system of protection, and, having examined, to perceive the failure of that system, and whose ready contributions have secured a wide circulation for the reports of Commissioner Wells and for the writings of other inquirers like myself, this book is dedicated with great respect.

CONTENTS.

INTRODUCTION.

TEN years ago a Representative in Congress, when called to account by his constituents for his vote on a tariff bill, replied, "I don't know any thing about the tariff, and I never pretended to." Yet this was a member from one of the largest commercial cities in the country, and nearly half of his constituents, by their votes soon afterward, testified that they preferred as their Representative a man who knew nothing about the tariff.

It has been fashionable to know nothing about this question. For nearly twenty years this country has been engaged in solving another problem, and men have been preferred for all positions, from lowest to highest, for qualifications quite distinct from those which enable a man to vote intelligently on a tariff bill. It has been fashionable, but it will be so no longer, to treat the tariff question as of little consequence. Everywhere men now begin to realize that business, industry, and individual well-being, are materially affected by legislation, and demand of each Representative not only the devoted loyalty of a patriot and the sincere purpose of an honest man, but the ability and the disposition to so shape legislation as to promote national prosperity. Labor conventions assemble; powerful leagues are formed in cities and States; audiences settle to the deepest attention whenever the speaker touches upon the method of taxation; official documents, crowded with statistics once thought dry, are sought for with unwonted eagerness; and public servants will henceforth need not only opinions but reasons for them. If any politicians fancy that a few well-turned phrases, or, at most, a few fragments of fact picked hurriedly from the ruins of theories overturned by the war, will serve their turn because "the people know nothing about this question, and never will understand it," they will surely learn their mistake. In some degree, the people have learned the responsibility which self-government imposes; they begin to see that men do not really govern themselves who do not understand the questions upon which they are voting, and they feel that, if they are to be fit to govern themselves, they must at least be able to determine whether the smooth speech or the spicy article contains fact or fallacy, sense or nonsense. Hence, from all quarters there is heard a demand for information upon this question, and those who examine it in earnest find it neither an inscrutable mystery nor an uninteresting topic.

I feel sure that my own experience has been that of many others. Born of Whig parents, trained under influences wholly favorable to the system of protection, and thrown, when I began life for myself, into editorial association with an able and experienced advocate of that policy, I rather borrowed than formed an honest belief that it was the wisest, and joined with sincerity, if not with clear understanding, in efforts to secure "protection for American industry." When the war closed, and we returned to peaceful pursuits, reconstruction engrossed attention. But, in the readjustment of industry, and in legislation since the war, prompted by frequent appeals by those interests which had been most favored, I saw reason to doubt whether the trial of the protective system had entirely justified the anticipations of its advocates. It seemed to me strange that, if protection had the desired effect, favored interests should be constantly demanding more protection, and I began to look into the question for myself. These pages are the result, and they are published in the hope that in some measure they may shorten the labor or aid the judgment of others who are honestly seeking to understand the tariff question.

It has not been my purpose to assail any theory, to defend any theory, or to set up any theory of my own. If any new idea is advanced, it is one which the facts have suggested. My object has been to ascertain facts. Having been somewhat familiar with writings of advocates and opponents of protection, I have been often annoyed at the incompleteness of the facts presented by each. When Prof. Perry exhibited a specimen of cloth, saying, "Duty eighty per cent.; excluded," I was hungry to know what a similar cloth of American manufacture cost now and under low duties. When Mr. Greeley stated that a yard of some woollen cloth cost not more in gold in 1869 than did the same quality in 1860, I did not dispute his fact, but regretted that he had not also stated how much the material cost per pound, how many pounds were used per yard, or how much similar cloth cost in other countries in 1860 and in 1869. He had given only one fragment of a fact; it seemed a pity that he had not given the whole fact. These morsels of information only sharpened but did not satisfy the appetite. With rare exceptions, men seemed to start with a theory fully formed, and to pick out here and there such facts as would support it, but did not give complete collocations of facts needed to decide questions at issue. Many honest debaters on either side seemed to have formed their opinions before they began to ascertain the facts. Now, a fixed theory possesses a more than magnetic power of drawing to itself congenial facts, and repelling all others. This world has all sorts of facts in it, and the man who searches with a fixed idea in his head will always find facts to fit that idea. In questions of political economy, this method may be called the seductive—and that science demands the inductive. He who would arrive at truth must invite all facts, and be content to take such theories as they may bring with them. I have honestly endeavored to follow this method; to obtain full records bearing upon each point of inquiry, and to present them with such suggestions as the facts themselves seem to warrant.

I need not say that the information gathered is far less complete than I wish. To those who have had experience of the difficulty of collecting statistics, who know what strange contradictions occur between authorities deemed most reliable; who have spent days in searching old pamphlets or musty files for a single item, I need not apologize for imperfections.

It should, however, be stated that this work was substantially completed and prepared for publication early in January, 1870, and, though other duties delayed arrangements for publication several months, I have not had time to gather and add statistics of later date than January 1st.

DOES PROTECTION PROTECT?

CHAPTER I.

NATURE AND OBJECT OF THE INQUIRY.

WE are living under a high "protective tariff." What does the phrase mean? The theory of its advocates is that the industry of this country cannot prosper in competition with "the pauper labor" of Europe, and that certain products of foreign labor must therefore be excluded, or so increased in cost that they cannot compete with similar products of domestic labor. The avowed object is to check or prevent competition. But, if competition is prevented, to that extent importation of foreign products must be prevented; and, if importation of any foreign products is prevented, to that extent revenue by duties on imports must be sacrificed. With the protective tariff, therefore, the controlling object is protection—restraint or prevention of competition. To that object it makes some sacrifice of revenue. With a revenue tariff, on the contrary, the controlling object is to secure duties with the least burden, and to that object it sacrifices the idea of excluding foreign competition. Every revenue-tariff protects as far as it prevents foreign competition, or checks its force by enhancing the cost of foreign products. But its duties are adjusted with intent to secure the largest revenue at the smallest cost to the people. On the other hand, a protective tariff secures revenue only by virtue of provisions which do not exclude competition. But the theory of its advocates is that, when our industry is fostered by preventing or checking competition, our people are so prosperous that they buy more largely of foreign articles not excluded by duties, and that the revenue is thus increased. The protective system seeks first to check competition. The revenue system seeks first to fill the treasury.

We have been living since 1861 under tariffs intended to be protective. Whenever it has appeared that an important industry was still exposed to serious competition, that fact has been usually regarded as justifying an increase of duties. Eleven changes of the tariff have thus been made since the adoption of the act of March 2, 1861, and these frequent changes and the present condition of our industry have aroused men to inquire whether the protective system itself is in fact beneficial to the country.

National economy presents three methods of testing the prosperity of a country. The first is by the balance-sheet between that and other countries. The second is by ascertaining the increase in the production of wealth. The third is by ascertaining the distribution of wealth. If a nation imports in the way of trade more than it exports, due allowance being made for the profits of trade and for freights, it is running into debt. But a debt-involving purchase may so increase the productive power of the purchaser as to enable him to pay with interest, and realize ample profit. The second inquiry, whether the production of wealth by domestic industry is increased, is thus suggested. But the true national economy regards the welfare of the individuals who compose the nation rather than the aggregate of wealth. England's wealth is England's shame, if, in spite of great accumulation of property, the proportion of paupers is increasing. In the end, the richest country will be that in which the average condition of the laboring population most steadily and rapidly improves; for in that country the productive energies of the people are most fully employed and stimulated. When the labor of a country is improving in condition, and thus gaining both the power and the desire to produce more largely, the nation is enlarging its sources of wealth, though the balance of trade may be against it, or its production of wealth may be temporarily checked. But when the natural improvement in the condition of the laboring people of any country is retarded or stopped, that country is growing poorer; the very sources of its wealth are choked; and only a change in the condition of its labor can save it from decay. It matters not, then, how largely the balance of trade may be in its favor, or how vast may be the accumulations of wealth in the hands of a class. The power of growth and progress dies with the deterioration of the laboring people, and the loss of opportunity or stimulus to employ their energies to the utmost. Hence, to ascertain the present condition of a country, we examine its balance of trade and its production of wealth. But, to determine whether seeming prosperity is real, whether its apparent progress involves future disaster, whether the country is living within its income, and adding to its productive power, or wasting its very capital, and drying up the sources of its wealth, we must study the condition of its laboring population.

Tried by these tests, how is the condition of this country affected by the system of protection? It is not denied that many unfavorable symptoms appear. The balance of trade is against us. Most important branches of industry are checked in their progress. The Special Commissioner of the Revenue, in his report of January, 1869, presented statements which attracted very general attention in regard to the condition of the laboring class. But it is said that each of these unfavorable symptoms is due to other causes, and that the tariff has not produced, but has greatly diminished disasters. To test the correctness of this reasoning, it is necessary to trace the effect of different tariff systems in other times, to ascertain whether, other causes being absent, similar duties have in other times produced results such as we now witness.

Taking each of the three tests in order—foreign trade, production of wealth, and distribution of wealth—we shall endeavor to ascertain what results have been produced in common by the present and by former protective tariffs, and to compare them with the effects of tariffs for revenue. In brief, does the protective system benefit American industry?

CHAPTER II.

PROTECTION DOES NOT PREVENT OVERTRADING.

DURING the twelve months ending June 30, 1869, we imported merchandise and specie of the invoiced value of $437,026,541 in gold. In the same time we exported foreign and domestic goods and specie valued at $438,999,349 in currency. Reducing this to gold, we have $343,233,932 of exports, against $437,026,541 of imports, and a balance against us for the year 1869 * of $93,792,609 in gold.

---

* In these pages, instead of "the fiscal year ending June 30, 18—," the phrase "the year 18—" will be commonly used.

It is true that exports, if trade between this and other countries be profitable, have a purchasing power in foreign ports considerably greater than their valuation in our own. The merchant who ships a cargo of wheat or cotton to Liverpool expects to sell it there for a sum larger than its value here—enough larger to cover the cost of freight and yield a profit. But a large share, both of freight-money and of profits, goes to foreigners. The report for the year 1869 states that 69 per cent. of our imports and 67 per cent. of our exports were in foreign vessels, but the proportion of freight-money paid to foreign vessels is still larger, for the more expensive transatlantic trade is done more largely in foreign bottoms than the traffic with Canada, the West Indies, Mexico, and South America. Treasury returns do not enable us to ascertain accurately either the aggregate of freight-money, or the proportion paid to foreign vessels, but the aggregate has been estimated at sixty millions, and, if that estimate is correct, more than forty millions must be yearly paid for freight to foreign vessels. Of the profits of foreign trade, it is probable that a proportion equally large goes to foreign dealers, who have many agencies and branch houses in New York. Whatever difference there may be between the returned value of our exports and their purchasing power when delivered abroad, not less than two-thirds of it goes to foreigners, either in the form of freight-money or of profits, and not more than one-third can be regarded as applied to payment for our imports. Omitting reëxports, and deducting them from foreign imports also, we have net imports for the year $411,896,374, and domestic exports $318,103,765 in gold. It will hardly be supposed that the exports were enhanced in value by transportation more than 18 per cent. in the average, and, if we add one-third of this, 6 per cent., or $19,086,225, to the value of domestic exports, we have $337,189,990 as the purchasing power of those exports delivered in foreign ports. But the goods purchased were valued in foreign ports at $411,896,374.

Not only are we buying each year more than we sell, but we have a large foreign debt on which we pay interest. It has been estimated that at least six hundred millions of United States bonds are held abroad, and we have also State and city, railroad, and other corporation bonds held in Europe to an amount not known, on which some interest is paid. In September Mr. Greeley estimated that our whole bonded indebtedness to Europe was over one thousand million dollars. In his report for 1870, Special Commissioner Wells estimates that indebtedness at $1,400,000,000. If we suppose the lower estimate approximately correct, the interest on this sum, about sixty millions, must be paid by our exports. Let us suppose that we actually send abroad for interest-money only fifty millions; deducting this sum from the purchasing value of our exports, we have $287,189,990 in gold to pay for imports valued at $411,896,374, and the balance of trade against us for the year appears to be $124,706,384. Not even this large sum, it is believed, fully represents the real balance against us. It is known that, in many cases, foreign goods are invoiced at prices below their true value, to escape part of the duty. A Secretary of the Treasury has declared his belief that this undervaluation amounts to not less than fifty millions yearly. The actual balance against us may upon these estimates be placed at one hundred and seventy-five millions in gold.

In the statement of domestic exports was included the sum of $37,301,426 in specie exported. If, instead of treating gold as merchandise, we regard it as money, the balance against us will appear still greater. Our net imports of merchandise exceeded our exports of merchandise of domestic production by $131,094,035. Making the same estimates as before for the increased value of exports, freight, profits, interest, and undervaluations, the balance due from this to other countries appears to have been not less than $212,007,810, of which we remitted $37,301,426 in specie.

Never before, since this nation first declared its independence, has the balance against us been as large. In 1864 the merchandise balance was larger by over eighteen millions, but we remitted over ninety-two millions of specie, and had much less to pay on account of interest. In 1866 our imports were larger, but we exported so largely that the merchandise balance was only eighty-nine millions, and we remitted over seventy-five millions in specie. Prior to the war, the merchandise balance against us was never sixty-two millions, and we were then exporting only our surplus of gold. In a word, our foreign trade has never before presented as unfavorable an aspect as in the fiscal year 1869.

The people of this country have been taught by the advocates of a protective tariff that it would check overtrading, diminish imports, and cause them to be exceeded by exports, and thus turn the balance of trade in our favor. From the earliest days, men deservedly honored for ability and sincere patriotism have argued that high duties on imports must check purchases of foreign goods, and stimulate the production of needed wares and fabrics at home. Through years of heated political strife, this was ever a main and very effective argument in behalf of the protective system. It seemed consistent with the teachings of common-sense. Plain men, who did not think they fully understood the tariff question, still thought it clear that a high duty on one foreign article must check its importation, and hastily jumped to the conclusion that high duties on all would check the importation of all. So widely has this argument gained lodgment in the minds of men that to-day, whenever it is shown that we are buying more than we can pay for, and running into debt to Europe, not a few instinctively say, " We must shut out these foreign goods by a higher tariff ! " Nor is this the reasoning of those only who have not studied the question. Mr. Greeley has been for many years prominent in discussion of this subject, and has gained much reputation by an adroit use of facts, which has seemed to many readers to prove that he was fully and correctly informed. Undoubtedly there are few men in the country who have given to the subject more labor. In his work on " Political Economy," the ripest fruit of many years of investigation, he constantly betrays the presence and mastery in his mind of one fixed idea, that a high tariff will diminish imports. Thus, in his seventeenth chapter, he says: " When we had low tariffs, we increased debts abroad," and urges adherence to the essential provisions of the existing tariff, " with no expectation of supplying all our wants from domestic sources, but with a resolute, firm, intelligent purpose that our exports shall soon be made to overbalance our imports, so that we may cease transmitting to Europe bonds."

We are living to-day under the highest tariff ever enforced in this country. Beginning with a law deemed fully protective in 1861, in order to still more effectually exclude foreign goods, we have made eleven amendments or revisions, each raising the duties on some articles, and several adding materially to the general average of duties. In 1868 the amount collected by duties was 44 per cent. of the entire value of imports, and 48 per cent. of the value of all dutiable imports. The attempt to shut out foreign goods and diminish importations has been faithfully made, and persisted in for nine years, and yet we find that in the last year the balance of trade against us is greater than it has ever been before, under any tariff, since the earliest settlement of the country. If, under the highest duties ever imposed, the balance of trade against us becomes larger than ever before, must we not conclude that a high tariff does *not* prevent overtrading ?

The advocates of the existing tariff reply that the excess of imports is caused entirely by the inflation of the currency and the recent war. The correctness of this explanation may be tested by examining the effect of similar tariffs, in times when there had been no recent war, and when the currency was not inflated. At the close of this chapter will be found a table of exports and imports since the organization of the government, with the excess of either.

When the war of the Revolution ended in acknowledgment of the independence of these colonies, we had no central government empowered to control commerce with foreign nations, and the power of taxing imports was exercised at pleasure by the different States. In those dark days, the comparative liberality of New York encouraged foreign trade, and laid the foundation of her commercial supremacy. With the formation of a government empowered to regulate commerce began the history of our tariffs. Much stress has been laid upon the fact that the founders of the republic imposed duties upon imports. Their example is not necessarily an unerring guide. The nation was then weak; its industry was in its infancy. It does not appear that, in all the discussions of those times, any of those prominent in the formation of the government ever advocated discriminating duties except as a temporary measure, adapted to the condition of a people just beginning national existence. Still less does it appear that of these patriots there was a single one who imagined that it was possible to protect every branch of industry at once. Arguments offered in favor of any protection whatever contemplated only a temporary discrimination in favor of a few of the most important branches of industry. Whether these fathers of the republic believed in duties prohibitive in purpose, or tariffs averaging 44 per cent., we may judge from the fact that until 1807, when those difficulties with European powers began which led to embargoes and war, the duties actually imposed never averaged higher than 16 per cent. of the value of imports, and were usually about 10 per cent., and in six years even less. Yet we had just emerged from the war of the Revolution, with a heavy debt, and were then, if ever in our history, in a position to need protection for infant industries. The result proved the wisdom of moderate duties. A vast carrying-trade fell into our hands; the commerce of the young nation excited the envy and roused the fear of the most powerful; our imports for the years 1800 to 1807, inclusive, exceeded eight hundred millions of dollars. Nearly forty years after, during the eight years ending with 1845, they were but little greater. Nor was this rapid growth of commerce due to the carrying-trade alone.

2

In those early days we exported domestic produce worth forty or fifty millions yearly, and our progress in domestic industry was yet more wonderful. "Never in the history of the world," says Seybert, "was there a more rapid and extraordinary prosperity." Those great branches of manufacture, which have since been thought to need so much aid, then rapidly advanced under competition, and in 1810 were thought to be firmly established. The war interrupted our commerce, and caused a fatal inflation of our currency. Its close was followed by the extravagant importations which inflation invites, by the depreciation and abandonment of the currency, by prostration of banks and of business, and by general distress. The first tariff for protection was passed in 1816. The fact that this distress followed it only deserves mention as showing that protective duties do not prevent the disastrous effects which naturally flow from a corruption of the currency and an overthrow of the banking system.

The detailed records of the Treasury commence with 1821. In that year the country was still suffering from the disorder already described. But, as soon as it began to revive, importations increased. Demands for heavier duties, to shut out foreign goods, were answered by the higher tariff of 1824. Four years proved that it was not satisfactory, and a still higher tariff was granted in 1828. In the first period, 1821 to 1824 inclusive, the imports were $303,955,539, and exports, $287,820,350; excess of imports, $16,135,189. In the second period, 1825 to 1828 inclusive, under higher duties, imports were $349,305,444, and exports, $331,720,223; excess of imports, $17,585,221. In spite of the increased duties, imports had increased more than exports. Then the extreme protective tariff was adopted, Congress being determined, it would seem, to test the theory then held by advocates of protection, and still adhered to by Mr. Greeley, that high duties would make our exports exceed our imports. Accordingly, with "a firm, intelligent purpose" of that sort, the experiment was made, and in the third period, 1829 to 1832 inclusive, imports were $349,589,837, and exports were only $314,695,705; excess of imports, $34,894,132. It is true, imports were reduced in the first and second years under this tariff, but in the third rose to a larger value than had ever been imported in any year since the war. Meanwhile, exports had been reduced, and the balance of trade against us was increased from the seventeen millions of the preceding period to nearly thirty-five millions.

Never in our history have we given to any policy a longer, more uninterrupted, and faithful trial than we then gave to the plan of causing exports to exceed imports by means of protective duties, increased from time to time at the desire of protected interests. Is it not plain that the effort failed? Our imports, three times temporarily checked, had each time recovered more than they had lost, and during the whole period of twelve years had largely increased. But our exports had been checked, and, as compared with 1818, when the second protective tariff was passed, or 1825, the year after the third increase of duties, had been actually reduced. Meanwhile, no inflation of the currency had existed to account for these events. The protective system had been thoroughly and fairly tried. If history teaches any thing, if fair trial can prove any thing, it surely was proved, by the experiments of 1818 to 1832, that high duties do not permanently shut out importations, but do check exports of domestic products; and that protection, therefore, does not cause exports to exceed imports. The people of that time, at any rate, seem to have learned the lesson, for they demanded and obtained a change of policy.

We are seeking to ascertain the effect of former protective tariffs, in times when the currency was not inflated. The tariff of 1833–1842 was not protective, and during the years 1833–1837 occurred a remarkable inflation of the currency, accompanied by excessive importations, which will be considered at a proper time. The currency was not restored to a proper level until the closing years of that tariff, when imports fell below exports, and the years 1840–1842 inclusive show a balance of twenty-three millions in our favor. Nor did the protective tariff of 1842 immediately work a change; for, in the first year of its operation, the balance in our favor was about twenty millions. But in 1844 this balance was reduced to less than three millions; in 1845 the situation was so changed that imports exceeded exports by nearly three millions; and in 1846 the balance against us was over eight millions. The system was then a second time abandoned. This second experiment, adopted at a time when exports exceeded imports, in its first year, by twenty millions, in less than four years worked such a change that imports exceeded exports by over eight millions. In this case, also, it is impossible to say that inflation of the currency produced the result. For the currency in circulation was actually less in 1846, when the excess of imports was eight millions, than it was in 1840, when the exports exceeded imports by twenty-five millions. And in this instance, too, the same phenomenon is a second time presented—imports increased in spite of duties intended to check them; but exports were checked, remained almost stationary during the four years, and were smaller in 1846 than they had been in 1840, and smaller for the last three years of that tariff than they had been for the last three years of the tariff of low duties which had preceded.

The non-protective tariff of 1846 continued in operation until 1857, and was then changed for another of similar character, but lower duties.   The closing years of this period, the seven years 1855 to 1861 inclusive, deserve mention as the first in our history in which the balance of trade was turned decidedly in our favor.   For the first time our exports exceeded our imports every year, and the balance in our favor during the seven years named was one hundred and eighty-four millions.   Thus ended the first serious trial of the non-protective policy.   And, whereas the mere approach of that policy in 1840–'42 gave us the first three years of peace in which the aggregate of exports exceeded the aggregate of imports, the fair trial of that policy gave us in its last seven years a balance of one hundred and eighty-four millions in our favor.   Toward the close of the fiscal year 1861, the protective system was again adopted.   Since that time we have endeavored most faithfully, by frequently-increased duties, to exclude foreign goods.   Both in frequency of changes and in severity of imposts, this period surpasses any other in our history.   Its result, reducing exports to gold values, and including specie, has been as follows: imports, $2,598,849,217; exports, $1,796,988,873; balance against us, $284,600,939.   But of this aggregate of exports $517,259,405 has been in gold.   The balance of trade, not counting gold as merchandise, has therefore been $801,860,344, or one hundred millions a year against us.   Or, comparing this period with the preceding period of non-protection, the account stands thus: Non-protection, seven years, balance one hundred and eighty-four millions in our favor; protection, eight years, balance two hundred and eighty-four millions against us.

The first period, 1821–1824, of moderate protection, gave a balance against us of sixteen millions.

The second period, 1825–1828, of higher duties, gave a balance against us of over seventeen millions.

The third period, 1829–1832, of extreme protection, gave a balance against us of nearly thirty-five millions.

The fourth period, 1843–1846, of high protection, changed the situation from a balance in our favor of twenty millions to a balance against us of eight millions.

The fifth period, 1862–'69, of increasing and extreme duties, has given a balance against us of two hundred and eighty-four millions, although in the seven years preceding, under low and non-protective duties, the balance in our favor was one hundred and eighty-four millions.

If it be possible for any theory to be refuted, conclusively and forever, by official records, surely the theory that high protective duties check overtrading, prevent imports, and turn the balance of trade in our favor, is so refuted. And any man who clings to the protective system, "with a firm, intelligent purpose" to cause exports to exceed imports, has studied facts with little benefit, and his right to call his purpose "intelligent" may well be doubted. Indeed, the facts are so conclusive that the ablest writers who support protection now maintain that a high tariff not only permits, but encourages and even causes increased importations, or, in the words of Mr. Carey, that a protective is the only true revenue tariff.

It will be observed that it is not denied that inflation of currency stimulates increased importations, nor that inflation has increased the recent extravagant overtrading. But, by comparison with other periods in which the currency was not inflated, it has appeared that high tariffs check importations only for a single year or two, if at all, and that the accompanying decrease of exports has left the balance of trade against us larger in each period of high duties than in a corresponding period of lower protective or non-protective duties. From these facts it follows, not only that high tariffs do not prevent overtrading, but that they do not effectually shelter our industries against competition. If, in spite of them, or as Mr. Carey reasons, because of them, our people buy more largely of foreign products in the aggregate under high duties than under low duties, is there not already reason to suspect that a protective tariff, from some cause or other, tends to defeat its own object? It aims to exclude foreign goods. The facts prove that in the aggregate it does not exclude, but permits, if it does not cause, an increased importation of them. If the importation of some is lessened, that of others is increased still more largely, and hence, while some interests may be favored, the competition which American industry in the aggregate has to meet from foreign industry is increased rather than diminished. That this inference is not erroneous, will appear when the progress of manufactures is examined.

"But can a high tariff possibly cause increased importations?" it will be asked. In two ways. It may increase prices, secure artificial profits to particular industries at the expense of the community at large, increase the cost of living and the cost of production and of materials, so that the cost of our manufactured product is increased more than the duty adds to the cost of the foreign article. On the other hand, Mr. Henry C. Carey, whose acknowledged ability and vigor have made him the leader of the modern advocates of protection, maintains that a high tariff confers such blessings on a people, so stimulates their industry, so fully employs their labor, and secures to all such ample reward, as to enable them to buy of foreign nations more than they can under any other system. Both of these theories so far accord with the actual increase of importations after the effect of high duties is felt, that we may ascribe them to some examination of facts, rather than to that preconceived notion of what a tariff ought to do which alone can account for the idea that high duties prevent overtrading. But the theory of Mr. Carey does not account for the decrease of exports. In 1817, we were exporting $87,671,560, and, at the close of the long era of progressive protection in 1832, we were exporting only $87,176,943. Yet during that time population had increased from 8,918,687 to 13,698,665. In the only period of long-continued low duties, our exports increased from one hundred and nine millions in 1846, to three hundred and seventy-four millions in 1861, a gain of more than two hundred per cent. in fifteen years, while in the fifteen years under protection exports actually decreased! Moreover, if Mr. Carey's theory be accepted, it proves too much, for imports were vastly greater in 1837 and 1857, under low duties, than in any year prior to the war under high duties. If we are to ascribe increase of importations to a condition of prosperity, in which labor is well rewarded, and people are able to buy largely, then a condition of far greater prosperity appears to have existed under low duties, in the years mentioned and others, than in any time of high duties. A different explanation is needed to account for all the facts.

Exports and Imports, Gross Value, from the Beginning of the Government to June 30, 1869.

YEAR.	EXPORTS.			Total Imports.	Excess Exp'ts.	Excess Imp'ts.
	Domestic.	Foreign.	Total.			
1790	$19,566,000	$539,156	$20,205,156	$23,000,000	....	$2,794,844
1791	18,500,000	512,041	19,012,041	29,200,000	....	10,187,959
1792	19,000,000	1,753,098	20,753,098	31,500,000	....	10,746,902
1793	24,000,000	2,109,572	26,109,572	31,100,000	....	4,990,423
1794	26,500,000	6,526,233	33,026,233	34,600,000	....	1,573,767
1795	39,500,000	8,489,472	47,989,472	69,756,268	....	21,766,796
1796	40,764,097	26,300,000	67,064,097	81,436,164	....	14,372,067
1797	29,850,206	27,000,000	56,850,206	75,379,406	....	18,529,200
1798	28,527,097	33,000,000	61,527,097	68,551,700	....	7,024,603
1799	33,142,522	45,523,000	78,665,522	79,069,148	....	403,626
1800	31,840,903	39,130,877	70,971,780	91,252,768	....	20,280,988
1801	47,473,204	46,642,721	94,115,925	111,363,511	....	17,247,586
1802	36,708,189	35,774,971	72,483,160	76,333,333	....	3,850,173
1803	42,205,961	13,594,072	55,800,033	64,666,666	....	8,866,633
1804	41,467,477	36,231,597	77,699,074	85,000,000	....	7,300,926
1805	42,387,002	53,179,019	95,566,021	120,600,000	....	25,033,979
1806	41,253,727	60,283,236	101,536,963	129,410,000	....	17,873,037
1807	48,699,592	59,643,558	108,343,150	138,500,000	....	30,156,850
1808	9,433,546	12,997,414	22,430,960	56,990,000	....	34,559,040
1809	31,405,702	20,797,531	52,203,233	59,400,000	....	7,196,767
1810	42,366,675	24,391,295	66,657,970	85,400,000	....	18,742,030
1811	45,294,043	16,022,790	61,316,833	53,400,000	$7,916,833	....
1812	30,032,109	8,495,127	38,527,236	77,030,000	....	38,502,764
1813	25,008,132	2,847,865	27,855,927	22,005,000	5,850,927	....
1814	6,782,272	145,169	6,927,441	12,965,000	....	6,041,559
1815	45,974,403	6,583,350	52,557,753	113,041,274	....	60,483,521
1816	64,781,896	17,138,156	81,920,452	147,103,000	....	65,182,548
1817	68,313,500	19,358,069	87,671,560	99,250,000	....	11,578,440
1818	73,854,437	19,426,696	93,281,133	121,750,000	....	28,468,867
1819	50,976,838	19,165,686	70,142,521	87,125,000	....	16,982,479
1820	51,683,640	18,008,029	69,691,669	74,450,000	....	4,758,331
1821	43,671,894	21,302,488	64,974,382	62,585,724	2,088,658	....
1822	49,874,079	22,286,202	72,160,281	83,241,541	....	11,081,260
1823	47,155,408	27,543,622	74,699,030	77,579,267	....	2,880,237
1824	50,649,500	25,337,157	75,986,657	89,549,007	....	13,562,350
1825	66,944,745	32,590,643	99,535,388	96,340,075	3,195,313	....
1826	53,055,710	24,530,612	77,595,322	84,974,477	....	7,379,155
1827	58,921,691	23,403,126	82,324,727	79,484,068	2,840,659	....
1828	50,669,669	21,595,017	72,264,686	88,509,824	....	16,245,138
1829	55,700,193	16,658,478	72,358,671	74,492,527	....	2,153,856
1830	59,462,029	14,387,479	73,849,506	70,876,920	2,972,588	....
1831	61,277,057	20,033,526	81,310,583	103,191,124	....	21,880,541
1832	63,137,470	24,039,473	87,176,943	101,029,266	....	13,852,323
1833	70,317,698	19,822,735	90,140,443	108,118,311	....	17,977,868
1834	81,024,162	23,312,811	104,336,973	126,521,332	....	22,184,359
1835	101,189,082	20,504,495	121,693,577	149,895,742	....	28,202,165
1836	106,916,680	21,746,360	128,663,040	189,980,035	....	61,316,995
1837	95,564,414	21,854,962	117,419,376	140,989,217	....	23,569,841
1838	96,033,821	12,452,795	108,486,616	113,717,404	....	5,230,788
1839	103,533,891	17,494,525	121,028,416	162,092,132	....	41,063,716
1840	113,895,634	18,190,312	132,085,936	107,141,519	24,944,417	....
1841	106,382,722	15,469,081	121,851,803	127,946,177	....	6,094,374
1842	92,969,996	11,721,538	104,691,534	100,162,087	4,529,447	....
1843	77,793,783	6,552,697	84,346,480	64,753,799	19,592,681	....
1844	99,715,179	11,484,867	111,200,046	108,435,035	2,765,011	....
1845	99,299,776	15,346,830	114,646,606	117,254,564	....	2,607,958
1846	102,841,893	11,346,623	113,488,516	121,691,797	....	8,203,281
1847	150,637,464	8,011,158	158,648,622	146,545,638	12,102,984	....
1848	132,904,121	21,128,010	154,032,131	154,998,928	....	966,797
1849	132,666,955	13,088,865	145,755,820	147,857,439	....	2,101,619
1850	136,946,912	14,951,808	151,898,720	178,138,318	....	26,239,598
1851	196,689,718	21,698,293	218,388,011	216,224,932	2,163,079	....
1852	192,368,984	17,289,382	209,658,366	212,945,442	....	3,287,076
1853	213,417,697	17,558,460	230,976,157	267,978,647	....	37,002,490
1854	253,390,870	24,850,194	278,241,064	304,562,381	....	26,321,317
1855	246,708,553	28,448,293	275,156,846	261,468,520	13,688,326	....
1856	310,586,330	16,378,578	326,964,908	314,639,942	12,324,966	....
1857	338,985,065	23,975,617	362,960,682	360,890,141	2,070,541	....
1858	293,758,279	30,886,142	324,644,421	282,613,150	42,031,271	....
1859	335,894,385	20,895,077	356,789,462	338,768,130	18,021,332	....
1860	346,256,252	26,933,022	373,189,274	362,166,254	11,023,020	....
1861	362,191,047	20,645,427	382,836,474*	352,739,387	30,097,097	....
1862	199,107,587*	14,145,973	213,253,560*	275,446,939	....	62,193,379
1863	214,283,928*	26,123,584	240,407,512*	252,919,920	....	12,512,408
1864	221,710,108*	20,256,940	241,967,048*	329,565,134	....	87,598,086
1865	164,121,298*	32,114,157	196,235,455*	248,555,652	....	52,320,197
1866	402,399,967*	14,742,117	417,142,084*	445,512,158	....	28,370,074
1867	313,739,145*	20,611,508	334,350,653*	411,733,309	....	77,382,656
1868	330,592,764*	22,195,438	352,788,202*	373,409,448	....	20,621,246
1869	318,103,765*	25,130,167	343,233,932*	437,026,541	....	93,792,609

* Merchandise exports since 1860, reduced to gold values.

EXPORTS AND IMPORTS, COIN AND MERCHANDISE, FROM 1821 TO 1868, INCLUSIVE.

YEAR.	IMPORT ENTRIES.		Total.	RE-EXPORTS.		Net Imports.	COIN.
	Specie.	Merchandise.		Specie.	Total.		Domestic Exp.
1821..	$8,064,890	$54,520,834	$62,585,724	$10,478,059	$21,302,488	$41,283,236	....
1822..	3,369,846	79,871,695	83,241,541	10,810,180	22,286,202	60,955,339	....
1823..	5,097,896	72,481,371	77,579,267	6,372,897	27,543,622	50,035,645	....
1824..	8,379,835	81,169,172	89,549,007	7,014,552	25,337,157	64,211,850	....
1825..	6,150,765	90,189,310	96,340,075	8,797,055	32,590,643	63,749,432	....
1826..	6,880,966	78,093,511	84,974,477	4,098,678	24 530,612	60,443,865	$605,855
1827..	8,151,130	71,332,938	79,484,068	6,971,306	23,403,136	56,080,932	1,043,574
1828..	7,489,741	81,020,083	88,509,824	7,550,439	21,595,017	66,914,807	693,037
1829..	7,403,612	67,088,915	74,492,527	4,311,123	16,658,478	57,834,049	612,886
1830..	8,155,964	62,720,956	70,876,920	1,241,622	14,387,479	56,489,441	937,151
1831..	7,305,945	95,885,179	103,191,124	6,956,457	20,033,526	83,157,598	2,058,474
1832..	5,907,504	95,121,762	101,029,266	4,245,399	24,039,473	76,989,793	1,410,941
1833..	7,070,368	101,047,943	108,118,311	2,244,859	19,822,735	88,295,576	366,842
1834..	17,911,632	108,609,700	126,521,332	1,676,258	23,312,811	103,208,521	400,500
1835..	13,131,447	136,764,295	149,895,742	5,748,174	20,504,495	129,391,247	729,601
1836..	13,400,881	176,579,154	189,980,035	3,978,598	21,746,360	168,233,675	345,738
1837..	10,516,414	130,472,803	140,989,217	4,692,730	21,854,962	119,134,255	1,239,519
1838..	17,747,116	95,970,288	113,717,404	3,035,105	12,452,795	101,264,609	472,941
1839..	5,595,176	156,496,956	162,092,132	6,868,385	17,494,525	144,597,607	1,938,358
1840..	8,882,813	98,258,706	107,141,519	6,181,941	18,190,312	88,951,207	2,235,073
1841..	4,988,633	122,957,544	127,946,177	7,287,846	15,469,081	112,477,096	2,746,487
1842..	4,087,016	96,075,071	100,162,087	3,642,785	11,721,538	88,440,549	1,170,754
1843..	22,390,559	42,363,240	64,753,799	1,413,362	6,552,697	58,201,102	107,429
1844..	5,830,429	102,604,606	108,435,035	5,270,809	11,484,867	96,950,168	133,405
1845..	4,070,242	113,184,322	117,254,564	7,762,049	15,346,830	101,907,734	844,446
1846..	3,777,732	117,914,065	121,691,797	3,481,417	11,346,623	110,345,174	423,851
1847..	24,121,289	122,424,349	146,545,638	1,844,404	8,011,158	138,534,480	62,620
1848..	6,360,284	148,638,644	154,999,928	13,141,204	21,128,010	133,870,918	2,700,412
1849..	6,651,240	141,206,199	147,857,439	4,447,774	13,088,865	134,768,574	956,874
1850..	4,628,792	173,509,526	178,138,318	5,476,315	14,951,808	163,186,510	2,046,679
1851..	5,453,592	210,771,340	216,224,932	11,403,172	21,698,293	194,526,639	18,069,580
1852..	5,505,044	207,440,398	212,945,442	5,236,298	17,289,382	195,656,060	37,437,837
1853..	4,201,382	263,777,265	267,978,647	3,933,340	17,558,460	250,420,187	23,548,535
1854..	6,939,342	297,623,039	304,562,381	3,218,934	23,748,514	280,813,867	38,062,570
1855..	3,659,812	257,808,708	261,468,520	2,289,925	26,448,293	235,020,227	53,957,418
1856..	4,207,632	310,432,310	314,639,942	1,597,206	16,378,578	298,261,364	44,148,279
1857..	12,461,799	348,428,342	360,890,141	9,058,570	23,975,617	336,914,524	60,078,352
1858..	19,274,496	263,338,654	282,613,150	10,225,901	30,886,142	251,727,008	42,407,246
1859..	7,484,789	331,333,341	338,768,130	6,385,106	20,895,077	317,873,053	57,502,305
1860..	8,550,135	353,616,119	362,166,254	9,599,388	26,933,022	335,233,232	56,946,851
1861..	46,339,611	306,399,776	352,739,387	5,991,210	20,645,427	332,093,960	23,799,870
1862..	16,415,052	259,031,887	275,446,939	5,842,989	14,145,973	261,300,966	31,044,651
1863..	9,584,105	243,335,815	252,919,920	8,163,049	26,123,584	226,796,336	55,993,562
1864..	13,115,612	316,449,522	329,565,134	4,922,979	20,256,940	309,308,194	100,321,371
1865..	9,810,072	238,745,580	248,555,652	3,025,102	32,114,157	216,441,495	64,618,124
1866..	10,700,092	434,812,066	445,512,158	3,400,697	14,742,117	430,770,041	82,643.374
1867..	22,070,475	389,662,834	411,733,309	5,892,176	20,611,508	391,121,801	54,976,196
1868..	13,702,923	359,706,520	373,409,448	10,038,127	22,195,438	351,214,010	83,746,161
1869..	....	....	437,026,541	....	25,130,167	411,896,374	....

CHAPTER III.

CURRENCY AND IMPORTS.

No one who attentively considers the record of our foreign trade will fail to observe that the influence of changes of tariff, either to check or to stimulate importations, has been much less than has commonly been supposed. Great changes in the current of trade, for which no tariff accounts, have already been observed. The geologist, as he searches the surface of the earth for traces of its history, finds here and there paltry mounds which human hands have reared; here and there ridges or indentations which tell of the action of winds or waters. But, when, in his journeyings, he reaches the frowning mountain-ranges, stretching from continent to continent, where the very foundations of the earth have been uplifted, he reads there the working of tremendous forces which lie imprisoned within the earth itself; compared with which the waves and their ridges, the currents and their indentations, and the human hands which have heaped up little mounds, seem alike insignificant. In searching the history of commerce, we find slight changes which may be traced to the action of tariffs, or to temporary conditions in this country or in Europe. But there are also mighty upheavals which tell of a power greater than any of these. The line of our commerce now rises, in majestic swell, for a period of many years, and then suddenly drops again, as if the very foundations of trade had given way. Reading the record in the light of tariffs only, we are like those who puzzle over some hieroglyphic writing of which the key is yet unknown. The growth of imports from 1830 to 1837, the sudden collapse in 1837 and 1838, the advance of fifty millions in 1839, and the fall of nearly sixty millions which followed—these changes are not consistent with the regular reduction of duties by only two per cent., and they tell of a power far greater than these paltry changes of tariff which then occurred. Equally inexplicable, if we have only the tariff to guide us, are the sudden fall of eighty millions in imports in the year 1858, and the sudden recovery in 1859. To explain these changes, we must seek for a power more mighty in its influence over the prosperity and commerce of a country than any changes of tariff. We all know that in 1837 and 1857 there were great changes in our currency. Prior to those years there had been expansion of currency, and our imports had also been largely increased. In those years the banks suspended, the currency was violently contracted, and imports were suddenly reduced. These coincidences suggest some comparison of the changes of currency with the changes in our importations.

During the War of 1812, our currency increased from about forty millions to about one hundred millions in 1816, and was then reduced, by general overthrow of banks, to about fifty-five millions in 1820. In like manner, our imports for domestic consumption, which in 1807 had been about seventy millions, as soon as the war closed rose to over one hundred millions, and to one hundred and thirty millions in 1816, and were then reduced to about sixty millions in 1820. From 1820 to 1833 the currency increased a little faster than population, and our imports increased in like proportion. From 1833 to 1837 the currency rose very rapidly to two hundred and twenty-two millions, and the imports were in like manner increased from eighty to one hundred and sixty-nine millions. From 1837 to 1843 the currency was contracted from two hundred and twenty-two to one hundred and twenty-eight millions, and imports shrank from one hundred and sixty-nine to fifty-eight millions. Again, from 1843 to 1857, the currency was expanded from one hundred and twenty-eight to four hundred and seventy-four millions, and the gross imports rose from sixty-four to three hundred and sixty millions. In 1857 the currency was violently contracted, and imports were instantly reduced. For more accurate comparison a diagram is necessary. The quantity of currency actually in circulation at different periods it is not possible to ascertain with certainty or exactness. But, from estimates by Secretaries of the Treasury, especially Gallatin and Crawford, from reports of congressional committees, and estimates of statistical writers, the following figures have been gathered, which probably approximate as closely to the actual circulation in the years mentioned as it is now possible to do. The figures are millions and decimals :

CIRCULATION.

YEARS.	Specie.	Paper.	Total.	Currency.	Imports.
1790...............	16.	3.	19.	22.	22.4
1792...............	12.	7.	19.	24.	29.7
1804...............	.17.5	13.	30.5	42.	48.7
1808...............	14.	22.7	36.7	60.7	78.8
1816...............	7.5	110.	117.5	136.	129.9
1819...............	8.	62.	70.	109.5	67.9
1820...............	16.	44.	60.	89.4	56.4
1829...............	8.5	52.7	61.2	95.7	57.8

The imports for 1807 are given; our trade in 1808 was interrupted by the embargo. No other reliable statistics or estimates have been found, except the estimates of Gallatin for the years 1814 and 1815, which are of no value for our purpose, for our foreign commerce in those years was not uninterrupted. It is not supposed that the figures given are absolutely correct, nor is it possible to obtain exact information of the amount of specie and paper in actual circulation in those early times, but the aggregates of actual circulation and of currency in the country are sufficiently reliable to show that there was a remarkable parallelism between the currency of the country and its imports for consumption. In every case an increase or decrease of circulation and of currency is accompanied by a corresponding increase or decrease of imports. Were statistics obtainable for the years of peace not given, it is probable that the coincidence would be still more striking. And the increase of imports bears a general proportion to the increase of currency, especially where the statistics of currency are most reliable.

From the year 1830 onward, more complete information of the amount of currency is obtained. The following table is based mainly upon one prepared from the official records, by the New York *Economist*. In this table only bank-notes and specie are included as currency. It has been carefully verified by comparison with such records as the writer has been able to obtain, additions having been made for the years 1829, 1831, 1832, and 1834, for which the *Economist* gave no figures. Treasury reports of 1834 and 1836, with a calculation of the quantity of specie in the country, and comparison of returns of the banks of the different States, as far as those could be found, supply data sufficiently complete to justify the figures given. Thus the returns of the Massachusetts banks (given at the close of the chapter) show an increase of circulation from $5,124,070 in 1830 to $7,739,317 in 1831, and a decrease to $7,122,856 in 1832. Returns of other banks show similar changes; while the specie in the country, estimated at thirty-three millions, in 1830, by Gallatin, was decreased $1,708,986 by exportation, but increased nearly as much by the discovery of gold in North Carolina, which increased the coinage at the mint to nearly four millions. In 1834 the circulation of the banks was reported as $94,839,570, and the specie in the country had been increased by January of that year, by imports and yield from the mines, then delivering a million a year, to over forty-four millions. With similar data the figures of the *Economist* have been compared, and their substantial correctness may be accepted with qualification as to the years 1838, 1839, 1840, and 1855. The quantity of paper-money in the country, after the first suspension of the banks in 1837, by no means accurately indicates the quantity accepted as currency, for the notes of many banks were altogether refused, while the notes of others were passed only at a discount. The specie in the country was increased by importation of $14,239,070, so that it was probably eighty-five millions by the beginning and about ninety-two millions by the middle of the year 1838; but the paper in circulation, reported as $116,138,910 at the beginning of the year, probably includes at least twenty millions of notes, which were actually refused, and not effective as currency. With these data, the effective currency for that year may probably be placed at one hundred and eighty-two millions. Nor were all the dead notes in circulation quickened by the temporary resumption of the next year, or accepted as currency; and, though the quantity of paper returned was $135,170,995, it is probable that, of paper effective for currency, there was not more than one hundred and fifteen millions, which, with eighty-nine or ninety millions of specie, would give an effective currency of two hundred and five millions. The second suspension reduced the paper circulation reported to $106,986,572; but of this quantity, again, it is probable that a considerable proportion was ineffective—perhaps twenty-five millions. The quantity of paper kept afloat by banks, which were not entirely thrown out before the year 1842, was only eighty-three millions; and, if we suppose that not more than eighty millions of the quantity in circulation in 1840 was accepted as currency, and add ninety millions of specie, we have an effective circulation of one hundred and seventy millions. For the year 1855 the figures of the *Economist* are four hundred and forty-four millions, an increase of twenty-six millions, as compared with 1854. But the paper in circulation was eighteen millions *less* in 1855 than in 1854, namely, only one hundred and seventy-eight millions. And the quantity of specie was reduced by the export of $52,587,531, while the coinage was also less than in 1854. No estimate of the quantity of specie in circulation will warrant placing the currency for 1855 higher than three hundred and ninety-four millions, and these figures are therefore substituted for those of the *Economist*. In the second column we have placed the imports of merchandise for consumption, and in the third and fourth are given the rate of currency per capita, and of imports per capita.

IMPORTS AND CURRENCY, PER CAPITA, FOR THIRTY-TWO YEARS, 1829-'61.

The dotted line—1837 to 1841—represents the supposed quantity of effective currency (gold and paper in circulation) during suspension of specie payments. It should be remembered that imports are for fiscal years, from September until 1843, and thence from June 30th. But estimates of currency and bank returns are mainly from January to January. Thus the currency, about January, 1837, was $222,000,000, but contraction began, and the banks suspended several months before the fiscal year 1837 closed.

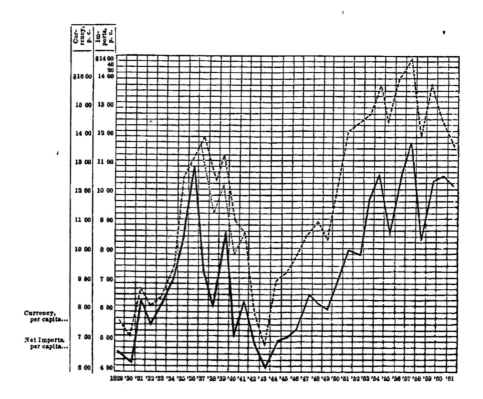

MOVEMENT OF CURRENCY AND IMPORTS COMPARED.

| YEAR. | Currency. | Imports. | PER CAPITA. | |
			Currency.	Imports.
1829.........	$95,700,000	$57,834,049	7.70	4.61
1830.........	93,000,000	56,489,441	7.20	4.31
1831.........	117,000,000	83,157,598	8.80	6.25
1832.........	112,000,000	76,989,793	8.20	5.61
1833.........	119,000,000	88,295,576	8.50	6.25
1834.........	139,000,000	103,208,521	9.60	7.09
1835.........	183,000,000	129,391,247	12.40	8.64
1836.........	205,000,000	168,233,675	13.30	10.93
1837.........	222,000,000	119,134,255	14.00	7.53
1838.........	203,000,000	101,264,609	12.50	6.23
1839.........	222,000,000	144,597,607	13.40	8.68
1840.........	190,000,000	88,951,207	11.20	5.21
1841.........	187,000,000	112,477,096	10.70	6.38
1842.........	143,700,000	88,440.549	8.00	4.87
1843.........	128,500,000	58,201,102	6.90	4.15
1844.........	175,000,000	96,950,168	9.10	5.03
1845.........	186,000,000	101,907,734	9.40	5.15
1846.........	202,500,000	110,354,174	9.90	5.42
1847.........	225,500,000	138,584,480	10.70	6.60
1848.........	240,000,000	133,870,918	11.10	6.25
1849.........	234,700,000	134,768,574	10.50	6.13
1850.........	285,000,000	163,186,510	12.20	7.03
1851.........	341,000,000	194,526,639	14.20	8.14
1852.........	360,000,000	195,656,060	14.50	7.95
1853.........	380,000,000	250,420,187	14.80	9.88
1854.........	418,600,000	280,813,867	15.80	10.71
1855.........	394,600,000	233,020,227	14.50	8.67
1856.........	446,200,000	298,261,364	16.10	10.77
1857.........	474,300,000	336,914,524	16.70	11.81
1858.........	406,600,000	251,727,008	14.00	8.57
1859.........	458,800,000	317,873,053	15.80	10.50
1860.........	457,000,000	335,233,232	14.50	10.80

The returns of imports are for fiscal years ending in September prior to 1843, and June 30th since; the statements of currency are from returns near the 1st of January in the years named.

It will at once be observed that there exists an astonishing correspondence between these records. Every expansion of currency is found to be accompanied by an increase of imports, and every contraction by a reduction of imports, except in the years 1840 and 1848. For 1840, if we substitute the estimate already given of effective currency, the correspondence is exact. The currency in 1848 was affected by the famine and disasters in Europe. In every other year since 1829, as in every year prior to that of which we have records of currency, a contraction of currency is accompanied by a reduction of imports and an expansion of currency by an increase of imports. But the relation of long columns of figures to each other is not easily borne in mind; therefore a diagram is given, representing by two lines the changes of currency and of imports, each per capita.

Both lines are drawn in fidelity to the table just given, and upon the same scale, though for convenience they are brought near each other the base-line representing $3 per capita for imports, and $5 per capita for currency. For 1838, 1839, and 1840, a dotted line is given for the effective currency per capita, according to the estimates already made.

No reasoning being can study this remarkable correspondence of facts without attributing it to a relation of cause and effect. One or two coincidences might be ascribed to chance. But chance does not trace such lines as these. Nothing less than an irresistible law by which one series of events has controlled the other, or both have been alike controlled by a third, can account for the fact that during thirty-two years, under tariffs of all kinds, from the highest to the lowest, in spite of the wonderful development of our resources and growth of our manufactures, and in spite of famines or commercial revulsions on either side of the ocean, the lines of imports and of currency follow each other in every rise and fall as if chained together. In *every* change, for, when such absolute correspondence appears elsewhere, the correctness of the estimates of effective currency in the years 1838–'42 is strongly confirmed by the fact that these estimates correspond, while the record of aggregate currency, effective and non-effective, does not correspond, with the changes of foreign trade in those years. But the correspondence at all other points, between records extending for thirty-two years, is surely convincing enough. If there can be absolute demonstration of cause and effect, we surely have it in this marvellous parallelism.*

Which is cause and which effect? Is the quantity of currency controlled by the increase or decrease of importations? A moment's

---

* Since this chapter was completed, the attention of the writer has been called to a very similar diagram and demonstration in the elaborate work of Hon. Amasa Walker, entitled "The Science of Wealth." Mr. Walker, however, includes as currency the bank circulation and deposits, so that the figures given differ materially. Yet the correspondence remains, and that writer holds it demonstrated "beyond cavil that the demand for foreign merchandise depends upon the quantity of currency in the country." It may justly be observed that this conclusion is not logically unavoidable; that some other cause may have controlled both the changes of the currency and the movement of imports. It is not the intention of this work to affirm or deny the conclusion at which Mr. Walker arrives; for the present purpose it is enough to prove that the movement of imports is not controlled by changes of the tariff, but corresponds so perfectly with changes of the currency as to demonstrate that imports are either controlled by the currency, or that both are controlled by some third cause independent of changes of the tariff.

IMPORTS AND TARIFFS CONTRASTED.

The dotted line shows the percentage of duties to total imports each year. The black line shows the value of net imports, per capita, each year. The lack of correspondence will be contrasted with the remarkable parallelism between the lines of currency and imports.

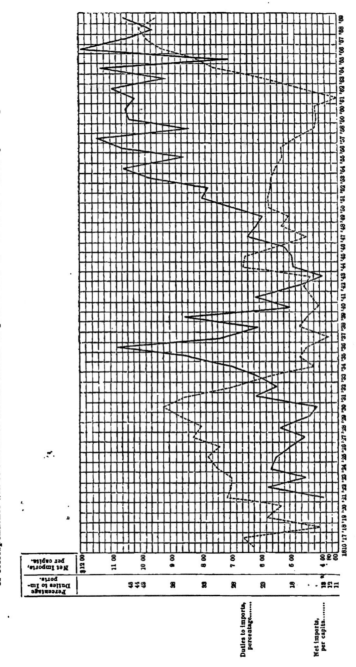

3

consideration will remove that idea from the mind. The currency is used in performing the domestic exchanges of the whole country, and these amount to thousands of millions in value, while importations amount only to hundreds of millions. In foreign exchanges, only a small part of our currency, namely, the specie, could be used, and it will appear that the quantity of specie in the country has varied very differently from the quantity of currency. Yet the changes of currency *not* used in foreign trade correspond exactly, while the quantity of specie which may be used in foreign trade does not correspond with the movement of imports. It is not reasonable to suppose that the variations of a currency used for domestic exchanges amounting to thousands of millions have been controlled by a foreign trade amounting to hundreds of millions only, in which that currency has not been used, while the movement of specie, which may have been used in those foreign exchanges, has not been so controlled. Yet the correspondence of facts demonstrates that some relation of cause and effect exists. We are forced to believe, either that the quantity of imports for consumption is controlled by the quantity of currency, or that both are alike controlled by some other cause. If the latter hypothesis be adopted, it is enough for the present purpose to know that this other cause cannot be the changes of the tariff. A comparison of the lines representing the movement of currency and of imports with the diagram showing the percentage of duties to imports under different tariffs will show how complete is the lack of correspondence, and will convince every mind that the controlling cause of fluctuations in the currency or in imports, whatever it may have been, has certainly not been the change in tariffs. These comparisons show that imports have repeatedly increased or decreased greatly, while the tariff has remained substantially the same, and that increase of duties has neither been followed uniformly by decrease nor by increase of imports, nor has decrease of duties been followed uniformly by increase or decrease of imports. In short, whatever the real cause of large importations may be, whenever that cause has existed, imports have increased in spite of high duties or low duties, tariff reduction or tariff increase, and, whenever that cause has been removed, imports have fallen off whether the duties have been heavy or light, increasing or decreasing. But, in each of these changes, imports have corresponded with the changes of currency.

When currency is expanded, money is plenty, and is easily obtained for the transaction of business—including the importation of foreign goods. High prices and expansion of currency occur contemporaneously, and when currency is contracted low prices prevail. But high prices invite the seller. Whenever prices in this country are higher than in other countries, importation becomes profitable, and goods rush hither for sale. At such times, also, abundance of money stimulates other branches of business, people feel able to consume more largely of foreign products, and have plenty of money with which to buy. There is an easy money-market for borrowers, a profitable margin for importations, and a quick sale. If water will run down-hill, foreign goods will flow into a country where these conditions exist. But, when the currency is contracted, and low prices prevail, the margin of profit in importations narrows or closes, the seller is repelled, money is scarce for borrowers, and there exists a general contraction of business and purchases. Thus it is easy to see that the condition of the currency must affect importations, while the facts prove that in all changes the correspondence has been complete. It is not necessary in this inquiry to enter upon that much-debated question whether expansion of currency is a cause or consequence of high prices, nor to ask whether some other cause, controlling at once domestic exchanges, foreign importations, and movements of currency, may not produce the parallelism observed in the phenomena. But the parallelism between these events, and the non-correspondence between changes of importations and changes of tariff, leave no room to doubt that the tariff does not control importations, and that they are controlled either by the currency or by some other influence coinciding and coöperating with that, and not coinciding with the tariff in effect.

It has been claimed that the great periods of inflation, speculation, and subsequent prostration, occurring under low tariffs, have been caused by the tariff; that excess of foreign importations has produced bankruptcy; and that these disorders can be prevented only by protective duties. If the conclusions be accepted to which facts have led us, it will be conceded that the excess of importations was a consequence and not a cause of the expansion of the currency; that changes in foreign trade amounting to hundreds of millions cannot have produced an inflation of the currency used in domestic exchanges amounting to thousands of millions; and that the low tariff, if it has in any manner contributed to cause the inflation, can have done so only by producing such activity of domestic business, such vigor of production, such a demand for consumption, and such rapidity of the societary circulation, as to bring about expansion of currency and rise of prices. In other words, low duties so greatly promoted the prosperity and stimulated the business and industry of the country, that men anticipated too bright a future, that credit was too widely extended, that currency expanded beyond the limit of safety, and some temporary revulsion became necessary to correct the evils engendered by a prosperity too great and too rapidly attained. If the advocate of protective duties is driven to this position, it will rest with him to show that we cannot secure all the wonderful growth resulting from low duties, without the disasters which have followed, by legislative barriers against undue expansion of the currency. It will rest with him to show that the evils which he ascribes to the tariff were not wholly attributable to the lack of a proper system of currency and banking. It will rest with him to show, also, that the marvellous progress under low duties was more than balanced by the disasters of subsequent prostration. But these periods of inflation deserve separate consideration.

COMMERCIAL CRISES.

No discussion of the tariff question is conducted without frequent reference to the great commercial disasters of 1817, 1837, and 1857. Other seasons of prostration have indeed occurred, but they have been less severe, less extended in effect upon different industries, and are therefore less frequently referred to in discussion. Before proceeding further, we may well notice briefly the nature and causes of these revulsions. It may appear that, in selecting these for frequent reference, both advocates and opponents of protection have given peculiar attention to those very disasters which were in the least degree produced by changes of duty. In each case, unnatural expansion of the currency and the credit system and the resulting failure of banks were the immediate causes of disaster, but it is maintained by writers of reputation that the speculation and expansion were produced or greatly increased by unrestricted importations, and that the flood of foreign goods, breaking down our domestic industry, caused the subsequent failure of banks and contraction of currency.

Of the revulsion of 1817, at least, this cannot be pretended with any regard to the facts. The expansion began, and extended so far as to cause general suspension of the banks, during the war, when our foreign trade was almost wholly interrupted. The suspension of banks began in Philadelphia, August 29, 1817, and the banks of New York and Maryland followed September 1st. In that same

year the imports were only $12,965,000—less than in any other year
in our whole history. The treaty of peace was signed on the 24th
of December, and in the next year, *after* the suspension of the banks,
the flood of foreign goods came in. It cannot be said, then, that the
expansion or suspension was caused by any excessive importations.
In fact, they were caused by the measures used by the government
to carry on the war; the loans amounting to over sixty-two millions
in the three preceding years, and to thirty-five millions in 1815;
the charter of countless banks, and the authorization of banking,
manufacturing, and even bridge corporations, to issue paper-money.
Forty-one banks were authorized in the State of Pennsylvania alone,
within the six months preceding the suspension. In consequence,
specie bore a premium of about twenty per cent. before the banks
failed, and the revival of foreign trade with a flood of depreciated
paper-money in circulation, and with all prices enormously high, was
necessarily most injurious to industries already much embarrassed.
Relieved of all obligation to pay in specie, the banks loaned without
measure, and increased their issues greatly, and a year or two of
fictitious prosperity followed, but the attempt to resume specie payments brought all the unsoundness to light, and caused terrible distress. The government refused to receive paper-money after February 20, 1817; the United States Bank and branches went into
operation at the same time, forcing other banks to resume; and in
the December previous the Bank of England, after suspension since
1797, began to pay specie for small notes. These measures brought
on a general bankruptcy, a suspension of business, domestic and
foreign, and severe sufferings, which lasted until 1820. This brief
review shows that no excess of foreign importations caused the inflation and the breaking of the banks, but it occurred under a suspension of foreign trade more complete than the highest tariff could have
produced; that the flood of foreign goods, which continued until the
resumption of specie payments and the violent contraction of the
currency, was caused by the inflation and the attendant high prices;
that the contraction was not caused by any change of tariff, but by
the refusal of paper by government and the United States Bank, and
that the contraction of currency brought with it bankruptcy and distress, as well as a decrease of importations.

Scarcely less clear is it that the inflation which culminated in the
panic of 1837 was caused not by the tariff, but by other agencies.
It occurred in a time of wonderful prosperity, and when duties had
been not violently but gradually reduced from the maximum at-

tained in 1832. That the reduction of duties caused neither the excessive importations nor the expansion of currency appears from the fact that both began, as has been shown, in 1830, before any reduction of duties took place (except on coffee, tea, and molasses, duties on which were reduced in that year), and that neither continued as the reduction of duties progressed after 1837. Indeed, so plain is it that excessive importations did not prostrate our industry, that Mr. Carey, in a pamphlet discussing the history of the iron manufacture, absolutely ignores the panic of 1837, and does not discover that there was any difficulty until 1839 or 1840. His readers were doubtless astonished to find the great collapse of 1837 suppressed by a writer so distinguished, but they will search his reply to Mr. Wells, and some other pamphlets by him, in vain for any evidence that he had ever heard of that event. The reason is obvious. The production of iron continued to increase, in spite of reduced duties and foreign importations, until 1839 or 1840, and that writer therefore found it inconvenient to refer to the prostration of 1837 without suggesting another and more reasonable cause for the embarrassments of 1840 than the reduction of duties.

By all writers of that time, the unsoundness of the currency is regarded as the main cause of the disaster. But, in the heated contests of those days, the cause of that unsoundness does not seem to have been clearly set forth. Intense hostility to the National Bank, or to the State banks selected for custody of the deposits, led people to ascribe all disasters to official action in one direction or another. Nor can it be doubted that the distribution of twenty-eight millions of the surplus revenue to certain State banks, with scarcely-needed injunction to loan it liberally, poured oil on flame already too fierce. But the main cause of the inflation, as the records of that time seem to prove beyond doubt, was the speculation in Western and Southern lands. This speculation was in part the effect of causes easily discovered. The Erie Canal, completed in 1825, soon began to increase very rapidly the value of Western lands, to attract immigration to the Western country, and to build up thriving towns along the lakes. In 1830 the steamboats on the Western rivers numbered 130, and their tonnage was 63,053; in 1834 the number was 230, and the tonnage 122,474; and in 1837 the tonnage had increased to 153,661. Thus the successful and extensive use of steam-vessels, and the building of canals, the Erie and others, had greatly increased the value of Western lands. At the same time the price of cotton rose in Liverpool from six to eight and ten cents for uplands, and the price of cotton lands was greatly increased. Every natural and legitimate increase in the value of a species of property induces speculation in that property in anticipation of further advance, and that speculation itself, increasing the demand, contributes to produce a further advance. Thus there sprang up a traffic in land of which the following record of the receipts from sale of public lands gives proof: *

RECEIPTS FROM SALE OF PUBLIC LANDS.†

Year.	Amount.	Year.	Amount.	Year.	Amount.
1796........	$4,836 13	1821........	$1,212,966 46	1845........	$2,077,022 30
1797........	83,540 60	1822........	1,803,581 54	1846....,....	2,694,452 48
1798........	11,963 11	1823........	916,523 10	1847........	2,498,355 20
1799........	....	1824........	984,418 15	1848........	3,328,642 56
1800........	443 75	1825........	1,216,090 56	1849........	1,688,959 55
1801........	167,726 06	1826........	1,393,785 09	1850........	1,859,894 25
1802........	188,628 02	1827........	1,495,845 26	1851........	2,352,305 30
1803........	165,675 69	1828........	1,018,308 75	1852........	2,043,239 58
1804........	487,526 79	1829........	1,517,175 13	1853........	1,667,084 99
1805........	540,193 80	1830........	2,329,356 14	1854........	8,470,798 39
1806........	765,245 73	1831........	3,210,815 48	1855........	11,497,049 07
1807........	466,163 27	1832........	2,623,381 03	1856........	8,917,644 93
1808........	647,939 06	1833........	3,967,682 55	1857........	3,829,486 64
1809........	442,252 33	1834........	4,857,600 69	1858........	3,513,715 87
1810........	696,548 82	1835........	14,757,600 75	1859........	1,756,687 30
1811........	1,040,237 53	1836........	24,877,179 86	1860........	1,778,557 71
1812........	710,427 78	1837........	6,766,236 52	1861........	870,658 54
1813........	835,655 14	1838........	3,081,939 47	1862........	152,203 77
1814........	1,135,971 09	1839........	7,076,447 35	1863........	167,617 17
1815........	1,287,959 28	1840........	3,292,683 29	1864........	583,333 29
1816........	1,717,985 03	1841........	1,365,627 42	1865........	966,553 31
1817........	1,991,226 06	1842........	1,335,797 52	1866........	665,031 03
1818........	2,606,564 77	1843........	897,818 11	1867........	1,163,575 76
1819........	3,274,422 78	1844........	2,059,939 80	1868........	1,348,715 41
1820........	1,035,871 61				

It appears that the receipts prior to 1830 had never been two mill- ions in any year except in 1818 and 1819, although the minimum price prior to 1820 was $2 per acre, and from 1820 onward only $1.25 per acre; that in the year 1830 there began a purchase of lands more than double the average of preceding years, doubtless owing to the actual enhancement in the value of Western lands by cheaper transportation; that in 1833 the receipts were about four millions, and in 1834 about five millions; that a speculative demand then grew up, and in 1835 the receipts mounted suddenly to over four- teen millions, and in 1836 to nearly twenty-five millions. During the whole decade prior to this speculation there had never been more than two millions of acres sold in a year, but in 1835 there were sold twelve millions, and in 1836 about twenty millions of acres. Not all the enormous immigration since that day, not all the excitement

---

* In the chapter on immigration, Diagram X., will be found a representation of the sales of public lands at different periods.

† Report of Secretary of the Treasury, 1868.

caused by the discovery of gold and silver, not even the enormous increase in the value of Western lands, after the building of new railroads in 1854 and 1855, caused sales of land in any year one-half as great as those of 1836. This record will recall to the minds of those who remember that time the mad speculation which raged throughout the country. The sales by government were but the beginning of transactions of enormous magnitude. Paper cities sprang up at the West and South by the hundred. The lands for which forty millions of dollars were paid to government in the two years 1835 and 1836 were quickly sold and sold again, doubtless for four or five times that sum, and for all these transactions the currency and the credit were supplied by the banks. Enormous sums were loaned upon real-estate security, and the lands were accepted at the imaginary value which speculation had given to them. Of the three hundred millions then loaned by the banks, much the greater part had no better security than government lands thus extravagantly valued, paper cities projected thereon, and corner lots and eligible locations in every Western and Southern city. For the speculation was not confined to wild land or cities " *in nubibus*," as may be inferred from the following record of the valuation of real estate in Mobile, and the assessment of property for taxation in New York City:

YEAR.	MOBILE.		NEW YORK.	YEAR.	MOBILE.		NEW YORK.
	Polls.	Real Estate.	Assessed Value.		Polls.	Real Estate.	Assessed Value.
1820...	88	$493,300	$69,530,753	1836..	617	$18,050,060	$309,500,920
1821...	211	403,200	68,285,070	1837..	836	27,482,961	263,837,350
1822...	287	419,550	71,289,144	1838..	1,487	20,407,435	264,152,941
1823...	332	989,350	83,431,170	1839..	1,725	21,098,915	266,789,130
1824...	512	832,125	87,480,026	1840..	1,453	13,441,783	252,843,163
1825...	334	1,519,765	101,160,046	1841..	1,372	17,601,950	251,771,702
1826...	407	1,535,640	107,447,781	1842..	1,615	16,138,643	237,806,901
1827...	471	1,408,327	112,211,926	1843..	855	14,773,470	228,001,889
1828...	527	1,488,168	111,130,240	1844..	452	14,053,056	235,960,047
1829...	402	1,891,760	112,526,016	1845..	943	12,622,085	239,995,517
1830...	531	2,162,770	125,288,518	1846..	....	12,854,650	244,952,404
1831...	417	1,294,810	139,280,314	1847..	....	8,638,250	247,152,303
1832...	764	2,623,110	146,302,618	1848..	1,217	8,943,810	254,192,027
1833...	898	3,377,649	166,495,187	1849..	1,607	9,300,930	256,217,093
1834...	980	4,611,950	186,548,511	1850..	1,400	8,577,025	286,085,416
1835...	788	6,414,425	218,723,703	1851..	1,554	11,698,045	320,108,358

The official assessments for taxation are given, the only records accessible, although they do not accord with actual values, because they probably bear nearly the same relation in different years to the supposed value. Mobile and New York probably represent two extremes; the former, a class of cities in which speculation was most wild, and the latter, those older cities which were affected by

the mania in a less degree. In New York, however, the valuation
began a natural increase in 1829, and, during the speculation, more
than doubled in four years. But in. Mobile, where the valuation
was larger than ever before in 1832, and was then only $2,623,110,
it rose to six and a half millions in 1835, to eighteen millions in
1836, and to twenty-seven millions in 1837. Not less than twenty
millions of this increase was imaginary, and the population, as indicated by the polls, had scarcely increased at all. If we suppose that
a large part of the land taken from government was held at similar
extravagant prices ; that land in other Western and Southern towns
and cities was bought and sold in the same wild fever ; and that
even in the oldest Eastern States the valuation of property doubled
in four years, we shall understand what pressure there was in every
quarter for loans of money, and on what imaginary security all loans
were based. To this insane passion for gambling in real estate, and
to the enormous loans made on property valued at fictitious rates,
whether in city, projected city, town, or prairie, are directly trace-
able the inflation and the subsequent explosion of 1837. Will any
one pretend that this speculation was caused by the tariff ? Was
there at that time any extravagant importation of foreign lands ?

By writers who do not trouble themselves to consult facts, it has
indeed been suggested that this speculation was caused by the withdrawal of capital from manufacturing, which importations, it is
imagined, had rendered unprofitable. But two facts make an end
of that theory. The speculation, increased valuation, and increased purchase of lands, as the statistics given prove, actually
commenced in 1830, two years before the tariff was changed; and
in every branch of manufactures there were great prosperity and
rapid growth during the whole period of inflation; so that more
capital was invested, and the product yearly increased, as will fully
appear when the progress of manufactures is discussed. Indeed,
it is because this increase in manufactures cannot be denied or
explained away that Mr. Carey takes pains to forget that there was
any panic in 1837 !

The cause of the inflation has been ascertained. It only remains
to show that the tariff was equally guiltless of the subsequent explosion. Indeed, no argument is needed to prove that the explosion
of such a bubble was an inevitable consequence, not of low duties
or large importations, but of the hollowness of the whole system
of currency and credit. Loans and paper-money alike had corner
lots in paper cities for their only security. Increase of the circula-

tion swelled values, and thus enticed thousands more into the mad whirlpool. Paper-money pervaded the air. The government threw its surplus revenue into the vortex, and begged the banks to lend it. For a few short months everybody went on getting enormously rich, in dreams, and then the bubble burst, and with it exploded almost every bank in the country. Shall we ask what caused the bubble to burst? What explodes the boiler when the captain has been sitting on the safety-valve? Failure of crops helped both to produce the explosion and to aggravate its effects. But the main cause was the steam in the boiler—the expansive force of a crazy land speculation.

A partial resumption was reached in 1838; but the volume of currency and the load of debt, sustained only by imaginary prosperity, were too vast. A second suspension was followed by a throwing out of worthless banks and their notes, and a shrinkage of currency and prices. Then, thousands of firms were driven to bankruptcy, and manufacturing establishments, which had thriven when foreign importations were large, went to ruin when those importations had almost ceased! And this prostration of industry, which did not precede, but followed the shrinkage of values and the bankruptcy of firms and banks, is the event which Mr. Carey regards as the cause of the disaster. Ignoring the panic of 1837, and the fact that our industry had continued to thrive until after foreign competition had been checked, that writer and others point to the prostration of 1841 and 1842 as proof that the tariff of 1833 was fatal to our manufactures.

With a like indifference to facts, they ascribe the subsequent recovery to the tariff of 1842. If a whole people stop gambling and wasting, and begin earning and saving, the inevitable effects are, first, dulness of trade and revival of industry; and second, steady and sure revival of both. The people had stopped gambling and wasting before the tariff of 1842 was adopted. They had begun to earn and to save. Many records prove that the revival of industry had already begun, and of these some will appear in connection with the history of manufactures. Two items here must suffice. In 1841 there were 224,176 tons of freight moved from Western States or Canada eastward over the Erie Canal, and in 1842 there were 221,477, though in 1840 there were only 158,148, and in 1839 only 121,671. Receipts of flour, wheat, and other products at Buffalo, from the West, also show a steady increase from 1840 onward. The number of vessels built for domestic trade, including sloops, canal-boats, and steamers, was largely increased in 1842, and 137 steamers were built in that year against 78 in 1841, and 63 in 1840. Our foreign trade revived less promptly; but the recuperation of domestic industry began as soon as the banks resumed specie payments, and that was before the tariff of 1842 went into effect. The sure revival came because people had begun to live economically, and to earn their living by honest labor. Knowing that economy had begun, that specie payments had been resumed, and that industry had revived months before the tariff went into operation, we may unhesitatingly assert that prosperity would have come had no change in the tariff been made. To doubt it is to doubt that honesty and industry will earn a living. To deny it is to deny that economy and faithful labor will secure prosperity to any people.

The panic of 1857 was neither long continued, nor did it materially affect the productive power of the country. It was a collapse of the credit system rather than of the currency, and its cause is easily ascertained. Those who ascribe it to the importations of the preceding years seem to forget that those imports were more than paid for by our exports of surplus products. It was not a bankruptcy caused by buying more than we could sell; on the contrary, our foreign trade was then in a peculiarly healthy condition. During the years 1851–1857 inclusive, we exported of merchandise, of domestic production, $1,476,672,650, and of specie, $269,616,413. The merchandise was valued in our own ports; its purchasing power or exchange value in foreign ports was, at least, 15 per cent. greater; and, adding this, we have merchandise valued abroad at $1,718,873,547 to exchange for imports valued abroad at $1,783,926,710. Thus, in these seven years we almost paid for our entire imports in exports of merchandise alone, without counting the surplus of gold. Nor was the gold needed here; our production was greatly in excess of our capacity to use it as currency or otherwise, and though $264,616,413 was exported—much of it to pay interest on loans, or dividends on investments, by European capitalists—there still remained in the country more than we could advantageously use.

The value of precious metals produced and added to our supply after the discovery of mines in California cannot be accurately ascertained, but official estimates place the product of the years 1848–1857 inclusive at not less than five hundred millions, and the records of the mint show that four hundred and thirty-eight millions had passed through that institution and its branches. It is safe to say that the product was, at least, four hundred and eighty millions; and, as only two hundred and eighty millions were exported, there were added to the circulation or supply of precious metals in this country not less than two hundred millions—a sum equal to the entire currency of the country, specie and paper included, in 1846. At the same time the paper circulation was also increased. The currency thus became greatly expanded; primarily, by the flood of gold thrown into circulation. Certainly no tariff caused, and none yet known among men could have prevented, this inflation; but, if the tariff of 1846 stimulated importations, and facilitated the exchange of this superfluous metal for iron rails, to that extent it checked the inflation, and lessened the consequent disaster. For every increase of currency, whether in specie or paper, tends to increase prices, and every increase of prices prompts to speculation in the hope of further increase. In its origin, then, the inflation prior to 1857 was a gold inflation.

But a second cause operated more powerfully to accelerate the expansion, and produced the subsequent explosion. With the settlement of new States, the rapid extension of the boundaries of civilization, the large immigration which followed the European famine of 1847, and the political disturbances on the Continent, came both the demand and the labor for the building of railroads. The flood of gold made money plenty. A low tariff made iron cheap. Roads built to supply the most immediate necessities were at once prosperous. Lands in the neighborhood were greatly enhanced in value. Then came a rush into railroad-building and land speculation. Statistics of receipts from sale of public lands already given (page 36) show that the amount more than quadrupled in 1854, reached eleven and a half millions in 1855, and was about nine millions in 1856. But this movement was altogether subordinate to the growth of the railroad system. On page 42 will be found statistics of the number of miles of railroad built each year, and the diagram, "Iron, Coal, and Railroads," page 350, will clearly present the facts to the eye. Only four hundred miles were built in 1848; then the number suddenly rose to 1,369 in 1849; to 1,656 in 1850; to 1,961 in 1851; to 1,926 in 1852; to 2,452 in 1853; and to 3,643 in 1856. In the years 1849 to 1857 inclusive, 18,212 miles of railroad were built, and the average outlay for track, rolling-stock, buildings, equipments, and repairs, was not less than $50,000 a mile. We have here an actual expenditure of $910,600,000 for railroad

RAILROAD-BUILDING.

Statement of the Number of Miles of Railroad in Operation, and Increase of Mileage each Year, since 1830.

YEAR.	Miles in Operation.	Increase of Mileage.	YEAR.	Miles in Operation.	Increase of Mileage.
1830...........	23		1850........	9,021	1,656
1831..........	95	72	1851........	10,982	1,961
1832..........	229	134	1852........	12,908	1,926
1833..........	380	151	1853........	15,360	2,452
1834..........	633	253	1854........	16,720	1,360
1835..........	1,098	465	1855........	18,374	1,654
1836..........	1,273	175	1856........	22,017	3,643
1837..........	1,497	224	1857........	24,508	2,491
1838..........	1,913	416	1858........	26,968	2,460
1839..........	2,302	389	1859........	28,789	1,821
1840..........	2,818	516	1860........	30,635	1,846
1841..........	3,535	717	1861........	31,256	621
1842..........	4,026	491	1862........	32,120	864
1843..........	4,185	159	1863........	33,170	1,050
1844..........	4,377	192	1864........	33,908	738
1845..........	4,633	256	1865........	35,085	1,177
1846..........	4,930	297	1866........	36,827	1,742
1847..........	5,599	669	1867........	39,276	2,449
1848..........	5,996	397	1868........	42,255	2,979
1849..........	7,365	1,069			

purposes. Of this vast sum, nearly one thousand millions, it is well known that a large proportion was invested in works not immediately profitable; indeed, few of the roads returned fair dividends until after the crash of 1857. A sum so enormous could not be directly withdrawn from the productive capital of the country, and, of necessity, most of the roads then built were constructed mainly on credit. Stocks and bonds were thrown upon the market, or used as securities to sustain loans, and to meet the demand the banks * expanded their circulation from one hundred and twenty-eight millions in 1848, to $214,778,822 in 1857, and their current credits from two hundred and eighty-one millions to four hundred and forty-five millions. Thus rapidly expanding to sustain these enterprises, the whole banking system soon came to depend for its stability upon the value of railroad securities. When loans were not made directly upon stocks or bonds, the banks loaned to individuals or corporations whose whole capital or more was so invested; brokers were sustained whose operations in stocks went far beyond their actual means; and thus, directly or indirectly, the whole credit system of the country became

* See table of the condition of the banks at different periods, following this chapter.

dependent upon the success of new railroads which were being built through half-settled regions at the rate of three thousand miles a year! Can any one wonder that the collapse came? Most of the railroads did not pay. The stocks and bonds lost value. Individuals and firms became bankrupt. Finally, with the fall of a prominent institution which had speculated largely, general prostration came. Yet this is the panic which Mr. Carey and others, with prodigious stride of logic, attribute to the reduction of duties in 1846, eleven years before!

Every reader will judge for himself whether the cause of this disaster was a foreign trade which gave a balance of two hundred millions in our favor—exchange value of merchandise being allowed —or the investment of one thousand millions of dollars in roads temporarily unprofitable.

It will, however, be said, and said with truth, that the country would not have built so many railroads had not the iron been admitted at low duty. It is true that, if iron had then cost what it costs now, the vast net-work of railroads built in 1849–'57 would not now be in existence. Would the country be the gainer? Thousands of men sunk their property in these enterprises, but was not the nation enriched and strengthened beyond all estimate? Let those answer whose farms have been quadrupled in value! Let those answer who have since been enabled, by those very railroads, to develop mines and erect factories and mills, in regions before inaccessible! The railroads constructed in that period have done more to protect American industry, by building up a home market and rendering possible an increased production of wealth, than all the tariffs, high or low, ever yet adopted. To those railroads we owe the growth of manufactures in spite of the war, in spite of embarrassing duties on almost every material, and in spite of large importations which an inflated currency has invited, and which no protective tariff can shut out. To them we owe no small share of the enormous immigration which adds yearly to our population a quarter of a million of workers. To them we owe, in no considerable measure, the stability of the Union itself, for the railroads of the North multiplied its forces, and made possible some of its best feats of generalship.

The phenomenon of 1837 was the explosion of a currency system corrupted by speculation in real estate. The phenomenon of 1857 was the explosion of a credit system built upon an investment of one thousand millions of dollars in eighteen thousand miles of new railroad through a half-settled country. The first originated in the legitimate increase in the value of Western lands by the opening of the Erie Canal and other improved facilities of communication. The second originated in the flood of gold from California. In both cases the increase of importations was a consequence and not a cause of the inflation, and the bursting of the bubble and suspension of the banks would have occurred, in both cases, as the suspension did in 1814, although foreign trade had been wholly stopped. In each case, also, the suspension was followed by an attempt to go on without material reduction of values, and by the failure of that attempt. In each case, the people came back, before any change of tariff, to more solid values, to more real business, and began again that sober industry and economical life which make prosperity certain.

BANKS OF THE UNITED STATES—CONDITION AT DIFFERENT TIMES.

YEAR.	Specie.	Circulation.	Deposits.	Current Credits.
1811......	$15,400,000	$28,100,000	....	....
1815......	17,000,000	45,500,000	....	....
1816......	19,000,000	68,000,000	....	....
1820......	19,820,240	44,863,344	$ 35,950,470	$80,813,814
1830......	22,114,917	61,323,898	55,559,928	116,863,826
1833.....	30,600,000	80,000,000	....	....
1834......	35,000,000	94,839,570	75,666,986	170,503,556
1835......	43,937,625	100,602,405	83,034,365	131,773,860
1836......	40,019,594	140,301,038	115,104,420	276,495,478
1837......	37,915,340	149,135,990	127,397,185	276,533,075
1838......	35,184,112	116,138,910	84,691,184	200,830,694
1839......	45,132,763	135,170,995	90,240,146	225,411,141
1840......	33,165,155	106,986,572	75,696,857	182,665,439
1841......	34,818,913	107,290,214	64,890,101	172,180,315
1842......	28,440,423	83,734,011	62,498,870	146,142,881
1843......	33,515,806	58,653,603	56,163,623	114,732,231
1844......	49,898,269	75,167,646	84,550,785	159,718,431
1845......	44,241,242	89,608,711	83,020,646	177,629,357
1846......	42,012,095	105,552,427	97,918,020	202,465,497
1847......	35,132,516	105,519,766	91,792,533	197,312,299
1848......	46,369,765	128,596,091	108,226,177	281,732,263
1849......	43,619,863	114,743,415	91,178,623	205,922,033
1850......	45,379,345	131,366,526	109,586,595	240,953,121
1851......	48,671,048	155,165,251	128,957,712	284,122,963
1854......	59,410,253	204,689,207	188,188,744	392,877,951
1855......	53,944,546	186,952,223	190,400,342	377,352,565
1856......	59,314,063	195,747,950	212,705,662	408,753,612
1857......	58,344,838	214,778,822	230,351,352	445,130,174
1858......	74,412,832	155,208,344	185,932,049	341,140,393
1859......	104,537,818	193,306,818	259,568,278	452,875,096
1860......	83,594,537	207,102,477	253,802,129	460,904,606
1861......	87,674,507	202,005,767	256,229,562	459,235,329
1862......	102,146,215	183,792,079	297,322,408	480,114,487
1863......	101,227,369	238,677,218	393,686,226	632,363,444

FOREIGN EXCHANGE.

Dotted line, total exports. Black line, total imports. Perpendicular lines, specie; black, imports; dotted, exports.

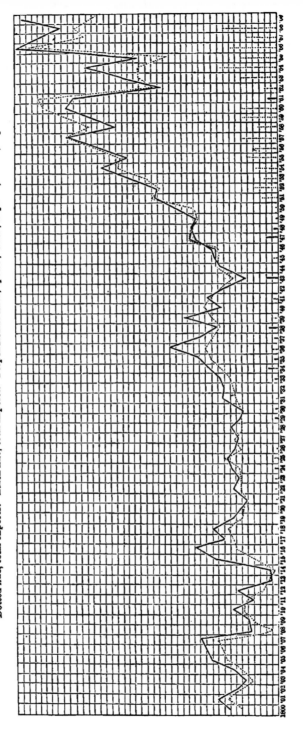

MASSACHUSETTS BANKS.

Year.	Bills in Circulation.	Year.	Bills in Circulation.
1815	$2,605,611 00	1834	$7,650,146 75
1816	2,332,100 00	1835	9,430,357 72
1817	2,482,500 00	1836	10,892,249 50
1818	2,631,150 00	1837	10,273,118 71
1819	2,437,802 00	1838	9,400,512 75
1820	2,562,000 00	1839	7,875,322 50
1821	2,859,540 00	1840	9,112,882 25
1822	3,096,800 00	1841	9,509,112 00
1823	3,145,010 00	1842	8,049,906 75
1824	3,742,231 00	1843	9,219,267 50
1825	3,508,100 00	1844	12,183,158 25
1826	3,644,400 00	1845	14,339,686 00
1827	5,567,606 50	1846	14,591,914 50
1828	5,034,593 50	1847	17,196,362 25
1829	4,747,784 50	1848	13,196,029 00
1830	5,124,090 00	1849	15,700,935 25
1831	7,739,317 00	1850	17,005,826 25
1832	7,122,856 00	1851	19,694,698 25
1833	7,889,110 67		

CHAPTER IV.

HIGH TARIFFS CHECK EXPORTS.

In every fluctuation imports follow currency. With the certainty of a law of Nature, goods are attracted to the market where expanded currency and high prices exist, just as water runs down-hill, or air forces its way into a vacuum. But it has already appeared that exports do not obey the same influence, and that in certain periods of high duties or high prices our exports have been checked, while our imports have increased, thus turning the balance of trade against us. What laws, then, govern our exports?

An examination of the table of total exports and imports will suggest the fact that, except under unusual circumstances, imports have always exceeded exports in such proportion as to indicate a mutual exchange of products. To present the facts to the eye, a diagram has been prepared (Plate II.), in which imports for each year since 1800 are represented by a full and exports by a dotted line, both being drawn on the same scale. The perpendicular lines opposite certain years indicate movements of specie; the full line, imports; and the dotted, exports, and are also in proportion to the aggregates. By this diagram, the history of our exchanges with other nations during the current century is presented in a form to be readily understood. The interruption of our commerce during the War of 1812, the depression of 1843, and the prostration during the recent war, at once attract attention, as well as the period of prosperity before the embargo of 1808, the inflations of 1816 and 1836, and the enormous development of our commerce during the decade 1850–'60. Less important changes next attract notice ; the year of prostration and the year of attempt to go forward without readjustment of values, which follow each inflation ; and the minor depressions of 1829 and 1830, of 1849 and 1855. Then the fact will be observed that, prior to 1855, when gold began to overflow, our imports always exceeded our exports, except in certain years. Omitting the period of the War of 1812, we find that exports first rose above imports in the year 1821, the year of greatest depression after the suspension of 1814. The next instance was in 1825, when a peculiar demand existed in Europe. For the same reason, 1847, the year of famine, may be omitted from further consideration. In 1827 and 1830 our industry was greatly depressed. In 1840 culminated the disasters caused by the land mania. Thus, prior to the overflow of gold, our imports never fell below our exports except in years of famine abroad or prostration and disaster at home. The years of prostration and disaster are years of extreme low prices, which favor exports but repel imports.

Our foreign trade, except in such periods of disaster, is an exchange of products, in which the imports valued abroad naturally exceed the exports valued here. Unless under stress of commercial disaster, we cannot sell more than we buy. But we can and do buy more than we sell, especially in every period of inflation. Then prices here are high, so that exportation of our products becomes unprofitable, except as the foreign price of those products may be controlled by our own. And, even then, the enhanced price tends to check foreign consumption. Accordingly, periods of inflation are those in which imports most largely exceed exports. High prices here, as compared with prices in other countries, favor the foreign industry and operate against our own industry.

It will, however, be said that this idea of exchange is not consistent with rules generally accepted; that Mr. Mill and other distinguished authors teach that a nation cannot buy more than it sells, and that our imports must therefore by controlled by our exports. It would, doubtless, be a mistake to suppose that any eminent writer had overlooked the fact that of two nations trading with each other it is impossible that the imports of each should be controlled by its exports. If we exchange cotton for cotton goods with England, a refusal on our part to take goods must cause England to diminish her purchases of raw cotton, until an equal market for her products should be opened elsewhere, and thus, in this case, our imports control our exports, while Britain's exports control its imports. But Mr. Mill undoubtedly teaches that in the long-run a nation's purchases will not exceed its power to pay by its exports. There is a feature in our condition which may render the rule less applicable to us than to older nations. This is a new and rapidly-growing country, and offers a peculiarly inviting field for foreign investments or loans of capital. In times of rapid development, when lands quickly double in value, when mines of vast wealth are opened, or when railroads are pushed forward, making business for themselves and creating civilization as they advance, it is natural that foreign capitalists desire to share in the enormous profits, and it is certain that our people, needing increased capital, have both sought and found it in Europe. The sale of bonds or shares, though not represented in our export account, is in fact an important and constant element in our transactions with Europe, and especially important in times of speculation or rapid development. Prices here being unnaturally-high, the importer, S., will import as largely as he can. Speculation being rife, the real estate, or railroad, or mining operator, R., will desire to place bonds or shares or to effect loans in Europe. Interest here being high, and the rapid growth of the country giving comparative certainty to enterprises which might otherwise be hazardous, European capitalists are prompted to invest. S. buys an enormous stock of goods, and at the same time R. sells abroad a quantity of shares or bonds. S. buys in the New-York market a draft on London to pay for his goods, and at the same time R. sells in the New-York market the draft which he has received in payment for bonds or shares. Thus it happens that the importer has not run into debt, but is doing a prosperous business, while the country has imported more than it can pay for; in other words, we have bought goods or iron, and paid in bonds or shares. Our imports may have created in England an increased demand for raw materials, and may thus increase exports as far as we supply that demand, but the same inflation has so enhanced the price of those of our products which can be elsewhere produced as to prevent our exports from rising in proportion to our imports. Precisely this phenomenon we have observed as occurring in 1836, and in recent years.

Not only in times of inflation, but under ordinary circumstances, our rapid growth and healthy progress invite investment of foreign capital. This country, always needing capital, constantly seeks to borrow as largely as anybody will lend. Nor is this altogether an evidence of folly : our resources yet undeveloped are so great, and our progress is so rapid, that many millions can at any time be invested in enterprises reasonably certain of ultimate profit, though, in older countries, similar undertakings might be most hazardous. Hence, as a nation, we are naturally and legitimately borrowers, and the loans of foreign capital form a fund upon which we can constantly draw for payment of imports in excess of exports. In the end, perhaps, we must repay in profits, dividends, interest, and principal, as much as we borrow ; but that fact has never yet restrained us from importing more than our exports; nor will it until this ceases to be a country where capital can be profitably invested. If these reasonings are correct, and applied to the condition of this country thus far they certainly accord with ascertained facts : it follows that, in any year, or during any ordinary term of years, our imports have not been limited by our exports, while our exports have been limited by the law of exchange.

Let us now inquire what effect, if any, tariffs have had upon our exports. It is plain that if they have diminished our importation of manufactured products, they may have checked the exportation of the materials; and, if they have increased prices, or caused inflation, they have checked exports, and placed our industry at a disadvantage in foreign markets. It is important, first, to separate the exports of specie from those of merchandise. No tariff gives us the specie-producing power. It may be doubted whether any tariff can cause specie to flow into a country, or arrest its outflow, and, whether, could either be done, it would be advantageous. Specie, beyond the quantity needed to facilitate exchanges, is a non-productive investment, and may be advantageously exchanged for any products of other countries which enable us to increase the production of wealth, which improve the condition of the people, or which, being necessary for use, can be obtained cheaper than we can produce them, thus enabling our own labor to be more profitably employed. The table on page 49, of exports and imports of specie since 1820, gives only the excess of either in each year, showing at a glance the movement at different periods, and in the third and fourth columns is shown, for each year, the aggregate excess of imports or exports from 1820 to 1869. These tables show that under the protective system,

MOVEMENT OF SPECIE.

YEAR.	Excess of Exports.	Excess of Imports.	Balance of Exports.	Balance of Imports.
1821............	$2,413,169	....	$2,413,169	....
1822............	7,440,334	....	9,853,503	....
1823............	1,275,091	....	11,128,594	....
1824............	....	$1,366,148	9,762,446	....
1825............	2,646,290	....	12,408,736	....
1826............	....	2,176,433	10,232,303	....
1827............	....	136,250	10,096,053	....
1828............	753,735	....	10,849,788	....
1829............	....	2,479,592	8,370,196	....
1830............	....	5,977,191	2,393,005	....
1831............	1,708,986	....	4,101,991	....
1832............	....	251,164	3,850,827	....
1833............	....	4,458,667	....	$607,840
1834............	....	15,834,874	....	16,442,714
1835............	....	6,633,672	....	23,076,386
1836............	....	9,076,545	....	32,152,931
1837............	....	4,540,165	....	36,693,096
1838............	....	14,239,070	....	50,932,166
1839............	3,181,567	....	....	47,950,599
1840............	....	465,799	....	48,216,398
1841............	5,045,699	....	....	43,170,699
1842............	726,523	....	....	42,444,176
1843............	....	20,869,768	....	63,313,944
1844............	....	376,215	....	63,690,159
1845............	4,536,253	....	....	59,164,906
1846............	127,536	....	....	59,037,370
1847............	....	22,214,265	....	81,251,635
1848............	9,481,392	....	....	71,770,243
1849............	....	1,246,592	....	73,016,835
1850............	2,894,202	....	....	70,122,633
1851............	24,019,160	....	....	46,103,473
1852............	37,169,091	....	....	8,934,382
1853............	23,285,493	....	14,351,111	....
1854............	34,342,162	....	48,693,273	....
1855............	52,587,531	....	101 280,804	....
1856............	41,537,853	....	142,818,657	....
1857............	56,675,123	....	199,493,780	....
1858............	33,358,651	....	232,852,431	....
1859............	56,452,622	....	289,305,053	....
1860............	57,996,104	....	347,301,157	....
1861............	....	16,548,431	330,752,726	....
1862	20,472,688	....	351,225,414	....
1863............	54,572,506	....	424,005,791	....
1864............	92,128,738	....	515,975,835	....
1865............	57,833,154	....	573,808,989	....
1866............	75,343,979	....	649,152,968	....
1867............	38,797,897	....	687,950,865	....
1868............	80,081,660	....	768,032,225	....
1869............	37,301,426	....	805,338,651	....

from 1820 to 1825 inclusive, gold flowed out of the country to the
amount of twelve and a half millions; that the higher tariff of 1824
but slightly reduced the excess of exports—to about eleven millions
in 1828; and that the extreme protective tariff then reduced it to

about four millions in 1832. The first year of the compromise tariff, 1833, is also the first year in which the balance was turned to the side of imports, and, from that time, imports, every year until 1838, raised the excess of imports to fifty-one millions. The years 1839 and 1841 reduced this excess by more than eight millions, but the year of extreme depression, 1843, raised it again to sixty-three millions. The other years of the tariff of 1842 caused a slight reduction; but the famine in England lifted the balance to $81,251,635—the highest point of excess of imports. At that point, the supply of California gold changed the current, and by the year 1854 the exports had again exceeded imports. Since 1850 we have been exporting gold largely in every year, except 1861—another year of great depression.

Since the discovery of gold in California, an outflow of that metal has been not only natural, but necessary. The effects of different tariff systems can only be inferred from the movement prior to that event. The record indicates a more steady influx of gold under the compromise tariff than under either of the protective tariffs; but it must be observed that the influx was greatest in the year of extreme prostration after the protective tariff of 1842 was adopted. These facts warrant only negative inferences—that an influx of gold is neither an unerring symptom of health, nor of disease; that it has not been caused exclusively by any form of tariff; and that the "drain of gold," which some writers ascribe to the system of low duties, has existed only in their imaginations—unless, indeed, they mistake the overflow since the opening of California mines for an unnatural drain. If so, the outflow since 1861 has been still greater. But, if we observe the large importations of gold in years of disaster —in 1829 and 1830, in 1838 and 1843, and in 1861—we shall, perhaps, be inclined to regard an influx of gold as a very questionable boon. Spain has done much to teach civilized nations the folly of trying to hoard gold. Her many and stringent laws, designed to prevent the outflow of precious metals, have not made Spain either prosperous or wealthy.

Having examined the movement of specie, we may now ascertain the effect of tariffs upon exports of other products of our industry. In a table at the close of this chapter will be found a statement of exports of domestic products, other than specie, each year since 1820—earlier Treasury records do not distinguish specie—compared with imports for consumption of foreign products, other than specie. For the present purpose, however, the following table will be more convenient, in which the rate per capita of net exports and imports of merchandise is presented, with the excess of net exports or imports of merchandise for each year. The exports since 1861 are reduced to specie values, and, as the Treasury year 1843 contained only nine months (September 30th to June 30th), the figures per capita given are four-thirds of the rate for actual exports and imports during these months. The table thus constructed gives a complete record of our exchanges of merchandise with foreign nations compared with the progress of population. It is proper to remark that, in many of the Treasury reports, in tables of "foreign merchandise consumed," specie has, by some curious error, been included.

EXCESS OF IMPORTS AND EXPORTS, AND THE RATE OF EACH PER CAPITA.

YEAR.	MERCHANDISE.		SAME, PER CAPITA.		YEAR.	MERCHANDISE.		SAME, PER CAPITA.	
	Excess Exports.	Excess Imp'ts.	Expt's.	Impt's.		Excess Exports.	Excess Imports.	Expt's.	Imp'ts.
1821..	....	$ 24.511	$4.38	$4.39	1846..	....	$8,331,817	$5.08	$5.50
1822..	....	18,521,594	4.84	6.64	1847..	$34,317,249	....	7.34	5.67
1823..	....	4,155,238	4.45	4.84	1848..	....	10,448,129	6.09	6.57
1824..	....	8,197,067	4.64	5.77	1849..	....	1,055,027	6.00	6.05
1825..	$549,023	....	5.98	5.92	1850..	....	29,133,800	5.87	7.13
1826..	....	5,202,722	4.56	5.01	1851..	....	21,856,081	7.50	8.42
1827..	2,977,009	....	4.86	4.58	1852..	....	40,456,167	6.30	7.94
1828..	....	16,998,873	4.09	5.49	1853..	....	60,287,983	7.50	9.89
1829..	345,736	....	4.40	4.38	1854..	....	61,937,155	8.27	10.65
1830..	8,949,779	....	4.53	3.91	1855..	....	38,899,205	7.19	8.64
1831..	....	23,589,527	4.45	6.22	1856..	....	29,212,887	9.61	10.67
1832..	....	13,601,159	4.50	5.50	1857..	....	54,604,582	9.78	11.70
1833..	....	13,519,211	4.99	5.96	1858.	8,672,620	....	8.58	8.28
1834..	....	6,349,485	5.56	5.99	1859..	....	38,431,290	9.21	10.49
1835..	....	21,548,492	6.69	8.13	1860..	....	20,040,062	10.07	10.71
1836..	....	52,240,550	6.92	10.31	1861..	67,291,045	....	11.09	9.02
1837..	....	19,029,676	5.97	7.17	1862..	....	68,519,944	7.75	10.66
1838..	9,008,282	....	5.97	5.41	1863..	....	40,961,330	7.50	9.23
1839..	....	44,245,283	6.12	8.79	1864..	....	150,469,884	5.24	11.11
1840..	25,410,226	....	6.56	5.07	1865..	....	78,039,194	4.39	6 99
1841..	....	11,140,073	5.92	6.56	1866..	....	88,971,936	9.42	11.92
1842..	3,801,924	....	5.09	4.88	1867..	....	95,569,045	7.65	10.27
1843..	40,462,449	....	*5.51	2.68	1868..	....	78,507,168	7.17	9.27
1844..	3,141,226	....	5.24	5.07	1869..	....	131,094,035	7.13	10.52
1845..	....	7,144,211	5.05	5.41					

There have been only twelve years in our history since 1820 in which the exports of domestic products have exceeded imports for consumption, and six of these were in times of protective duties; but all, except 1847, were years of panic, distress, or prostration of our industry, and 1847 was the year of famine in Europe. Those who cherish "a firm and intelligent purpose" that our exports shall exceed our imports, must therefore desire to bring about a state of perpetual prostration, a chronic paralysis of our industry.

---

* Four-thirds of the actual rate.

Under the protective system, from 1821 to 1832, inclusive, our exports barely kept pace with the increase of population. They were $4.38 per capita in 1821, and only $4.50 per capita in 1832. In like manner, the protective tariff of 1842 only reduced our exports from $5.09 in that year, and $5.51 in 1843 (allowing for twelve months instead of nine), to $5.08 in 1846, the last year of its operation. And under the protective system now in force our exports have been reduced from $11.09 in 1861, to $7.13 per capita in 1869. This was not because our imports had been stopped, so that the law of exchange restrained exports. For in 1821 our imports were $4.39 per capita, and, though twice temporarily checked in their natural increase, they were $5.50 in 1832. In 1843 they were $2.68 per capita (for the nine months only $2.01), and in 1846 they were $5.50. In 1861 they were $9.02 per capita, and, in spite of eleven additions to the tariff, in 1869 they were $10.52 per capita. With a natural and unrestricted exchange, imports increasing would have caused a larger exportation of our products. But the high tariffs, while their power to stop importations is quickly expended, so that in the long-run they do not prevent increased imports, do have this effect: they prevent any like increase of exports. Intended to prevent purchases of foreign goods, the protective tariff, reduced to its simplest terms, says to the American producer, "Thou shalt not export!"

As a nation progresses in growth, refinement, prosperity, and individual well-being, its people desire new or increased supplies of foreign products, and become able to consume a larger quantity in proportion to population. If they are truly prosperous, they must in like proportion increase in their power to produce a surplus of goods to exchange with foreign nations for those which they desire. Thus a reasonable and healthy increase per capita of exports and of imports is at once a result and a proof of the progress of a country in civilization and real prosperity. In every period of relaxation of duties, a rapid increase of exports bears testimony to the vigor of our industry and the increased prosperity of our people. When the protective system was abandoned in 1832, our exports instantly rose from $4.50 per capita in 1832 to $4.99 per capita in 1833, to $6.56 per capita in 1840, and, in spite of the depression of our industry, were $5.09 in 1842. Again, upon the second abandonment of the system, our exports rose from $5.08 in 1846 to $11.09 in 1861. These contrasts, and the changes of each year, may be most easily observed in the accompanying diagram, in which the rate of net exports and imports per capita, specie ex-

MERCHANDISE, IMPORTS, AND EXPORTS, PER CAPITA, SPECIE EXCLUDED, WITH EXPORTS OF MANUFACTURED PRODUCTS, PER CAPITA.

Black line, imports. Dotted line, exports.

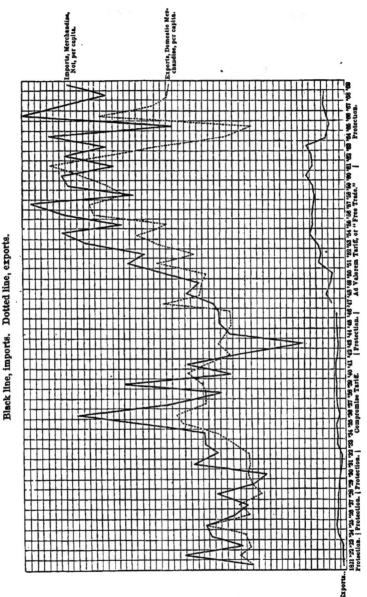

Manufactured Exports....

Imports, Merchandise, Net, per capita.

Exports, Domestic Merchandise, per capita.

1821 '20 '22 '23 '24 '25 '26 '27 '28 '29 '30 '31 '32 '33 '34 '35 '36 '37 '38 '39 '40 '41 '42 '43 '44 '45 '46 '47 '48 '49 '50 '51 '52 '53 '54 '55 '56 '57 '58 '59 '60 '61 '62 '63 '64 '65 '66 '67 '68 '69

Protection. | Protection. | Protection. | Compromise Tariff. | Protection. | Ad Valorem Tariff, or "Free Trade." | Protection.

clubed, is traced year by year according to the table already given. The lower line also represents the exports of manufactured products, to which we shall presently refer. Remembering that the years 1825 and 1847 were years of peculiar demand from Europe for our products, and that the sudden rise in 1866 was largely owing to the escape of cotton worth over two hundred and eighty millions of dollars, much of which had been confined during the war, we may trace year by year the effects of the currency on the one hand, and of tariffs on the other, upon our exports and imports.

During the twelve years of protection, with which the record begins, our imports, repeatedly depressed for one year or two, always recovered, and were higher per capita at the end than at the beginning of the period. But our exports, in spite of the increase of currency in 1831, remained about the same during the whole period, though, as soon as the duties were removed, they rose rapidly, and in 1834 reached the natural limit of exchange value. The expansion which followed increased them some, but imports far more, and the depression of exports which followed was due in part to failure of crops. Again, through all the tariff of 1842, our exports slightly declined in rate per capita, although imports, forced down to the lowest point in 1843, the first year of the tariff, more than recovered at once, and were higher at its close than in 1842. But the instant that tariff was removed, exports rose rapidly—not only in the year of famine, for they were higher in 1850 than in any year under protection—and from that time moved naturally and regularly in sympathy with imports, year by year, until the panic of 1858. Here the law of exchange was free to operate, and exports and imports both increased rapidly and harmoniously. But under each protective tariff that law of exchange has been interrupted; imports, obeying laws more powerful than any tariff, have risen in spite of temporary depression, while the natural tendency to increase exports in like proportion has been thwarted. Omitting the year 1866, for the reason given, we find that our exports since the war are lower than they were in any year since 1853, before the war. But our imports, cut down in 1861 to $9.02 per capita, instantly rose to $10.66. Higher duties cut them down to $9.23, but in the very next year they rose again to $11.11. Then came one more effort to shut out foreign goods, and duties, intended and believed to be almost prohibitory, cut down imports to $6.99 per capita. But in the very next year they rose to $11.92—higher than ever before in our history. And the last tariff, which reduced imports to $9.27 in 1868, seems already to have lost nearly all its force, for in 1869 we find an increase to $10.52. Meanwhile our exports are decreasing, and the gap to be filled every year with gold and bonds grows wider. Is it not wide enough already?

It will be said, however, that the recent decrease of exports is owing to the changes at the South, which have reduced the cotton crop. During the war, when our exports sank to $4.39 per capita—almost precisely the point at which the record starts, forty-eight years ago—the cotton crop was indeed interrupted. But it must be observed that the records before us are of values, not quantities, and the cotton crop since the war has actually sold for nearly as much money, and therefore added nearly as much to our exports per capita, as it did in the years before the war. In 1866 our exports of cotton were valued at two hundred and eighty-one millions, or in gold at two hundred and two millions; in 1860 at only one hundred and ninety-one millions. During the four years 1866–'69, inclusive, we have exported cotton valued at seven hundred and ninety-seven millions, or in gold at five hundred and seventy-four millions. During the four years 1857–'60, inclusive, we exported cotton worth six hundred and sixteen millions, so that the loss on this crop is only forty-two millions in four years, or ten millions a year—less than thirty cents per capita. Neither has the loss been in tobacco; in 1869 we exported of that article more than twenty millions' worth, and in 1860 less than sixteen millions. Nor has it been in breadstuffs. In 1860 we exported of wheat to the value of four millions, of flour fifteen millions, and of corn two and a half millions; in 1869 we exported of wheat over twenty-four millions, of flour nearly nineteen millions, and of corn nearly seven millions. And in 1868 the values were: of wheat, thirty millions; of flour, twenty millions; and of corn, thirteen millions.

It is the theory of the advocates of protection that by high duties we build up a home market for the farmer, enable the country to consume its own breadstuffs, and thus save the transportation to Europe on these and other bulky products, while we export more of finished products of industry. It is very plain that protection for eight years has not rendered our farmers more independent of foreign markets for their breadstuffs. It is very plain that the reduction of our exports has not been in the raw materials chiefly exported. Let us see whether the tariff actually does enable us to export a larger proportion of manufactured products, and a smaller proportion of raw materials. It must be admitted that this is a crucial test. If protection has failed in this, it has utterly failed to justify the theory of its advocates.

It has been stoutly asserted by Mr. Carey and others that our exports of manufactured products are now greater than ever before. If this were true, it would not sustain their reasoning. As a nation grows in population and in commerce, its exports of manufactured products ought to increase in at least equal ratio, and, if it progresses at all in civilization and mechanic arts, in a greater ratio. Were the statement true, therefore, it would only prove that our manufactures have not been conspicuously prostrated by a system especially designed to develop them. But it is not the fact!

At first glance, the records published by the Treasury Department seem to sustain the assertion. The aggregate value of the exported articles now classed as manufactures is reported as greater than the reported value of articles exported before the war, and then classed as manufactures. Thus when the Treasury tables assert that the value of manufactured exports in 1867 was $74,796,531, we look in vain to any former year for figures as large. In 1860 the reported value was only $48,090,640. But a moment's reflection suggests that the exports of 1867 were valued in a currency worth only seventy-one cents to the dollar, and, reducing the seventy-four millions in paper to gold values, we have only fifty-three millions—an increase of only five millions in nine years. Now, the nation has increased more than ten per cent. in population, and would naturally have increased more than ten per cent. in productive power.

But when we look into the items now classed as manufactures, and compare them with those of manufactured exports in 1860, we find that the tables are quite curiously constructed. The eye presently reaches the item, "Petroleum"—exported over twenty-four millions in 1867! Now, we did not export, nor in any considerable quantity produce, petroleum in 1860. This enormous item is simply added to our exports of manufactured articles, and the record is then quoted with infinite zest, as proving that our industries have been vastly benefited by high duties. What tariff, then, claims the honor of Drake's discovery? What tariff has bored wells to the great reservoirs of oil? Or did some very high protective tariff, far back in ages of the world's infancy, store away in caverns for the use of man these inexhaustible deposits of light and heat? Only by this addition of all exports of petroleum, crude or refined, have our exports of manufactures been thus apparently increased. Such a table evidently gives no just test of the effect of the present system upon our manufactures. Further, it appears that all exports of lumber, timber, masts, spars, shooks, staves, and headings, are now classed as manufactures. Whether such classification be proper or not, it is certainly not calculated to help to a correct understanding of the progress of what are usually regarded as manufactures. And it will be observed that exports of lumber have increased from six millions in 1860 to over ten millions in 1867 and 1868, so that, deducting these and the exports of petroleum, we have, in 1860, exports valued at forty-two millions in gold, against exports, in 1867, valued at forty millions in paper, and in 1868 valued at forty-one millions in paper. Now, the forty-two millions of exports in 1860, of articles legitimately classed as manufactured products, were 13¼ per cent. of our whole domestic exports in that year. But the forty-one millions in paper, or twenty-nine millions in gold, of manufactured exports in 1868, were only 10 per cent. of our domestic exports for that year. So that the exact result of nine years of protection has been to reduce the proportion of our manufactured exports, and increase the proportion of exports of raw materials. It happens, indeed, that these nine years of protection have pushed us back farther than we were in 1846, for then, after only four years of protection, our exports of the same manufactured articles were only $11,139,582, or almost 11 per cent. of our domestic exports. From that time to 1860, without protection, our manufactured exports advanced from 11 to over 13 per cent., and, from 1860 to 1868, the export of the same articles has declined to only 10 per cent.! Surely these facts do not justify the assertion that our exports have been checked by the tariff only because we have been sending away less of raw materials. For the contrary is proved by the statistics: the tariff has not only checked exports, but it has retarded our exports of manufactured more than our exports of raw products.

But it will be said that these selected facts may not fairly represent the whole history, and that there has been just complaint of other writers on that score. Let us, then, present a complete record of our exports of manufactures, from the earliest day. The following table is compiled from official records: * the data for the years prior to 1847 are taken from the Treasury reports of that period, and do

---

* On Diagram III. (page 52), the lower line represents the exports of manufactured products.

not include exports of lumber, timber, and shooks ; the data for the
years subsequent to 1847 are taken from the Treasury reports of
1866 and later, and do include exports of lumber, timber, shooks,
and also two small items, ashes and sperm candles, which were not
classed as manufactures prior to 1847. There is thus a break in the
continuity of the record at that point—an apparent increase caused
by including for the first time the articles named. The values for
recent years are reduced to gold, and exports of petroleum are of
course excluded—not because refined petroleum may not be called a
manufactured product, but because the object is to compare the effect
of tariffs in different years upon those branches of industry commonly
spoken of as manufactures, and which may be affected by them.
Against the amount exported each year, since 1821, will be found in
another column the amount per capita.

VALUE OF MANUFACTURED PRODUCTS EXPORTED.

YEAR.	Value per Cap.	Value.	YEAR.	Value per Cap.	Value.
1821.........	$ .28	$2,752,631	1845..........	$ .53	$10,329,701
1822.........	.30	3,121,030	1846..........	.55	11,139,582
1823.........	.29	3,139,598	†1847..........	.76	15,756,814
1824.........	.45	4,841,383	1848..........	.89	19,249,896
1825.........	.51	5,729,797	1849..........	.73	16,116,400
1826.........	.48	5,495,130	1850..........	.67	15,414,222
1827.........	.47	5,536,651	1851..........	1.15	27,317,107
1828.........	.44	5,548,359	1852..........	1.02	25,284,123
1829.........	.42	5,412,320	1853..........	1.12	29,255,104
1830.........	.41	5,320,980	1854..........	1.40	36,380,397
1831.........	.38	5,086,890	1855..........	1.34	35,999,387
1832.........	.36	5,050,633	1856..........	1.32	36,612,053
1833.........	.46	5,557,080	1857..........	1.29	36,655,296
1834.........	.43	6,247,893	1858..........	1.23	35,853,693
1835.........	.51	7,694,073	1859..........	1.32	39,934,373
1836.........	.40	6,107,528	1860..........	1.53	48,090,640
1837.........	.46	7,136,997	1861..........	1.33	43,190,497
1838.........	.51	8,397,078	1862..........	‡1.36	32,026,250
1839.........	.50	8,325,082	1863..........	1.54	37,549,508
1840.........	.58	9,873,462	1864..........	.88	24,122,859
1841.........	.57	9,953,020	1865..........	.79	23,932,073
1842.........	.47	8,410,699	1866..........	.81	29,019,254
1843.........	*.48	6,779,527	1867..........	.98	35,818,949
1844.........	.50	9,579,724	1868..........	.96	37,163,465

In 1803, prior to the complete Treasury records, it is mentioned
that the exports of manufactured products were but $1,355,000,

---

* For the year 1843 four-thirds are allowed, the Treasury year embracing only
nine months.

† Change of items included.

‡ Population within military lines, as per table elsewhere ; values reduced to gold.

5

or 23 cents per capita, and that they then rose, before our commerce was interrupted, to $2,963,000, or 45 cents per capita in 1806. This was without any such tariff as is now called protective, either to help or to embarrass. The seas were not free to our commerce again until 1815, and in that year the record starts with only $2,051,000, or 24 cents per capita, increased the next year to 27 cents, and the next to 28. But at this point begin the first duties for protective purposes, and, after an increase to 30 cents in 1818, there is a sudden decrease. From 1821 the records of the Treasury are complete, and we find that manufactured exports again rose to 45 cents per capita in 1824, and to 51 cents in 1825, when the protective tariff of 1824 began to be felt. From that time, with increasing duties to protect our manufactures, there is a curiously steady and regular decrease, a little every year, in the power of our manufacturers to compete in foreign markets. Exports of manufactured products fell from $5,729,797, or 51 cents per capita in 1825, to $5,050,633, or 36 cents per capita in 1832, the last year of that tariff. Instead of decreasing, they should have increased, if natural progress of industry had been left to work its legitimate results.

It is equally interesting to notice how promptly exports of manufactured products increase when the duties begin to decline. In 1833, the first year of the compromise tariff, the exports increased over a million and a half, or from 36 to 46 cents per capita. The inflation of 1836 and 1837, and the consequent panic, checked this progress, but in 1840 we were exporting of manufactured products $9,873,462, and in 1841, $9,953,020. Thus, in spite of the great panic, our export of manufactures had almost doubled in nine years. We shall see that a still more surprising progress followed the removal of protection in 1846.

During the tariff of 1843–'46, as has been already explained, the country was steadily recovering from the effects of the bank explosion, and exports of manufactures rose from ten millions in 1841 to eleven millions in 1846. The low figures for 1843, it will be remembered, represent only nine months. A gain of little more than a million in five years, or, population growing more rapidly, a decrease per capita from 58 to 55 is the result in that period.

In the next year the ad valorem tariff took effect, and we have also a change in the items, as already stated. Starting, then, with lumber, ashes, and sperm candles included, we have in 1847 an export of $15,756,814, or 76 cents per capita. For three years our manufactures were affected by foreign competition, but then began to grow in earnest. By 1854 our exports of the same products had reached $36,380,397, or an increase of nearly 150 per cent. in four years. The exports per capita reached the highest point then ever attained, $1.40 per capita, and, though interrupted again by the disaster of 1857, they more than kept pace with population, reaching $1.53 per capita in 1860. At that time the export of the manufactured products was $48,090,640, an increase of more than 200 per cent. in ten years.

We have now to observe the steady decline under protection to $23,932,070 in 1865, a loss of more than 50 per cent. in five years. But it is unjust to ascribe this wholly to the tariff; it is also the effect of the withdrawal of a large number of men from production, and of the high prices caused by an inflated currency. The amount per capita is calculated for the number of persons estimated in Treasory reports as being within our military lines and supplied by our trade each year, and this causes the figure for 1863 to rise too high, as compared with other years. During the war, when the Southern population, never largely engaged in manufacturing, was not consuming, while the force producing was not materially diminished by their isolation, and the population by which we divide was much reduced, the rate per capita was high, but the restoration of the Southern population to the computation makes the test of comparison of years since with the years before the war a fair one. Though we have been slowly recovering in exports of manufactured products, we are still more than eleven millions behind the point reached in 1860, and in 1868 exported only 96 cents per capita. The diagram (opposite page 52) will enable every reader to mark, first, the steady decrease under protection to 1832, and the rapid increase following the abandonment of protection; second, the slight increase under the tariff of 1842, compared with the rapid growth after 1850; and, finally, the condition to which our industry has now been brought by nine years of protection, as compared with the progress attained under low duties prior to 1860.

Is not this test a decisive proof that high duties render our industries less able to compete in open markets with those of other countries? Is it not proof that high duties do *not*, as has been claimed, reduce our exports of raw materials and increase our exports of manufactured products? Does it not clearly appear that the protective system thus fails, tested by facts, to sustain the expectations of its advocates?

NET IMPORTS AND EXPORTS OF MERCHANDISE ONLY.

YEAR.	Exports.	Per Capita.	Imports.	Per Capita.
1821.........	$43,671,894	$4.38	$43,696,405	$4.39
1822.........	49,874,079	4.84	68,395,673	6.64
1823.........	47,155,408	4.45	51,310,646.	4.84
1824.........	50,649,500	4.64	53,846,567	4.89
1825.·.......	66,944,745	5.98	66,395,722	5.92
1826.........	52,449,855	4.56	57,661,577 ·	5.01
1827.........	57,878,117	4.86	54,901,108	4.58
1828.........	49,976,632	4.09	66,975,505	5.49
1829.........	55,087,307	4.40	54,741,571	4.38
1830.........	58,524,878	4.53	49,575,099	3.91
1831.........	59,218,583	4.45	82,808,110	6.22
1832.........	61,726,529	4.50	75,327,688	5.50
1833.........	89,950,856	4.99	83,470,067	5.96
1834.........	80,623,662	5.56	86,973,147	5.99
1835.........	100,459,481	6.69	122,007,974	8.13
1836.........	106,570,942	6.92	158,811,492	10.31
1837.........	94,280,895	5.97	113,310,571	7.17
1838.........	95,560,880	5.97	86,552,598	5.41
1839.........	101,625,523	6.12	145,870,816	8.79
1840.........	111,660,561	6.56	86,250,335	5.07
1841.........	103,636,236	5.92	114,776,309	6.56
1842.........	91,799,242	5.09	87,996,318	4.88
1843.........	77,686,354	*4.21	37,223,905	2.01
1844.........	99,531,774	5.24	96,390,548	5.07
1845.........	98,455,330	5.05	105,599,541	5.41
1846.........	101,718,042	5.08	110,048,859	5.50
1847.........	150,574,844	7.34	116,257,595	5.67
1848.........	130,203,709	6.09	140,651,838	6.57
1849.........	131,510,081	6.00	132,565,108	6.05
1850.........	134,900,233	5.87	164,034,033	7.13
1851.........	178,620,138	7.50	200,476,219	8.42
1852.........	154,931,147	6.30	195,387,319	7.94
1853.........	189,869,162	7.50	250,151,145	9.89
1854.........	215,156,304	8.27	277,093,459	10.65
1855.........	192,751,135	7.19	231,650,340	8.64
1856.........	266,438,051	9.61	295,650,938	10.67
1857.........	278,906,713	9.78	333,511,295	11.70
1858.........	251,351,033	8.58	242,678,413	8.28
1859.........	278,392,080	9.21	316,823,370	10.49
1860.........	316,242,423	10.07	336,282,485	10.71
1861.........	359,036,604	11.09	291,745,559	9.02
1862.........	182,208,909	7.75	250,728,903	10.66
1863.........	184,413,850	7.56	225,375,280	9.23
1864.........	141,645,677	5.24	301,115,561	11.11
1865.........	131,617,331	4.39	209,656,525	6.99
1866.........	334,498,710	9.42	423,470,646	11.92
1867.........	279,374,457	7.65	374,943,502	10.27
1868.........	269,042,041	7.17	347,549,209	9.27
1869.........	275,187,799	7.13	406,281,834	10.52

* Per capita estimated for number within United States lines during the war, as per table of population. Rate for 1843, if four-thirds of the year be allowed: Exports, $5.51; imports, $2.68.

The examination of our exchanges with foreign nations has established certain facts:

1. That the protective system does not prevent overtrading.

2. That high duties check imports only temporarily, and their effect is lost after one or two years.

3. That any decrease of imports so caused is purchased at the cost of a greater decrease of exports.

4. That every period of high duties has checked the natural increase of our exports.

5. That in every such period our exports of manufactured products have been checked, and our industry has been rendered less able to compete with that of other nations.

6. That the present tariff has increased the proportion of raw materials, and decreased the proportion of manufactured products exported, and rendered the farmer more largely dependent upon foreign markets for his products than he was before the war.

CHAPTER V.

SHIP-BUILDING.

IT may now be confidently asserted that our prosperity, as affected by foreign exchanges, is not increased, but is retarded in its natural growth, by high duties on imports. Yet it may be true that those duties so stimulate home industry and domestic commerce as to confer benefits more than compensating for disadvantages resulting. "Protection to home industry"—the idea has an almost magical fascination. By many the policy bearing that name is thought to have a magical effect. Some have called it the American policy, but neither its virtues nor its vices are our own. It comes from Europe, was practised by European nations long before this nation was born; and has descended to us of modern times, a relic of the dark ages when the germs of civilization, struggling up through the mould of barbarism and the wreck of feudalism, deemed it necessary to shelter every industry with the strictest laws. Indeed, it has in spirit, if not in form, a still older exemplar in that nation which protected her industries by walls of stone instead of legislative barriers. Unconsciously, they borrow Celestial ideas who say, "What need we care for foreign commerce? Let us build up within this country industries to supply all our wants, for thus only can we achieve, in peace or in war, a true national independence."

One industry, however, we do not stimulate. To the enlightened protectionist, foreign commerce is a waste of human effort, and ships are a waste of the raw material. The object of his system is to eliminate the cost of transportation, and a perfectly protected country ought to have no use for a sailor. So much, at least, we might almost infer from the coolness with which the advocate of protection contemplates the decline of our shipping and ship-building. Our ship-yards become desolate; our seamen seek service under other flags; and our best vessels find owners in foreign ports; but Mr. Greeley quietly remarks that this interest cannot be expected to prosper at present. Yet our naval power depends upon the growth of our commercial shipping. Our fisheries, so long encouraged with liberality by government as a school for seamen, no longer meet the needs of modern times. Our coasting service has been greatly contracted by the rapid growth of railroad communications. Our foreign merchant-ships alone provide the trained seamen who can be called to man our vessels in time of conflict. Foreign commerce alone can keep in existence those magnificent ship-yards from which, in former time, went forth stanch and swift vessels, everywhere envied in peace and dreaded in war. No one who wishes to see our flag respected by foreign powers can witness without regret the decline of our shipping interest, the abandonment of yards, the sale of ships, and the expatriation of hardy and trained seamen. What manufacture deserves protection more than the manufacture of ships? No small share of our success in the recent struggle we owe to the readiness of our ship-yards, the genius of our architects, and the skill of our mechanics. But to-day that great interest—the only arm with which we can strike any foe of importance—is crippled, and that industry is almost annihilated. The immense yards and iron-works, from which years ago we sent ships and engines of matchless excellence to all countries, are closed and silent. In September there were but two sea-going steamers for commercial purposes being built in all our ports. Nor is this strange. The wonder is that any are built, when the cost of every material, iron, copper, cordage, duck, and timber, is so great. It is a singular proof of the superiority of our workmen, that, in spite of these disadvantages, they can still build any class of vessels within 20 per cent. of the cost in foreign ports. In Nova Scotia, wooden vessels can be built, it is stated, nearly 30 per cent. cheaper than in this country. On the Clyde, for miles, the ear is stunned with the clang of hammers, and iron ships by the hundred are built at rates with which our builders cannot now compete.

If it is desirable or possible to "protect American industry," this particular industry of all others deserves its full share of favor. The artisans of our ship-yards, the machinists of our great iron-works, were not these also American laborers? Were not they entitled to some thought from a paternal government which holds it a duty to secure plenty of work at high wages to American workmen? Or do we intentionally select, as the one industry which we will not protect, that very one upon which our national honor and safety most depend?

Prior to 1855, wooden vessels were mainly used; since that time they have been rapidly superseded by iron. At the point of change, during the years 1856 and 1857, our foreign tonnage declined, but it began to recover again in 1858, and increased in 1859, 1860, and 1861, iron ships being built with success in our ship-yards. The two periods, then, are to be considered separately, and in the following table will be found the registered tonnage for each year since the War of 1812, the proportion of tonnage to population expressed in thousandths of a ton per capita, and the number of ships, barks, and brigs, built each year since 1821. Of schooners, sloops, and steamers, a large proportion has been used in the coasting, lake, or river traffic, and it is with foreign tonnage only that we have to do at this time.

TONNAGE—VESSELS BUILT.

YEAR.	Registered.	Tonnage per Cap.	Ships and Barks.	Brigs.	YEAR.	Registered.	Tonnage per Cap.	Ships and Barks.	Brigs.
1815...	854,294	.101	..	..	1840...	899,765	.053	97	109
1816...	800,760	.092	..	..	1841...	845,803	.048	114	101
1817...	809,725	.091	..	..	1842...	975,359	.054	116	91
1818...	606,089	.067	..	..	1843...	1,009,315	.054	58	34
1819...	612,930	.065	..	..	1844...	1,068,765	.056	73	47
1820...	619,047	.064	..	..	1845...	1,095,173	.056	124	87
1821...	619,896	.062	..	..	1846...	1,130,286	.056	100	164
1822...	628,150	.061	64	131	1847...	1,241,313	.060	151	168
1823...	639,921	.060	55	127	1848...	1,360,887	.663	254	174
1824...	669,973	.060	56	156	1849...	1,438,942	.065	198	148
1825...	700,787	.062	56	197	1850...	1,585,711	.069	247	117
1826...	737,978	.064	71	187	1851...	1,726,307	.072	211	65
1827...	747,170	.062	55	153	1852...	1,899,448	.077	255	79
1828...	812,619	.066	73	108	1853...	2,108,674	.080	269	95
1829...	650,142	.052	44	58	1854...	2,333,819	.089	334	112
1830...	576,675	.045	25	56	1855...	2,535,136	.094	381	126
1831...	620,452	.047	72	95	1856...	2,491,402	.090	306	103
1832...	686,989	.050	132	143	1857...	2,463,967	.086	251	58
1833...	750,026	.053	144	169	1858...	2,499,742	.085	122	46
1834...	857,438	.059	98	94	1859...	2,507,402	.083	89	28
1835...	885,822	.060	25	50	1860...	2,546,237	.081	110	36
1836...	897,774	.058	93	65	1861...	2,642,628	.081	110	38
1837...	810,447	.051	67	72	1862...	2,291,251	..	60	17
1838...	822,592	.051	66	79	1863...	2,026,114	..	97	34
1839...	834,244	.050	83	89					

At the close of the War of 1812, our registered tonnage was 854,294 tons, or $\frac{101}{1000}$ of a ton per capita. As there is no other method of reaching, even approximately, the amount of tonnage employed in foreign trade, we may treat the registered tonnage as foreign, and may suppose that the number of ships, barks, and brigs built affords a fair basis of comparison for the whole number of sea-going vessels put afloat. Never, since 1815, has our registered tonnage been as great in proportion to population as it was in that year. Under the tariff of 1816 there was a sudden decline to 606,089 tons, or $\frac{87}{1000}$ per capita in 1818; and from this time until 1828 there was an increase almost exactly proportioned to that of population—from $\frac{87}{1000}$ to $\frac{88}{1000}$ of a ton per capita. The tariff of 1828 affected this interest just as it did others; it produced a rapid decline and general prostration in 1829 and 1830, after which imports revived, and shipping also. In 1830, tonnage fell to 576,675, or $\frac{46}{1000}$ per capita, its lowest point in our history since the war. Fourteen years of protection had reduced our foreign tonnage from 800,716, in 1816, to 576,675, in 1830, and from $\frac{88}{1000}$ to $\frac{45}{1000}$. It is difficult to avoid the inference prompted by the fact that this, the lowest point in our history, was reached under the heaviest duties on iron, hemp, cordage, duck, copper, and other materials. Nor will the singularly steady and regular decline be overlooked, which followed the duties placed on iron in 1818. The rate per capita changed thus: 67, 65, 64, 62, 61, 60. The subsequent increase under the tariff of 1824, though not large, is, nevertheless, noteworthy, because it was in spite of duties still higher, and it may, perhaps, be ascribed to an increase of the cotton crop, from 560,000 bales in 1824 to 957,000 bales in 1827, that the higher duties did not cause a further decline of tonnage. The actual increase was less than that of the cotton crop. The decrease in 1830 of 236,000 tons since 1828 cannot be wholly explained by a decrease in the cotton crop, from 957,000 bales in 1827 to 870,415 in 1829, and in 1830 the crop was 976,845, and in 1831 it was, for the first time, over one million bales, which in part explains the recovery of tonnage in 1831 and 1832. Taking the whole period of sixteen years of protection, we have an actual decrease of foreign tonnage, from 854,294 tons in 1815 to 686,989 tons in 1832, and from $\frac{101}{1000}$ to $\frac{50}{1000}$. And this was in spite of the fact that our cotton crop had grown from almost nothing to one million bales. It certainly cannot be denied that such a change gives proof that our shipping and shipbuilding were affected most unfavorably then, as they are now, by high duties on the materials used.

In anticipation of reduction of duties and revival of commerce, a large number of ships were built in the year 1832, and a still larger number in the year 1833, and, under the compromise tariff, tonnage rose to 885,822 in 1835, or from 50 to 60 per capita. In the same time, the cotton crop had increased in the same ratio. The financial disasters prevented further increase after 1836, until the return to specie, but there was then an increase, and in 1842 the tonnage was 975,359, or 54 per capita. Taking this period as a whole, therefore, its results are an increase from 686,989 to 975,359 tons, slightly greater than that of population—from $\frac{68}{1000}$ to $\frac{64}{1000}$ per capita. Under the protective tariff there was also a very slight increase, from 54 to 56 per capita. But, with the return to a non-protective policy in 1847, the tonnage gained in two years more than it had in four years under protection, and the rate per capita gained in one year more than it had in four. Thenceforward an increase is maintained with great regularity, until 1855. In those nine years tonnage increased from 1,130,286 in 1846 to 2,535,136 in 1855, or more than doubled. Let us now compare the fifteen years under protection, from 1816 to 1830 inclusive, with the nine years under non-protection, from 1847 to 1855 inclusive. In the protective period we have a decrease from 854,294 in 1815 to 576,675 in 1830. In the non-protective period we have an increase from 1,130,286 in 1846 to 2,535,819 in 1855. And these are the only periods in our history during which long-continued adherence to either policy, without inflation of currency, fully tested its effect.

It will be said, however, that the tonnage declined during the remaining years of the non-protective period. It did, indeed, increase less rapidly than population, and the cause, as has been remarked, was the substitution of iron for wooden vessels. But the commercial disorders of 1857 also had a depressing effect.

It will be reasoned that the rapid increase of our cotton crop and of exports of cotton caused the increase of tonnage from 1847 onward. If this were so, the reply would be ready that it is the avowed object of protection to diminish the quantity of raw material sent abroad for manufacture; and that, had that policy been in force, and had it produced such effects as its advocates desire, it would have prevented this increase of shipping. But the facts do not fully sustain this plausible explanation of the increase. For, first, if it were the true one, our tonnage should have increased far more from 1855 to 1860 than in the previous years, because our cotton exports increased from one thousand to seventeen hundred

million pounds in that period.   But tonnage did not increase in the
same time, and the increased exportation was done in foreign vessels.
And, again, if the increased exportation of cotton is to account for
the increase of tonnage between 1846 and 1855, then there should
be some proportion between them.   But there is not, for the exports
of cotton were eight hundred and seventy-three million pounds in
1845, and eight hundred and fourteen million pounds in 1848 (the
crops were short in the years 1846 and 1847), while they were only one
thousand million pounds in 1855, and only nine hundred and eighty-
seven million pounds in 1854.   Increase of cotton exports, from
eight hundred and fourteen to one thousand million pounds, or 25
per cent. ; increase of tonnage, from eleven hundred to twenty-five
hundred thousand tons, or 225 per cent.—surely, these facts do not
sustain to each other the relation of cause to effect !

By no such reasoning can the inference be avoided, that under a
non-protective policy our ship-building was stimulated to vigorous
progress by profitable employment for our ships in foreign commerce,
while under a protective policy that interest was retarded, both by
that decline of our exports which we have traced as an effect of
that policy, and by the unnatural enhancement of the cost of materials used in ship-building.

The record of ships built strongly confirms the same conclusion.
We suppose that ships, barks, and brigs, were mainly used in
foreign trade, and that taken together they afford a fair test of the
amount of shipping built each year for ocean service.   The number
built under the tariff of 1824 was 931 (1824 to 1827 inclusive), and
the number built under the higher protective tariff of 1828 (1828
to 1832) was only 533—a loss of four-ninths.   The number built in
1832 may, perhaps, fairly be attributed in part to the expectation
of a more prosperous trade from the change of tariff then rendered
certain by the elections.   And the number in that year and the years
1833 and 1834, before inflation of currency had greatly increased
prices, was 880—more by 60 per cent. in three years than had been
built in four years under protection.   Again, though building had
revived after the inflation and panic, so that 628 vessels were built
in the three years 1840, 1841, and 1842, it was instantly checked by
the tariff of 1843, so that only 587 were built during the four years
of its operation.   And, after the expiration of that tariff, in the next
four years (1847 to 1850 inclusive) the number built rose to 1,457—
an increase of more than 250 per cent. !   In the years 1852 to 1856
inclusive there were built, of ships and barks only, 1,645, or nearly

three times the number of ships, barks, and brigs, built under the protective tariff, and almost five times that of ships and barks!

No comments can add to the force of these figures. They demonstrate that high tariffs are injurious to our ship-building interest. They demonstrate that, when we claim to be protecting American industry, there is at least one branch of American industry, and that not the least important, which we protect well-nigh to death. Is there any reason why the thousands of workmen in our forests and ship-yards, and the tens of thousands of sailors and of people dependent upon their trade in our maritime towns, should be selected from all other laborers by our government, and sentenced to starvation or a change of employment?

This great interest cannot longer be safely ignored or trampled down. For, since the change from wooden ships to iron, the effect of the protective policy is more injurious than ever before. The wooden ships of twenty years ago required, for one of five hundred tons, about fifty-two thousand pounds of iron, twenty thousand pounds of cordage, three thousand five hundred pounds of copper, and fifty-two pieces of sail-duck; and on smaller vessels the quantity required of these articles, though less, was much larger in proportion to tonnage—thus a schooner of only one hundred tons required fifteen thousand pounds of iron, eight hundred pounds of copper, five thousand pounds of cordage, and twenty-four pieces of sail-duck. It was estimated that the tariff of 1844 enhanced the prices of those articles alone $2,290 for a five hundred ton ship, or $4.58 to the ton; and, as ship-building had cost prior to that tariff not far from $35 a ton, the tariff added about one-ninth to the cost of the ships by the duties on those articles only. But the burden is still greater now. It would cost to build the same vessels now about $70 a ton in gold,* while builders in New Brunswick will build for any customer at $40 a ton. The iron needed, which before the war could be bought for $45 a ton, now commands $85; the hemp then costing 4½ cents, now costs 12; the copper, then 22 cents, is now 34; hackmatack knees, then costing $1.25 and $1.50 a-piece, now cost $2.50 to $3; oak timber, then 28 cents per foot, now costs 60; white pine, then 22 cents, is now 45; and yellow pine, then 23, is now 35 cents per foot. The present prices are stated in currency, but it will readily be seen that they are far higher now in gold than they were in 1860. It is noticeable that ship-carpenters do not share in the benefits of the tariff, for before the war they received $2.25 to

* These and other figures following give prices in the fall of 1869.

$2.50 per day, and now they get only $3.25 to $3.50 in currency, and a great part of them are idle even at that.

But in the building of iron ships the disadvantage is fatally great. Iron for that use cost before the war $45 a ton, and now (1869) it costs $85 in currency, or about $60 in gold. This alone would add nearly one-third to the cost of the ship, while the cost of iron to other builders in Great Britain and elsewhere has been reduced by improvements in manufacture. Before the war our builders of iron vessels were beginning to compete vigorously with foreign builders; but it needs no elaborate reasoning to show that they work to-day under such a load as must crush all enterprise.

The history of England in this matter is instructive. Prior to 1848, through centuries of battle with the world, England tried by every form of legislative aid to help her shipping interest, and had the mortification to see young America fairly rival her in number of vessels, and outstrip her in excellence. In 1848 England adopted free trade in shipping, and, after freeing from import duty all foreign timber, copper, iron, hemp, rope, and naval stores, took away the futile legislative helps and told her ship-builders to fight for themselves. The consequence was that her tonnage quickly rose from about 3,000,000 tons entered in her ports in 1848, to 5,388,953 in 1859, and to 7,299,417 in 1863; while in the years 1853 to 1862, inclusive, there were built of steam vessels alone in Great Britain 1,940, of which 1,499 were of iron. To-day we have eight steamers in all sailing from our ports to Europe, while England alone has sixty-eight steamers sailing to American ports, France has six, and North Germany has twenty-four.

Here, then, is one great branch of American industry which we are protecting to death. And it is that upon which depend the honor of our flag in war, and, in a large degree, the commercial prosperity of our country in peace.

CHAPTER VI.

INTERFERENCE WITH NATURAL LAWS.

THE inquiry thus far has not touched those points upon which advocates of the protective system mainly depend. Shipping and ship-building are important interests, but they are so allied with foreign commerce that it is impossible to repress that commerce without unfavorably affecting them. If it be proved that high tariffs do not prevent over-trading, since they check imports only at the expense of a greater reduction of exports, it will be replied that they may nevertheless have given needed aid to our industries. If it be proved that any high tariff to check imports quickly spends its force, the reply is that it gives at least a temporary advantage, which, by frequent additions to duties, can be prolonged. If it be proved that our manufactures, tested by the power to compete in foreign markets, have progressed more rapidly under low than under high duties, the answer is that protection does not look to foreign markets.

There is something grand in the attitude of a people who deliberately make voluntary sacrifices, resolutely spurn the allurement of goods offered at lower prices, and with unflinching fidelity to their purpose tax themselves, year after year, in order to build up a nationality complete in every industry, armed at all points, and sufficient unto itself. Other nations have borne such taxes when imposed by rulers, but few, if any, themselves have imposed them. Whether the effort has succeeded or has failed, there has been a certain heroism in making it. Perhaps even the failure may place in a brighter light the heroism of the endeavor; as the Spartans at Thermopylæ, or the six hundred at Balaklava, were not the less glorious in their death. But, honorable as it may be in a people to make voluntary sacrifices for the public good, the time has come when we must ask whether the endeavor has succeeded; if so, at what cost; if not, whether it has reasonable prospect of success; in short, whether an enlightened desire for the public welfare still demands that the effort shall be continued. We cannot always afford to waste the nation's strength in honorable but futile exertions. If the idea has been a mistaken one, its patriotic purpose is a sufficient justification in the past; but, when it shall appear mistaken, the same patriotism will prompt to its abandonment.

Briefly stated, the idea of the advocate of protection is that high and discriminating duties, in spite of some disadvantages, greatly benefit the country by building up within it such diversified industry as to render it comparatively independent of other countries.

Independence is not always and necessarily a blessing. The savage tribes of some Pacific islands were wholly independent of the rest of the world, but their condition has improved since their independence was destroyed. China and Japan, by exclusion of foreign trade, built up wonderfully complete and self-sustaining civilizations, but we do not envy them. Already greater dependence upon the outside world is giving to them the benefits of a civilization less isolated and stagnant. Yet, if mere protection to home industry could ever confer blessings, those nations should have been most blessed. If mere diversification of industry, without regard to its cost, is the one thing needful, those nations gained it. If the perfect condition is that in which a nation produces every thing it wants and has no foreign commerce, deeming that a useless waste of material and effort, then China and Japan were for centuries models of perfection.

These phrases, by which the system of protection is defended, tempt the mind to overlook two important considerations : first, whether the desired diversification and independence can at this time be secured except at a cost greater than their value ; and, second, whether these ends can be obtained more speedily, surely, and cheaply, by a system which seeks to exclude foreign competition than by one which permits that competition as an additional stimulus to our industry. Protection is not a blessing in itself, for it involves denial of freedom to satisfy all wants at the least cost. Diversification of industry is not a blessing in itself, for it would cost a great sacrifice of labor and capital to produce on our own soil all the natural products of the tropics. Diversification, attainable at a future time without cost, may now be attainable only by a wasteful sacrifice. He who advocates the encouragement of any industry by legislation, ought, therefore, to show that it will not grow up as fast as the country can afford to sustain it without encouragement. And, the cost being considered, he is also bound to show that the industry in question will be more healthy and valuable to the country if sheltered from foreign competition, than if subjected to that stimulus. Not all plants can be grown under glass to advantage. Oaks do not become tough and sturdy in a hot-house.

These two considerations—cost to the country, and effect upon industry of competition or its absence—must be taken into account when we attempt to decide whether the protection of any branch of industry has been successful. In other words, we must not only ascertain whether the production of wealth has on the whole been increased under protective duties, but whether it has been increased more rapidly and surely under those duties than under the non-protective system.

It will hardly be denied that every interference with natural laws involves some disadvantage. If it be only a difference of a cent in the pound of an article of food or a material of industry, it causes some inconvenience to somebody. However slight it may be, that inconvenience is an element in the cost, and, if there are many, the aggregate may not be slight.

Every change from one form or degree of interference with trade to another also involves loss to somebody. If it increases or lessens the value of a stock on hand, or the cost of filling a contract, there is loss to somebody; and, when there is a general change in the rate of duties, there are a great many losses on a great many different articles. The disadvantages and losses which result from the changes themselves are an important element in the cost of a protective system. If by the prospect of frequent changes men are discouraged from attempting the production of wealth, the cost is still further increased.

The policy of interfering with the laws of trade has now been tried for more than eighty years. Absolute free trade this country has never tried. The lowest ad valorem tariffs have operated to some extent as a tax upon all industries and as an encouragement to many. Ever since our government had being, it has been making artificial conditions for trade and industry; sometimes with equal or level tariffs, and sometimes with unequal or discriminating; sometimes with high duties and sometimes with low; sometimes with specific, and sometimes with ad valorem duties; but always in one way or another interfering with natural laws. Thirty-five distinct tariff laws have been passed, each changing in some way the conditions of trade and production. It will be admitted by all that such fluctuation is in itself a great evil. No one, who attentively considers the effect upon commerce, manufactures, investments and profits of capital, and employment of labor, can fail to realize that these changes have been terribly injurious. Thirty-five alterations of the very basis upon which industry and capital must build—thirty-five earthquakes, each shattering some structures, destroying some, and trying all—thirty-five changes, each involving to one class or another loss or gain, bankruptcy or sudden wealth—how can such fluctuations occur without imparting to all business something of the character of gambling? The sober and cautious method, the true enterprise of quick sales and small profits, must give place to something else. Large profits must be realized to make up for expected losses; the lender must charge twice, once for use of money, and once for risk; timid capital must shrink from productive enterprise; the rate of interest and the charges for exchange of commodities must rise.

All these consequences must result, in a greater or less degree, from a system which changes the conditions of trade and the very basis of industry thirty-five times in eighty years, and introduces the element of chance into the most legitimate business.

But is not this frequency of change a natural effect of the attempt to set aside or modify natural laws? Does not interference with natural relations breed more interference? No tariff can please everybody, and, if we interfere for the benefit of one, another may ask aid with equal justice. The favor to one interest is a detriment to some other. Men are not omniscient; not all the consequences of any measure can be foreseen. If in any respect it works badly, the result is a new interference, this again begetting still another. And, the higher the duties, the more decided the discrimination between some interests and others, the stronger will naturally be the tendency to frequent changes.

Since the War of 1812 there have been twenty-four tariffs adopted. Twenty of these have been protective in their object. Only four were non-protective, and one of these scarcely went into operation before it was repealed by a protective tariff. But the three non-protective tariffs lasted over twenty-three years. The twenty protective tariffs lasted less than twenty-nine years. Beginning with the protective period of 1816–'32, we find that new tariffs were adopted in 1816, 1818, 1819, 1824, 1828, 1830, and 1832—the last a protective tariff, though succeeded early in the next year by the compromise act of 1833. For this period of seventeen years, seven tariffs were necessary. The protective tariff of 1842 lasted four years without change, because the elections in 1844 precluded all hope of increase. The third protective period began March 2, 1861, and including the act of that date we have had twelve changes in eight years. Compare the proportion of duties to the whole value of imports and dutiable imports, for each period, with the duration of each tariff!

NON-PROTECTIVE TARIFFS.

Date of Tariff.	Duration.	PERCENTAGE OF	
		Duties to dutiable Imports.	Duties to whole Imports.
1846—August 6.............	10 years 7 mos.	24.	20.4
1857—March 3..............	4 "	19.	13.8
1833—March 2.............	8 " 6 "	31.9	15.4
1841—Sept. 11..............	11 "	23.1	16.6
Four tariffs..................	24 years.		

PROTECTION BEGETS FREQUENT CHANGES.

Twenty Protective Tariffs, duration, twenty-eight years nine months; average duration, seventeen months and eight days. Four Non-Protective Tariffs, duration, twenty-four years; average duration, six years,

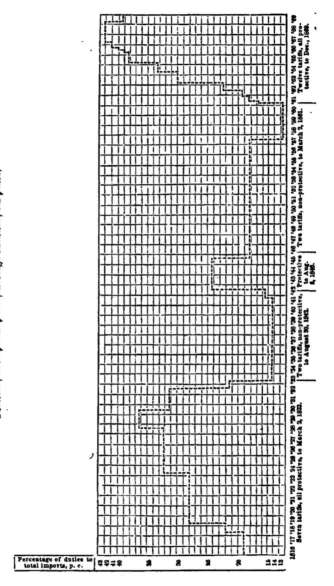

PROTECTIVE TARIFFS.

Date of Tariff.	Duration.	PERCENTAGE OF	
		Duties to dutiable Imports.	Duties to whole Imports.
1816—April 27...............	2 years.	....	20.
1818—April 20...............	...... 11 mos.	....	23.
1819—March 3...............	5 " 2 "	34.4	29.
1824—May 22................	4 "	38.1	33.1
1828—May 19................	2 "	46.5	38.5
1830—May 20................	2 " 2 "	41.1	32.2
1832—July 14................	...... 7½ "	31.9	22.4
First period, seven acts........	16 years 10¼ mos.		
1842—August 30.............	3 years 11 mos.	32.4	25.2
1861—March 2...............	...... 5 mos. ⎫		
1861—August 5..............	...... 4½ " ⎬	26.7	17.7
1861—Dec. 24...............	...... 7 " ⎭		
1862—July 14...............	...... 7½ "	33.2	23.7
1863—March 3...............	1 year 4 "	37.2	31.
1864—June 30...............	...... 8 "	43.7	34.2
1865—March 3...............	1 year ¼ "	47.06	40.2
1866—March 14..............	...... 2 " ⎫		
1866—May 16................	...... 2½ " ⎬	47.34	42.8
1866—July 28...............	...... 7 " ⎭		
1867—March 2...............	2 years.	47.86	44.
1869—Feb. 24...............	1 year.		
Third period, twelve acts.......	9 years.		

It appears that the longest period without change of laws, ten years and seven months, and the next in duration, eight years and six months, were under a non-protective policy. Under the act of 1833 there were changes of duty, but no change of system, the design being to reach a purely revenue standard; and the act of 1841, extending low duties to the free list, effected no material change in industrial relations. The other non-protective period, also, properly extends from August 6, 1846, to March 2, 1861, fourteen years and seven months, for the change of duties in 1857 was but slight, from 30 to 24 per cent. These are the periods of low duties and non-protection, and their long duration without essential change is evidence that such tariffs tend less strongly than those of a different character to produce frequent fluctuations. For, excepting the tariff of 1842, which was virtually condemned to repeal by the popular vote when it had been in operation hardly two years, other high tariffs have invariably led to clamors for still higher duties, or protection to additional interests. At the same time, they have roused an intense desire for their repeal. By these contending forces, legislation has been constantly threatened, and obtained with such frequency, that the average duration of protective tariffs without change is less than eighteen months, while the average duration of non-protective tariffs is six years.

The chief cause of frequency of change under protection is the increased cost of production here, as compared with a reduced cost elsewhere, in consequence of which the advantage of duties is soon neutralized. It is important that this statement should not be misunderstood. It is not intended to repeat that notorious untruth, that duties always enhance to their full amount prices of domestic products. Nor is it true that an absolute increase of price follows every duty. Instances can be and have been given of an actual reduction of price after protective duties had been imposed on the corresponding foreign article, sometimes because, as protectionists maintain, home competition has sufficed to reduce the price, and sometimes because less costly raw material or improvements in manufacture, here and in other countries, have caused a great reduction of cost, a part of which appears in a lower price, while another part appears in larger profits of the manufacture. But it must be remembered that in the latter case the cost here, though not absolutely, is relatively increased; the margin between the cost here and the cost in other countries is made wider. It will not be denied that the general object of protective duties is to enable the manufacturer to receive more for his products than the cost of like foreign products, and their general effect is therefore to make prices higher here than they would have been without the duties. Not all prices, but some unquestionably, are enhanced; and the cost of production is therefore affected. If iron is dear, the cost of machinery is affected; if coal is dear, the cost of power or fuel is affected; if dye-stuffs are dear, the cost of cloths is affected; and in like manner the price of lumber affects the cost of buildings, and the price of clothing and food, the cost of labor. These many items make a large aggregate, and each of them is swelled by the large profits which every transporter, merchant, or middle-man, must charge to cover his own increased risk from fluctuations, or expense from enhancement of prices. Let us now suppose that, with cotton at twenty cents, a maker of cotton goods, four yards to the pound, could sell them at eight cents a yard without loss, the manufacture costing twelve cents to the pound, or three cents a yard, and that British goods cost eight and a half cents imported. The manufacturer can make a profit of one-half cent a yard. If we now add a tariff of one cent a yard it simply enables him to make three times as large a profit, *at first*. But other articles are also protected, and presently his machinery costs more, his coal more, his dyes more, his buildings more, and each item is increased by higher charges of middle-men, and his labor needs higher wages to meet increased cost of living. Let us suppose that the cost of working up a pound of cotton rises to sixteen cents, or four cents to the yard; the benefit of the tariff is then fully neutralized. He has to sell at nine and a half cents to get a profit of one-half a cent a yard. Meanwhile, the British manufacturer, forced by competition, steadily reduces his cost of manufacture by improvements or greater skill. If he reduces the cost one-half cent, the profit of the American manufacturer must vanish, competition from abroad overwhelming him. Were there no tariff, he would be forced to keep pace with others in skill; but, since government has taught him to look to legislation for success, he flies to Congress, represents with truth that the foreign competition is crushing him, and obtains a duty of two cents a yard. How many such instances have we seen! How often, in the record of foreign trade, have we observed that importations were at first checked by high duties, but presently rose higher than ever! Every such increase shows that the duties have in some way neutralized themselves, and the method just described is, perhaps, the most common.

To show how this loss of the effect of duties may occur while the price of the product here is not absolutely, but only relatively increased, let us suppose that cotton falls from 20 to 12 cents a pound while the high duty is in force. Both in England and here the cost of the goods is reduced. Our manufacturer now pays three cents for his material to the yard, though he formerly paid five, and, though the cost of manufacture has been increased by the tariff to four cents a yard, he can now sell without loss at seven cents, or lower than he could at first. But the British manufacturer has his cotton cheaper also, so that the goods which could be delivered here for eight and a half cents now cost six and a half, or, with the duty, seven and a half. And the natural progress in skill and machinery, under pressure of competition, has enabled him to reduce the cost of production one half cent, so that foreign goods can be sold here, duty paid, at seven cents. The American can make no profit. He flies to Congress, states with truth that competition is crushing his industry, and, by way of proving that the high tariff has not taxed the people at all, he points to the prices when cotton was twenty cents, and says with truth, "The same goods which I sold before the tariff for eight and a half cents, I sell now at seven and a half; but the pauper labor of Europe undersells me, and drives me from the market." Then, Congress, convinced that high duties make low prices, gives him a larger duty, and he goes home again to manufacture until that duty also has neutralized itself. What is the fact? The price is absolutely lower, but relatively higher. If the cost of production had not been increased by a tariff, and if the manufacturer, forced by competition, had kept pace with others, the cost of production, originally three, would have fallen to two and a half cents a yard, and, the cost of material having fallen to three cents, the goods actually ought to be sold as low as six cents, yielding to the manufacturer a profit even then of one half cent a yard. What, then, is the result in the case supposed? The goods sell at seven cents, the people are taxed one cent a yard, the manufacturer makes no profit, and British competition crushes him. Everybody is taxed; nobody is benefited; and our industry clamors for a still higher tariff.

This is an imaginary case. But it shows precisely what the effect must be, when the cost of production is increased fully as much as the duty increases the cost of foreign goods. Now, any tariff which affects the prices of thousands of articles must increase the cost of production in some measure. And every such increase, whether much or little, tends to neutralize the effect of the duty, and to drive the manufacturer to Congress, seeking higher duties. That this effect does follow, we may infer from the frequency of changes under the protective system, and from the fact that imports, temporarily checked by high duties, have always become larger than ever after those duties have been in force one or two years. When the history of separate industries shall be examined, a multitude of facts will illustrate this principle.

Other causes contribute to bring about frequent changes. Not all manufacturers are enterprising or careful in management. Interference in behalf of any interest invites all who are not successful in that business to ask further aid. The less enterprising and capable, finding themselves unable to realize large profits, represent that the industry, as a whole, is still depressed by foreign competition, and needs higher duties. The capable and enterprising manufacturer, not averse to still larger profits, joins the demand, or rarely opposes it. A third cause of dissatisfaction is that the manufacturers, in anticipation of higher duties, prepare and hold as large stocks as possible, to be thrown upon the market when the new duties cause higher prices. But so many take this course, straining their capital to carry large stocks, that the market is depressed for a time, and, indeed, in some cases, great losses have occurred. Finally, the expectation of large profits invites capital to a favored industry. Men rush into it without experience or skill, and with insufficient capital, who cannot produce at a cost much below the artificial limit fixed by duties, and cannot afford to wait in an unfavorable condition of the market. Production is suddenly increased; the market is overstocked; prices fall a little, and that little suffices to break the new adventurers, and, perhaps, older manufacturers who have been holding back heavy stocks. The broken firms cease producing; the production falls once more below the demand; and, after sacrificing the entire capital of many firms, the country is in the hands of a monopoly, which points to the distress and ruin of many as proof that duties still higher are needed. He who will attentively examine any faithful history of either industry, however strongly it may advocate protection, will find examples of the workings of these principles. "Bishop's History of Manufactures," a work which no protectionist will consider unfriendly, says (vol. 2, p. 336) of the year 1829, immediately following the passage of the high tariff of 1828 with its minimum of 35 per cent. on cotton goods:

"An unusual degree of distress prevailed at this time among the manufacturers of New England, particularly in the cotton branch, producing numerous failures and great depreciation of the value of stocks. The cause was by some ascribed to the disappearance of specie, and by others to over-speculation, which had tempted great numbers into manufacturing with insufficient capital and consequent over-production."

And the same result is noticed as the first effect of the tariff of 1842, which caused such a deluge of goods on the market in 1843, that many manufacturers, who had survived all the pressure of foreign competition, were then ruined. Prices were then temporarily depressed remarkably; but, when the market had cleared itself, they rose again higher than before, and those manufacturers who had survived made large profits. The history of the past eight years is full of illustrations of the same principles—of demands for new duties from the less capable, when the majority of manufacturers were already thriving; of demands from all, caused by increased cost of production; of stoppage of factories in consequence of over-production; of failures and losses caused by fluctuations of price. And every change has induced a new appeal to Congress for aid. Accordingly, the changes of tariff have been more frequent than ever before.

It needs no argument to prove that these continual changes are most injurious to industry. Said one of the shrewdest manufacturers of New England, protesting against the proposed increase of duties in 1866: "Your constant changes of tariff do more harm than any possible foreign competition. Give us any system, with duties low or high, but let it only be permanent, and the business of the country will adapt itself to the circumstances and will prosper." That he did not exaggerate the benefits of a steady and enduring policy may be inferred from the fact that the progress of the country in wealth, production, and prosperity, was never as great in any decade in its history as in the decade 1850 to 1860, the only one during which the same tariff policy prevailed, with only one slight change of duties. In like manner, speaking in behalf of the agricultural interest, Henry S. Randall, who will be recognized by the farmers as high authority, said in 1845:

"If the same settled and steady character could be given to our tariff laws, our prosperity would be greatly augmented. The farmer wants to know what to depend upon. He asks that the fruits of his labor shall not be subject to constant variations in value, by reason of vacillating legislation; he asks that his government shall not one year enact laws to encourage him to embark his capital in one branch of industry, and the next, by adverse legislation, destroy or depreciate the value of the investment. In a word, he asks that the tariff be settled on a fixed and permanent basis—one admitting of no fluctuations but those rendered indispensable by important natural changes, or discoveries developing new interests, or modifying existing ones."

Mr. Randall's judicious words will be most heartily indorsed by the ablest representatives of every other producing interest. Constant fluctuations can benefit only the gambler. The producer, no matter of what branch, needs for prosperity a steady and settled basis for his calculations. We have seen that high duties, and especially protective and increasing duties, tend to cause fluctuations, and that this is an almost inevitable result of the nature of that system. We have seen that low duties alone have endured for more than five years, and that non-protective tariffs tend to prevent frequent changes. It may fairly be asked at the outset, whether a system which involves frequent changes, however much it may momentarily benefit particular interests, must not of necessity produce by its fluctuations greater evil than can result from duties lower and more steady.

CHAPTER VII.

POPULATION AND WEALTH.

" In spite of frequent changes, the production of wealth is even now increasing," it may be said. It certainly is! During the war, when half a million of men were withdrawn from useful labor, and when heavy burdens rested upon every back, and a fearful uncertainty filled the air—even then the production of wealth increased. But we do not suppose that the war caused the increase.

There has never been a period in the history of this country, of which any statistical evidence can be given, during which the aggregate production of wealth has not increased. Single years can be found, in which widely extended commercial disaster or failure of crops occurred; but of no period, long enough to test the working of any policy or measure, can it be said that it witnessed a decrease in the aggregate production of wealth. The reason is obvious. We have an inexhaustible supply of natural resources, land both rich and cheap, mines of wonderful productiveness, forests scarcely less than continental in area. In consequence, the time never has been when any large proportion of our population were reduced to want, or when any considerable share of our labor was more than temporarily unemployed. Our population is increasing at the rate of three and a third per cent. yearly, and, unless that proportion of the laboring population were deprived of employment for a whole year, the aggregate number of laborers and the aggregate production of wealth must have increased. But there is no period, regarding which statistics are attainable, in which the wealth of the country has not increased faster than population. The proportion of labor which has at any time been kept out of employment has been very small; but the increase in the productiveness of labor, by means of inventions, facilities for transportation, development of resources, and settlement of the country, has been very rapid. Disaster in one employment has only driven a small surplus of labor to seek another. Perhaps a more considerable change of this character was caused when the war broke out than at any other time; but even then the aggregate production of wealth in the Northern States was probably reduced not more than one year, and certainly not more than two.

No period of tariff, whether high or low, protective or "free trade" in character, has ever diminished the production of wealth. The only changes effected have been in the mode of production, and in the rapidity of increase. This fact it is of essential importance to keep in mind, for if in every period wealth has increased faster than population, a mere increase of production under any duty proves nothing; the test is the rapidity of increase in one as compared with other periods.

The population of the country has increased with very great regularity. Immigration and the acquisition of a vast territory swelled the increase during the decade 1800–'10—that of the Louisiana purchase—to 36½ per cent., and during the decade 1840–'50—that of the acquisition of Texas, New Mexico, and California—to 35½ per cent. Large immigration during the last decade, 1850–'60, made the increase 35½ per cent. Its lowest rate was in the decade of 1830–'40, when it was only 32.67 per cent.; but no inference valuable to our inquiry can be drawn from this fact, for the loss in that decade was wholly in the slave population, the white population having increased more rapidly than in either of the two decades preceding. The increase of the white and total population during the seven decades since 1790 has been as follows:

YEAR.	White.	Total.
1790–1800	35.68	35.02
1800–1810	36.18	36.45
1810–1820	34.11	33.13
1820–1830	34.03	33.49
1830–1840	34.72	32.62
1840–1850	37.74	35.87
1850–1860	37.97	35.46

The increase of colored population has been affected by causes not pertinent to this inquiry, and the increase of white population has been mainly affected by other causes than changes of tariff. It happens, however, that the only decade during the whole of which the protective policy was in force is the one in which the increase was smaller than in any other, 1820–'30; and the only decade during which no protective duties of any kind were in force is the one in which the increase is greater than in any other, 1850–'60. Indeed, if we remember that the decades 1800–'10 and 1840–'50 were marked by annexation of territory, the difference between the last decade of low duties and any former decade will be quite impressive.

No accurate statistics of the aggregate wealth of the country in earlier decades enable us to make comparisons. The property valued for taxation in 1789 was $619,977,247.92, and an increase at the rate of little more than 40 per cent. in a decade would give about the valuation estimated from the census of 1830, or $2,591,000,000. From 1830 to 1840 the increase was 53 per cent., and the valuation of 1840 about $3,964,322,000. From 1840 to 1850 the increase was 80 per cent., and the valuation of 1850 was $7,135,780,228. But from 1850 to 1860 the increase was 126 per cent., and the valuation of 1860 was $16,159,616,068. Incomplete as these statistics must necessarily be, they suffice to prove, first, that in every period there has been a productive power in constant and vigorous activity ; and second, that the increase has been far more rapid in that decade in which there were low duties and no material changes of tariff, than in any other in our history. Even if we suppose the natural increase of wealth to gain in a regular ratio, that gain was greater in the last than in any former decade—50 per cent. from 1830–'40 to 1840–'50, and 57½ per cent. from 1840–'50 to 1850–'60. But it must be remembered that the acquisition of a vast and rich territory, and the opening of California mines in the decade 1840–'50, account for a portion of the increase of wealth in that decade. The contrast between the last decade, of low duties and no material changes of tariff, and any preceding decade, then becomes still stronger. We may fairly say that the increase of wealth from 1850 to 1860, from causes other than the acquisition of territory, was nearly double that of any former decade. It appears, then, that the same period in which our population gained most rapidly is also that in which the production of wealth was most largely increased. It happens to be the only decade of continuous low duties; the only one in which nothing like protection was attempted.

Of the progress of the whole country in wealth since 1860 no complete and reliable statistics can be given. The Secretary of the Treasury has recently made an estimate, which, however, was not based upon any ascertainment of facts, but upon the supposition that the increase has been about as great since 1860 as it was during the preceding decade. Mr. Wells, the Special Commissioner of the Revenue, in the report just published, gives an estimate confessedly based only upon a supposed continuation of the increase at the rate of the increase during the preceding decade, with allowance for property destroyed and productive industry diverted in consequence of the war. But both these estimates take for granted the very thing in question—whether the rate of increase has been as great since 1860, allowance being made for the war and its effects, as it was before.   Always faithful to facts when he can ascertain them, however, Mr. Wells has presented statistics which, if they do not suffice for a reliable estimate of the present wealth of the country, at least suffice to prove conclusively that the supposition above mentioned is quite unwarranted.

These statistics are records of valuations of property, real and personal, in several of the richest States, according to assessments for taxation by State authority.   That these assessments never represent the full value of property is true; but it may fairly be supposed that as to real estate, at least, they are likely to bear about the same relation to the actual value in different years.   As to personal property, which can more easily be concealed from assessment, the disposition to conceal it has undoubtedly been increased by the increase of taxation since 1861; but, on the other hand, the efforts to discover property have been stimulated by the same cause, and that work has been greatly aided by the laws passed and the efforts made by the Federal Government to reach property for taxation. On the whole, however, it is probable that assessments do not now reach quite as large a share of personal property, other than United States bonds, as they did in 1861; but the difference in the relation of aggregate assessments of real and personal property to actual value cannot be material.   But the property invested in United States bonds is important, and a material difference in the calculation must be made for the fact that so large a value of personal property is now in form not subject to taxation.   Of a bonded debt of about twenty-one hundred millions, it is estimated by the best authorities that not less than one thousand millions are now held in foreign countries, and three hundred and forty-two millions held as security for bank circulation are represented in the capital of the banks, and the property thus invested is therefore within reach of taxation.   Deducting these, there remain about seven hundred and fifty millions of United States bonds held in this country, an investment of property not liable to taxation or assessment by State authority.   For this withdrawal of property from assessment, allowance must be made in any estimate based upon assessments in 1861 and 1868.*

---

* Since this was written, I have learned that in at least one of the States named the valuation includes United States bonds, though I supposed they were not included in either.

Mr. Wells gives the assessments in Massachusetts, Rhode Island, Connecticut, Ohio, Indiana, and New York, for 1861 and 1868, as follows :

STATES.	Valuation, Real and Personal.	
	1861.	1868.
Massachusetts....................	$861,485,418	$1,220,498,939
Rhode Island...................	121,118,126	187,697,591
Connecticut....................	224,962,514	312,574,408
Ohio..........................	892,850,084	1,143,461,386
Indiana.......................	441,562,339	587,970,549
New York.....................	1,441,769,430	1,766,089,140
Total....................	$3,983,747,911	$5,218,292,013

In these States the nominal increase has been $1,234,544,102, or 31 per cent. But during the year 1868 the premium on gold was 39.8 per cent., so that the gold valuation of property for assessment in these six States was actually less in 1868 than in 1861 ! Yet these States embrace no small share of the wealth of the whole country. In 1860, according to the census, their wealth was $28\frac{5.8}{100}$ per cent. of the entire valuation reported. They represent mainly that very branch of industry which it is the object of the protective system to promote; and in States like these, if anywhere, the recent tariffs must have caused a more rapid production of wealth. If the country has increased in wealth while these States have declined, it may be said with certainty that the increase has not been in consequence of any development of manufactures—that it has been in spite, and not because of the tariff. But no one will suppose that the aggregate wealth of the country has increased in ratio materially different from that in the six States named. Reducing the valuation for 1868 to gold at 139, we have this comparison :

Valuation six States, 1861........................	$3,983,747,911
Valuation six States, 1868.......................	3,757,170,249
Loss in seven years........................	$226,577,662

This shows a loss of 6 per cent. in seven years. If the wealth of the whole country has decreased in like proportion, the loss has been $850,000,000, a sum larger than the whole amount invested in United States bonds not reached by assessment. If this calculation were absolutely correct, what would follow ? This, simply, that the destruction of wealth by the war has been as great as the entire increase by the production of wealth up to the year 1868.

Mr. Wells estimates the " destruction of wealth, or diversion of industry which would have produced wealth," at nine thousand millions of dollars. But in this estimate he counts all money expended by the Government in supporting men under arms, and, at the same time, counts the loss of their industry. The men must have been fed and clothed, had there been no war. He counts all the money applied by them to the support of families; but those families also must have been supported, and would probably have consumed as much, had there been no war. He counts all that soldiers saved from their pay, and sailors from their prize-money, and all the money paid in bounties or yet to be paid in pensions, as so much wealth absolutely destroyed, whereas it was simply transferred from one person to another. Much more than half the expenses of Government, in feeding, clothing, and paying the army and navy, must be deducted, with all pensions and bounties paid, and all the bonded debt now held in this country, which is simply property in another form. With these corrections, the cost of the war, as a reduction of the wealth of the country, was not more than four thousand millions, accepting the estimates of Mr. Wells in other respects, and those estimates are certainly liberal.

Had there been no war, then the country should have been four thousand millions richer than it is; or, since it seems to have gained not more than the war has cost, the increase by production of wealth has been apparently about four thousand millions, or 28 per cent. in eight years. This estimate would show an increase during the decade of not more than 35 per cent., against 126 per cent. in the previous decade; and, of that 35 per cent., 28 per cent. would be cancelled by the losses and the waste of war.

It is not pretended that this estimate is altogether reliable. Any calculation based upon assessments for taxation must be accepted only with many reservations. But one thing it does seem to prove: that, after making full allowance for property which is now invested in bonds, and after making full allowance for the waste and destruction of property and diversion of industry caused by the war, the increase of wealth during the decade now drawing to a close must have been less than the increase during the decade 1850–'60 under a revenue tariff. The estimate may vary widely from the truth, but it can hardly vary as widely as the supposed increase differs from the ascertained increase of that decade.

POPULATION OF THE UNITED STATES.

YEAR.	Population.	YEAR.	Population.	YEAR.	Population.
1791........	4,067,371	1818........	9,158,513	1844........	19,034,332
1792........	4,205,404	1819........	9,398,339	1845........	19,525,749
1793........	4,343,457	1820........	9,638,166	1846........	20,017,155
1794........	4,481,500	1821........	9,959,965	1847........	20,508,582
1795........	4,619,553	1822........	10,281,765	1848........	21,413,890
1796........	4,757,586	1823........	10,603,565	1849........	21,956,945
1797........	4,895,629	1824........	10,925,365	1850........	23,191,876
1798........	5,033,672	1825........	11,247,165	1851........	23,887,632
1799........	5,171,715	1826........	11,568,965	1852........	24,604,261
1800........	5,379,788	1827........	11,890,765	1853........	25,342,388
1801........	5,502,772	1828........	12,212,565	1854........	26,102,659
1802........	5,695,787	1829........	12,534,365	1855........	26,885,738
1803........	5,888,801	1830........	12,856,165	1856........	27,692,310
1804........	6,081,816	1831........	13,277,415	1857........	28,523,079
1805........	6,274,830	1832........	13,698,665	1858........	29,378,771
1806........	6,467,845	1833........	14,119,915	1859........	30,260,134
1807........	6,660,859	1834........	14,541,165	1860........	31,429,891
1808........	6,853,874	1835........	14,962,415	1861........	32,373,388
1809........	7,047,888	1836........	15,383,665	1862........	23,500,000
1810........	7,239,908	1837........	15,804,915	1863........	24,400,000
1811........	7,479,729	1838........	16,226,165	1864........	27,000,000
1812........	7,719,555	1839........	16,649,415	1865........	30,000,000
1813........	7,959,381	1840........	17,068,665	1866........	35,500,000
1814........	8,199,208	1841........	17,560,082	1867........	36,500,000
1815........	8,439,034	1842........	18,051,499	1868........	37,500,000
1816........	8,678,860	1843........	18,542,915	1869........	38,640,000
1817........	8,918,687				

The population given for the years 1862–'65, inclusive, is the Treasury estimate of persons within the military lines, and in all calculations of exports or imports, production or consumption per capita, these figures are used, with the estimates given for the subsequent years, as approximately correct.

CHAPTER VIII.

AGRICULTURE.

By far the greater part of our production of wealth is by means of agriculture. The annual product of that branch of industry, according to the census of 1860, was about $2,598,393,364. The product of manufactures, mining, and fisheries, was $1,885,861,676; but the cost of raw material consumed was $1,031,605,092, so that the wealth produced by those industries was $854,256,584—less than one-third of the amount produced by agricultural labor.

In a scientific rather than a popular sense, trade and transportation produce wealth, it is true, by adding to the value of products of other industries. But these employments depend upon the industries commonly called productive; and, since it will not be claimed that legislation injurious to agriculture, mining, manufactures, and fisheries, in the aggregate can have increased the production of wealth, and it is impossible to distinguish in statistics between the increased value given to foreign and the increased value given to domestic products by exchange or transportation, it will be sufficient for the purpose of this inquiry to consider the effect of tariffs upon those popularly known as producers. Thus agriculture, mining, manufactures, and fisheries, may be regarded as the wealth-producing industries, and of their production more than three-fourths is by means of agriculture.

The protective system is designed to aid manufactures and mining. Its theory is that those operations in which large capital and costly machinery are needed must be stimulated by legislation, while the abundance of cheap land renders it unnecessary to stimulate or shelter agriculture. But, when the farmer began to feel the burdens which the protective system imposes, men sought to reconcile farmers to their burdens by pretending to give them a share of the benefits. Duties were imposed on wool for the North, and sugar and tobacco for the South; and in due time other duties, of no effect whatever except in localities close to our northern border, were added. The tariff under which we now live imposes duties of twenty cents a bushel on wheat, fifteen cents on rye and barley, ten cents on oats and corn, and twenty-five cents a bushel on potatoes, the potato interest being thus peculiarly protected! It can hardly be said that we owe the existence of the potato industry to this beneficent duty; for in 1860, under a revenue tariff, we raised 153,000,000 bushels of that crop, and in 1867, under protection, it yielded only 97,000,000, and, in 1868, only 106,000,000 bushels. Nor can it be said that the market is flooded with foreign potatoes grown by pauper labor; for in 1868 we imported only 194,905 bushels, or less than one very small potato to each bushel of domestic production. If any farmer supposes that his crop is increased in value by this duty, he may observe that the average price of potatoes for New York, the State most exposed to this flood of foreign potatoes, according to the Agricultural Bureau, is lower in currency than the price paid in gold in 1860, before this peculiar form of protection began. It is amazing, too, that a crop so important as that of Indian corn receives no better protection than a duty of ten cents a bushel; and yet, though exposed in this manner it amounts to 768,000,000 bushels. Strange it is that our production has not been stopped by the flood of corn from Canada, whence we received in 1868 just 43,042 bushels, costing seventy-one cents a bushel in gold !

Of the duty on wool we shall inquire in another chapter, and it will appear that in every instance the protective duties have deprived the grower of a part of the value of his fleece. Duties on sugar and tobacco would be imposed for revenue rather than protection. On every other agricultural product except potatoes, the duties are lower now, under an extreme protective tariff, than they were under the purely revenue tariff of 1846—a fact which suffices to prove that the protective system is not meant to protect the farmer, and that the duties imposed on the great products of agriculture are merely legislative tubs thrown to political whales. Under the level ad valorem tariff those products then paid 30 per cent., while they now pay only 20, 15, or 10 cents, as already stated; flax pays only 4 per cent., Russian hemp 23, and Manilla 20 per cent. Wheat then paid 30, and in 1868 only 12 per cent., and not one of the grains pays as large a duty as was imposed by the revenue system. Perhaps potatoes, the duty on which has been raised from 30 to 56 per cent., are specially protected, because their bulk makes them least likely to be imported. No sensible man supposes that the farmers of this country get a better price for their crops because of these duties. It is an insult to the farmer, if his intelligence is supposed to be unequal to the task of discovering that they do not really benefit him. The plain truth is that these duties are put into a bill for the benefit of manufacturers, in the hope that some farmers may be so ignorant as to suppose themselves blessed thereby. Indeed, in 1844 it was gravely argued by one of the advocates of the tariff then in force, that our farmers were in need of a protective duty, lest their industry might be destroyed by the importation of wheat from Russia ! The farmers who vote for such members chiefly need protection against their own ignorance.

From the earliest times the large majority of farmers in this country have looked upon the protective system as injurious to their interests. They could well understand that a people, with land as cheap and as rich as ours, could not be and did not need to be protected in agriculture against any other country. They could see the effects of the protective system upon the prices of manufactured products of which they were consumers, and they held that the system could in no way benefit, while, to some extent, it manifestly taxed them. Moreover, an opinion widely prevailed that the prices

7

of agricultural products were lower under the operation of the protective system than under other tariffs.

To overcome this opposition, it has been argued that protection will in some way prevent the exhaustion of the soil, and facilitate the return to it of the elements withdrawn in crops sent to market. If it were true that under non-protective duties we exported ten times more largely of breadstuffs and raw materials than under protective duties, this reasoning would still be absurd. To the farmer it makes no difference whether his wheat or his cotton is sent to New York, New England, or to Liverpool. The possibility of a return of its fertilizing elements to the soil is not greater in one case than in the other. Farmers within short distances of cities or towns, whether manufacturing or not, may, by some possibility, receive again in the form of manure the identical elements of their crops, or an equivalent to some extent; but farmers so located would also do this, whether the tariff were protective or not, and they are in number not to be considered in comparison with the millions of farmers who never bring from any city a single peck of manure, or who use only such fertilizers as guano. Throughout the great producing region no fertilizer is needed or used, and the crop sent to eastern consumers might as well be sent to England or China. But even at the East or nearest cities and towns, of the fertilizers used, guano, gypsum, plaster, lime, ashes, bone or fish, it is difficult to see how the supply of a single one can be affected by the quantity of wheat exported, or by the tariff. No protective duty has caused the birds to visit particular islands of the sea, or placed in the earth the deposits of stone, or caused the people of towns to burn wood or to gather bone for grinding. It is hard to give serious treatment to such evanescent will-o'-the-wisps of argument. The farmer, be he east or west, will hardly raise good crops who looks to Congress to fertilize his fields by law. In practical effect on his soil, he will find one dead fish worth a million tariffs.

Others have reasoned that agriculture will become over-crowded, and the prices of its products depressed, by the withdrawal of labor from other occupations. In reply to this argument, facts will be presented showing conclusively that the prices of agricultural products have increased during the longest period of low duties, and that the number of persons employed in manufactures, mining, and the fisheries, and in trade and transportation, during that same period, increased more rapidly than the whole population. If, during fourteen years of a non-protective policy, and of lower duties than have been in force in any other period since 1816, the proportion of persons attracted to other occupations increased, and the price of agricultural products rose, it must be conceded that the fear of an overcrowding of agriculture, as a consequence of low duties, is groundless. The census returns for 1850 and 1860 show that, during that period, the number of persons engaged in manufactures, mining, and fisheries, increased from 956,000 to 1,310,000, or more than 37 per cent., population meanwhile increasing only 35½ per cent. In view of these facts, the apprehension of overcrowding agriculture may be dismissed as chimerical.

The most common and plausible argument to prove that the protective system will benefit agriculture is, that it will build up a local home market for agricultural products. It has this basis of truth, that farmers in the immediate neighborhood of manufacturing towns are enabled to raise bulky or perishable crops for that market, which they find highly profitable. Hence, it is somewhat hastily inferred that the protective system will give to all farmers this advantage. But it is the proximity to a town, and not the protection, from which the advantage comes. Other towns, as well as the manufacturing centres, give it. Unless protection can build up towns in immediate proximity to every farm—unless, in short, it can bring one-half of our population to live packed together in cities, while millions of acres of rich and wild land remain uncultivated—the argument is deceptive. But somebody must grow wheat, corn, and cotton, and those other crops which will not be produced on costly land near a large market. The country cannot do without these crops to have every farmer raising garden vegetables and strawberries; and a nation composed two-thirds of operatives and mechanics living entirely on the costly vegetables which farmers can afford to raise for a city market, however beautiful it might seem to the eye of the speculative philosopher of the protective school, would scarcely find anybody to consume its wares and fabrics. The absurdity of this, which may be called the garden-sauce theory of political economy, is sufficiently made manifest by the fact that in 1860 the entire returned value of market gardens and orchard products was only thirty-five millions; only this quantity was required to supply the consumption of a body of over two millions of persons engaged in manufactures, mining, fisheries, trade, and transportation. If two millions of consumers required $35,000,000, more or less, of garden products, how many millions of consumers must we have to enable all our farmers to raise vegetables and fruits for a city market?

Laughably unimportant as this branch of production is, compared with the great crops of agriculture, it does not appear that even the garden-sauce interest can in any way be promoted by protective duties, unless those duties will increase in the aggregate the number of persons engaged in manufacturing, and, at the same time, disperse them about the country in such a manner as to create towns where none existed before. Certain natural facilities determine the selection of localities for manufacturing establishments. The presence of a natural water-power, proximity to coal mines, or mines of mineral, and lines of communication which afford the cheapest transportation for materials and products—these determine the location of the great manufacturing centres, and in the nature of the case such centres are few in number. Around such natural centres cluster many minor and dependent branches of manufacture. But by far the greater number of persons engaged in manufacturing have their locations fixed by the lines and centres of trade, and gather of necessity in those towns which the lines of trade create. From time to time new mines are opened; but by far the greater portion of the increase in the number of persons employed in manufactures is simply an increase in the population of a few large cities or manufacturing centres. That increase of population benefits, by creating increased demand for garden or orchard products, only the farmers who already own lands near such localities, and the increase by opening of iron mines affords a market only to the few farmers who own lands adjacent to these. · The great bulk of the farming population remains beyond the reach of benefit in that way, whether the increase of manufactures be rapid or tardy. Manufacturing, limited in its choice of location by natural facilities or lines of trade, tends peculiarly to a compact and concentrated growth around great centres of industry; and the expectation of building up a factory on every farm, if by anybody seriously entertained, is doomed to disappointment.

To all these curious theories of the benefit to be derived by agriculture from the protective system, a few statistics conclusively reply. The census returns of 1840, 1850, and 1860, if not absolutely correct, are sufficiently accurate in regard to this industry to enable us to test its progress. The decade 1840–'50 embraced the protective period of 1843–'46. The decade 1850–'60 was one of low and non-protective duties throughout. The accompanying tables show whether this industry progressed more rapidly in the decade which includes a protective period than in the decade of unbroken non-protection.

AGRICULTURAL PRODUCTS—QUANTITIES.

CROP.	1840.	1850.	1860.	1867.	1868.
Corn, bushels......	377,492,388	592,071,104	838,792,740	768,320,000	906,527,000
Wheat, "	84,821,065	100,485,944	173,104,924	212,948,390	224,036,600
Rye, "	18,640,466	14,188,813	21,101,380	23,184,000	22,504,800
Oats, "	123,054,992	146,584,179	172,643,185	278,698,000	254,960,800
Barley, "	4,161,210	5,167,015	15,825,898	25,727,000	22,896,100
Buckw't, "	7,291,371	8,956,912	17,571,818	21,359,000	19,863,700
Potatoes, "	104,285,435	104,066,044	153,243,893	97,783,000	106,090,000
Hay, tons..........	10,246,777	13,838,642	19,083,896	26,277,000	26,141,900
Tobacco, lbs.......	219,607,739	199,752,655	434,209,461	313,724,000	320,982,000
Cotton, bales......	1,513,543	2,445,793	5,387,052	2,450,000	2,500,000

AGRICULTURAL PRODUCTS—VALUES.

CROP.	1850.	1860.	1867.	1868.	1868 (gold).
Corn..............	$296,035,552	$503,275,644	$610,948,390	$569,512,460	$410,048,971
Wheat............	100,485,944	216,381,155	421,796,561	319,195,290	229,820,609
Rye..............	7,803,847	12,660,828	32,499,790	28,683,677	20,652,247
Oats..............	43,975,253	57,547,728	172,472,970	142,484,910	102,589,135
Barley............	3,616,910	7,912,949	23,850,130	29,809,931	21,463,150
Buckwheat........	6,969,838	14,057,454	23,469,650	20,814,315	14,986,307
Potatoes....	45,453,232	76,621,946	89,276,880	84,150,040	60,588,029
Hay..............	96,870,494	190,838,960	372,864,670	351,941,930	253,398,190
Total..............	$601,211,070	$1,079,296.664	$1,746,178,800	$1,546,592,553	$1,113,546,638
Cotton	98,603,720	215,480,000	220,000.000	225,000,000	162,000,000
Tobacco............	13,982,686	43,420,946	41,283,431	40,081,942	28,858,998
Total	$713,797,476	$1,338,197,610	$2,007,462,231	$1,811,674,495	$1,304,405,636

The crop of corn increased over two hundred millions in each of the periods under comparison; that of wheat increased sixteen millions, or 19 per cent., in the period 1840-'50, and seventy-three millions, or 72 per cent., in the period 1850-'60; rye decreased in the first period four and a half millions, and increased in the second seven millions; oats increased twenty-three and a half millions in the first, and twenty-six millions in the second period; barley increased one million in the first, and ten millions in the second period; buckwheat increased less than two millions in the first, and over eight millions in the second; tobacco decreased about twenty millions in the first, and increased two hundred and thirty-four millions in the second; and cotton increased nine hundred thousand bales, or 60 per cent., in the first, and nearly three million bales, or about 125 per cent., in the second. These crops, however, are produced largely for exportation; let us see how those fared which depend wholly or mainly upon a home market. In hay, the increase was three and a half million tons in the first period, or 33 per cent., but in the second period it was 5,245,000, or 38 per cent. The home market appears to have been the better in the non-protective period. Again, in potatoes there was an absolute decrease in the first period, but in the second an increase of forty-nine millions of bushels. Very clearly, this crop also found an encouraging home market under low duties. It may be added, as evidence that the production of crops for a home market exclusively was by no means retarded during this long period of low duties, that the quantity of butter produced increased from three hundred and thirteen millions to four hundred and fifty-nine million pounds; of peas and beans, from nine to fifteen million bushels; hops, from three and a half to eleven million pounds; clover seed, from 468,973 to 956,188 bushels; grass seed, from 416,921 to 900,040 bushels. The value of orchard products increased five and a quarter millions in the first, and 7,190,000 in the second period, a larger increase, but smaller percentage. But the value of market gardens increased in the first period about two and a half millions, or 100 per cent., and in the second about ten millions, or 200 per cent. This comparison must satisfy those who look at political economy from a market-garden point of view, that protection is a grave mistake !

For comparing values, the census of 1840 does not give complete data; but from 1850 to 1860, the value of slaughtered animals increased over one hundred millions, or 90 per cent.; the value of live stock over five hundred millions, or about 100 per cent.; the value of farm implements and machinery about ninety-five millions, or 60 per cent.; and the value of farms more than three thousand three hundred and seventy millions, or over 103 per cent. The entire wealth of the country in 1840 was nearly four thousand millions. The increase between 1840 and 1850 in the value of farms can by no computation be estimated higher than eleven hundred millions, or 52 per cent. But the increase in the decade of unbroken low duties was about twice as great.

It will not be forgotten that this enormous increase in the production of wealth by agriculture was not caused by the change of laborers to that pursuit from others, or at the expense of a reduced price of agricultural products. We have stated that during the same decade of low duties the increase of laborers in manufacturing industry was more rapid than the increase of population, proving that, in spite of non-protection, a larger share of the population was drawn to manufacturing for employment. Yet the quantity of agricultural products increased, as has been shown, with great rapidity, and the value of farms, by which their productive power may be measured, increased over 103 per cent. The actual value of the leading crops above mentioned increased from seven hundred and fourteen millions to one thousand three hundred and thirty-eight millions, or over 80 per cent.

But what has been the effect of the recent protective duties? It may be supposed that the decade 1840–'50 was an exceptionally unfavorable one for the agricultural interest, or that, as it comprised only four years of protective duties, the comparison is unjust. Of the progress since 1860 we have no more reliable statistics than those of the Agricultural Bureau, and the latest published report is that of 1868. Its statements, therefore, may be accepted as the best and latest evidence attainable as to the progress of agriculture under the recent extreme protective duties. The figures are given in comparison with those of 1840, 1850, 1860, and 1867. In the production of corn there is a decrease in 1867 of seventy millions, but in 1868 an increase of about sixty-eight millions of bushels, or about 8 per cent. The crops of tobacco and cotton have largely decreased, but in part from causes not connected with this inquiry. The increase in wheat, since 1860, has been forty millions in 1867, and fifty-one millions in 1868, a gain of 29 per cent. in eight years; while in the ten years preceding 1860 the gain was 73 per cent. The crop for the year 1869, though not accurately known, is estimated in the papers at two hundred and fifty millions of bushels, a gain of 43 per cent. since 1860. In rye, the increase has been scarcely 7 per cent. against 50 per cent. in the last decade. The crop of oats has increased about 48 per cent., and is the only one of the principal crops which has increased as rapidly as it did in the decade ending in 1860. Barley has increased about 40 per cent. in 8 years, against 200 per cent. in ten years. Buckwheat has increased about 13 per cent., against nearly 100 per cent. in the last decade. Hay has increased about 36 per cent. against 38 per cent. Potatoes, notwithstanding "protection," have decreased about forty-seven millions, or nearly one-third. It is very plain that agriculture has not advanced as rapidly by any means in the present as it did in the last decade. But it may be said that the increase in value of crops may have compensated for a loss in quantity. This has been in part the case with cotton and tobacco; these crops together, though much reduced in quantity, command so much larger prices, that the value realized in currency is about seven millions more than it was in 1860 in gold. But other crops have fared quite otherwise. In the tables given for values, the estimates of the Bureau are accepted for 1867 and 1868, though the prices are much higher than the average allowed for 1860 and 1850. The figures for 1850 are from De Bow's Compendium of the Census, and those for 1860 are prepared on the same plan, allowing for the average value throughout the country the same proportionate reduction from the prices at New York in 1860. In the last column, the values for 1868 are reduced to gold at 139, a little less than the average premium for the year. It appears that the crop of corn, though somewhat larger, was worth nearly one hundred millions less in gold than the crop of 1860, while that crop was worth over two hundred millions more than the crop of 1850; that the crop of wheat increased in value only about 6 per cent. in eight years, against an increase of 116 per cent. in the last decade; that the crop of buckwheat has increased less than one million in value, against a gain of over 100 per cent.; that the crop of potatoes has decreased sixteen millions in value, against an increase of over 60 per cent.; and that the crop of hay has increased in value only 33 per cent. in the last eight years, while the increase during the last decade was almost 100 per cent. The aggregate value of the principal crops, except cotton and tobacco, increased only $46,250,000, or 4½ per cent. in eight years, while the value of the same crops increased from 1850 to 1860 over four hundred and seventy-eight millions, or about 79 per cent. in ten years.

No possible correction of these estimates can affect the conclusion to which they irresistibly lead—that the increase in the production of wealth by means of agriculture has been arrested in a most remarkable manner during the past eight years. Instead of the rapid and healthy progress of the last decade, by which the wealth of the country was more than doubled, though manufactures at the same time increased with about the same rapidity—in value of product from one thousand to nineteen hundred millions—there has been during the eight years ending with 1868 scarcely any increase whatever in the value of Northern agricultural products, with a positive decrease in aggregate value, if cotton and tobacco are included. Two other items, for which the Agricultural Bureau furnishes statistics, confirm, in the most striking manner, these conclusions. The value of live stock increased a little more than 100 per cent. from 1850 to 1860. But from 1860 to 1867 the apparent increase was only three hundred and seven millions, less than the difference between currency and gold, and the value given by the Bureau, $1,337,111,822, for 1868, reduced to gold at 139, is only $962,720,511, against $1,089,329,915 in 1860. Again, the report of 1867 contains a very elaborate statement of the value of farming lands in that year, as compared with 1860, from which it appears that in only one of the old States there has been an increase equal to the difference between gold and currency, and in that State, Delaware, the improvement was due to new railroads. In Illinois the nominal increase was 42 per cent., or 2 per cent. actual increase; in Michigan, 70 per cent., or 30 per cent. actual; in Wisconsin, 50 per cent., or 10 per cent. actual, and in Iowa 75 per cent., or 35 per cent. actual. But in these States the great increase of population and railroad facilities has caused the improvement. The value of farming lands is determined by the net value of their annual products. The fact that in all the great agricultural States there has been an actual decrease in gold values, except in the newer Western States named, and in Illinois so small an increase, conclusively proves that the value of agricultural products has not advanced as fast as the actual cost of production, so that the farms are absolutely less profitable, and can produce less wealth now than they could in 1860.

It is indeed true that the crops of 1869 have been generally larger than those of 1868, but the very remarkable fact appears that this increase of crop has caused a corresponding decrease of price. The country is to-day not able to consume as many bushels of grain and potatoes, per capita, as it could consume in 1860, *at higher prices in gold!*

For the aggregate quantity of grain and potatoes produced in 1868 was 1,656,879,000 bushels, or 42 bushels per capita, while in 1860 the aggregate quantity was 1,392,283,838 bushels, or 45 bushels per capita. But in 1868 the aggregate value of those crops was $860,148,448 in gold, and in 1860 the aggregate value was $888,457,704 in gold. And the crops of 1869, a little larger in quantity, at once depressed prices materially.

This is the decisive fact in the discussion of the tariff question. By all parties the truth is acknowledged that any system which involves injury to agriculture, that industry by which three-fourths of our wealth is produced, must be injurious to the whole country. Hence it is claimed that the protective system will create "a home market" for agricultural products—establish in this country such a body of consumers that a larger crop of agricultural products can be consumed here at better prices. The low tariff in force from 1850 to 1860 did so develop manufactures, mechanic arts, commerce, trade, and transportation, that crops from 50 to 100 per cent. larger in quantity were consumed at prices 10 to 50 per cent. higher, so that the aggregate value of the principal crops increased from $713,797,476 in 1850, to $1,338,197,610 in 1860.   But the high protective tariffs in force since 1860 have in some way so retarded the natural growth of this home market that crops not as large per capita as those of 1860 were consumed in 1868, at a cost twenty-eight millions less than that of 1860, and a small additional increase of the crop in quantity instantly forces down prices below the cost of production and much below the gold values of 1860.

But the advocates of protection will reply that, although the growing of wheat, cotton, and other principal crops may be discouraged, the farmers are enabled to grow garden produce and green crops for consumption in cities and manufacturing villages, and to obtain better prices for these than they could for principal crops.   No statistics are obtainable of the product of such crops in recent years; but, if the absurdity of this theory has not been already sufficiently demonstrated, the records of the Agricultural Bureau give it the *coup de grace*.   If the farmer can produce a more valuable crop, his farm becomes more valuable.   The Bureau gives statistics which prove that the farms of the chief manufacturing States are actually worth less money to-day in gold than they were in 1860.   The report for 1867, p. 119, gives the following summary of "the increase or decrease of nominal values of farm lands in the several States since 1860," and it is only necessary to remember that the premium on gold in 1867 was 40 per cent.:

STATES.	Increase per cent.	Decrease per cent.	STATES.	Increase per cent.	Decrease per cent.
Maine	19	..	Mississippi	..	65
New Hampshire	17	..	Louisiana	..	70
Vermont	17	..	Texas	..	28
Massachusetts	17	..	Arkansas	..	55
Rhode Island	18	..	Tennessee	..	18
Connecticut	20	..	West Virginia	32	..
New York	28	..	Kentucky	10	..
New Jersey	30	..	Missouri	32	..
Pennsylvania	25	..	Illinois	42	..
Delaware	66	..	Indiana	27	..
Maryland	20	..	Ohio	32	..
Virginia	..	27	Michigan	70	..
North Carolina	..	50	Wisconsin	50	..
South Carolina	..	60	Minnesota	100	..
Georgia	..	55	Iowa	75	..
Florida	..	55	Kansas	150	..
Alabama	..	60	Nebraska	175	..

The increase in the Western States is due to settlement and extended railroad facilities.   The increase in States like Ohio, Illinois, Indiana, Michigan, and Delaware, is fully accounted for, also, by the increase of railroad facilities.   But the remarkable fact remains that in every one of the great manufacturing States the cash value of farms is absolutely less than it was in 1860. Reducing the statement of the Bureau to gold values, it appears that the actual value, in 1867, of land worth $100, in 1860, was in the several States as follows:

Maine.....	$85 68	Pennsylvania..........	$90 00
New Hampshire..........	84 24	Maryland	86 40
Vermont	84 24	West Virginia..........	95 04
Massachusetts	84 24	Kentucky	79 20
Rhode Island..........	84 24	Missouri..........	95 04
Connecticut..........	86 40	Illinois..........	100 80
New York......	92 16	Indiana	91 44
New Jersey..........	93 60	Ohio..........	95 04

From this statement, the farmers of the manufacturing States can learn exactly how much protection has cost them in the value of their farms. In Massachusetts it has cost them $15 76 on every $100; in New York $7 84, and in Pennsylvania just $10 on every $100. Can there be a more conclusive demonstration of the fact that, even in the largest manufacturing States, the cost of production has increased more largely than the value of crops raised even for a market close at hand? For population has unquestionably increased in these States, manufacturing has made progress, new towns and villages have grown up, and there must of necessity be a larger demand for those products which can be raised only for markets near at hand. But the value of a farm must depend upon the profit which can be realized by working it, and that depends upon the value of products raised, compared with cost of production. If the actual value of farms is less than it was in 1860, the conclusion is unavoidable that the cost of production has increased more rapidly than the value of products which can be sold in an enlarged market. There is no reason to doubt the accuracy of the statement given by the Bureau. But the conclusion to which it leads is absolutely fatal to the whole system of protective duties.

For to no other cause can the injury to agriculture be ascribed. The comparison of crops and values in former years is conclusive. Similar comparisons for earlier periods are not possible, for want of statistics of minor crops; but the crop of wheat is by all regarded as a fairer test than any other of the general progress of agriculture, and of that crop the production at different periods is thus stated:

YEARS.	Crop.	Increase per cent.	Bushels per capita.	YEARS.	Crop.	Increase per cent.	Bushels per capita.
1790........	17,000,000	....	4.19	1840......	84,321,065	.69	4.96
1800........	22,000,000	.29	4.15	1850......	100,485,944	.19	4.33
1810......	80,000,000	.36	4.16	1860......	173,104,924	.72	5.51
1820......	38,000,000	.27	3.95	1868......	224,036,600	.29	5.97
1830........	50,000,000	.31	3.88				

7

These records show that the production of wheat, as compared with population, declined during the forty years from 1790 to 1830, from 4.19 bushels per capita to 3.88 bushels per capita; and that, during nearly forty years since, it has increased to 5.97 per capita. The year 1830 was just before the close of the long protective period, and prior to the beginning of that experiment were the embargo of 1808 and the War of 1812, so that our commerce was almost unceasingly interrupted, by war, high tariffs, or other blessings, from 1808 to 1832.   But from 1810 to 1830 the production of wheat declined from 4.16 bushels per capita to 3.88 per capita.   Again, the progress from 1830 to 1860 is broken by a marked decrease in the decade 1840–'50, and it happens that in that decade, and in no other after 1832, until 1861, there was a protective tariff in force, from 1843–'6 inclusive.   Finally, during the eight years since 1860, the increase of population having been retarded by war, there is a slight increase in the production of wheat, from 5.50 to 5.97 per capita. But the two periods in which we have increased most rapidly have been the very decades during which non-protective tariffs were the rule, namely: the decade of the compromise tariff, 1832 to 1840, and the decade of the revenue tariff, 1850 to 1860; and in those decades the increase was 69 and 72 per cent., and in no other period was the increase more than one-half as great.

Did agriculture become overcrowded in these periods, so that its products declined in price?   Statistics are attainable with which to answer that question also, and as the precise inquiry before us is whether the protective or the non-protective system causes the greater increase, not in the production of crops, but in the production of wealth by agriculture, the comparison of values is indeed the more correct one.   As it is not well with the farmer when he raises a great crop but has no market for it, so the production of wealth by agriculture may decrease, though crops increase, in quantity.   We may, indeed, infer that production will only temporarily increase beyond the demand, and that rapid increase during any period is proof that the labor so employed has been well repaid.   But statistics are better than syllogisms.   The price of wheat in all parts of the country is determined, first, by the price in a market for export; second, by the price in chief markets for consumption, and third, by cost of transportation to those markets.   We shall presently see that the cost of transportation has been very materially reduced by the more rapid increase of facilities for transportation under non-protective than under protective tariffs.   But, setting aside that topic for the moment, let us first take the New York prices of wheat, and suppose that these have borne the same ratio to the actual value to the farmer in different years. The following statement does not give the actual value of the crops, but the value at which they could have been sold in the principal market for export, New York:

YEAR.	Price.	Value of Crop.	Increase.	Per cent.
1820......................	1.00	38,000,000	....	....
1830......................	1.06	53,000,000	15,000,000	.36
1840......................	1.10	93,303,000	40,303,000	.76
1850......................	1.25	125,600,000	32,297,000	.35
1860......................	1.50	259,656,000	134,056,000	1.07
1869 (currency)............	1.37	342,000,000	82,000,000	.32
1869 (gold)..............	1.06	265,000,000	5,344,000	2½

The crop of 1869, supposed to be about two hundred and fifty millions of bushels, is included at the prices prevailing in New York since it has begun to be delivered. It will be observed that, in every period until the present, the price of wheat has risen, so that the increase in the production, not of wheat but of wealth by wheat-growing, in the last decade, was 107 per cent.; that this was three times as great as the increase in either of the periods, 1820–'30, wholly protective, or 1840–'50, partially protective; and that the increase in the other decade of low duties, 1830 to 1840, was also very large. But the contrast between these periods of rapid progress and the present period of protection is very striking. In currency, the increase in value since 1860 has been about 32 per cent., but in gold the increase has been only 2½ per cent. in nine years. Nor will the result be materially changed if, instead of the large crop and low price of 1869, we insert the higher price and smaller crop of 1868, for the increase of value would then be only thirty millions in gold, or about 11 per cent. in eight years, against 107 per cent. in the last decade.

The advocate of protection does not wish to see wheat exported, or sent to any market for export; let us therefore ascertain what its price has been in the principal markets for home consumption. Let us take the price of flour in that market where it is bought and sold not for export but for consumption; that market by which the largest number of persons employed in manufacturing is supplied. We shall thus test the truth of the theory that high duties, by building up a home market for the farmer, have increased the value of his products. The city of Philadelphia is the centre of the largest manufacturing region in the country, where almost all branches of manufacture flourish. From that city go the supplies of flour to miners and iron-workers by the thousand, and to a vast body of workers in other branches of manufacture, while in the city itself almost every branch is represented. At the same time, Philadelphia exports so little flour, as compared with other large cities, that we may suppose that there, if anywhere, the price will be governed rather by the "home market" of which so much is said than by export demand. Fortunately, an accurate record of the price of extra fall wheat flour, for every month since 1790, has been preserved by the Philadelphia Board of Trade. Diagram No. V. presents to the eye, at a glance, the changes of price from 1800 to 1867, the average each year, and for different periods. The record of the Board of Trade is given in currency, but for the diagram the currency prices are reduced to gold at the average rates for each month.

It will at once be seen that the imaginary "home market" has not secured to the farmer high prices for flour in times of high tariffs, even in this market, the centre of supply for a vast manufacturing region. On the contrary, the ugly fact is very plainly presented, that high tariffs have given low prices to the farmer for his wheat, and that low tariffs have given high prices.

The period from 1800 to 1815 was one of low duties and of high prices for flour—higher than have ever ruled since. But it must be remembered that the War of 1812, and the great inflation and depreciation of currency which followed, account in part for the high prices, as the collapse of the currency and the prostration which followed account in part for the extreme low price of 1821. Nevertheless, the first great fall in the price is coincident with the adoption of the iron protective tariff in 1818. From that time the price declined, and, though it recovered a little after the panic had passed, the tariff of 1824 gave an average price of $5.09 a barrel, and the tariff of 1828, with two short crops, gave an average of only $5.63, while from 1820 to 1824 it was $5.91. We have here the first test: eight years of extreme protection did not lift the price of flour in this manufacturing centre, but simply reduced it, as compared with the average price of previous years. The increase of price in the years 1835, 1836, and 1837, was partly due to the inflation of currency. In the years of contraction and hard times, 1839, 1840, 1841, and 1842, the average price was about $5.45. After the passage of the high tariff in August, 1842, it fell from $5.45 to $4.12, and early in 1843 to $3.75. During the four years of that tariff, the average price was very low, not more than $4.46. It has never been as low during any period of years in our whole history, *except during the*

PRICE OF FLOUR.—AVERAGE FOR EACH YEAR, AND FOR SEVERAL PERIODS, ACCORDING TO RECORD OF
BOARD OF TRADE, PHILADELPHIA.

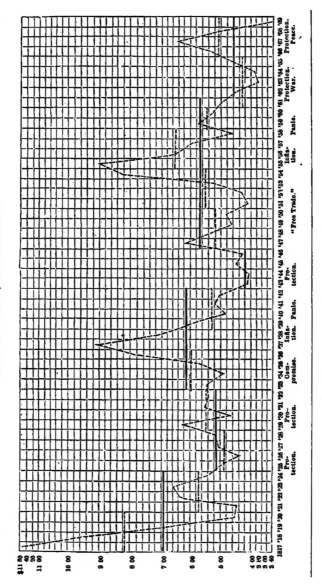

Average price.—1817–'24, $7.13 ; 1825–'32, $5.36 ; 1833–'42, $6.33 ; 1843–'46, $4.46 ; 1847–'61, $5.86 ; 1862–'69, $4.79.
Average twenty years' protection, $4.95 ; twenty-five years' non-protection, $6.04.
The prices for 1868 and 1869 are taken from published quotations ; the latest record of the Board of Trade which I have
seen, ends with 1867.

high tariff now in force. The diagram shows, at a glance, this contrast, and the fact that under the high protective tariff the average price of flour was lower, during the whole period, than it was even in the hard times and extreme prostration which followed the panic of 1837. As soon as the tariff was removed, we find that the price rose in the next year to $8.25, but part of this increase was due to the famine in Europe, and the peculiar demand. Nevertheless, it never fell again, until protection was revived, as low as it had been in 1846, and the average for the first period of low duties, 1847–'50, inclusive, was $5.37. Even the panic of 1857 did not cause the price to fall as low as the average for the whole protective period ending in 1846. But the passage of the protective tariff of 1861 was instantly followed by a fall, and the price under the successive additional tariffs since imposed is most conclusive proof that high tariffs do not help the farmer to higher prices for his produce, *even in the very heart of the manufacturing region.*

The diagram, with its frequent fluctuations, speaks to the eye, but a brief statement of the figures for certain periods may serve to aid the comparison. The first non-protective period ended in the years of hard times, in which, if ever, we should expect prices of flour in a great manufacturing centre to be depressed. Yet, taking the lowest price each month, the averages for the first and last half of each year, for each year, and for the whole period, are as follows:

	First Half.	Last Half.	Year.
1839	$7.46	$5.48	$6.16
1840	5.08	5.00	5.04
1841	4.65	6.15	5.40
1842	5.74	4.66	5.20

Average for the four years, $5.45.

This, then, is the measure of the effect of extreme hard times, when occurring under a non-protective system. Compare these four years, the worst under that tariff, or under any system of low duties, with the record of the protective tariff which followed:

	First Half.	Last Half.	Year.
1843	$4.16	$4.53	$4.35
1844	4.53	4.08	4.31
1845	4.44	4.84	4.64
1846	4.68	4.42	4.55

Average for the four years, $4.46.

As compared with the extreme hard times which preceded, then, the tariff of 1842–'46 cost the farmer just *one dollar a barrel* in re-

8

duced price of his product ! And this is the effect, in the greatest manufacturing centre in the country, of that system which is to " build up a home market ! "

Let us compare two other periods. We throw aside the earlier years of the tariff of 1846, because the price was then affected, on the one hand, by the European famine, and on the other by the depressed condition of business in 1851, and take the eight closing years of that tariff to compare with the six years of protection which followed. It must be remembered that this period includes the panic of 1857, which seriously reduced the price for six months. The average of monthly prices is as follows :

	First Half.	Last Half.	Year.
1854	$8.44	$8.47	$8.45
1855	9.78	8.68	9.23
1856	6.87	6.56	6.71
1857	6.57	5.78	.17
1858	4.47	5.15	4.81
1859	6.40	5.28	5.84
1860	5.48	5.35	5.41
1861	5.29	5.05	5.17

Average for eight years, $6.47.

We include 1861, though it reduces the average, because the effects of the tariff were not felt in its earlier months. Observe how quickly the price recovered from the depression in the winter of 1857-'58, and observe also that the average is *just two dollars a barrel more* than the producer received under the tariff of 1842-'46.

The quotations since the adoption of the protective system in 1861 have been reduced to gold, at the rates current each month, and are as follows :

	First Half.	Last Half.	Year.
1862	$4.89	$4.52	$4.70
1863	4.01	3.86	3.93
1864	3.91	4.20	4.05
1865	4.42	5.23	4.81

Average for four years, $4.37.

1866	$5.30	$5.72	$5.51
1867	7.89	5.43	6.66

Average for six years, $4.94.

The published table closes with the year 1867, but it is well known that the price during the year 1869 has been so low that, were the monthly quotations given, the average for the whole eight years would be even lower than the average for the six years given.

It appears that, during four years of protection, the average price, at Philadelphia, was lower than it had ever been during any preceding period. Moreover, during this period of six years, as compared with the non-protective period preceding, the loss to the farmer on each barrel of flour was $1.53. The four periods compare thus:

Average price of flour during

Four years, from 1839 to 1842 ("free trade") $5.45.
"   "   "   1843 " 1846 ("protection") 4.46.
Eight "   "   1854 " 1861 ("free trade") 6.47.
Six   "   "   1862 " 1867 ("protection") 4.94.

Average price for twelve years, under "free trade," $6.13.
Average price for ten years, under "protection," $4.75.

The system of high duties, therefore, costs the agricultural interest an average yearly of one dollar and thirty-eight cents on every barrel of flour produced, which means, of course, an average of nearly thirty cents a bushel on every bushel of wheat grown. Yet these are the prices in the greatest manufacturing region in the country, and, if "the home market" is not a myth, there we should see its effects most conspicuously displayed! If we call the crop of wheat two hundred and fifty millions of bushels, protection costs us this year seventy-five millions of dollars, in the value of that product alone. And this is only one of the many products of the farmer, though its price is by all accepted as the best test of the general prosperity of the agricultural interest.

If agriculture has ever been overcrowded to that degree that its products have exceeded the ability of this country to consume, or of other countries to buy them at remunerative rates, that event has happened under the heaviest protective duties ever imposed in this country. In periods of low duties, the production by agriculture increased nearly or over 70 per cent. in a decade; and yet our ability to consume at fair prices was so much more rapidly increased that the price rose, and the production of wealth was swelled 76 and 107 per cent. But in this latest and most faithful trial of the protective system an increase in quantity of products of not more than 40 per cent. has been met by such an inability to consume at fair rates that the prices fall, and the increase in the production of wealth shrinks to a smaller proportion than ever before since the War of 1212 and the protective system first interfered with a prosperous foreign commerce.

Startling and conclusive as these facts are, they by no means represent the full injury done to the agricultural interest by high tariffs.   We have thus far considered only the price in the principal markets for export or consumption, because by these, it is well known, prices in all parts of the country are governed.   But to every farmer another consideration is of vital importance—the cost of transportation to those markets.   If transportation for wheat from Columbus to New York costs 18 cents, and wheat is selling in New York at $1.28, it is certain that it cannot bring more than $1.10 at Columbus, and the actual price is still further reduced by charges of shippers and middle-men.   Thus to every farmer a saving of ten cents a bushel in the cost of transporting his grain to the principal markets results in an increase of nearly ten cents in the price which he receives.   It is, therefore, of vital importance to the farmer that facilities for transportation shall increase with rapidity.

Increase there must be in any case, in a country as new and rapidly growing as this.   Not a year has passed, however complete the prostration of industry, in which no improvements have extended facilities for transporting our products to market.   But that increase has been greater in some periods than in others, and in a very remarkable degree it has been greater in times of low than in times of high duties.

In the earliest times of which we have record, the interior tonnage was not distinguished from the foreign, but from 1815 we can trace the progress of ship-building on Western lakes and rivers.   In 1815, 1816, and 1817, the average was about one thousand tons yearly; in 1817 there were built vessels measuring 1,250 tons. Then the tariffs of 1816 and 1818 were felt, and in 1818, 1819, 1820, 1821, and 1822, the lake tonnage was increased only 189, 267, 88, 249, and 105 tons respectively, the aggregate for five years being less than the tonnage built in the single year 1817.   In 1823, for the first time, we have record of steamers built for the Western rivers, 663 tons, making the aggregate for lakes and rivers in that year, 1,066.   It then increased rapidly, reaching 5,000 in 1827, falling to 3,027 in 1828, rising to 6,044 in 1829, and falling to 5,222 in 1831. The average for these eight years of protective duty, 1824 to 1831, inclusive, was about 4,300 tons yearly.   The tariff bill passed July, 1832, greatly reducing duties, though it did not immediately take effect, appears to have stimulated ship-building enormously, internal as well as foreign, for in that year the foreign tonnage built was over 100,000, more than twice as great as that of the year before, while the lake and river tonnage built amounted to 14,475, more than double that of any previous year.   Nor did it recede in any year afterward as low as the highest point reached under protection. The average under the seven years of compromise. duties, 1833–'39, inclusive, in spite of a decrease of nearly one-half after the panic of 1837, was 14,456 tons. In the hard times of 1840 it fell to 8,693, but recovered to 15,318 the next year, and to 20,782 in 1842, so that the average for the whole period was 14,598, an increase of more than 200 per cent. on the average of the eight years of protection.

The rapid increase noticed in 1841 and 1842 continuing, the tonnage built rose to 38,872 in 1846, the average for the four years of protection being 31,708, a gain of 100 per cent. on the average of ten preceding years, and of 50 per cent. on the last year of low duties. But in 1847, the first year after the removal of the protective system, the tonnage built for the rivers and lakes jumped to 58,240, an increase of more than 50 per cent. in a single year. And by 1856, before it was reduced by the panic, it rose to 100,713, a gain of 200 per cent. on the average of the protective period. The panic of 1857 reduced the Western tonnage built to 23,308 in 1859, but it recovered to 43,056 in 1860, and to 53,427 in 1861.

Again, if we observe the number of steamers built, we find that in 1823 there were 15, and in 1824 there were 26; that the yearly average for the four years under the tariff of 1829 was 38, and the yearly average under the tariff of 1829–'32 was 53½—including the year 1832, in which alone there were 100 built. The reduction of duty was then certain, and the average without that year was only 38—just the same as that of the preceding tariff. But under the reduced duties the average for the four years 1833–'36 was 72 a year, and for the next four years, 1837–'40, it was 103 a year, in spite of the panic. For the last two years of this tariff, 1841 and 1842, the average was 107½. Here is an increase of about 150 per cent., as compared with the average of eight years under protection. Again, from 1842–'46, inclusive, the average was 157½, a gain of less than 50 per cent. But the four years which followed under low duties, 1847–'50, show an average of 185 yearly, and the period 1851–'54 shows an average of 261 yearly. After the panic the number so decreased that the average for 1859 and 1860 is only 233.

Let us next consider the progress in railroad-building. The influence of railroads in increasing the value of farming products and of farming land has been most wonderful, and every farmer will understand that, if the building of railroads has been materially checked or retarded by any tariff system, that system has cursed the farmer and retarded the whole agricultural interest of the country. In the years 1829–'32, under protection, we built 229 miles of road, an average of 76 miles yearly. A table at the close of this chapter gives the number of miles of railroad built each year, and the same record is presented in Diagram, "Iron, Coal and Railroads" (p. 206). In the years 1833–'36, under reduced duties, we built 1,044 miles, an average of 261 miles yearly; in 1837–'40, with duties still lower, we built 1,545 miles, an average of 386 miles yearly; and in the two years, 1841 and 1842, duties being at the lowest point, though business was depressed, we built 1,208 miles, or 604 yearly! But it will be said that this increase was natural, the country being new and greatly in need of railroad facilities. True; but observe how suddenly the tariff of 1843 cuts down this progress, from 717 miles built in 1841, to 159 miles in 1843! The whole number of miles built under that tariff was only 904, an average of 226 miles yearly— less than had been built ten years before under lower duties! Observe, again, how the progress is resumed instantly when the load of duties is removed! In 1847 the number of miles built was 669, more than double the number built in 1846, and in 1849 it had doubled again. The whole number of miles built in the four years after the removal of the tariff was 4,091—more than four times as many as were built in the four years of protection just preceding! The average for 1847–'50 was 1,023 miles yearly, and for the next period, 1851–'54, it was 1,925 yearly, 7,699 miles being built; and for the next period, 1855–'58, it was 2,562 miles yearly, 10,248 miles being built. The panic reduced the yearly average to 1,833 for the years 1859 and 1860, but the tariff of 1861 reduced it still more. Though government needed and built roads for military purposes, and gave enormous subsidies to others, the whole number of miles built during the years 1861–'64 was 3,273, an average of 818 yearly. But these were years of war. Take, then, the latest years of peace, 1865–'68, inclusive, during which the average was 2,087—less than the average of the period 1855–'58, ten years before! Nor is this a fair comparison; for within the last four years more than 3,000 miles of road have been built by government land grants and subsidies, involving a debt of over fifty millions of dollars. Yet the whole number of miles built was only 8,347, and a portion of these were built by government aid. Deducting these, the yearly average for these four years under protection is less than the average twenty years ago, during the first period after the tariff of 1842 expired!

In short, there have been built in fifteen years of protection, without government subsidies, 9,750 miles, an average of 650 miles yearly. But in twenty-four years of revenue tariff we have built 29,502 miles, an average of 1,229 miles yearly. Does "protection" protect the agricultural interest?

The most accurate measure of the benefit conferred by railroads upon the farmers is the increase in the value of farm lands. A farm is worth that sum upon which its net products, with allowance for value of labor, will pay a fair interest; and an improvement which reduces the cost of transporting these products to a market, thus adding to the price which the farmer can obtain for them, directly increases the yearly value of the farm. Statistics of hundreds of counties, in different parts of the country, prove that the opening of a railroad into a county, not previously blessed with such means of transportation, has ordinarily increased the average value of lands in the county nearly 100 per cent. within a few years. Under the tariff of 1842 only 904 miles of railroad were built in four years; and, if we suppose that the value of farming land for fifteen miles on each side was doubled, 27,120 square miles of land were thus raised in value. But the average number of miles built every year after that tariff was repealed was greater than the whole number built during four years of its operation, and in the four years, 1855–'58, under low duties, we built 2,562 miles yearly, and thus doubled the value each year of 76,860 square miles of land, a territory one-fourth larger than the old State of Virginia. During the decade 1850–'60, under low duties, there were built 21,613 miles of road; and, had these nowhere conflicted with each other, about 650,000 square miles of land would have been raised in value—a territory more than one-fifth as large as the entire domain of the United States. These figures serve only to give some idea of the importance of railroad-building to the agricultural interest, and it may easily be inferred that a protective system which makes the rails alone for every mile of railroad cost $8,000, when far better rails could be procured, did no tariff hinder, at a cost of $5,000, and enhances the cost of other materials in like proportion, must greatly retard the progress of railroads, and consequently the progress of agriculture. Men who have five millions of money at command can iron one thousand miles of road if no tariff interferes; but a protective tariff reduces them to 625 miles, or compels them to defer the undertaking altogether.

The examination of the effect of the protective system upon agriculture has been somewhat lengthy, but it is repaid by the extreme importance of the facts established. It is proved, beyond question, that the system of protective duties does very materially retard the production of wealth by agriculture. It reduces the export price of products. It reduces the prices of agricultural products in the great manufacturing centres. It reduces the value of farming land in the chief manufacturing States. It has rendered the country unable to consume crops scarcely larger than those of 1860, at prices lower in gold. It has produced similar results, as to the general progress of that branch of industry, in every period in which it has been tried since 1790, so that the increase in non-protective periods has been fully twice as great as the increase in protective periods. It has checked the growth of facilities for transportation, thus depriving the farmer of a part of even that low price which his products could in protective times have brought in markets for export or consumption. Within the last decade, the increase in the production of wealth by agriculture was fully 100 per cent., but during eight years, under protective duties, the increase has been, measured by the quantity of wheat, about 40 per cent.; measured by the value of wheat produced, 2½ per cent.; measured by the value of all the principal crops, nothing; measured by the value of Northern crops, 4¼ per cent.; measured by the value of live-stock, nothing; measured by the value of farm lands, less than nothing.

But by agriculture three-fourths of all our wealth has been produced. If the production of wealth by that industry has been retarded by at least one-half of its natural growth during every protective period, and if under the present tariff the progress has been yet more seriously retarded—if not arrested altogether—what has the country lost? The annual product in 1860 was about twenty-six hundred millions. If the progress of the last decade had been maintained, the yearly product would now be five thousand millions. If there has been no progress, we have lost in yearly product by agriculture alone a sum as large as the whole national debt. If the progress of agriculture generally has been retarded no more than the crop of wheat, we have lost in the product of this year only a sum half as large as that debt. And if, in the year 1870, it shall appear that the production of wealth by agriculture has increased 40 per cent.—a rate more rapid than that of any other protective period in our history—we shall then have lost, upon the product of a single year, not less than $1,500,000,000, a sum nearly twice as great as the entire production of wealth by all other forms of industry in the year 1860. To compensate for that loss, the production of wealth by manufactures and mining must have increased threefold.

The following tables show, first, the number of miles of railway built, and the number in operation each year since 1830; second, the price of flour each month, according to the report of the Philadelphia Corn Exchange; third, the averages for different periods of the lowest quotations each month, those since 1861 being reduced to gold values; fourth, the number of ships, barks, brigs, schooners, sloops, and steamers built, and the total tonnage each year from 1815 to 1862, inclusive. The Philadelphia quotations are for extra fall wheat flour, and the published report ends with 1867. In the next table the averages of the lowest quotations are given, for the first half of each year, for the last half, for the year, for periods of several years, and under each tariff. For the years 1868 and 1869 newspaper quotations of January 1st, and July 1st, reduced to gold, are averaged for the first half, and quotations for July 1st and January 1st, for the last half of each year.

RAILROADS.

Statement of the Number of Miles of Railroad Built each Year.—(From Poor's Railway Manual.)

YEAR.	Built.	Total in Oper'n.	YEAR.	Built.	Total in Oper'n.
1830	23	23	1850	1,654	9,021
1831	72	95	1851	1,961	10,982
1832	134	229	1852	1,926	12,908
1833	151	380	1853	2,452	15,360
1834	253	633	1854	1,360	16,720
1835	465	1,098	1855	1,654	18,374
1836	175	1,273	1856	3,643	22,017
1837	224	1,497	1857	2,491	24,508
1838	416	1,913	1858	2,460	26,968
1839	389	2,302	1859	1,821	28,789
1840	516	2,818	1860	1,846	30,635
1841	717	3,535	1861	621	31,256
1842	491	4,026	1862	864	32,120
1843	159	4,185	1863	1,050	33,170
1844	192	4,377	1864	738	33,908
1845	256	4,633	1865	1,177	35,085
1846	297	4,930	1866	1,742	36,827
1847	669	5,599	1867	2,449	39,276
1848	397	5,996	1868	2,979	42,255
1849	1,369	7,365			

The number of miles built in 1869, after Poor's work was issued, was very large—it is said nearly six thousand miles. But a large part of this was built by government aid, and at heavy expense to the people, either in subsidies or land grants. But for the Pacific roads, and those constructed to give access to or connection with them, the contrast in railroad building between the present period and that of low duties which preceded would be very striking.

Highest and Lowest Price for Flour in Each Month for Eighty-one Years—From 1786 to 1867.

Years.	January.	February.	March.	April.	May.	June.
1786..	....	42s. 0d.	41s. 6d.	40s. 6d.	40s. 0d.	43s. 0d.
1787..	40s. 0d.	40s. 0d.	40s. 0d.	40s. 0d.	40s. 0d.	42s. 6d.
1788..	....	....	35s. 0d.	36s. 0d.	37s. 0d.	37s. 0d.
1789..	35s. 0d.	34s. 0d.	35s. 0d.	35s. 0d.	40s. 0d.	42s. 6d.
1790..	44s. 6d.	....	....	....	....	....
1791..	45s. 0d.	45s. 0d.	40s. 0d.	38s. 0d.	40s. 0d.	40s. 0d.
1792..	37s. 6d.	37s. 6d.	37s. 6d.	37s. 6d.	37s. 0d.	37s. 6d.
1793..	45s. 0d.	45s. 0d.	....	....	....	45s. 0d.
1794..	....	56s. 0d.	48s. 2d.	....	50s. 0d.	50s. 0d.
1795..	....	....	....	75s. 0d.	82s. 6d.	80s. 3d.
1796..	$12 00	$13 50	$15 00	$14 00	$14 00	$12 50
1797..	10 00	10 00	10 00@ 9 25	9 00@ 8 50	9 00	8 50
1798..	8 50	8 50	8 50	8 50@ 7 50	7 00	6 75
1799..	9 50	9 50	9 25	9 25	9 50	9 50
1800..	....	....	....	9 50	9 75	10 00
1801..	11 50	11 25	11 50@ 9 50	11 00	11 50	11 50
1802..	7 00	7 00	7 00	7 00	7 00	7 00
1803..	6 50	6 50	6 50	6 00	6 00	6 00@ 6 50
1804..	7 50	7 50	7 00	6 00	6 50	6 50@ 7 75
1805..	11 00	....	12 00@13 00	17 00	11 75	11 00
1806..	7 50	7 00	7 00@ 6 75	6 50@ 7 00	7 00@ 8 00	8 00
1807..	7 50	7 50	7 25	7 25	7 25	7 25@ 7 00
1808..	6 00	5 75	5 75	5 18¾	5 00	5 00
1809..	5 50	7 00	7 00	6 25	7 00	6 50@ 7 00
1810..	7 75	8 00	8 25	8 25	9 00	9 00
1811..	11 00	10 50	10 50	10 50	10 25	10 12
1812..	....	10 12	9 75@ 9 25	9 00@ 7 00	7 25@ 8 50	8 50
1813..	12 00	10 50	9 50	9 75@10 00	8 50@ 7 25	8 00@ 8 50
1814..	....	....	....	....	7 50@ 7 00	6 75.
1815..	8 00	8 00	7 75	7 75	8 50	8 50@ 9 00
1816..	9 00	9 00	8 00	7 75	7 87	8 75@10 50
1817..	13 50	13 75	14 00@14 75	14 00@14 25	14 50@14 00	11 50@11 00
1818..	9 25@10 00	10 50@10 75	10 50	10 00	10 00	10 25
1819..	9 00	8 75	8 00	7 25	6 37	6 00
1820..	6 00@5 37½	5 50@5 12½	5 00@ 4 75	4 75	4 37@ 4 87	4 50@ 4 75
1821..	4 00	4 00	3 62@ 3 75	4 00	4 00	4 09
1822..	6 25	6 25	6 25	6 50	7 12	6 75@ 7 00
1823..	6 50@ 7 00	6 50@ 7 00	7 00	7 25	7 37	7 50
1824..	6 00	6 00	6 00@ 6 50	6 12	6 00	6 00@ 5 75
1825..	4 87½	5 12	5 12	5 00	6 00	5 50@ 5 00
1826..	4 75	4 62	4 50	4 25	4 25	4 25@ 4 75
1827..	5 25@ 6 00	6 00@ 5 75	5 75@ 5 12	5 12@ 5 00	5 00	5 00
1828..	5 00@ 4 75	4 87½@ 4 75	4 75	4 75	4 75	4 50
1829..	8 25	8 25@ 8 00	8 00@ 7 50	7 50@ 6 75	6 60@ 6 75	6 75@ 6 25
1830..	4 62½@ 4 50	4 50	4 50	4 50@ 5 00	4 75	4 75@ 4 50
1831..	6 25@ 6 00	6 00	6 25@ 7 00	6 37@ 7 00	6 50@ 5 50	5 75@ 5 25
1832..	5 50	5 50	5 25@ 5 00	5 25@ 5 50	5 50	5 75@ 6 25
1833..	5 75	5 00@ 5 19	5 25	5 25	5 50	5 50@ 5 75
1834..	5 25	4 87	4 62	4 75@ 5 25	5 25@ 5 50	5 50
1835..	4 93¾	5 09	5 00	5 18¾	6 00	6 25
1836..	6 62½	6 75	7 00	6 81¼	6 50	6 81¼
1837..	11 00@11 25	10 50@11 00	10 50@10 75	9 31¼	9 00	9 00@ 9 37
1838..	8 12½@8 62½	7 50@8 06¼	7 50@ 8 00	7 50@ 8 00	7 71@ 7 90	7 50@ 7 75
1839..	8 25@8 50	8 50	7 50@ 8 62	7 37@ 7 50	7 00@ 7 50	6 12@ 6 32
1840..	5 75	5 50	5 00	4 87	4 62	4 75
1841..	4 65@5 25	4 50@5 06¼	4 50@ 4 93	4 62@ 5 00	4 65@ 5 00	5 00
1842..	6 06¼	5 90@6 12	5 60@ 5 81	5 62@ 5 80	5 75	5 50@ 5 62
1843..	3 98	3 75@3 92	3 79@ 3 91	4 22	4 25@ 4 40	5 00@ 5 12
1844..	4 50	4 80	4 75	4 68	4 37@ 4 57	4 10@ 4 30
1845..	4 15	4 31¼	4 31¼	5 38	4 45	4 25@ 4 40
1846..	5 31¼	4 90	4 83	4 81	4 31	3 91
1847..	4 83½	6 17	5 93¾	6 87	7 90	8 25@ 8 40
1848..	6 06¼	5 87½	6 06¼	5 93¾	5 87	5 44
1849..	5 21	5 00	4 75@ 5 12	4 50	4 68	4 55
1850..	5 00	4 78	4 79	5 00	6 18	5 27
1851..	4 66	4 25@4 56¼	4 12	4 50	4 26	4 25
1852..	4 25	5 55	4 18¾	4 06¼	4 20	4 20
1853..	5 37½	5 20	4 93¾	4 90	4 18	4 62
1854..	7 59	8 12	7 45	8 08	8 69	8 72@ 8 90
1855..	9 18¾	8 94	9 06¼	10 25	10 75	10 52
1856..	8 33	7 31	7 00	6 57½	6 06¼	5 94
1857..	6·32	6 37½	6 12½	6 00	7 19	7 45
1858..	4 73	4 46	4 46	4 40½	4 44	4 31¼
1859..	5 75	5 81	6 73	6 25	7 25	6 62
1860..	5 44	5 00	5 00	6 00	5 94	5 50
1861..	5 31	5 12	5 12	5 37	5 56	5 25
1862..	5 31¼	5 31¼	5 00	5 12½	4 87½	4 75
1863..	6 25	6 25	6 12	6 12	5 87	5 75
1864..	6 25	6 25	6 00	7 00	7 25	7 50
1865..	9 75	9 75	8 25	7 50	6 25	6 25
1866..	7 25	6 50	6 75	7 25	8 00	8 50
1867..	11 25@13 50	10 25@11 25	10 00@11 00	12 00@14 00	11 00@12 50	10 00@15 25

Highest and Lowest Price for Flour in Each Month for Eighty-one Years—From 1786 to 1867 (*Continued*).

Years.	July.	August.	September.	October.	November.	December.
1786..	43s. 0d.	43s. 0d.	42s. 6d.	42s. 6d.	42s. 0d.	40s. 0d.
1787..	42s. 6d.	36s. 6d.	33s. 0d.	33s. 0d.	....	....
1788..	35s. 0d.	35s. 0d.	35s. 0d.	34s. 6d.	34s. 0d.	35s. 0d.
1789..	38s. 8d.	41s. 0d.	42s. 0d.	42s. 6d.	40s. 0d.	42s. 6d.
1790..	....	53s. 6d.	45s. 0d.	43s. 3d.	46s. 0d.	46s. 0d.
1791..	40s. 0d.	35s. 0d.	36s. 0d.	36s. 0d.	37s. 6d.	37s. 6d.
1792..	37s. 6d.	37s. 6d.	39s. 0d.	38s. 6d.	38s. 6d.	38s. 6d.
1793..	....	48s. 6d.	47s. 6d.	47s. 6d.	47s. 6d.	47s. 6d.
1794..	54s. 0d.	53s. 0d.	52s. 6d.	56s. 0d.	59s. 0d.	69s. 0d.
1795..	86s. 3d.	90s. 0d.	90s. 6d.	$13 00	$13 00	$13 75
1796..	$11 75	$11 00	$12 00	12 00	12 00@11 50	11 50@10 50
1797..	8 50	8 50	8 50	8 50	8 50	8 50
1798..	6 75	8 00@ 8 50	8 50	8 50	8 50@ 9 50	9 50@10 00
1799..	10 00@ 9 50	9 50	9 50	9 50@10 00	10 50@11 00	10 00
1800..	10 25	10 75	10 50@ 9 75	9 50	10 50	11 00
1801..	11 50@11 00	11 00	10 00@ 9 50	9 25	9 00	8 00@ 6 50
1802..	7 25	7 25	7 00@ 6 50	6 50	6 50	6 50
1803..	7 00	7 00@ 7 75	7 75@ 7 50	7 50	7 50	7 50
1804..	7 75	8 00	9 75@10 00	9 00	10 00@10 50	11 00
1805..	10 75@ 9 00	9 00@ 8 00	8 00	8 00	8 00@ 8 50	8 25
1806..	8 00	7 50@ 6 75	7 00	6 75	7 00@ 7 50	7 50
1807..	6 75	6 75	7 12@ 7 50	7 25@ 6 75	7 00	6 75
1808..	5 00@ 5 75	5 25	5 00@ 6 00	6 00	6 00@ 5 50	5 50@ 6 00
1809..	6 12@ 7 00	6 75	6 75@ 7 25	7 25	7 50@ 8 00	7 50
1810..	10 00@11 00	11 00@12 00	11 00@10 75	10 75@11 50	10 25	11 25
1811..	10 00@11 00	10 75@10 00	9 00	8 50	9 50	10 00
1812..	8 50	8 25@ 9 00	9 00@10 00	10 25@10 00	11 50@10 50	10 25
1813..	7 50	7 00@ 8 00	8 25@ 8 75	9 25@ 8 25	8 50@10 00	10 00@ 7 50
1814..	7 00@ 7 25	7 25@ 8 50	8 50	8 75	8 75	8 00
1815..	9 25@ 8 75	8 62	8 75	9 00	9 50	9 25
1816..	11 00	10 75@ 9 50	9 75	10 00@11 00	11 50@12 50	12 50@13 50
1817..	10 50@11 50	11 50@10 00	9 50	9 00	9 50@10 00	9 75@ 9 00
1818..	10 25	10 50@10 75	9 75	9 75	9 25	9 00
1819..	6 00	6 00@ 6 25	6 50	6 50	6 12	6 00@ 6 25
1820..	4 50@ 4 75	4 50	4 50	4 25	4 25	4 50
1821..	4 00@ 4 50	4 62@ 5 00	5 25@ 5 50	5 50@ 7 50	7 00@ 6 00	6 00@ 6 50
1822..	6 75@ 6 25	6 25@ 7 00	7 00	6 62	6 50	6 50
1823..	7 00	6 50	6 50	6 75	6 62	6 25@ 6 00
1824..	5 25	5 25	5 12@ 5 50	5 12	5 50@ 5 00	4 75@ 5 00
1825..	5 50@ 4 50	5 00	5 00	5 00@ 5 12	5 12@ 5 00	4 87
1826..	4 37@ 4 50	4 50	4 50@ 5 00	5 00@ 4 25	5 50	5 25
1827..	5 00	5 00	5 00@ 5 25	5 25	5 25@ 5 50	5 00
1828..	4 50@ 4 75	5 00@ 5 50	5 50@ 7 00	6 25@ 7 00	7 25@ 9 00	7 75@ 8 25
1829..	6 00@ 5 00	5 00@ 5 50	5 50@ 5 75	5 25@ 5 00	5 00@ 5 25	5 25@ 4 62
1830..	4 50@ 5 25	5 25@ 5 75	5 50@ 5 25	5 25@ 5 00	5 00	5 00@ 5 62
1831..	5 37@ 4 75	4 75	5 25@ 5 50	5 50	5 50@ 5 25	5 25
1832..	6 00	6 37@ 6 25	6 37@ 5 50	5 50@ 6 00	5 25@ 6 12	5 75@ 5 50
1833..	6 00@ 6 50	6 12@ 6 00	6 00	5 87@ 5 75	5 75	5 50@ 5 25
1834..	5 25@ 5 50	5 50	5 50@ 5 25	5 25	5 25@ 5 12	5 00@ 4 80
1835..	6 81	6 06¼	6 12	6 06¼	6 37	6 75
1836..	7 00	8 37	9 37	9 31	10 62	11 00
1837..	9 50@ 9 95	9 00@ 8 53	8 00@ 8 50	8 25@ 9 00	9 31@ 9 81	9 50@ 9 75
1838..	6 43@ 6 12	6 12@ 7 12	6 90@ 8 45	8 25@ 8 40	8 00@ 8 12	8 31@ 8 50
1839.	5 59@ 5 12	5 75@ 6 12	5 87@ 6 12	5 87@ 6 00	6 25	5 56@ 5 90
1840..	5 25	5 00	5 00	5 00	5 00	4 75@ 5 25
1841..	5 25@ 5 50	6 06@ 6 84	6 62@ 6 87	6 12@ 6 30	6 47@ 6 96	6 42
1842..	5 50@ 5 37	5 25@ 5 45	4 56¼	4 19	4 12@ 4 37	4 37@ 4 62
1843..	5 25@ 5 37	4 75@ 5 06	4 44	4 25@ 4 50	4 25@ 4 37	4 25@ 4 50
1844..	4 00@ 4 37	3 91@ 4 19	3 89@ 4 33	4 00@ 4 50	4 37	4 29
1845..	4 22@ 4 62	4 18¾	4 60	4 06¼	5 91	6 06¼
1846..	3 84	3 83	3 82@ 4 12	5 18	5 10	4 76
1847..	5 91	6 03	5 50	6 45	6 31	6 49
1848..	5 25	5 22	5 67	5 42	5 25	5 14
1849..	4 56¼	4 87@ 5 12	5 02	5 10	5 06¼	4 87
1850..	5 06¼	5 12@ 5 37	5 00	4 83	4 85	4 71
1851..	4 25	3 97	3 96	4 12	3 97	4 15
1852..	4 12	4 20	4 44	4 48	4 90	5 16
1853..	5 00	5 33	5 70	6 61	6 90@ 7 45	6 72@ 7 00
1854..	8 06@ 8 29	8 13@ 8 53	8 50@ 8 81	8 33@ 8 58	8 68@ 8 90	9 12@ 9 25
1855..	9 31	8 81	7 47	8 37	9 31	8 82@ 8 90
1856..	6 56½	6 52½	6 40	6 50	6 62½	6 60
1857..	6 87½	6 50	5 62½	5 25	5 31¼	5 12½
1858..	4 37½	5 25	5 59	5 42	5 15	5 12½
1859..	5 87	5 12	5 00	5 12	5 25	5 31¼
1860..	5 31	5 56	5 69	5 75	4 94	4 87
1861..	4 75	4 42	5 12	5 44	5 27	5 31
1862..	4 87½	5 25	5 00	6 12½	6 12½	6 12½
1863..	5 50	4 75	5 06	5 62	5 75	6 00
1864..	9 75	10 25	10 25	9 75	10 00	10 00
1865..	7 00	7 00	8 25	8 25	8 00	7 25
1866..	7 00	8 25	8 50	9 00	8 50	8 75
1867..	8 75@10 00	8 00@ 8 75	7 25@ 9 50	8 25@ 8 75	7 00@ 8 50	....

PRICE OF FLOUR.

Average of the Lowest Quotations Each Month for Certain Periods.

YEAR.	First Half.	Last.	Year.	Period.	Tariff.	Remarks.
1817..........	$13 54	$9 96	$11 75	....	....	Inflation.
1818..........	10 08	9 75	9 91	....	....	"
1819..........	7 89	6 19	7 04	....	....	Contraction.
1820..........	5 02	4 42	4 71	$8 35	....	"
1821..........	3 94	5 39	4 66	....	....	"
1822..........	6 56	6 60	6 58	....	....	....
1823..........	7 02	6 60	6 81	....	.... '	....
1824..........	6 02	5 16	5 59	5 91	$7 13	....
1825..........	5 27	5 08	5 17	....	....	....
1826..........	4 43	4 85	4 64	....	....	....
1827..........	5 35	5 08	5 21	....	....	....
1828..........	4 77	5 96	5 36	5 09	....	....
1829..........	7 56	5 33	6 45	....	....	....
1830..........	4 60	5 03	4 81	....	....	....
1831..........	6 19	5 27	5 73	....	....	....
1832..........	5 47	5 74	5 60	5 63	5 36	....
1833..........	5 37	5 87	5 62	....	....	....
1834..........	5 04	5 29	5 16	....	....	....
1835..........	5 39	6 36	5 87	....	....	....
1836..........	6 75	9 28	8 01	6 16	....	Inflation.
1837..........	9 72	8 93	9 32	....	....	"
1838..........	7 64	7 33	7 48	8 40	....	"
1839..........	7 46	5 48	6 16	....	....	Contraction.
1840..........	5 08	5 00	5 04	....	....	"
1841..........	5 65	6 15	5 40	....	....	"
1842..........	5 74	4 66	5 20	5 45	6 32	"
1843..........	4 16	4 53	4 35	....	....	....
1844..........	4 53	4 08	4 31	....	....	....
1845..........	4 44	4 84	4 64	....	....	....
1846..........	4 68	4 42	4 55	4 46	4 46	....
1847..........	6 66	6 11	6 38	....	....	Irish Famine.
1848..........	5 87	5 32	5 59	....	....	....
1849..........	4 78	4 91	4 85	....	....	....
1850..........	5 17	4 93	5 05	5 37	....	....
1851..........	4 51	4 07	4 29	....	....	....
1852..........	4 56	4 55	4 55	....	....	....
1853..........	4 87	6 04	5 45	....	....	....
1854..........	8 44	8 47	8 45	5 69	....	....
1855..........	9 78	8 68	9 23	....	....	....
1856..........	6 87	6 56	6 71	....	....	....
1857..........	6 57	5 78	6 17	....	....	....
1858..........	4 47	5 15	4 81	6 70	....	Panic.
1859..........	6 40	5 28	5 84	....	....	....
1860..........	5 48	5 35	5 41	5 62	5 86	....
1861..........	5 29	5 05	5 17	....	....	War.
1862..........	4 89	4 52	4 70	....	....	"
1863..........	4 01	3 86	3 93	....	....	"
1864..........	3 91	4 20	4 05	....	....	"
1865..........	4 42	5 23	4 81	4 53	....	Short Crop.
1866..........	5 30	5 72	5 51	....	....	"
1867..........	7 89	5 43	6 66	....	....	"
1868..........	5 10	4 17	4 63	....	....	....
1869..........	3 44	3 42	3 43	5 ·05	4 79	....

SHIP-BUILDING.

The Number and Class of Vessels built, and the Tonnage thereof, from 1815 to 1862.

YEAR.	CLASS OF VESSELS.					Total No. of Vessels built.	Total Tonnage.
	Ships and Barks.	Brigs.	Schooners	Sloops and Canal B'ts.	Steamers.		
							Tons. 95ths.
1815....	136	224	681	274	..	1,315	154,624.39
1816....	76	122	781	424	..	1,403	131,668.04
1817....	34	86	559	394	..	1,073	86,393.37
1818....	·53	85	428	332	..	898	82,421.20
1819....	53	82	473	243	..	851	79,817.86
1820....	21	60	301	152	..	534	47,784.01
1821....	43	89	247	127	..	506	55,856.01
1822....	64	131	260	168	..	623	75,346.93
1823....	55	127	260	165	15	622	75,007.57
1824....	56	156	377	166	26	781	90,939.00
1825....	56	197	538	168	35	994	114,997.25
1826....	71	187	482	227	45	1,012	126,438.35
1827....	55	153	464	241	38	951	104,342.67
1828....	73	108 ·	474	196	33	884	93,375.58
1829....	44	68	485	145	43	785	77,098.65
1830....	25	56	403	116	37	637	58,094.24
1831....	72	95	416	94	34	711	85,962.68
1832....	132	143	568	122	100	1,065	144,539.16
1833....	144	169	625	185	65	1,188	161,626.36
1834....	98	94	497	180	68	937	118,330.37
1835....	25	50	301	100	30	506	46,238.52
1836....	93	65	444	164	124	890	113,627.49
1837....	67	72	507	168	135	949	122,987.22
1838....	66	79	501	153	90	889	113,135.44
1839....	83	89	439	122	125	858	120,989.34
1840....	97	109	378	224	64	872	118,309.23
1841....	114	101	310	157	78	760	118,893.71
1842....	116	91	273	404	137	1,021	129,083.64
1843....	58	34	138	173	79	452	43,617.77
1844....	73	47	204	279	163	766	103,537.29
1845....	124	87	322	342	163	1,038	146,018.02
1846....	100	164	576	355	225	1,420	188,203.93
1847....	151	168	689	392	198	1,598	243,732.67
1848....	254	174	701	547	175	1,851	318,075.54
1849....	198	148	623	370	208	1,547	256,577.47
1850....	247	117	547	290	159	1,360	272,218.54
1851....	211	65	522	326	233	1,367	298,203.60
1852....	255	79	584	267	259	1,444	351,493.41
1853....	269	95	681	394	271	1,710	425,571.49
1854....	334	112	661	386	281	1,774	535,616.01
1855....	381	126	605	669	253	2,037	583,450.04
1856....	306	103	594	479	221	1,703	469,393.73
1857....	251	58	504	258	263	1,334	378,804.70
1858....	222	46	431	400	226	1,225	242,286.69
1859....	89	28	297	284	172	870	156,601.33
1860....	110	36	372	289	264	1,071	212,892.45
1861....	110	38	360	371	264	1,143	233,194.35
1862 ...	60	17	207	397	183	864	175,075.84

CHAPTER IX.

MECHANICS AND NATURAL MANUFACTURES.

Has the production of wealth by manufactures increased more largely under protective than under non-protective duties? And, if so, has that increase been so great as to compensate for an ascertained loss in a branch of industry to this country three times as important?

We approach questions which have not usually been considered, in discussions of the tariff, with that attention which their importance invites. Some have argued with force that this country ought to build up a diversified industry. Others, with equal force, have argued that the effort costs heavily. But the question, "Does protection protect?" may not have received as much attention as it deserves. By many, at least, it has been taken for granted that the system of protective duties must at least stimulate manufactures.

If protection does protect anybody, then it confers some benefit, even though it may injure others more. But if, with all its disadvantages to other interests, the protective system results in no healthy and permanent development of manufactures, greater than would be attained without it; if, with reference to that interest alone, protection is a failure and a mistake; if the supposed protection has proved unreal, and the supposed stimulus only a hindrance, then all the arguments in favor of a diversified industry become arguments for a non-protective policy.

What production of wealth actually results from manufacturing industry, and to what extent is that industry supposed to be within reach of protection? The census report of 1860, volume "Manufactures," includes the statistics of mining and fisheries. The mining of iron, coal, and other metals than gold and silver, may the more properly be classed with manufactures, as the mining and the manufacture are frequently combined. . But the mining of gold and silver is not supposed to be protected. Fisheries are included, no doubt, only because they are too unimportant for a separate schedule. Deducting the products and materials reported for these industries from the aggregates given in the census return, we have as the product of manufactures, or mining other than of gold and silver, $1,822,234,031, while the raw material used cost $1,009,972,896, and the production of wealth, therefore, amounted to $812,261,135.

But there are also included as manufactures many branches of industry which may, perhaps, properly be termed mechanic arts. Masons, carpenters, and painters, if manufacturers at all, do not belong to that class whose relations to the tariff we are especially investigating. Some classification of the branches of industry included by the census under the head of manufactures is necessary. Yet the vagueness of the entries in the census returns renders any rigorous classification impossible. Thus under the single head of "Lumber sawed" are entered over 19,000 establishments, employing over 71,000 hands, and yielding a product of over ninety-three millions yearly. Evidently, every variety of establishment, from the smallest and most primitive saw-mill to the largest works of our chief lumber-markets, is here included. Whatever may be thought of the wisdom of duties on timber and lumber, it will not by any one be seriously supposed that the existence of this industry depends upon duties, the less as we export largely of lumber and its manufactures. Under the heads of "Boots and shoes" are included 12,486 establishments, and 123,026 hands, whose product was about ninety-two millions. Every village has its shoemaker, and in this entry are evidently included all those who make boots and shoes to order, as well as the larger establishments more properly called manufacturing. Under the head "Clothing" are included over 4,000 establishments, employing over 120,000 persons, whose product was nearly ninety millions. The wholesale maker and the village tailor are indistinguishable here. But, while accurate classification is not possible, a few general principles may enable us to reach a fair approximation.

A country mainly agricultural in its industry needs no duty to protect its flour-mills and provision-packers. The product of our flour-mills was $248,580,365, and the material cost $208,497,309. The product of provision-packing was $31,986,433, and the material cost $24,894,624. No one will apprehend that we may import our bakers' bread, and the bakers produced $16,980,012, and their material cost $10,634,199. Mill-wrights will also find employment as long as we raise our own wheat, and the ice dealer will scarcely need protection until there is an increased supply of pauper labor about the North Pole.

Whatever may be thought of the duty upon lumber, it will by no one be seriously supposed that this country is in danger of depending upon foreign forests for its main supply of wood. But in some parts of the country, at least, the duty does increase the cost of lumber, and in consequence a manufacture is retarded which is as necessary as any other to every country, which could be subjected to no serious competition if all duties were repealed, and which employs a large share of our industry—the manufacture of wood. We cannot import the hundredth part of our lumber; and saw-mills must exist in which to cut our own forest-trees. The simple fact that they did exist, in number quite as great as ever before or since, during the time when lumber from Canada was admitted free of duty under the reciprocity treaty, must end all dispute as to the necessity of protecting this manufacture. But if the sawing of trees into lumber is beyond the reach of protection, the manufacture of lumber into houses, furniture, and household articles, is still more independent. We cannot import our own houses, or the repairs on them, our barns, or our fences. Except in a few of the most costly articles, this country is beyond the possibility of competition in the matter of furniture; indeed, we have for many years sent to other countries large quantities of furniture for sale, and, with lumber increased in cost, are still exporting not less than ten millions' worth of wood and its manufactures. But the manufacture is incomparably more important than that small fraction of the lumber interest which can be benefited by duties on Canadian products. If those duties enhance the cost of lumber in the least degree, they benefit only a few owners of forests near the Canada border, while they injure a manufacture employing a quarter of a million of skilled mechanics, and yielding a product quite incalculable in value, since no census return attempts to ascertain the cost of houses or barns built, or the value of additions and repairs. Still less does any census give the value of fences, yet farmers on western prairies know to their sorrow how large a share of the expense of farming is caused by the cost of lumber. And the cost of all furniture made of Northern lumber is in like manner affected. Whatever makes a product more costly, other things being equal, diminishes consumption of that product and injures the manufacture. But statistics prove beyond question that the duty on Canada lumber does affect the price in our largest and most important markets. The price of lumber at Albany and at Chicago has largely increased since the expiration of the reciprocity treaty in the spring of 1866.* The owners of certain timber-lands have thus been benefited. But one of our most important manu-

---

* Commissioner Wells, in the report published since this volume was mainly completed, gives tables showing that the increase at Chicago was from $14.80 per M. to $17.70 per M., and at Albany from $22.12 per M. to $29.83 per M. The general fact that there has been an increase, however, is undenied and undeniable.

factures has been retarded, and consumers in all parts of the country dependent upon those markets have been taxed, while the cost of furniture has necessarily been somewhat affected. This manufacture, since it cannot be aided by duties on foreign houses or barns, fences or furniture, and has been to some extent injured by increased cost of its material, must be classed with the non-protected industries. In the table of manufactures of 1860, it includes 139,000 persons; raw materials, $74,100,000; products, $167,600,000.

We are as likely to import foreign houses, as the bricks or the dressed stone of which they are built. Nor can masons, joiners, plasterers, carpenters, painters, plumbers, roofers, whitewashers, paper-hangers, upholsterers, or locksmiths, be protected in their industry, because no foreign competition is possible. Unless we can import foreign gas, the makers and gas-fitters must also be classed as unprotected. But each of these is to some extent retarded in his industry by duties on lime, lead, paints, lumber, tools, or paper, and the gas-manufacturers, especially in Eastern cities, having to pay heavy duties on foreign gas-coal, find the consumption of their product in some degree restricted by its increased cost. To these, which may be classed as house-building employments, may be added the dressing of marble, not separable from stone-cutting in census returns, for we are not likely to import our tombstones engraved to order. These branches, in 1860, employed 59,188 persons, used material costing $15,300,000, and produced to the value of $56,200,000.

Of necessity, the manufacture of clothing must be injured by a system which undeniably increases the cost of some of its materials. Without entering at present upon the question whether woollen, cotton, silk, or linen goods are generally rendered more costly by high duties, it is not denied that they are in many cases. But, whenever the materials are rendered more costly, the increased cost of clothing must to some extent affect its use, and limit the consumption. It is perfectly true that this injury does not follow all duties, but certain that it does result from some; perfectly true that it is not always apparent, since other circumstances, such as an inflated currency, may prompt people to consume more largely in spite of the cost, but the fact remains that even then they would have consumed still more largely, had the clothing cost less. Any increase in the cost of materials also increases the capital necessary to transact the same business, and thus reduces its profits, causing a smaller production of wealth in proportion to the capital and labor invested. A single fact proves that it is not even intended by the protective

9

system to confer any benefit upon the tailor, and the manufacturer of clothing: the duty on clothing is only 54 per cent. if of wool, and 35 per cent. if of cotton, while the duty on woollen cloths ranges from 56 per cent., upward, and the duty on cotton cloths, of qualities inported, is from 40 per cent. upward. In fact, so much does the clothing manufacture depend upon taste, style, changes of the fashion, and the form or habit of the wearer, that Congress has very correctly inferred that it could not be exposed to any serious competition, and, in spite of the duty on the uncut cloth larger than the duty on the finished article, we imported in 1868 less than $200,000 worth of woollen clothing of all kinds. Adding ladies' dress-making, dying, and bleaching, the returns for 1860 include, under manufactures of clothing, 128,488 persons employed, $51,400,000 of materials, and $98,000,000 of product.

The manufacture of leather needs no protection, because this country possesses materials superior to those of any European country, and has so perfected the manufacture, that in 1845 it was testified, by men in that business, that leather could be made here cheaper than in Europe. It may be considered certain that an agricultural country, amply supplied with the best materials for dressing leather, will not throw away its hides, or send them abroad to be dressed. But this important manufacture is also impeded by the duty on foreign hides and materials used. The hides produced in this country supply less than three-fourths of the consumption, and the hides from South America and elsewhere, thus required for our own use, are rendered more costly; currying oil is increased in cost, and in some localities hemlock-bark is also made more expensive. The resulting injury to the whole leather manufacture may be slight, but it affects an industry of vast importance, and the increased cost of leather in turn injures another manufacture of the very first rank—the making of boots and shoes. In 1868, according to estimates by the trade, given by Commissioner Wells, there were made 51,500,000 pairs of boots and shoes for males, and 47,000,000 pairs for females, the aggregate value being about $228,250,000, and statistics are published by him, to show that the cost of these products is increased by more than fifteen million dollars by the duties on hides, bark, oils, lasting, serge, and rubber webbing, so that men's boots cost $42.38 a dozen, and would cost only $39.37 without the duties; and cheap gaiters for women, sold before the war for 60 cents, now cost $1.05. The result is, that an export trade in boots and shoes, which has existed for many years under all changes of style, and which, after the removal of the protection tariff of 1842, increased from $93,140, in 1847, to more than two millions in 1865, is now reduced to $475,053, the trade with South and Central America, Mexico, and the West Indies, being almost entirely lost. It need not be added that workmen in New England are suffering from lack of employment and low wages, and the organ of that industry states that they are now employed on an average only ten months in the year. Since leather and boots and shoes can be made here cheaper than anywhere else, and could therefore be profitably exported, while no duty can aid the workmen in this industry, duties which enhance the cost of its materials must inevitably injure it, rendering it less able to compete in foreign markets. Only a part of the shoemakers are included under manufacturers in the census tables of 1860, but, of persons so included in all branches of leather manufacture, there were 161,563; raw material, $99,000,000; product, $182,000,000.

Enough has been said to show that ship-building has been seriously injured by the system of protection. It employed 9,560 persons, materials worth $10,500,000; and its products are valued at $21,000,000. Carriages, cars, omnibuses and wagons, from their bulk, are not readily imported, and so superior is our manufacture that, in spite of the cost of transportation and materials, we have shipped American vehicles of many kinds to foreign countries, and even to Europe. But no other interest is more directly injured by high duties, which affect the cost of the iron and steel, the paint and the varnish, the woollen cloth and silk trimmings, and some varieties of leather, the cost of which forms a large part of the cost of the finished carriage. In this industry 40,638 persons used materials costing $13,800,000, and produced to the value of $40,200,000. To these may be added, as manufactures, natural and necessary to the country, which cannot be helped by duties on foreign products, the production and refining of coal-oil, kerosene, and turpentine, the manufacture of soap and candles, and the taking of photographic likenesses, which we are not likely to import. These branches in 1860 employed 13,689 persons; used $20,100,000 of materials, and produced to the value of $32,300,000.

But there still remain important branches of industry which must be set aside in any inquiry as to the effect of protective duties. For revenue purposes only, duties are imposed in nearly all countries, and with assent of all parties in this country, upon a class of articles which may be termed natural objects of taxation—liquors, tobacco, jewelry, silks, sugar, and coffee. Extreme protectionists and extreme free-traders agree that a part of the revenue needed by government may advantageously be raised by duties on such articles; and those duties, whether they affect favorably or unfavorably the manufacture in this country, are not properly classed with those of a protective character, and need not be considered in an examination of the protective system. In these branches of manufacture 63,164 persons were employed, and the raw material used cost $105,000,000, and the product was $171,000,000.

It will not be seriously argued that we are in danger of importing our daily and weekly newspapers, or our handbills, posters, and advertising cards. The great majority of our printers are employed in newspaper or in job offices—not depending upon the publication of books or magazines for success. Of books originating here, not one in twenty would, under any circumstances, be published in foreign countries, and by far the greater part of that business also is beyond the reach of any foreign competition. But, in the publication of foreign books, the American has an advantage in the fact that the foreign publisher has to pay the authors. The proportion of the publishing business which depends upon protective duties is therefore small. But, while the publication of books is but a small part of the printing business, and but a small part of that can be helped by protective duties, all publishers in all their business are injured by duties which increase the cost of paper, ink, machinery, types, and labor. Even those few publishers who print works of foreign origin are probably injured more than they are benefited by the duties, while the much larger proportion, including the whole force of job and newspaper publishers, are injured materially and are not benefited at all. It is reasonable, therefore, to class the printing business, as a whole, with those branches of industry which are in no degree protected by duties on corresponding foreign products. It employed, in 1860, among those returned in the table of manufactures, 28,150 persons, using material costing $15,000,000, and its product was $38,000,000.

The industries already specified yielded, in 1860, a product of $1,104,000,000, and the raw material cost $648,000,000. Nearly two-thirds of the entire product of manufactures, therefore, is derived from branches not benefited by duties upon corresponding importations, protective in design. But, besides those enumerated, there are others in great number, each yielding a small product, though the aggregate is over one hundred and fifty millions, which are indeed protected by duties on foreign products, but are injured to a much greater extent by the duties designed to aid the great branches of manufacture, and by the consequent increase in cost of materials. Thus the manufacture of looking-glass frames is in no considerable degree aided by duties, because the glass is almost of necessity framed near the place of use, but it is retarded by duties ranging from 20 to 90 per cent. on the silvered glass which is imported, and manufacturers of the silvered glass are in turn impeded by duties ranging from 20 to 90 per cent. on glass, added to a duty of 15 per cent. on quicksilver. In the time of low duties, American oil-cloth gained a deserved reputation for its excellence, and our workmen are so superior that we could manufacture largely for export if the cloth and the paints were not rendered costly, especially by duties ranging from 50 to 200 per cent. on the most important paints. The preparation of medicines has been peculiarly successful in this country as a branch of manufacturing, but it has to meet most extraordinary duties on drugs and barks, in addition to revenue duties or excises upon alcohol in all forms. The manufacture of rubber goods, by patents of American invention, has grown up in spite of duties on the imported raw material, and still is so flourishing that notwithstanding those duties we export largely of rubber goods. American pianos are by our makers so skilfully adapted to our climate that they are in no danger of foreign competition, the less as our makers have won premiums, at European expositions, for their excellent workmanship; but the cost of materials is somewhat enhanced by duties. American invention has distanced competition in the manufacture of buttons, and in producing silk hats our workmen are only retarded by the duties on materials, while the manufacture of wool hats, even in colonial times, had progressed so rapidly that the British Parliament, at the appeal of London workmen, prohibited the exportation of felt goods from these colonies in order to protect the British manufacturer from competition, and ever since our independence we have exported of such goods. American clocks may be found in every part of the world; brooms, baskets, boxes, lamps, matches, and other such articles, no one imagines that we shall ever cease to make for ourselves; billiard-tables are made better here than anywhere else; tinware is too bulky for importation, nor is there any danger that we shall import our coffins, send our soiled clothes to European laundries, or our wood and coal to Europe to be made into charcoal and coke.

Space does not serve even to enumerate the many minor branches of manufactures, but enough has been said to show the relative im-

portance of those which are recognized as especial objects of legislative aid.   These are the manufactures of iron, and of articles
of which iron is the material of chief cost, the manufactures of cotton, of wool, of paper, of glass, of salt, copper, brass, linen, flax,
lead, and hemp.   The unprotected branches of manufacture—those
which cannot be aided by duties, or are necessarily injured more than
they are aided—employ not less than two-thirds of the hands, and
yield not less than two-thirds of the annual product, of all manufacturing industry.   Before passing to an examination of separate
branches of industry, it is well to fix attention upon the inquiry,
" Does the system of protection increase the production of wealth ?"
Three-fourths of our production is by agriculture, and is not increased
but retarded by this system.   Of the remaining fourth, it now appears that a large share is derived from industries not protected, or
seriously injured by high duties.   Not more than six hundred millions in the aggregate, or, deducting cost of material, not more than
two hundred and sixty millions of annual product, is derived from all
these branches of industry which are supposed to be sustained or
aided by the tariff.   It is therefore necessary to inquire, not merely
whether these have been aided, but whether the production of wealth
by these industries has been so enormously increased as to compensate, first, for the injury to agriculture, producing nearly ten times
as much ; and second, for the injury to other manufactures producing
more than twice as much.   About seven per cent. of our annual
production was derived, in 1860, from industries supposed to depend
upon protection.   How vastly must their product be increased, to
balance any injury to industries yielding 93 per cent. of that annual
protection !

CHAPTER X.

THE COTTON MANUFACTURE.

Four hundred years before Christ, Herodotus, the father of history, learned of India that its trees bore fleeces, which the Indians
made into cloth.   But Herodotus does not tell us that the manufacture owed its existence to any protective tariff.   The cultivation and
manufacture of cotton in Persia are spoken of by Strabo, and Pliny
recorded that cotton clothes had been made in Egypt.   Nor is it
doubted that calico-printing by blocks, and the use of mineral dyes,

were known to the Egyptians. Early in the Christian era, cotton stuffs from India were transported to Europe for sale; indeed, long before that time, the vestal virgin had preserved the last sparks of sacred fire on the altar, by casting upon it her head-dress of "carbasus." When civilized travellers first penetrated to the interior of Africa, they found broad fields cultivated in cotton, by dusky natives dressed in its soft fabrics. When Columbus first gazed upon the wonders of a new world, he saw women clothed in coats of cotton; the earliest discoverers found the plant growing wild as far inland as the Mississippi; and Cortez sent back, among his earliest spoils from Mexico, cotton cloths woven into beautiful figures, "mantles, some all white, others mixed with white and black or red, green and yellow, and blue; waistcoats, handkerchiefs, counterpanes, tapestries, and carpets of cotton." Those who suppose that the working of cotton into fabrics is due in this country to protective duties, or that it would not now survive without them, must suppose that the ingenious and skilful American has less of that wonder-working power on which civilization is based than the natives of Hindostan, less than the Persians, less than the negroes of the wilds of Africa, less than the copper-colored savages, and far less than the ancient Aztecs.

Long before any legislative aid had been given to it, this industry existed in this country. Early in the history of the colonies, women and children carded and spun the raw cotton, while the father of the family plied the loom; and in 1645 the General Court of Massachusetts, with a patriotic desire to direct the industries of the people, which may be called the very germ of American protection, declared in a general order that the towns should take measures for the importation of sheep, because "those who had provided their families with cotton cloth (not being able to get the other) have by that means had some of their children much scorched by fire, yea, divers burned to death." So little did this industry then need aid, that it was thought necessary to discourage it, and, by this and many other acts, to compel the making of woollen goods. In New Amsterdam and in Virginia, the utmost efforts were also made to stimulate the making of other cloth, but in the acts of that period the cotton industry is treated as not in need of similar care. In all parts of the country, the manufacture of cotton had grown up with the colonies, and existed prior to the Revolution. The cloth used by the people was mainly of their own manufacture, and after the Revolution the domestic supply continued to increase so greatly that the

importations of goods were largely reduced. Indeed, Bishop, in his
"History of American Manufactures," notices this fact, and adds, " It
may be questioned if the people of that day were not as really independent of other countries for such necessaries as are their descendants at present." Yet the same writer ascribes the subsequent progress of the manufacture to the stimulus afforded by legislation !
Until that time (1790) the Arkwright machinery had not been introduced, while it was largely used and had materially reduced the cost
of the cloth in England ; and yet, in spite of that advantage, the increase of the domestic manufacture was rapidly driving out the foreign goods. Is it reasonable to suppose that, with the machinery
then introduced, we should not have sustained this industry had no
legislative aid been given it ?

In 1790, Samuel Slater set up in this country two Arkwright
frames of thirty-two spindles ; and, in 1791, a duty of 7½ per cent.
was laid on all imported manufactures of cotton. This would hardly
be called a protective duty now, and, in his report of that year,
Hamilton explains that the duty previously imposed of three cents
a pound on the raw cotton, then largely brought from the West
Indies, " was a serious obstacle " to the manufacture. The duty on
goods was, perhaps, designed to counterbalance this disadvantage ;
but in 1794 it was raised to 12½ per cent. At that time Slater was
selling American yarn, No. 20, at $1.21. After six years of pro-
tection, we find that the price of Slater's yarn, No. 20, had increased in 1800 to $1.36, although, during the same period, the
price of yarn in England had been reduced—No. 100, from 15s.
1d. to 8s. 9d. per pound. Accordingly, in 1802, there were petitions
from calico-printers for legislative aid. And, until our commerce
was interrupted by embargo in 1808, the price of yarn and goods
continued about the same—yarn, No. 20, being 131 cents, sheeting,
in 1805, 50 cents a yard, and gingham 70 cents, although the price
of United States upland cotton had fallen in Liverpool from 38d., in
1799, to 14d. in 1804, and the price of yarn, No. 100, in England,
had fallen to 7s. 10d. In consequence, the imports of British goods
increased largely—to about nineteen millions in 1807. Under no
duties at all, and without machinery, the domestic manufacture had
reduced imports. With machinery of the same style as the English,
and with duties to aid the manufacture, the imports of cotton increased. For, under the operation of duties, the price of yarn here
actually increased from 121 cents to 131, although the cotton had
fallen in price, and the yarn in England had been reduced in cost

from 15s. to 7s. 10d.   Is there not, in this brief history of the manufacture prior to the embargo, a complete illustration of the failure of duties on imports to build up a manufacture or to exclude foreign goods ?

During the embargo and the war with England, the manufacture of cotton grew rapidly on both sides of the ocean.   In England and in this country the power-loom was invented and successfully applied, but with this difference : in England, sharp competition forced every manufacturer to adopt the best methods; in this country, the manufacture was shut out from all competition, and adhered, generally, to the old hand-loom.   The power-loom, invented by Mr. Lowell, was applied with success, in the first large establishment for spinning and weaving combined, by the Waltham Company, and the price of yarn was reduced to less than one dollar before the war closed, but very few establishments had made similar improvements.   When the peace brought our manufacturers to the test of competition with those of England, and cargoes of goods were sent to our markets for sale, what was the effect ?

The power-loom of Mr. Lowell held its ground so well that in 1816 its proprietors stated to Congress that *they were making a profit of 25 per cent., and stood in no need of further protection.*   Other enterprising manufacturers either had adopted improved machines or quickly did so.   Mr. Bemis, of Boston, who had begun the manufacture of sail-duck in 1809, was still using the hand-loom and selling his duck at a dollar a yard in 1815.   But, under the pressure of competition, he introduced the power-loom in 1816, and, not long after, we find that he was selling the same quality of duck at 35 cents a yard.   Other mills did likewise, and new mills were put up in the years 1815 and 1816, in spite of the utmost efforts of the British manufacturers to break down this industry.

But, while men of enterprise were only stimulated by competition to new effort and progress, a large majority of the manufacturers were still using the hand-loom, and, instead of seizing upon improvements, they appealed loudly to government for aid.   Seven years of great prosperity, entire freedom from competition, and consequent large profits, had indeed enormously increased the number of mills, but had led the majority to no such improvements as had been made in England, or in this country by a few men of enterprise.   To help them, they asked and obtained the first tariff in which the minimum principle was applied : all cotton goods were deemed by the law to have cost at least 25 cents a yard, and were subjected to a duty of

25 per cent. on this assumed cost. It was intended to be, and in effect it was, absolutely prohibitory as to low-priced goods.

It is important to observe the real difficulty which led to the adoption of this tariff. It was not that the raw material had risen in price, or that the currency had greatly depreciated—those disadvantages, serious as they were, affected the Waltham Company as well as others, and did not prevent it from making a profit of 25 per cent. It was simply the failure to adopt new and improved machinery, either during the war, when the manufacture yielded great profits, or after its close, when foreign competition rendered weaving by hand-looms unprofitable. The minimum tariff was devised to protect these old methods, to sustain men in their adherence to old machines, to help men who had refused to help themselves. The first heavy shirtings, unbleached, made by the Waltham Company during the war, sold for 30 cents a yard, but, in 1816, shirtings, from yarn, No. 12, sold in New York for 23 cents, and, at that price, the Waltham spinners were making a profit of 25 per cent., while goods made on the hand-loom could not be sold at a profit. Their testimony to Congress proves that the duty was not needed to protect them or others who had adopted new looms. Was not the tariff a premium for laziness and want of enterprise? Have we not the right to infer that, if all manufacturers had then been forced to adopt the best machines, and to win success as the Waltham Company did, by keeping pace with the progress in other countries, this industry would not then have needed any protection, and its growth would have been more sure, more healthy, and thenceforward independent of artificial aid?

The effect of this tariff was not such as to encourage other efforts in the same direction. British mills quite generally changed from United States to the cheaper Bengal and Surat cotton, and the price of cotton here declined from over 20d. to about 11d. in 1819, and 9½d. in 1820. The losses of shippers and planters were severe, and a similar decline in breadstuffs of fully 50 per cent. combined to reduce the agricultural interest, then even more than now the basis of all prosperity, to great distress, and affected shippers and merchants not less. When farmers stop buying, mills must stop producing. "A general paralysis fell upon all branches of industry," writes Bishop; "the distress became more general and severe than had ever before been known; farms were mortgaged and sold at one-half and one-third their cost," and factories and workshops were everywhere closed." In the Pennsylvania courts, there were 14,537 actions for debt in 1819, and 1,800 imprisonments for debt in the county of Philadelphia alone. These disasters were not caused by the excess of foreign importations, for those had greatly declined. The manufacturing interest was not the basis; it employed but a small part of the people. Neither is it claimed that the tariff was the principal cause; the condition of the currency, already explained, was undoubtedly the main trouble. But, in view of the peculiar prostration of agriculture, it is not easy to avoid the conclusion that this disaster was immediately brought on and greatly aggravated by the decline in our great exported staples, cotton and breadstuffs.

In the midst of the prostration then prevailing, when mills had generally suspended, and prices had fallen 50 per cent., the Waltham Company went forth cash in hand to seek a site for a much larger establishment, and in 1820 bought the site now occupied by the city of Lowell. These gentlemen had not suspended. Others were calling on government to help them. But these had helped themselves by enterprise. They had testified that they did not need the tariff of 1816 with its minimum, nor would others had they relied upon themselves and not upon government. Others, in the midst of the prostration, were begging for higher duties. But the Waltham makers, understanding that their only sure reliance was in the invention and enterprise of American industry, "were supposed to be unfavorable to an increase of duties," say records of that time. Accordingly, while others were begging for aid, they were putting up at great cost the largest establishment in the United States, which went into operation in 1823, and in 1825 "made its first dividend of $160 per share, and the company had also built three new mills!" As early as 1823, the "domestics" of this company had become so popular that they were counterfeited by foreign manufacturers, and as early as 1827 it is recorded that "the demand for American cottons in Brazil was considerably affected by imitations of them made in Manchester, and offered there" (in Brazil) "at lower prices, although they could be made as cheaply in the United States as the same quality could be produced in that city."—(Bishop, ii., 317.) In view of the progress of this company, is it not plain that the act of 1816 was unnecessary to protect the enterprising manufacturer? If to protect him it was unnecessary, it was simply a protection to others against the consequences of their own lack of enterprise, and a discouragement to those who might by peculiar energy and skill have commanded a larger share of the home market.

If the act of 1818 was not necessary, what shall we say of the act of 1824, with its increased duties? By that act the minimum was raised from 25 to 35 cents, in face of the fact that the Lowell mills were then making that profit of $160 per share in two years! What shall be said of it in view of the fact that, after the prostration, the great prosperity of the cotton manufacture was acknowledged, and new mills had been established in every direction prior to 1824—thirty-six in New York alone in the years 1821–1824? Although American cottons were largely exported, and were counterfeited by foreigners both for our own and for other markets, although the manufacture was already increasing faster than the demand for its products, this increased duty was by some demanded, and by Congress granted.

The effect was such as to instruct those not wilfully blind. Within less than five years (in 1829) we find it recorded that great distress prevailed "among the manufacturers of New England, particularly in the cotton branch," and that "at a meeting of the manufacturers of Philadelphia on 3d February (1829) resolutions were adopted to establish one or more private houses for the sale of their goods, and to discontinue sales at public auction, as having a tendency to reduce prices below value." Here we have the first recorded instance of combination to keep up the price of goods, in spite of competition and over-production. The tariff, therefore, had worked thus: first, profits to the manufacturer, "$160 per share in two years;" second, great numbers of new mills started; third, great distress among the manufacturers because of over-production; fourth, combinations of the manufacturers to prevent reduction of the price.

It is the constant argument of those who favor the protective policy, that it cannot increase the price of manufactured products, because competition will invariably keep down that price. But at every step will be found proof that manufacturers can combine in this country as well as in England, and that, when they are protected against foreign rivalry, they constantly do combine to keep up the price, the rate being fixed not by the progress of the most skilful, but by the negligence of the most unenterprising. Thus the least deserving and useful are kept alive to "cumber the ground;" and, though the quantity of goods made is increased often beyond the demand, the method of manufacture is not improved and the cost reduced, by weeding out the incompetent and yielding returns only to those who advance toward perfection. Those whose unskilful manufacture is a sheer loss to the country continue to share the

THE COTTON MANUFACTURE.

The quantity of Cotton produced, and the quantity consumed, in this country, in pounds, per capita, with the average export price, from 1827 to 1861, inclusive.

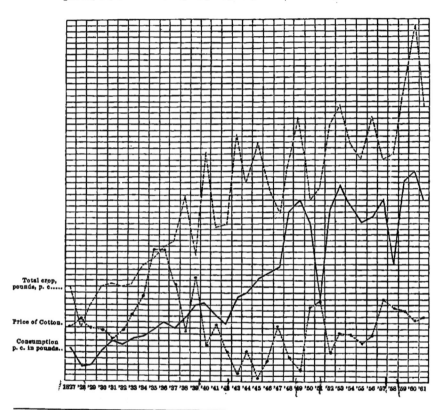

NOTE—I. The extreme low price during the tariff of 1842-'46.

    II. That the manufacture has been governed, in almost every increase or decrease of consumption, by the quantity of crop and the price.

    III. That the short crops and high prices of 1850 and 1851 fully account for the reduced consumption.

    IV. That the short crops of 1841 and 1842, rather than any state of tariff, explain the small consumption.

    V. That in 1847, under low duties, it happened for the first and only time, that two short crops did not reduce the manufacture.

profits and divide the market; and the more enterprising, unable to extend their sales freely to foreign markets because of a cost of production artificially increased, are themselves subjected to frequent losses and prostration by the overcrowding of the home market. Thus repeated disasters, shared by all, have to do the work which natural competition would do more surely, confining its effect to those who fail to keep pace with the times; they are crushed from time to time, but by prostrations which affect others as well. Meanwhile, all classes are trained to rely, not upon ceaseless improvement, but upon frequent interpositions of government.

The consumption of cotton, which, according to Bishop, had reached 150,000 bales in 1826, and according to the statistics of the Cotton Association was 149,516 bales in 1827, declined in 1828 to 120,593, and in 1829 to 118,853 bales, a loss of nearly one-fifth. This was not caused by a failure of crops, or by an increase of price. The crop of 1827 was the largest then ever produced by more than 200,000 bales, and except in that year none had ever been produced larger than those of 1828 and 1829. The price of cotton was 6½d. in Liverpool in 1827, and fell to 5¾d. in 1829. The duties on imported goods were higher than ever before; on sheetings about 145 per cent., checks 109, shirtings and chintzes 43, and calicoes about 72 per cent. Yet this prostration was more severe in effect upon the cotton interest than that produced by the terrible currency explosion of 1837. But it evidently had a good result. It forced into bankruptcy a great many concerns which had been kept alive by protection, and were a constant impediment to the progress of the manufacture; though it inflicted heavy losses upon the more enterprising as well, it left this branch of industry in a more healthy condition. For thenceforward, during many changes of duty, it continued a steady and rapid progress.

From this time onward we are able to trace with accuracy the progress of this manufacture by the aid of statistics. The following table presents the crop of each year since 1827, the quantity exported, the quantity consumed each year in this country, the proportion of the crop consumed here, the number of pounds consumed per capita, the price of uplands in Liverpool in pence, and the average price of all cotton exported in our own ports in cents. To render this table more intelligible, the accompanying diagram has been drawn, showing the crop, consumption, and price. By comparing these lines, the cause of every considerable change in the production of cotton goods may at once be traced:

THE COTTON MANUFACTURE.

YEAR.	TAKEN FOR CONSUMPTION.			EXPORTED.	TOTAL CROP.	PRICE.		Crop in lbs., per Cap.	CONSUMED	
	Bales.	Weight.	Pounds.	Bales.	Bales.	Export.	Liverpool Uplands.		Per Cent.	Per Cap. lbs.
1820....	....	..	....	127,800,000 lbs	....	16 c.	9½d.	..	..	..
1821....	....	..	....	124,900,000 lbs	180,000,000 lbs	16	8¼	..	..	..
1822 ...	....	..	....	144,700,000 lbs	210,000,000 lbs	16.6	8¼	..	..	..
1823....	....	..	....	173,700.000 lbs	....	11.8	8¼	..	..	..
1824....	....	..	....	142,400,000 lbs	....	15.4	8¼	..	..	..
1825....	....	..	....	176,500.000 lbs	255,000,000 lbs	20.9	11½	..	..	..
1826....	150,000	..	....	204,500,000 lbs	720,000 bales.	12.2	6¾	..	..	..
				Bales.	Bales.					
1827....	149,516	331	49,489,796	854,000	957,281	10	6½	26	15	4.22
1828....	120,593	335	40,398,655	600,000	720,593	10.7	6⅝	19	16	3.30
1829....	118,853	341	40,528,873	740,000	870,415	10	5¾	23	13½	3.31
1830....	126,512	339	53,887,568	839,000	976.845	9.9	6⅞	26	13½	4.19
1831....	182,142	341	62,110,422	773,000	1,068,847	9.1	6	26½	17	4.67
1832....	173,800	360	62,568,000	892,000	987,477	9.8	6⅝	26	17	4.56
1833....	194,412	350	68,044,200	867,000	1,070,438	11.1	8½	26½	18	4.81
1834....	196,413	363	71,297,919	1,028,000	1,205,394	12.8	8⅝	30	16	4.90
1835....	216,888	367	79,597,896	1,023,500	1,254,328	16.8	10¼	31	17	5.31
1836....	236,733	373	88,301,409	1,116,000	1,360,725	16.8	9⅞	33	17	5.73
1837....	222,540	379	84,342,660	1,169,000	1,423,930	14.2	7	34	15	5.33
1838....	246.063	379	93,262,877	1,575,000	1,801,497	10.2	7	42	14	5.74
1839....	276,018	384	105,990,912	1,074,000	1,360,532	14.8	7⅞	31½	20	6.36
1840....	295,193	383	113,058,919	1,876,000	2,177,835	8.5	6	49	13	6.68
1841....	297,288	394	107,131,472	1,313,500	1,634,954	10.3	6¼	36½	18	6.08
1842....	267,850	397	106,336,450	1,465,500	1,683,574	8.1	5⅜	37	16	5.85
1843....	325,129	409	132.977,761	2,010,000	2,378,875	6.2	4⅝	52½	13	7.11
1844....	346,750	412	142,861,000	1,629,500	2,030,409	8.1	4⅞	44	17	7.42
1845....	389,000	415	161,435,000	2,083.700	2,394,503	5.9	4⅜	51	16	8 15
1846....	422,600	411	173,688,600	1,666,700	2,100,537	7.8	4⅞	43	20	8.54
1847....	428,000	431	184,468,000	1,241,200	1,778,651	10.3	6⅜	37	24	8.87
1848....	616,044	417	256,890,348	1.858,000	2,439.786	7.6	4¼	47	25	11.99
1849....	642,485	436	280,123.460	2,228,000	2,866.983	6.4	5⅛	56½	22½	12.75
1850....	613,498	429	[illegible]63,190,642	1,590.200	2,233,718	11.3	7¼	41	27	11.34
1851....	485,614	416	162,015,424	1,988,710	2,454,442	12.1	5¾	43	19½	6.78
1852....	699,603	428	299.430,084	2,443,646	3,126.310	8	5⅜	54	22	12.16
1853....	803,725	428	343,994,300	2,528,400	3,416,214	9.8	5⅜	57½	23½	13.57
1854....	737,236	430	317,011.480	2,319,148	3.074,979	9.5	5⅜	50½	24	12.16
1855....	706,412	434	306,582,808	2,244,209	2,982,634	8.74	5¾	48	24	11.40
1856....	770,739	420	323,710.380	2.954,606	3,665,557	9.49	6	55½	21	11.70
1857....	819,936	444	364,162,584	2,252,657	3.093,737	12.55	7¼	48	26½	.12.76
1858....	595,562	442	263,238,404	2,590,455	3,257,239	11.70	6¼	49	18	8.95
1859....	927,651	447	414.659.997	3,021,403	4,018,914	11.64	6¼	59	23	13.70
1860....	978,043	461	450,877,823	3,774,173	4,861,292	10.89	5½	71	20	14.32
1861....	843,740	477	401,263.980	3,127,568	3,849.469	11.07	8¼	57	22	12.39
1862....	370,000	..	170,200,000	....	1,600,000	23.18	17⅝	..	..	7.24
1863....	288,000	..	120,960,000	....	450,000	42.57	23½	..	..	4.99
1864....	220,000	..	92,400,000	....	300,000	52.72	27¼	..	..	3.42
1865....	345.000	423	145,935,000	....	2,130,000	38.05	19	..	..	5.21
1866....	731,725	441	322,690,725	1,554,664	2,342,116	80.67	15½	29	31	9.09
1867....	940,039	444	417,377,316	1,557,054	2,318,660	21.59	11	28	40	11.49
1868....	968,165	445	425,992,600	1,655,816	2,599,241	....	9⅞	34	39	11.36
1869....	968,000	..	447,216,000	1,447,643	2,439,039	....	13½	..	39	11.57

The crop of 1819–'20 is entered as 1820, and so for each year. The estimate of consumption in 1826 is Bishop's.

The figures for 1869–'70 are from the *Financial Chronicle;* another statement gives the quantity consumed as 995,127 bales, or 11.94 pounds per capita, and the total crop as 2,260,557 bales.

Since 1829, until the recent war, the progress of the cotton manufacture has been rapid and generally steady, without regard to any changes of duty whatever. The compromise tariff of 1832, with its great reduction of duties, did not prevent the consumption advancing from 173,800 bales in 1832, to 297,288 bales in 1841, or from 4.67 lbs. per capita to 6.68 lbs. in 1840, and 6.08 in 1841. Nor was this advance caused or accompanied by any sacrifice of the producer of cotton, for the price was 9.8 cents in 1832 and 10.2 cents in 1841. The severe shock given to all industry, by the currency explosion of 1837, only reduced consumption 14,000 bales—less than one-fifteenth; and, in the extreme depression of the return to specie payments, the consumption was reduced less than 30,000 bales, or about one-tenth. This progress, therefore—steady, rapid, and sure-footed enough to be little shaken by the greatest industrial prostration—was not gained at the expense of the producer.

Neither was it gained at the expense of the consumer. Tables of prices, which will be found in Chapter XXI., show that there was a very considerable reduction in the prices of all kinds of cotton goods, from 1835 to 1841, amounting, in the average, to about one-third of the price in 1835, and a further reduction in 1842, so that nearly 40 per cent. of the cost to the consumer was removed during these eight years of non-protection. The cost of manufacture to the pound of cotton was reduced, it was stated by manufacturers in 1845, from 33 cents in 1828, to 14½ in 1841; and, as the price of cotton was more than 60 per cent. higher in 1835 than in 1841, it is plain that the reduction of price was not disastrous to the manufacturer, but that his profits at the prices of 1841 were probably about as large as they were at the prices of 1835. It is easy to understand, also, why the extreme depression of business after the resumption of specie payments did not more seriously prostrate this manufacture, for it found a ready outlet in exports for its surplus product whenever domestic consumption was checked. Grower, consumer, and manufacturer, were all benefited during this period.

In the next period it was otherwise. In 1843 the price in Liverpool fell below 5d., and so remained until the tariff of 1842 expired. The price here dropped to six cents, and during those four years averaged only seven cents. With a reduction of price from 15 cents in 1839, to 6 cents in 1845, and less than 8 cents in 1846, it is not strange that the consumption here advanced from 276,000 bales to 422,000 bales, an increase of just one-sixth in seven years. Indeed, this increase of the manufactures was not more rapid than the in-

10

crease of the crop, for in 1839 we consumed 20 per cent. of the entire crop, and in 1846 exactly the same proportion. The consumption per capita increased under this tariff from 6.68 in 1840 to 8.54 in 1846, or about two pounds per capita, and this was at an expense of two cents a pound on the value of the whole crop, or sixteen million dollars. Whether the tariff of 1842 caused the low price or not, the diagram shows that, in every period of protection until the war, the price has been low. The essential point is, that the consumption increased only in proportion to the crop, and in connection with prices extremely favorable to the manufacture, and extremely unfavorable to the grower.

It is also necessary to observe that this progress was made at the expense of the consumer of cotton goods. The tables of prices in Chapter XXI. show that the progressive reduction of price, which had been quite rapid from 1836 to 1842, was suddenly arrested during this tariff; that the low price of cotton was not permitted to inure to the benefit of the consumers of cotton goods, and that the prices of a large majority of the qualities there named were higher in 1846, at the close of the protective tariff, than they had been in 1842, before its adoption, or in 1843, its first year. Buying cotton at $10\frac{2}{10}$ cents in 1841, the manufacturer made Chicopee brown sheetings, three yards to the pound, so that they were sold in 1842 at $7\frac{8}{100}$ cents a yard, and the cost of manufacture and profits were then not greater than eleven cents to the pound of cotton worked. But the same establishment, buying cotton at $5\frac{9}{10}$ cents, in 1845, sold the same quality of sheeting in 1846 for eight cents a yard; so that the cost of manufacture and profits were then $18\frac{1}{10}$ cents to the pound of cotton manufactured. It will elsewhere appear that wages were not higher in 1845 than in 1841 or 1842, but the cost of manufacture may in many other ways have been increased in consequence of the tariff. Yet it is reasonable to suppose that the great part of the increased tax then borne by consumers—amounting to $7\frac{1}{10}$ cents to the pound of cotton used—went in the form of increased profits to the manufacturer. The grower, therefore, was injured, the consumer was taxed, and the manufacture increased at the expense of both classes. If profits were very large, they went not to the benefit of labor, but to the capitalist. May it not fairly be doubted whether progress so gained was wisely gained?

Under the "free-trade tariff" which followed, the manufacture progressed far more rapidly, while the cotton-grower received better prices, and the consumer obtained his cloths at a great reduction of cost. By reference to the table of prices it will be found that the cost of every quality of cotton goods was reduced from 1846 to 1849, the average reduction being about one-sixth. The same quality of sheetings already mentioned was sold in 1849 for $6\frac{90}{100}$ cents, a reduction of $1\frac{1}{10}$ cents, but the grower in that year received $6\frac{4}{10}$ cents, and in 1848 he received $7\frac{8}{10}$ cents a pound, while in 1845 the price was $5\frac{9}{10}$ cents, and in 1846 it was $7\frac{8}{10}$ cents. Two enormous crops pushed down the price in 1849 ; but in no other year thenceforward was the price as low as the average for the whole tariff of 1842. Stimulated by the reduced price of goods, the consumption advanced from 422,600 bales in 1846, the last year of protection, to 642,485 in 1849, a gain of more than one-half in three years, and the consumption per capita from 8.54 lbs. to 12.75 lbs., about one-half. Moreover, this increase was not caused by an increase of crop alone, for in 1846 we consumed 20, and in 1850 we consumed 27 per cent. of the whole crop. The short crops of that year and the next, however, causing the price to rise to twelve cents, temporarily reduced consumption, and imports of cotton goods were increased, England having the advantage of other and cheaper supplies of cotton. But, the instant that advantage was removed, by recovery of our crop, the manufacture rose in 1852 to 699,603 bales, and in 1853 to 803,725 bales, 13.57 pounds per capita. Thus, in seven years, the quantity manufactured in this country had increased under low duties nearly 100 per cent., and the proportion of the crop consumed here had increased from 20 to $23\frac{1}{2}$ per cent., while the price of cotton to the producer had risen from 7.8 cents to 9.8 cents a pound—just two cents. With many millions gained to the grower, the manufacture doubled, and cotton goods cheapened, this tariff cannot be said to have injured the country.

Thenceforward, until the war, the cotton manufacture varied almost precisely in proportion to the crop, rising from 803,725 bales in 1853, to 978,043 bales in 1860, or from 13.57 lbs. per capita to 14.34 lbs., the price meanwhile also rising to about eleven cents. The main variation caused by the panic of 1857 was a loss in consumption of about one-quarter in 1858, which was more than recovered in the next year. Taking this tariff period as a whole, the gain from 1846 to 1860 was in consumption from 422,600 bales to 978,043 bales, or 130 per cent., and to the grower from 7.8 cents a pound to 10.8 cents a pound, or over fifty million dollars on the crop of 1860.

The war cut off the supply of cotton and reduced the manufacture greatly, but since peace was restored it is again vigorously advancing. The consumption per capita, however, has not yet reached the quantity consumed before the war, and the great increase in the growth of cotton elsewhere has made England comparatively less dependent upon our crop for supply. In consequence of this fact, and of the reduced crop, we consume a larger proportion of the crop than we did before the war, though the manufacture does not as yet supply to consumers as large a quantity of goods per capita as it then did. As the crop is less than one-half as large as it was in 1860, the grower gets much higher prices, so that the production of wealth by the growth of cotton has not been materially diminished. Nor, if we consider the manufacture as productive of wealth in proportion to the quantity of cotton which it transforms into fabrics, can we say that the production of wealth by this branch of industry has increased. But the effect of the present tariff cannot be decisively distinguished from the effects of other causes upon both growth and manufacture. To the periods prior to the war we must look for proof whether the cotton manufacture has been aided by the protective system. The review of facts, we think, has fully demonstrated—

I. That the manufacture, like the growth of cotton, is indigenous to this country, and has never owed its existence to protection.

II. That protective duties, even in the earlier years, were desired only by the less enterprising, to shield them from the effects of lack of enterprise.

III. That those duties were a premium to bad management, and kept alive the less useful establishments, a hinderance to progress.

IV. That severe prostration, the disasters of which were shared by the best and the worst, were needed to weed out these concerns, and prepare the manufacture for healthy growth—a work which natural competition would have done with less detriment to others.

V. That since 1829, under all changes of duty, the growth in this manufacture has been such as to demonstrate its independence of legislative aid.

VI. That the manufacture has progressed, since that time, in proportion to the growth of the crop, but a little more rapidly in times of non-protective than in times of protective duties.

VII. That progress in the manufacture has been accompanied with loss to the grower of cotton and to the consumer of goods under protective duties, but under non-protection a more rapid progress has been made, with gain to the grower and to the consumer.

VIII. That the production of wealth by cotton manufacture progressed more rapidly under the low revenue tariff of 1846–'60 than at any other time in our history.

————◦••◦————

CHAPTER XI.

THE WOOLLEN MANUFACTURE.

THE condition of the woollen interest in this country is very remarkable. During the past year many large mills have stopped, and very few of the manufacturers have worked full time. The business, it is generally acknowledged, was never in a more unsatisfactory condition, and fine factories are for sale at great sacrifice. Some of the largest and most intelligent manufacturers openly appeal to Congress to repeal the protective duties, and give them a moderate revenue tariff. Yet this disastrous condition of the manufacture is not caused by high prices of the raw material, and is not accompanied with any benefit to the wool-grower, for the prices of almost all varieties of American wool are lower than they were in 1860, and of the most important grades lower in currency than they were in 1860 in gold. In consequence, the wool-growers are slaughtering their sheep by thousands, and the clip of wool for the year 1869 is said to be fully forty millions less than that of 1868. While the manufacturer is ruined and the wool-grower slaughters his sheep, the consumer is taxed from fifty to one hundred and fifty per cent. for his clothing, blankets, and carpets. Surely this cannot be considered a successful policy, which ruins manufacturers, slaughters sheep, and fleeces consumers !

"How can these results possibly occur under the same tariff?" Yet they actually do occur ; here they are, to be witnessed by any man : mills silent or bankrupt ; growers feeding hogs ; consumers paying nine dollars a pair for blankets which cost not more than five in 1860. Nor is this the worst phase of the matter. We imported in 1869 of wool and woollens about as much in value, and of woollens far more in quantity, than we did in 1860, under lower duties. Yet many important kinds of woollen goods are absolutely excluded, and the manufacturer here has absolute control of the market. No advocate of protection can be persuaded that a system which entirely excludes a foreign article can benefit nobody, yet who is benefited here ? No advocate of that system will admit that duties which ruin the manufacturer and the grower can at the same time tax the consumer, yet here are duties which unquestionably injure grower, consumer, and manufacturer. It is for no lack of protection that these disasters occur. The tariff under which we live was shaped by a convention of wool-growers and wool-manufacturers, and unanimously demanded by both, as absolutely necessary to keep those interests from destruction. Congress, as if legislating for them alone, and for the millions of consumers not at all, granted what they asked. How can the results be explained ?

Three causes have combined to that end : There has been a large increase here in the manufacture of those goods of which, prior to protection, consumption was mainly or wholly supplied by our own mills, rather than of those of which consumption was not so supplied. The cost of production here has been increased, while the cost of the raw material elsewhere, partly because of our tariff, has been greatly reduced. The cotton manufacture has recovered from its extreme depression during the war.

To a considerable extent, the woollen and the cotton manufacture compete to supply the same consumption. When the supply of cotton failed during the war, the woollen manufacture was very largely increased. A similar increase, less in degree, occurred in other countries, where the consumption of cotton was checked. In this and in other countries an enormous demand for wool was created, and production rapidly increased. But the revival of the cotton supply and manufacture, after the war, diminished the consumption of woollen goods, and the supply exceeded the demand. Consequently, in other countries as well as in this, the woollen manufacture has been reduced or compelled to accept lower prices, and the wool-grower has also been compelled to reduce production, or sell at lower rates.

When this cause began in all countries to affect both the growth and manufacture of wool, people in other countries adjusted their industry to the facts. If they could sell at lower prices or manufacture more cheaply, they did so. But in this country they went to government for aid. Already both grower and manufacturer had been aided, first by the Morrill protective tariff of 1861—as perfect a piece of work of its kind as ever was devised—and, that having failed, by the higher tariff of 1864. Instructed thus to rely upon legislation to cure all industrial ills, they asked and obtained a still higher duty in 1866, and finally the wool tariff, framed by wool-growers and manufacturers, the blessings of which we and they now experience. How higher duties could be expected to increase consumption, or relieve a market already overstocked with the wools and goods mainly produced here, we do not see. But, in some such strange hope, Congress granted the extreme duties desired, and grower and manufacturer were permitted to ruin themselves at the public expense.

When the cotton supply fell short and prices of woollen goods went extravagantly high, many people were attracted to the-growth and manufacture of wool. Quite naturally, they preferred to grow that class of wool which had been found most profitable here, instead of other qualities more really needed, but less profitable. The manufacturer, also, having promise of control of the home market, preferred to make goods for which our wool was suitable, rather than those which required the use of foreign wools bearing high duties. Thus both growth and manufacture progressed rapidly *in one direction*, without extending greatly in others. Of wools which we naturally produce because they are supposed to be the most profitable, we produced more. Of goods which we naturally make because they can be made of American wools, we produced more. And, of these wools and woollens, the supply quickly equalled or exceeded the demand. But, for other wools and other qualities of woollen goods, we remained as dependent as ever upon foreign supply. This did not please legislators, nor yet gentlemen who wanted to exclude foreign products entirely, and, therefore, duties were raised still higher. This promised larger profits, and accordingly more people rushed into the growing of the same wools and the manufacture of the same goods. Then the markets were overstocked, and losses followed, while we continued as dependent as before, for other goods and wools, upon foreign supply. Now, protection makes it the business of government to apply a remedy whenever any protected interest is losing. Wherefore, the remedy was applied—higher duties. With special determination to shut out foreign wools, on mestiza, then selling at 13 cents in gold, a duty of 11¼ cents was imposed. To help the manufacturer, duties of fifty cents a pound and thirty-five per cent. ad valorem were imposed on the goods. These promised great profits, and more people still began to grow the same wools and to manufacture the same goods. And now we have factories idle or for sale, and sheep slaughtered by the million. Yet we are still importing wool and woollens to the value of over forty millions; for the manufacture, extended mainly in those directions in which we do *not* compete with foreign products, has but slightly diminished our importations.

"But how can it be that an overcrowded manufacture of certain goods does not reduce the prices of those goods?" It does reduce the prices *of some* below the cost of manufacture, but not below the cost in 1860, when wool was dearer, but the manufacture cost much less, and not at all to compare with the reduction of cost in other countries. The attempt to exclude mestiza wool from our ports has thrown it upon the markets of Europe at a greatly reduced price. The English manufacturer, getting his wool cheaper than before, can produce cloths cheaper. Thus our tariff has operated to protect the foreign manufacturer, and so great has been the reduction of cost that he can now pay the duty of "fifty cents a pound, and 35 per cent. ad valorem," amounting, in some cases, to nearly 150 per cent., and still sell some goods in our market at prices little above those of 1860. But our manufacturer, with his increased cost of manufacture, and with no cheap foreign wool to mix profitably with our own, cannot sell lower than he did in 1860 without a ruinous sacrifice. Of the qualities which are sold at the prices of 1860 in gold, some are sold at a sacrifice, and even then the consumer is heavily taxed because foreign goods cost much less. But the goods sold at or near the prices of 1860 in gold are few. At the sale after the exhibition at Cincinnati in August, the prices paid to the manufacturers direct, in large quantities and not by the piece, were for flannels plain, 50 to 65 cents; red, 52½; plaid, from 40 to 52½; cassimeres, $1.12½, $1.25, and $1.35; blankets, from $9 to $11 a pair; shawls (long), $7.25; jeans, from 50 to 82½ cents. Similar goods sold in 1860—flannels, 26 to 36 cents; cassimeres, 66 to 90 cents; blankets, $3 to $6 a pair; shawls, $7.*

---

* In the report for 1870, received after this chapter was prepared, Mr. Wells gives tables of prices (quoted p. 153), which more fully illustrate the principles above stated than any statistics which I had been able to obtain. He gives, first, the selling prices at Stewart's, New York, of the most important articles of domestic manufacture, in 1860 and in 1869; and, second, the importing prices of certain French goods. These tables show that the prices of American goods have been increased from 10 to 80 per cent. since 1860, though many of them now sell for less in gold than they then did, but at the same time the cost of goods has been reduced in other countries very greatly. I add, at the close of this chapter, another table, prepared by Mr. Greeley to prove that many qualities of domestic-made goods actually sell for less or little more in gold than they cost in 1860—which is true of some goods which can be advantageously made of American wool only, because the price of American wool is much lower in gold than it was in 1860. But of other goods

But these are the goods which we most successfully manufacture, sold at auction in large quantities by the manufacturers direct. Of others the price has been much more increased—so much that the foreign manufacturers supply quite as large a share of the consumption as they have ever done. The reason is, that the wool of this country is not suited to the production of such goods, and foreign wool of that quality has not been admitted at such terms that our manufacturers could compete with others who have their wool free of duty.

Nearly all the wool produced in this country is of the merino of medium grades, suitable for the manufacture of card-wool tissues—flannels, blankets, shawls, cloakings, satinets, and cassimeres. But of the fine clothing wools from which broadcloths and doeskins can be made, this country produces no supply. Of combing wool, that quality by which the vast manufacture of England is mainly sustained, a long wool necessary to the worsted manufacture, we produce no supply. So small is the quantity produced of either of these qualities, that we might as well not produce them at all. Neither have we the Cheviot wool, a mixture of which gives their peculiar character to the Scotch tweeds, cassimeres, and coarser shawls and blankets. Nor have we those finest qualities of merino wool such as enable the French to excel all nations in dress-goods for women.

The American wool is costly, and, though superior in quality for many purposes, can even for those be often most economically used in mixture with foreign wools. A free supply of cheap wool from other countries, therefore, enables the manufacturer to consume a larger quantity of American wool, and retain command of the market. Manufacturers in other countries have this opportunity to choose from many qualities of wool the best and most economical

---

it is not true. And while Mr. Greeley introduces this table to prove that consumers in this country are not taxed by the tariff on woollen goods, he carefully conceals the fact that prices of goods in other countries have been so much reduced that duties of 80 per cent. do not shut out importations nearly as large as those of 1860; and he also conceals the fact that the cost of American wool here has been so depressed that the material for a yard of cloth, which cost in 1860 just \$1.08$\frac{1}{4}$ (wool 50 cents 2$\frac{1}{8}$ lbs.) now costs only 84$\frac{1}{4}$ cents (wool 39 cents 2$\frac{1}{8}$ lbs.), a difference of 24 cts. in gold in a yard of cloth. It is plain, then, that if the cost of manufacture has not been increased, the cloth costing one dollar and a half a yard in 1860 ought now to be sold for one dollar and a quarter in gold. It is not worthy of Mr. Greeley's reputation to suppress these essential facts, which prove that the people *are* taxed, and that heavily.

mixture. The policy of our government has always denied to our manufacturers that opportunity. The "protection"—the advantage thus given to the foreign manufacturer—is so great as to be absolutely decisive of itself in a contest between national industries. But another advantage, not less great, is the power of changing from one class of goods to another, as the state of the market may require. With free and amply supply of wools of all kinds, the foreign manufacturer, if he finds the market overstocked with goods of any kind, can change to others for a time. But the manufacturer here, when foreign wools are either excluded or by duties made too costly for profitable use, is forced to confine himself to the production of such goods as can be made wholly or mainly of American wool; and, whenever the market for these few qualities is supplied, he must close his mills or work at a sacrifice.

These few facts are the key to the whole history of the woollen interest. It was impossible for the manufacturer to compete on even terms with those of other countries, without free supply of all kinds of wool. But that supply has not been given a single year since 1824. Consequently the manufacture has always been at a disadvantage, and, in the attempt to produce goods other than those for which American wool alone can be profitably used, that disadvantage has been fatal. Even in the use of American wool, freedom to mix with others being denied, our manufacturer has been unable to produce as cheaply as that of other countries, except in a few articles; and thus, while the manufacture of some fabrics has been repeatedly prostrated by an excess of production over demand, the industry as a whole has been narrowed, weakened, and rendered unable to consume as largely of American wool as it otherwise might have done.

When to these disadvantages is added the increased cost of machinery, of buildings, of power, and of dyes, under a protective tariff, it will be realized that the cost of production here has been artificially raised above the cost in other countries. Hence, this great industry is the weakest of all leading branches of manufacture, and demands the heaviest duties to shelter it against competition; and, having those duties, finds itself worse off than ever before. In plain terms, it has been "protected" almost to death.

Instead of leaving it free to enjoy such success as it could honestly win and surely hold, unimpeded by legislative interference with the cost of materials and of production, we have been trying almost without cessation for forty-five years to compensate the manufacture for protection to the wool-grower and others, and have shut it out from supplies of wool absolutely necessary to make it permanently successful.

"But this has been done to benefit the wool-grower," it will be said. The only market for American wool must come from American manufacture, and that manufacture will be able to consume American wool at fair prices only when it has attained a healthy condition, a solid and enduring success. We shall presently inquire what protection has done for the grower. Let us first ascertain how it has affected the manufacture. A review of statistics will prove, first, that the woollen manufacture, never needing protection as to such goods as can be best produced from American wool, has never by protection been so extended as to materially diminish our dependence upon foreign countries for other goods; and second, that the manufacture has been retarded and crushed by repeated and mistaken efforts to protect wool-growers.

Under all tariffs prior to 1824, wool was free. Light revenue duties were imposed on carpets, of $7\frac{1}{2}$ per cent. in 1791, of 10 per cent. in 1792, of 15 per cent. in 1794, and in 1800 of $12\frac{1}{2}$ per cent., and in 1804 of 15 per cent. on other manufactured goods. Under these trifling duties the manufacture grew up. Arthur Schofield established the mill at Pittsfield from which goods were soon sent to New York, sold for British broadcloths, and brought back for sale by a dealer of that same town in which they were manufactured. He was soon followed by others, and in many quarters, before the embargo of 1808, woollen goods were made for $1.06 which were declared to be equal in fineness and superior in wear to British goods of double width costing $3.50 a yard. Thus British goods, if free of duty then, would have cost $1.50 for the same quantity and an inferior quality, compared with goods manufactured here at $1.06. But this was before we began to protect wool-growers. During the war, the woollen manufacture greatly increased, but wool was so scarce as to be sold for $4 a pound, and broadcloths sold as high as $18 a yard. When the war closed, and these fictitious prices in the then inflated currency were brought in contact with those of other countries, the manufacturer, having wool free, adjusted himself accordingly; and it is recorded that new and large woollen mills were built after the close of the war, until the prostration produced in 1819 by the great disorder and contraction of the currency, already described. In that disaster the woollen manufacture shared, yet not more largely than that of cotton, and it recovered quite as vigorously. Under the tariff of 1816, imported woollen goods bore a duty of 25 per cent., blankets, worsteds, and stuffs, bearing 15 per cent.; but these duties did not prevent the subsequent prostration.

A table of the importations of woollen goods, from 1821 to 1845 inclusive, classified, is taken from the Treasury report of 1845 (Table No. 5 at the close of this chapter), and preceding (Table No. 4) is also a table of wool, woollens, and carpets, imported since 1845. From these records it appears that in 1821, when the country was just beginning to recover from depression, the value of woollen goods imported was nearly seven and a half millions, of which five millions were of cloths, shawls, etc., and a million and three-quarters of worsted goods. But, of blankets, the importation was less than half a million, and of hosiery, gloves, etc., less than $200,000. It is evident that the importation of worsteds and of fine woollen cloths supplied a large part of the consumption, while of blankets, hose, and the coarser cloths, very much the greater part consumed was then produced here. The importations of 1822 were much heavier, but those of 1823 and 1824 were about eight and a quarter millions, and the proportions of different articles were about the same. At that time the whole consumption of woollens was about $43,000,000, of which $8,386,597 was imported in 1824, the last fiscal year preceding a change of duty, or less than one-fifth.

In 1824 the first attempt was made to protect the grower, and the manufacturers, to balance the duty on the raw material, received largely increased protection, the minimum principle being then applied to woollen goods. All goods costing less than 33⅓ cents a yard bore a duty of 25 cents a yard, and goods costing more a duty of 33⅓ per cent. This system, to the astonishment of its advocates, greatly prostrated the woollen manufacturer, and reduced the price of wool to the grower from 32½ to 25 cents! The reason is plain: the manufacturer was prostrated by denial of his choice of wools. That effect alone was so injurious, that, in spite of a reduced cost of nearly one-quarter in American wool, and an increased duty on foreign goods, the importations increased in the very next year, 1825, to over $11,000,000, and were $8,679,505 in 1828, the last (fiscal) year of this tariff. Demonstration cannot be clearer; the prostration of the manufacturer cannot possibly be ascribed to any other cause except the inability to compete without free choice of wool. It cannot be ascribed to increased cost of American wool. It cannot be ascribed to importations merely, for those only reached in 1828 about one-fifth of the total consumption. But the manufacturers themselves testified before a congressional committee to their losses. Thirteen of those who were examined in 1828 declared that they had been losing money since 1825; some largely, and only one, a maker of flannels, reported success. And they stated the real difficulty: they were dependent upon imported wools, which cost, Saxony, 61 cents to $1.60; Spanish, 35 to 85 cents; merino, 30 cents to $1.25; Italian, 32¼ cents; German coarse, 16 to 20 cents; Russian, 13 cents; Smyrna, 16 to 22 cents per pound, while the common American was selling for 20 to 25 cents. Its value had depreciated, they truly testified, because of "the depressed state of the manufacture."

Here are to be observed, as consequences of the first protective tariff on wool, nearly the same results as are now witnessed; manufacturers ruined, wool depreciated in price, consumers taxed, and importations increased. But Congress, failing to see that protection itself was the cause of these disasters, or believing in the maxim "*Similia similibus curantur,*" prescribed another dose of protection. On wool the duty was 4 cents a pound, and 40 per cent. for one year; then 45 per cent. for one year, and then 50 per cent. On woollens minimums were established of 50 cents, $1, $2.50, and $4, with a duty of 40 per cent. for one year on such arbitrary valuation, and after that of 45 per cent. If it is possible to exclude foreign goods, and give to domestic manufacturers an absolute monopoly, by any form of tariff, it would be supposed that this tariff would have that effect. The practical object of it was to impose upon the four classes of goods such duties as to establish in this country a fixed price, so that no reduction in the cost of the goods abroad could affect the price here. For if goods costing four dollars a yard should be reduced by improvements in manufacture to $2.51, they would still be valued at the custom-house at four dollars, and a duty of $1.80 a yard would be exacted. No improvement in manufacture abroad, it was intended, should ever inure to the benefit of any American consumer by affecting the duty. At the time this extraordinary tariff was passed we were importing of woollens $8,679,505. Three years after, in 1831, we imported $12,627,229. This increase, it is important to observe, was mainly in those qualities of goods which are not well manufactured from American wool, namely, fine cloths and worsteds. The importation of cloths increased from $4,315,714 to $6,121,442, and the importation of worsteds from $1,446,146 to $3,392,037. Instead of supplying any larger part of the consumption of these articles, the domestic manufacturer actually lost ground as to these, and supplied a smaller proportion, the importation of such goods being much larger in proportion to population, when this tariff closed, than when it was adopted. Here is illustrated the futility of attempting to force the manufacture into other channels than those to which the supply of American wool directs it. But it is equally important to observe that the importation of blankets increased from $624,239 in 1828 to $1,180,478 in 1831. "Blankets can be made wholly of American wool, but its cost has always been too high," said a manufacturer before the committee in 1824. Hence some mixture of cheap or foreign wool was useful, but the tariff tried to exclude that wool. Accordingly, the foreign wool came in the form of blankets!

During these four years it does not appear from the most minute records of the manufacture that a single new woollen-mill was established, or that it was extended or improved in any noteworthy respect. If individuals made money, they made it in spite of disadvantages which all felt, not the least of these being the increased cost of woollen goods to the consumer, which tended to check consumption, the increased cost of iron and its products, and of manufacture as compared with the cost in other countries where it was being constantly reduced. Once more, the consumer was taxed, and the manufacture not developed or extended, and yet the grower was worse off than ever. The price of wool during the years 1829 and 1830 was very low; in 1830 common sold for 18 cents in July; and in 1831 for $22\frac{1}{2}$ cents in May. If the grower was not benefited; if the manufacture was not developed in any healthy sense; if the consumer was heavily taxed, and if foreign importations increased from eight to twelve millions, in what sense can this tariff be called successful?

In 1832 a tariff was passed reducing duties on nearly all articles materially, abandoning the minimum principle on woollens, and putting very low duties on cheap woollen cloths, worsteds, flannels, and on ordinary carpets and hosiery only 25 per cent. Meanwhile wool. costing less than 8 cents was admitted free, and other wool reduced to 4 cents and 40 per cent. duty; dye-stuffs were also made free. In the next year Mr. Clay's compromise tariff was adopted, which provided for a gradual reduction of all duties, by abating every second year one-tenth of the excess above 20 per cent., until 1841, when one-half of the residue of such excess should be abated.

It is impossible to distinguish the effects of this tariff from those of the great ebb and flow of currency induced by the land speculation already described. It would be unfair to ascribe the general prosperity of the manufacturer until 1841 altogether to the large reduction of duties, and equally unfair to ascribe the subsequent depressoin altogether to the continued reduction. The extreme contraction of the currency and the general distress fully account for the prostration of the manufacture in 1842, while foreign importations do not, for those were less in either of the years 1840–'42 inclusive, than in the years 1831–'33 inclusive. The aggregate value of woollens imported for the three years 1831–'33 was nearly thirty-six millions, and the aggregate value imported for the three years 1840–'42 inclusive, when the duties were lowest, was twenty-eight and a third millions. The prostration of this interest at that time cannot, therefore, be ascribed to the effect of foreign competition. It is worthy of note, also, that the imports continued to be almost wholly of qualities of goods not manufactured here with success, namely, worsteds and fine cloths. The importation of blankets, notwithstanding the low duty, had fallen to $500,000, and of carpets to about $250,000, and of flannels to $90,289. The manufacture of these articles, especially of carpets and flannels, was so established that only the more costly kinds were imported under any rate of duty, and while the domestic manufacture supplied of carpets as early as 1834 fully 1,147,500 yards, of the qualities for ordinary use, besides great quantities which were made in families, the quantity imported under the reduced duty in 1833 was only 344,173 yards. The average price of all carpets made in this country, in factories, was then about a dollar a yard. The proportion of carpets imported was less in 1842, when this tariff closed, and under the lowest duties, than in 1833, when it began, and when duties were highest, and the same was true of flannels and blankets. But the importation of woollen cloths and worsteds varied with the general prosperity of the country, and was largest in the years 1835 and 1836, when the domestic manufacture of woollens was also most prosperous. These facts confirm the view already taken, that the importation was mainly of such articles as are not produced here; that the manufacture was aided by the admission of cheap wool free, and the reduction of duty on all wool, and that its subsequent depression was due not to importations or reduction of duties, but to changes of currency and of the general condition of the country.

Tables given in Chapter XXI. show that the prices of woollen goods made with success in this country were greatly reduced under the operation of this tariff. The price of Salisbury 38-inch flannels was reduced from 44 cents in 1835 to 40 cents in 1838, and 33 cents in 1840; Lowell carpets were reduced in price from $1.10 in 1835 to 90 cents in 1841; linseys were reduced from 28 to 22 cents; cassimeres from $2 to $1.70 per yard; broadcloths from $4.25 to $4 per yard; and blankets from $5.25 to $4.25 a pair. A further reduction of price followed the return to specie in 1841, caused not only by the depression of business, but by the low price of wool. But, prior to this change, the consumer had been greatly benefited by the reduction in the cost of goods; the wool-grower, in spite of the admission of cheap foreign wool free of duty, had received very high prices for his wool, and the manufacture had advanced with very great rapidity. In Massachusetts the value of woollen goods produced increased 60 per cent. in the five years from 1832 to 1837.

The restoration of the currency was followed by a revival of all industry, and, because the protective tariff of 1842 was adopted soon after that event, the tariff has been credited by its advocates with the revival of industry and the restoration of currency itself. For the present purpose, it is essential only to observe that under this tariff, as before, the importation of woollens increased with the increase of the manufacture here, so that the progress of our industry cannot be ascribed to the exclusion of foreign goods. The increase of importations was from $8,375,725 in 1842, to $10,083,819 in 1846, the last year of this tariff, and it was in every quality of goods, as follows:

YEAR.	Cloths.	Worsted.	Blankets.	Hosiery.
1842.......	$4,180,875	$2,366,132	$566,233	$375,297
1846.......	4,488,434	2,658,023	633,745	838,866

YEAR.	Yarn.	Carpets.	Flannels.	All other.
1842..........	$217,611	$242,309	$90,289	$336 989
1846..........	266,330	253,543	156,851	788,027

The importations, in 1845, of cloths, blankets, and carpets, were much higher than in 1846. No statistics are attainable of the quantity of woollen goods manufactured in these years, but it is known that it increased rapidly after the revival of industry, and that the manufacture of broadcloths was quite generally attempted. The duty on such cloths was 40 per cent., and the duty on wool, costing less than seven cents, was but 5 per cent., while on other wool it was three cents a pound, and 30 per cent. Under these circumstances, the growth of fine wool and the manufacture of fine cloth were undertaken, and in 1844 the finest wools commanded a high price.

But these and all other wools thenceforward fell rapidly in price, while the importations of woollen cloths slightly increased.

It appears that the American supply of the fine wools was entirely insufficient, and that the manufacturers depended very largely upon foreign supplies; and Mr. Randall, in a statement in 1845, said: "Numerous specimens of wool, equalling our choicest Saxon, are in the hands of various individuals throughout the country, which men of well-known standing and veracity allege they obtained of importers and manufacturers—such importers stating that they were from bales of South American wool admitted under the 5 per cent. ad valorem duty, and conceding that large quantities of a similar quality were received by them from the same source. It is alleged that some of the smaller manufactories of good cloths receive their principal supply in this way." In that same year we imported, of wool, no less than 23,833,050 pounds, and in the next year 16,558,247. Whether this wool was or was not fraudulently admitted, does not affect the inference that its admission under merely nominal duty was the advantage which enabled the manufacturer to extend his efforts to the finer cloths for which the American wool did not suffice.

Convincing evidence that this was in fact the cause of the temporary success of that branch of the manufacture is afforded by its immediate abandonment in 1847, when the duty on all foreign wools was changed to 30 per cent. Thus this tariff, though called a "free-trade" tariff, was in this particular eminently a protective tariff —it excluded the foreign wool upon which the manufacture of fine cloths had depended, and stopped that manufacture so that the committee of wool manufacturers and growers say in their memorial to Congress of 1866: "The manufacturers of fine cloths found it in vain to struggle against foreign wools, who, in addition to cheap interest and cheap labor, had the crowning advantage of free wool. The higher branches of the manufacture were abandoned; soon every one of the eighteen hundred broadcloth houses in the country ceased work. The branches of the manufacture continued with activity were those like flannels, which were supplied by the common wool of this country—so superior in its spinning qualities as in itself to afford an advantage over the foreign manufacturer. There was no longer a demand for any but common wools. The Saxon wool-husbandry ceased with the manufacture of fine cloths which had called it into existence." It seems to be very satisfactorily established by this concurrent testimony of both parties interested, the growers and manufacturers, that the increased duty on foreign wools at this

11

point destroyed the manufacture of fine cloths, and with it the demand for and culture of the Saxon wools.

Returning to the tariff of 1842, it appears that in other branches the manufacture made no such progress as to supply a better market for American wool at its close than had existed in the year of prostration with which it commenced, and that the price of goods was not reduced in proportion to the reduction in the cost of wool. Northampton broadcloth sold for $3 a yard without change for four years, and some other qualities of broadcloth were increased in price; satinet was increased in price from 50 to 65 cents; Lowell carpets were raised a little; flannels were slightly higher in 1846 than in 1843, and blankets were raised 50 cents a pair; yet all grades of wool were cheaper in the last year of this tariff than in its first. The tables already mentioned (Chapter XXI.) show that the consumer and the wool-grower were taxed to support the manufacturer, and that after the repeal of this tariff the price of wool materially improved, while the cost of goods to the consumer was lessened.

Notwithstanding the lamentable effect of the tariff of 1846 upon the broadcloth manufacture—an effect due, as has been stated, to a protective feature in a tariff generally non-protective in character— the manufacture of those qualities of woollen goods for which the American wool suffices so increased that a larger quantity of that wool was used at higher prices than it had obtained since the inflation in 1837.

The tariff of 1857 was marked by an entirely different policy. The duties on manufactured goods were reduced to 24 per cent., and all wool costing 18 cents or less was admitted free, other wool bearing only a 24 per cent. duty. Under the first provision was admitted nearly every kind of wool upon which our manufacture had depended. The tariff went into effect, however, at a time when industry was much disordered, and the panic which occurred in that year deferred for some months the improvement, but the subsequent progress was very rapid. So great, indeed, was the demand for wools of all kinds, that the prices of all grades of American rose higher than ever before since the War of 1812, although it was believed that fully 95,000,000 lbs. of foreign wool were imported within the three years; and the census of 1869 shows that about 98,379,785 lbs. of wool were consumed in the manufactures, of which about $51,516,959 were of domestic growth.

In that year the product of this manufacture was in value about eighty millions, and consisted of 124,897,862 yards of cloth,

6,401,206 lbs. of yarn, 296,874 pairs of blankets, 616,400 shawls.   In value the product had increased 42 per cent. since 1850, and a large part of that increase had been effected within the years 1858–'60, under the lowest duties on both wool and woollens.   The product in cloth was nearly four yards to each inhabitant, and in value $1.97 per capita; but the quantity of cloth exceeded the quantity manufactured in 1850 by 42,691,210 yards, or 52 per cent., showing that while quantity and value had both increased faster than population, the cost of a given quantity had been reduced.   Under this tariff, therefore, the manufacture grew with great rapidity, the wool-grower received the highest prices for his wool, and the consumer had cheaper cloth.   But this was during the period of the lowest duties, both on wool and woollens, ever imposed since 1824.   And, though no official records show the quantity of goods manufactured in the whole country, except in years of census, the State census of Massachusetts discloses the following facts, as to the value of the product of woollen manufacture in that State, at different periods:

1832	$6,500,000	....
1837	10,399,807	Increase, 60 per cent.
1845	8,877,478	Decrease, ...
1850	12,781,514	Increase, 44 per cent.
1855	12,105,514	Decrease, ...
1860	19,655,787	Increase, 62 per cent.

As Massachusetts is by far the larger producer of woollens, the value of the goods produced made in that State being nearly one-third of the value made in the whole country, and as there is no reason to suppose that, in either of these periods, the manufacture increased or decreased except under the influence of causes affecting in like manner other wool-manufacturing States, these figures give quite conclusive proof, first, of the large increase in the manufacture after the abandonment of the protective system in 1832—the increase having been 60 per cent. in five years; second, of the great depression caused by the disorders of currency; third, of the great increase in the manufacture as a whole, after the abandonment of the protective system in 1846, notwithstanding the defeat of the broadcloth experiment already described; fourth, of a decrease in the manufacture from 1850 to 1855, caused, apparently, by the pressure of competition from foreign mills enjoying cheap wool, while our mills were forced to pay 30 per cent. duty on their foreign wool—a competition the extent of which will be seen from the table of imports of woollens, which shows that over eighty-five millions in value were imported in the three years ending 1855—and finally, of the very rapid increase from 1855 to 1860, which was more than 62 per cent. Of this increase nearly the whole occurred after the removal of duty from wool of 18 cents a pound or less, in 1857. In view of these facts, it must be admitted that the greatest increase ever attained in the woollen manufacture was during the two periods when a large share of foreign wool was admitted free, while duties on woollen goods were low or rapidly reduced. Of the two periods, that increase was largest in the period when duties were lowest.

These are the conclusions compelled by a review of the history of this manufacture prior to the war. Since 1860 its growth has been greatly affected, first favorably and then unfavorably, by the changes in the production of cotton goods. The enormous increase prior to 1865 was by no means due entirely to the admission of foreign wool at low rates, on the one hand; nor on the other to the high duties on imports. Its great depression since 1865 has been in part caused by the revival of the cotton manufacture, but still more by the duties imposed on foreign wool. Very potent in its influence was the repeal of the reciprocity treaty. By that change, the worsted manufacture was remarkably affected, and the cost of making carpets greatly increased.

It has been stated that in this country no wool is grown from which worsteds are made. In 1866 the wool-manufacturers reported that "the American production of worsted combing wool is not sufficient to supply one mill"—say three hundred thousand pounds. At that time it was estimated that the quantity of combing wool consumed in the worsted-mills was four million pounds. This wool, grown in Canada far more largely than it has there been consumed, when admitted free, enabled us to build up a branch of manufacture not only important in itself, but exceedingly beneficial to the American wool-grower, because it increased the consumption of our own qualities of wool. But the tariff of 1864 subjected this wool, after the reciprocity ceased, to a duty of 37 to 40 per cent. The effect upon our manufacture may easily be imagined—it was entirely prostrated. The manufacturers were not wrong in saying, in January, 1866, "A duty on Canada wools would crush an industry which has already assumed a truly national importance," as the importation of worsteds worth about fourteen millions in that year indicated. In the manufacture of Brussels carpets, also, it was then made clear that the duty was a serious disadvantage.

But Congress, instead of giving to the manufacturer free wool, attempted to compensate for the higher cost of the material by higher duties on the product, and the result is before us in the depression now existing. Of the effect of the tariff of 1867, two witnesses may testify. The *Providence Journal*, edited by Senator Anthony, of Rhode Island, an advocate of the protective system, speaks of some mestiza wool thus:

No American wool has ever been found which will make so nice a finish, or felt so well. The tariff at the time this wool was purchased was six cents a pound. At the revision of the tariff a duty was placed upon it of 10 cents per pound in gold, and 13 per cent. on the valuation. This makes from 11 to 12 cents per pound duty on the wool in the grease, and is absolutely prohibitive. In consequence of this duty, the price of wool has been so brought down in Europe, that the manufacturers in Germany, England, and France, can obtain it at a much less rate than before we were deprived of it. In fact, much of it can be bought by them for the same price per pound that would be paid by us in duties. This enables them to send into the United States their fine goods, which only pay a duty to our government of 60 per cent., whereas the duty paid to this government on much of the same kind of wool amounts to from 100 to 120 per cent., leaving our manufacturers from 40 to 50 per cent. worse off than they would be under a free-trade system.

To the same purport, but more explicitly, writes Mr. Edward Harris, one of the largest woollen manufacturers in New England:

This (the duty) has put down the price of fine wool in Europe so low, that it enables their manufacturers to produce their fine goods so low that they can and will eventually drive us out of the market. It is worse to the American manufacturers than free trade, by 50 to 60 per cent., while the poor wool-grower is killing off his fine-wool sheep. . . . I venture to suggest that we have a tariff simply for revenue, that the reciprocity treaty be renewed, and that all duties on the raw material be repealed.

If manufacturers themselves are driven to such conclusions and confessions, must it not be admitted that the system which has taxed the consumer heavily has rendered no permanent service to this branch of industry? But it will be said that these admitted evils spring only from ill-adjustment of the protective tariff, and can be remedied by further legislation. So it was reasoned in 1866, when the wool-growers and manufacturers met in convention, and selected committees of their ablest men to frame a tariff. So faithfully did Congress echo their demands in legislation, that it might, without exaggeration, be said that in this instance the wool interest itself was permitted to make laws for the rest of the country, Congress having abdicated in its favor. If the very men who most thoroughly understand the wants and circumstances of this interest have found it impossible to frame a law with better results to themselves than those now witnessed, may we not begin to doubt the possibility of improving upon natural laws by finite wisdom? Is there not, in short, something in protection — interference with those natural laws—which defeats itself?

As to the wool manufacture, it is plain that duties for its benefit prompt the grower to demand like favors. Say the committees, in their joint memorial of 1866: "The obvious disadvantage to the manufacturer of the policy of the tariff of 1857 was its inherent instability. The manufacturer, investing large capital in structures and machinery which cannot be diverted to other purposes, and which may not give returns until years of operation, demands above all things stability of legislation. This he could never expect under a system which made the agricultural interest secondary to his." Is not that the inevitable result of any and every policy which taxes the agricultural interest for the benefit of the manufacturing? Is there not in every protective tariff this obvious and fatal disadvantage—"inherent instability?" The more thoroughly it discriminates in favor of an interest, the greater the probability of speedy change. Whoever will glance at the record of changes of the tariff, already given, will see reason to believe that tariffs are short-lived in proportion as they are " protective." The tariff of 1857, though the lowest revenue tariff ever adopted since 1816, was regarded by the wool-grower as a discriminating or protective tariff in favor of the manufacturer. Statistics have shown that under it the manufacture did increase more rapidly than under any other form of duty. But its " inherent instability " was obvious because it was supposed to discriminate in favor of the manufacture, although in fact it gave the wool-grower higher prices for his wool than he had ever received since "protection" began. It must at least be admitted that the system which succeeded it did not display any inherent stability, for we have had twelve changes in eight years. Is it not time for the manufacturer to seriously consider whether low duties for revenue, raw materials free, and stability, will not confer greater benefits upon him in the end than high duties for protection, with producers of raw materials also demanding protection, and twelve tariffs in eight years?

NO. 1.—MR. GREELEY'S TABLE.

The prices of the most important woollen fabrics ten years ago, when we had comparative free trade in wool and in woollens, and now, are as follows:

FABRICS.	Price in 1859.	Price in 1869.*	Currency price, 1869.
Flannels, per yard—			
A. & T. white	$0 18	$0 16	$0 21
H. A. F. scarlet	26	23	30
J. R. F. twilled scarlet	30	29	37½
B. twilled scarlet	26	25	32½
Double weight scarlet twilled	27½	30¾	40
F. & C.	36	34½	44½
Talbot R¾ plain scarlet	26	25	32½
G. M. & Co. twilled scarlet	23	20¾	27
E. S.	25	23	30
N. A. M	25	23	30
Ballam bale 4-4 white, No. 1	75	65¼	85
Ballam bale 4-4 white, No. 2	60	53½	70
Ballam bale 4-4 white, No. 3	45	40¾	52½
Ballam bale 4-4, white, No. 4	40	34½	45
Ballam bale 4-4 white, No. 5	35	32¾	42½
Blankets, per pair—			
Holland 10-4, all wool	3 50	4 23	5 50
Holland 11-4, all wool	5 00	5 38	7 00
Cocheco 11-4, ex. super.	6 00	6 15	8 00
Cocheco 12-4, ex. super.	7 50	7 30	9 50
Cumberland 10-4	3 00	3 46	4 50
Cumberland	4 00	4 23	5 50
Rochdale 10-4, super. extra super.	3 50	3 27	4 25
Rochdale 11-4, super. extra super.	4 50	4 08	5 25
Rochdale 12-4, super. extra super.	5 50	4 80	6 25
Rochdale 10-4, premium	4 50	4 23	5 50
Rochdale 11-4, premium	5 50	5 00	6 50
Rochdale 12-4, premium	6 50	5 77	7 50
Cassimeres, per yard—			
Broadbrook Co.'s fancy Cassimeres, 14 oz.	1 62½@1 75	1 34@1 44	1 75@1 87½
Hamilton Woollen Co.'s (1860) per yard	66 27/100	52¾	68 44/100
Shawls—Middlesex Co.'s.	7 00	5 38	7 00
De Laines—Hamilton Woollen Co.'s (1860)	16 80/100	13	17 80/100
Salisbury Mills Boys' Checks, per yard (1860)	58¾	45½	59¾
Salisbury Mills Eugenie Cloths (1860)	94	69	90¾
Salisbury Mills Silk Codrington (1860)	1 52¾	1 18½	1 54¾
Crossly Co.'s, Conn., Tapestry Carpet.	....	96	1 25
The imported article sold in 1859 for 95c.			

NO. 2.—WOOLLEN GOODS.

The following table, prepared at the request of Commissioner D. A. Wells, by the house of A. T. Stewart & Co., of New York, shows the selling price of certain leading varieties of woollen goods in 1860 and 1869, respectively:

FABRICS.	1860.	1869.
Cadet Cloths, Government standard, per yard	$2 75	$3 25
Harris Cassimeres, 14 oz., per yard	1 37½@1 50	1 75@2 00
Cotton Warp Cloths, 14 oz., per yard	1.00 @1 25	1 75
All-wool Cloths, 14 oz., per yard	1 50	2 75
Middlesex Sackings, per yard	1 10	1 25
Middlesex Doeskins, per yard	1 05	1 15
Middlesex Shawls, each	7 00	7 00
Middlesex Beavers, per yard	3 75	4 25
Middlesex Opera Flannels, per yard	47½	50
Broadbrook Cassimeres, per yard	1 62½@1 75	1 75
Broadbrook Beavers, per yard	2 75	3 00
Spring Cassimeres, 8 to 9 oz., per yard	1 12½@1 25	1 25@1 37½
Glenham Repellants, per yard	1 10 @1 15	1 20
Glenham Sackings, per yard	1 05	1 15
Swift River Fancies, 11 to 12 oz., per yard	90	1 00@1 10
Royalston Cassimeres, per yard, average	1 07½	1 25
Fitchburg Cassimeres, per yard, "	1 07½	1 25

* Equivalent in gold (gold at 130). October average.

NO. 3.—FRENCH GOODS.

Importing Prices.   Report 1869, p. 104.

FABRICS.	1859.	1866.	1869.
	Francs.	Francs.	Francs.
French Merinos, all worsted............ {	2 62 3 08 3 22	2 40 3 00 3 15	1 90 2 00 2 40
Dyed Mousseline de Laines, all worsted. {	1 13 1 22	98 1 06	79 85
French dyed Poplins, all worsted........ {	....	1 75 2 15	1 19 1 69

IMPORTS OF WOOL AND WOOLLENS.

YEAR.	UNMANUFACTURED.		Carpets.	Other Manuf's.	Value Manuf's.
	Quantity.	Value.			
1841...............	15,006,410	....	....	....	$11,001,989
1842...............	11,420,958	....	....	....	8,375,725
1843...............	3,517,100	....	....	....	2,472,154
1844...............	14,008,000	....	....	....	9,475,702
1845...............	23,833,040	....	....	....	10,666,176
1846...............	16,558,247	$1,134,226	$253,543	$9,830,307	10,083,850
1847...............	8,460,109	555,822	289,881	10,709,052	10,998,933
1848...............	11,341,429	857,034	643,187	14,597,696	15,240,683
1849...............	17,869,022	1,177,347	493,058	13,211,548	13,704,606
1850...............	18,669,794	1,681,691	790,604	16,360,905	17,151,509
1851...............	32,548,461	3,833,157	996,781	18,510,528	19,507,309
1852...............	18,341,298	1,930,711	730,967	16,842,727	17,573,694
1853...............	21,599,079	2,669,718	1,217,279	26,404,632	27,621,911
1854...............	20,200,110	2,822,185	2,268,815	30,113,779	32,382,594
1855...............	18,534,415	2,072,139	1,506,577	22,897,572	24,404,149
1856...............	14,737,393	1,665,064	2,212,318	29,749,475	31,961,793
1857...............	16,502,060	2,125,744	2,181,290	29,104,828	31,286,118
1858...............	Estimated	4,022,635	1,542,600	24,943,491	26,486,091
1859...............	95,000,000	4,444,954	2,200,164	31,321,792	33,521,956
1860...............		4,842,152	2,542,523	85,394,422	37,936,945
1861...............	36,000,000	....	....	....	28,261,039
1862...............	43,571,026	....	....	....	14,884,394
1863...............	73,897,807	....	....	....	20,411,625
1864...............	90,396,104	....	....	....	32,139,336
1865...............	43,858,154	....	....	....	20,347,563
1866...............	67,917,081	10,068,533	2,854,097	54,261,804	57,115,901
1867...............	33,482,155	5,565,279	....	....	45,776,475
1868...............	24,474,307	3,868,137	2,766,291	29,694,593	32,460,884

MANUFACTURES OF WOOL IMPORTED.

From Treasury Report, 1845.

Year.	Cloths, etc.	Blankets.	Hosiery, etc.	Worsteds.	Woollen Yarn.	Carpeting.	Flannels.	All Other.	Total Value.
1821	$5,038,255	$434,256	$198,783	$1,766,443	....	....	....	....	$7,437,737
1822	8,491,935	991,147	433,309	2,269,513	....	....	....	....	12,185,904
1823	5,844,068	604,896	314,605	1,504,469	....	....	....	....	8,268,038
1824	5,202,009	526,023	317,778	2,158,080	....	$37,834	....	$144,273	8,386,597
1825	5,264,562	891,197	369,747	2,277,480	....	515,391	$1,065,609	1,208,272	11,302,264
1826	4,546,714	527,784	189,993	1,143,166	....	545,148	586,823	892,346	8,481,974
1827	4,285,413	703,477	376,927	1,382,875	....	511,186	587,260	895,573	8,742,701
1828	4,315,714	624,239	365,339	1,446,146	....	581,946	667,722	678,399	8,679,505
1829	3,335,994	455,467	230,986	1,600,622	....	323,254	383,208	551,958	6,881,489
1830	2,854,339	594,044	133,453	1,397,545	....	201,649	266,060	319,306	5,766,396
1831	6,121,442	1,180,478	325,856	3,392,037	....	421,099	695,666	490,651	12,627,229
1832	5,101,841	602,796	260,553	2,615,124	....	557,775	503,193	351,132	9,992,424
1833	6,133,443	1,165,260	463,348	4,281,309	$102,719	319,692	286,299	510,539	13,262,609
1834	4,364,340	1,068,065	383,977	5,056,121	166,507	596,868	240,663	203,787	11,879,328
1835	7,048,334	1,865,344	652,680	6,549,278	262,515	603,084	399,785	453,404	17,834,424
1836	8,945,509	2,397,822	700,530	6,669,312	212,706	964,655	475,712	713,757	21,080,003
1837	3,015,783	959,814	177,092	3,350,266	172,462	623,101	111,249	90,625	8,500,202
1838	5,348,928	946,546	356,965	3,993,455	136,689	315,353	159,979	315,005	11,512,920
1839	7,361,373	1,356,086	1,037,096	7,025,898	368,958	612,607	291,373	522,554	18,575,945
1840	4,823,138	570,417	506,452	2,387,338	104,738	338,501	118,715	221,885	9,071,184
1841	5,042,045	691,895	471,877	3,712,206	158,224	346,488	84,911	395,293	11,001,939
1842	4,180,875	566,233	375,297	2,366,122	217,611	242,309	90,289	336,989	8,375,725
1843	1,398,064	201,454	61,073	1,456,051	60,961	181,810	37,449	75,292	2,472,154
1844	5,049,474	1,004,826	662,905	1,835,875	159,020	289,475	78,009	396,178	9,475,762
1845	5,638,167	998,914	741,242	1,938,109	187,975	431,914	176,387	553,468	10,666,176

The fiscal year 1843 includes only nine months.

A letter from Mr. Edward Harris, the "veteran, eminent, and successful manufacturer," as Mr. Greeley publicly states, has recently appeared in the *Tribune*, and deserves notice. He says:

I am a woollen and cotton manufacturer, and use annually a large amount of coal for producing motive-power, and am otherwise employing quite a large number of persons in skilled labor. I have, and can now use, bituminous coal from the British possessions; but I am met with a duty of $1.25 in gold per ton,- which is equal in currency to $1.50 per ton. There is no escaping this tax; and, it being so high, I can use but very little of this coal; consequently, I am obliged to purchase my coal from the Pennsylvania mines, and pay not only such a price as the miners may charge, but also, in addition, such a price as those who transport the coal to me may charge; which sums, added together, make it very high.

Thus you can see that, so far as the item of coal is concerned—which is a very heavy one—I cannot compete with those establishments situated near the coal-fields.

Thus a very heavy burden is legislated not only upon me, but upon a vast and varied interest, comprising a large section of our country, and giving employment to hundreds of thousands of our citizens.

And for whose benefit is this duty imposed? Not for the poor men who work in the mines; for demand and supply fix their wages, and those who work the mines are importing laborers daily at a small expense, and without paying a duty on the hands so imported. And even, for *argument*, if it *did* give these poor laborers a little more pay—it is nothing in comparison to the detriment of the many who are benefited by the use of the coal.

I have only alluded to the use of coal for producing motive-power. Think of the thousands of poor families which suffer for the want of fuel to keep soul and body together. The reasons for a repeal of this duty are numerous, and the benefits of continuing the duty are not apparent.

Now for the duty on fine wool. I will here state, without fear of contradiction, that fine nap goods cannot be made to advantage in this country without the use of foreign fine wools, which can be mixed to advantage with our American wools, and produce an article which will favorably compare with foreign goods. But here I am met with a duty of over 100 per cent. on this article, as I can prove to you by the Liverpool prices current. I quote from one published by John L. Bowes & Brother for the month of November, 1869: Buenos Ayres No. 1 wool, average shrinkage 70 to 72 per cent.; 5¼d. per pound. Call this, reduced to gold, 11 cents per pound. The duty on this wool is specific, 10 cents per pound, and 11 per cent., making a little over 100 per cent. duty; whereas the duty on fine woollen goods will not exceed 45 or 50 per cent. at most. This leaves a net balance of at least 50 per cent. against the American manufacturer, so far as the wool is concerned, which is much the heaviest item in the cost of the goods.

To simplify the matter, it is 50 per cent. worse than free trade to the manufacturer.

Now, I ask, how can any American grower of fine wools receive any advantage whatever from such a tariff, when, instead of the fine wools being brought to this country, we receive the fine goods smuggled and brought into this country in every direction?

This tariff has shut us out of the foreign markets for fine wool, and consequently reduced the price so low to the foreign manufacturers, and has given increased activity to their business, and enabled them to raise the price of their labor. In fact, it has acted as a bounty on smuggling; and, if continued, will ere long transfer the manufacture of fine goods from this country to foreign countries entirely. As an instance of the bad effects of this tariff upon the fine wool-growers of this country, we see their sheep disappearing in every direction.

I believe, if the duty was taken off from fine wool, that the price of that article would advance in Europe to such an extent that the manufacturers there would not be able to produce fine goods at such extreme low prices as to enable them to send the same into this country, and destroy our business in spite of any tariff which can be enforced.

If our wool-growers, by this unjust tariff on scoured wool of 32 cents per pound and 11 per centum in gold, succeed in keeping the fine foreign wool out of this country, they cannot keep out the fine goods of foreign manufacture; and no American manufacturer can afford to pay them any higher price for their wool than these fine foreign goods will warrant, as they will govern the price of American goods.

I will only add, I am of the opinion that the best minds of New England are coming to these conclusions.

With great respect, I remain your friend,

EDWARD HARRIS,

Woonsocket, R. I., January 19, 1870.

CHAPTER XII.

THE WOOL-GROWER.

Do protective tariffs benefit the wool-grower? The question is one of fact, easily answered by statistics of the most reliable character. At the close of this chapter will be found tables giving the price of wool of different qualities at New York, according to the official report of the Treasury Department of 1863, and at Boston, according to Mr. Livermore. The diagram indicates by two lines the prices of merino and common fleece in the New York market, with every monthly variation since 1824 until the close of 1861, when variations of currency began to affect the price.

In 1824 the first duty on wool was imposed—15 per cent. on wool worth 10 cents or less, and on other wool 20 per cent., until 1826, and afterward 30 per cent. As a consequence, in 1825 and the earlier half of 1826 the price was slightly reduced and afterward fell rapidly. The loss under that tariff was in New York 10 cents for common, 15 to 20 for full-blood merino, and 5 to 10 cents for pulled.

According to Mr. Livermore's tables, the prices at Boston declined 1 cent for long, 4 cents for middle, and 14 cents for fine wool. What is the explanation? The manufacture, shut out for the first time from cheap supply of foreign wool, was depressed and unable to consume as largely as before.

The first attempt to benefit the grower having resulted thus unfavorably, on the 19th of May, 1828, duties were imposed of 4 cents a pound and 40 per cent. until June 30, 1829, 45 per cent. until June 30, 1830, afterward 4 cents and 50 per cent. At once the manufacture was prostrated, and the prices of all grades fell still lower. The production of wool very readily adapts itself to the demand, and with production reduced, the reviving manufacture gave higher prices in 1831 and 1832. But in 1832, after eight years of protection, the prices were still lower than they were when it began, thus:

	Common.	Merino.	Pulled.
1825	30–38	50–62	25–44
1832	25–30	40–45	37–40 (No. 1.)

We have seen that the consumer was taxed. We have seen that the manufacturer was worse off at the end than at the beginning of this period of eight years. We now see that protection deprived the grower of a part of the value of his wool. In 1832 wool worth 8 cents a pound was admitted free, and the duty on more costly wool was reduced to 4 cents and 40 per cent., with gradual reduction afterward. It is interesting to note how the prices of American wool rose under this relaxation of duties. We have seen that the manufacture in Massachusetts increased 60 per cent in five years. The tables show that the prices of all grades increased both in Boston and New York, according to the official record, thus:

	Common.	Merino.	Pulled.
1832	25–30	40–45	37–40
1836	40–50	50–68	52–58

Thus the increase of price kept pace with the increase of the manufacture. And in like manner, when the manufacture was prostrated during the disorder of currency, the price of wool fell very low. Yet the average for this period is higher than that of the protective period which preceded it.

In 1842 another protective period commenced, with duties of 5 per cent. on wool costing 7 cents or less, and on other wool 3 cents and 30 per cent. It is curious to observe how the momentary improvement in prices in 1844 was followed by a decrease to as low a point as had ever been reached. Growers expected great profits, evidently, and held their wool for a few months, hoping to realize them. They realized the loss which awaits everybody who tries to mend natural laws by human legislation. The American wool was rejected while the manufacturer obtained from South America wool—as fine "as our choicest Saxon," says Mr. Randall; "no American wool has ever been found which will make so fine a finish," says the *Providence Journal* —necessary for the success of the broadcloth experiment. The result of this tariff to the grower was:

	New York.			Boston.		
	Common.	Merino.	Pulled.	Fine.	Middle.	Long.
1842....	19	29	27	42	37	30
1846....	20½	27½	22½	40	33	27

Thus the closing year of the great protective tariff of 1842 gave to the wool-grower lower prices than he received in the extreme "hard times" in 1842, and the average for the whole period was lower than that of any other, protective or non-protective, in our history.

With 1847 went into operation the "destructive British free-trade tariff," as Mr. Carey calls it—a level, 30 per cent. ad-valorem tariff, which remained unchanged until 1857. This raised the duty on wools costing less than 7 cents, but removed from those costing more than 7 cents a duty of 3 cents a pound. The broadcloth manufacture stopped, but people began to work up American wool with profit to the grower. The statistics have exhibited the increase of the manufacture from 1845 to 1850. The following figures show how the grower fared:

	New York.			Boston.		
	Common.	Merino.	Pulled.	Fine.	Middle.	Long.
1846...........	20½	27½	22½	40	33	27
1850...........	33½	40½	34½	45	38	32

Nor was this an increase for a single year only; for, though the manufacture did not greatly increase after this time until 1857, it continued to consume American wool at these rates or higher. Thus the prices of 1850 and of 1856 were:

	New York.			Boston.		
	Common.	Merino.	Pulled.	Fine.	Middle.	Long.
1850.........	33½	40½	34½	45	38	32
1856.........	32	42½	32½	57	48	41

It is not improbable that the high price of the material, as compared with reduced prices in other countries, did much to cause that slight decrease of the manufacture which has been observed, and the rapid growth of the cotton manufacture contributed to the same result. The only true remedy for this evil was to give a free supply of cheap foreign wool to mix with the American in use, and that remedy Congress applied in 1857, by a tariff admitting free all wool costing 18 cents a pound or less, which Mr. Stanton, of Ohio, denounced as "a blow at the wool-grower." How severe a blow, let the prices prove! The record shows that the prices of common and merino were higher during the whole of that period, 1857–'60, inclusive, except during the panic, than they were before the change of duty. Taking the New York record, because monthly prices are given, the average price of common wool was:

1853	41	1857	37
1854	32½	1858	30
1855	29½	1859	38
1856	33½	1860	36¾
Average	34½	Average	35¼

In spite of the reduced price during the panic in 1858, the average under this tariff was higher than before. Nor was this true at New York only, but in Western markets. The Chicago record, in spite of the very high price of 1853, gives the following average of prices for August:

1853	40	1857	36½
1854	25	1858	29½
1855	31½	1859	33½
1856	28½	1860	36
Average	31	Average	34

Returning to the New York table, it is interesting to compare the average prices for different periods.

	Common.	Merino.	Pulled.
1825–'28	28¼	42¾	27
1829–'32	26	44¾	38¼
1833–'41	34	49	42
1842–'46	23½	32	27
1847–'56	32	39½	31
1857–'60	35¼	44½	28½

It must now be conceded, since facts indisputably prove, that under the system of protective duties the price of wool has been lower than under non-protective tariffs; that the American wool has risen in price when the manufacture has been encouraged by the free admission of foreign wools, or by low duties on them, coupled with a revenue duty only on the woollen goods; and that it has been depressed in price whenever the manufacture has been retarded by high duties on foreign wool, or pushed by protection to attempt branches of the manufacture not naturally sustained by our own quality of wool. But to the wool-grower there is another consideration of especial importance. The essential thing is not that he shall get high prices in a single year; still less that he shall see high quotations for a single month; he needs, and must have, to make the culture of sheep profitable, a price remaining steadily at or above a certain limit, and never falling below it in any year so continuously that he cannot dispose of his clip of wool for that year at fair rates. The diagram will show at a glance when such periods of sustained prices have occurred. The first was from January, 1833, to February, 1840, eight years, during which common fleece never fell below 32 cents, except for a month in 1833, the winter of 1834, and a part of 1835. In any one of these eight consecutive years, the grower could obtain at least 32 cents for his common fleece, and in the same years he could obtain 49 cents for merino, though only in the last month of 1838. But this was a period of "free trade," during which cheap foreign wool was admitted free, and all duties were reduced. The next period of sustained high prices was from 1849 to 1861, thirteen years; and in any one of these years the grower could have sold common fleece for 30 cents, and the price fell below that mark only in parts of four years. Merino, also, never fell below 36 cents during that period, and in every year after 1849 the grower could have obtained at least 40 cents. But this was also a period of "free trade," and during the closing years wool worth less than 18 cents was admitted free. During the thirty-six years which these tables cover, no other periods of sustained prices occurred; and these facts, with the averages already given, prove that low duties on foreign wool, and free admission of cheap foreign wool, have secured higher and more steady prices to the American grower than any other form of tariff tried during that period.

But wool is consumed by manufacturing, and the manufacturer can pay more when prosperous than when embarrassed. Do not these facts prove that the wool manufacture possessed greater ability to consume wool at fair prices, under low and non-protective duties, than under protection? The domestic supply of wool has not controlled the price, for this country has never produced as much as it has consumed; the tendency has therefore been at all times to secure to the grower as high prices as the manufacturer could afford to pay. When he is able to pay 30 cents for common, as he was in the periods 1833–'40, and 1849–'61, then the farmer asks and obtains it; but when he is not able to consume wool profitably at that price, as he was not in the protective periods, 1824–'32 and 1843–'46, then the farmer has to accept less. The facts prove, then, that the manufacturers of wool in this country have been able to consume wool at the best prices when they have been least protected!

To those who still believe that protection must protect, the proposition will be somewhat startling. But it accords precisely with the incidents already observed in the history of the manufacture, and especially with the records of foreign importations. When high duties deprive the manufacturer of a variety of cheap foreign wools, he is placed at a fatal disadvantage as compared with manufacturers of other countries. Forced to use American wool exclusively, he must abandon the making of articles which can be most profitably made by mixture of wools, or must see himself undersold by foreign goods. When high tariffs prompt manufacturers to attempt work in which countries with free wool have the greatest advantage, they tempt them with delusive hopes. The foreign competition is shut out only for a short time. Soon the flood of foreign goods rushes in again, and the capitalist, who has been tempted to build on a quicksand, sinks.

It remains to consider the effect of recent tariffs. Protective duties were imposed in 1861 of 5 per cent. on wool worth 18 cents a pound or less, 3 cents a pound on wool worth 24 cents to 18 cents, and 9 cents a pound on wool worth over 24 cents. Under the act of 1865, wool worth $12\frac{1}{2}$ cents a pound or less bore a duty of 3 cents a pound. Under the act of 1866, the same wool was, by additional charges, held to have cost over 12 cents a pound. Under the act of 1867, the duties imposed were, on clothing or combing wools, value 32 cents per pound or less, 10 cents a pound and 11 per cent. ad valorem; on such wools of higher price, 12 cents a pound and 10 per cent.; on carpet wools, costing 12 cents a pound or less, 3 cents a pound, and costing over 12 cents, a duty of 6 cents a pound.

What effect have these extraordinary duties had upon the prices of American and foreign wool? It is admitted by all that the price of American wool is lower than it was in 1860. Mr. Greeley states the fact as a proof " that protection inevitably tends, by stimu'ating home production, to a reduction of price," but neglects to state that this same protection, within the very year in which his essays were written, instead of " stimulating home production," actually caused a reduction of forty millions of pounds in the clip; caused no less than four million sheep to be slaughtered, according to one statement of the Agricultural Bureau,* and the number actually killed must have been still greater; and, *in spite of this greatly-reduced production, also caused prices of wool to fall even lower than the ruinous rates of* 1868. These facts, which would, indeed, have sadly marred the beauty of his theory, Mr. Greeley remembered to forget. In a table, at the close of this chapter, will be found prices of different grades of wool at New York, October 31st, in 1860, and since; but the price of wool and the rate of gold have quite recently changed.

The prices, October 31, 1860, and December 25, 1869, gold then selling at 120, compare thus ·

	1860.	1869.	1869.
	Gold.	Currency.	Gold.
Saxony Fleece...... ...	54–58	55–60	46 –50
Full-blood Merino.......	48–52	47–53	39 –44
½ and ¾.............	40–46	46–50	38 –42
Extra Pulled...........	42–46	39–45	32½–37½
Superfine Pulled........	37–40	42–46	35 –38
No. 1 Pulled...........	28–30	30–33	25 –27½
California, unwashed....	24–32	26–30	22 –25

Every grade of American wool is selling at a price considerably lower in gold, and scarcely higher in currency, than it commanded at the close of the long free-trade period. The loss has been eight cents a pound on Saxony, eight and a half cents on blood merino, ten cents a pound on extra pulled, and about five cents on California wool. Inspection of the table referred to will show that meanwhile foreign goods have been somewhat increased in price in this country, in spite of the very great decrease in price elsewhere. African unwashed sold in New York for 9–18 cents, and washed from 16–28 cents, in 1860. African unwashed now sells for 16–19, and Cape of Good Hope unwashed for 33–34 cents. But the price at the place of export has decreased from 18 to 11 cents, and the foreign manufacturers have the benefit of that advantage, while ours do not. Mestiza then sold for 16–25 cents in New York, and it now sells for 20–30

---

* In another statement (March and April report, 1869) the decrease since 1866 is declared to be " not less than 20 per cent.," which would imply a slaughter of at least *eight millions.*

12

cents, but the cost to the foreign manufacturer has declined so greatly that good qualities are bought in England for sixpence a pound—just about the sum which our manufacturer would have to pay in duties alone.   Smyrna unwashed sold, in 1860, in New York, for 11–18 cents, and washed for 22–28, but the same qualities now cost 20–23 cents and 33–35 cents.   These facts show—

I. That, in the manufacture of any goods requiring foreign or a mixture of foreign wool, the foreign manufacturer has an advantage absolutely fatal to our industry.

II. That, in the manufacture of goods from American wool alone, the manufacturer lives only by depressing the price of American wool lower than was paid in 1860, under "free trade."

Paying eight to ten cents a pound less for wool than in 1860, the manufacturer ought to be able to make a yard of cloth eighteen to twenty-two cents cheaper; but he does not and cannot.   The foreign manufacturer, with wool still lower, can and does make cheaper cloth.   Hence, our mills meet a competition almost as great as they did in 1860; the people have to pay twice as much for their clothes as they should; and the unhappy, much-protected wool-grower slaughters his sheep.   He has been plundered doubly: ten cents a pound has been taken from the price of his wool, and twenty cents a yard has *not* been taken from the price of his cloth.   Yet there are farmers who meet in convention and resolve that the duty on wool ought not to be removed!   Do not these men show less good sense than the sheep whose wool they clip?   For the sheep never insist upon being shorn, and never solemnly resolve that they like it.

In this country we have never yet produced either the quantity or the variety of wool needed to sustain a vigorous manufacture, and the ability of the manufacturer to consume American wool at fair prices depends upon a free choice and ample supply of cheap foreign wool.   Those who advocate protection to the wool-grower maintain that it will cause the growth of other needed qualities.   But it is well known that the effort has been entirely unsuccessful; that the increase in production has been almost exclusively in those qualities which we already produce quite as largely as they can be consumed. The reason is plain: the farmer, rightly or wrongly, believes that the growth of those qualities is the most profitable, and he persists, and will persist, as long as duties encourage him to do so, in growing sheep for the wool alone, and in striving for weight instead of quality of fleece.   If a removal of all duties would make it no longer profitable in Eastern States to grow sheep, except for wool and mutton, the culture of breeds such as those which sustain the manufactures of England, France, and Germany, might soon be generally undertaken in the States where land is costly, and where proximity to markets secures a fair price for flesh and lambs. But high duties and hopes of profit only encourage the farmer to multiply his flocks of the American merino. Tariffs do not induce men to grow rye on land which will produce wheat in equal quantity. Neither tariffs on wool nor appeals from manufacturers will persuade the farmer to grow fleeces weighing three pounds as long as the duties promise him a profit on fleece and yolk weighing from seven to twenty pounds.

Why should we encourage, at public expense, the growing of sheep in Eastern States for the wool alone? Can it be that this culture is the most useful employment of land as costly and labor as dear as ours? We have in Texas, New Mexico, and California, lands less valuable, and peculiarly adapted to the sheep-culture, and thither, if no artificial system prevented, the growing of sheep, for wool only, would naturally be transferred, while the English breeds of sheep would be found in well-settled States, and the manufacture would have a solid footing. Is it indeed desirable for a great and well-settled country to go back as far as possible toward a patriarchal form of industry? Ought the country to pay men for employing costly land and costly labor in such a fashion? To " protect American industry," must we employ it as nearly as possible after the methods of the South American or African pampas? We are simply trying to prevent a natural progress from semi-barbarism to the highest civilization; trying to prevent the growing of sheep in Texas and New Mexico, where it will always be profitable, and to force in New England, New York, and Ohio, a growth of sheep for wool only. Whatever the purpose, eight years of protection has only induced an excessive development of a culture which, in many localities, is a sheer waste of land and labor. Nature frowns upon all attempts to arrest the progress of mankind. Disaster after disaster has driven the farmer to Congress for more aid, which when granted, has only proved a new Pandora's box of evils. Meanwhile, he has been taught to rely much upon Congress, and little upon common-sense. Such lessons have to be unlearned, and experience is a severe teacher.

In brief, the protection of wool and woollen manufactures has never enabled us to shut out any important part of foreign importations, but has retarded natural growth in the working of American and foreign wools. It has never caused the growth of new and needed varieties of wool, but has only hindered a natural adaptation of sheep-culture to the condition and needs of the country. More than once it has tempted the capitalist into ruinous undertakings, and the grower into a waste of land and labor. It has taxed the people many millions, has taken money from the farmer's pocket, and has deprived both grower and manufacturer of that measure of solid prosperity which, under low duties and with free wool, both had attained.

PRICE OF WOOL.

Common Fleece, New York, Highest and Lowest Each Month, with Average for Year, and Duty.

Year	Duty.	Jan.	Feb.	Mar.	April.	May.	June.	July.	Aug.	Sept.	Oct.	Nov.	Dec.	Average.
1825	20 p.c.	30@35	30@35	30@35	30@38	30@38	30@33	30@38	30@38	30@38	30@38	30@38	30@38	33 1/2
1826		30@38	30@38	30@38	30@38	28@30	28@30	28@30	28@30	28@30	28@30	28@30	20@30	30
1827		20@30	20@30	20@30	20@30	20@30	20@30	20@30	20@30	20@30	20@30	20@30	20@30	25
1828		20@30	20@30	20@30	20@30	20@30	20@30	20@30	20@30	20@30	20@30	20@30	20@29	25
1829	4-45	18@27	18@25	18@25	18@25	18@25	18@25	18@25	18@25	18@25	18@25	18@25	18@25	21 1/3
1830	4-50	18@25	18@25	16@22	16@22	16@22	16@22	16@22	20@30	20@30	20@30	20@30	20@30	22
1831		20@30	20@28	20@28	20@28	20@25	25@35	25@35	25@35	25@35	25@35	25@35	25@35	27 1/2
1832		25@35	25@35	25@35	25@35	25@35	20@30	20@25	20@25	20@25	25@30	25@30	30@35	27 3/4
1833	4-40	30@35	30@35	30@35	30@35	30@35	30@35	27@32	30@35	30@35	30@35	30@35	30@35	31 1/2
1834	4-38	30@35	30@35	30@35	30@35	30@35	30@33	30@33	30@33	25@30	25@30	25@30	25@30	30 1/4
1835	4-36	25@30	25@30	25@30	30@35	30@35	30@35	35@40	35@40	35@40	35@40	35@40	35@40	33 5/6
1836	4-34	35@40	35@40	35@40	40@50	40@50	40@50	40@50	40@50	40@50	40@50	40@50	40@45	43
1837	4-32	40@50	40@50	40@50	40@50	40@50	40@50	40@50	40@50	40@50	40@50	40@50	28@32	43 1/3
1838	4-30	28@32	28@32	28@32	28@32	28@32	28@32	28@32	28@32	28@32	28@32	28@32	37@40	30 5/6
1839	4-28	37@40	37@40	37@40	37@40	37@40	37@40	37@40	37@40	37@40	37@40	37@40	37@40	38 1/3
1840	4-26	30@35	30@35	30@35	30@35	30@35	30@35	20@25	20@23	20@23	20@23	25@30	25@30	28
1841	4-24	25@30	25@30	25@30	25@30	25@30	25@30	25@30	25@30	25@30	25@30	25@30	20@24	27
1842	4-22	18@22	18@22	18@22	18@22	18@20	18@20	18@20	18@20	18@20	18@20	18@20	18@20	19 1/3
1843	3-30	18@20	18@20	18@20	18@20	18@20	19@21	20@22	20@22	20@22	20@22	22@24	22@24	20 1/3
1844	3-30	25@27	27@29	27@29	27@29	27@29	27@29	27@29	35@37	35@37	32@34	32@34	28@30	30
1845	3-30	28@30	28@30	28@30	28@30	28@30	27@29	24@26	24@26	24@25	24@25	24@27	26@28	27
1846	3-30	26@28	26@28	26@28	26@28	26@28	25@27	18@20	20@22	20@21	20@21	20@21	22@24	23 1/2
1847	30 p.c.	22@24	22@25	23@25	25@27	25@27	25@27	25@27	26@28	26@28	28@30	28@30	28@30	26 1/4
1848		28@30	28@30	28@30	28@30	27@30	27@30	24@26	22@25	20@22	20@22	23@24	25@27	26 1/4
1849		25@27	28@30	30@31	30@31	30@31	26@28	27@30	26@29	28@30	30@32	30@32	30@32	29 1/4
1850		30@32	33@35	33@35	32@34	31@33	30@31	30@33	30@33	32@35	32@35	32@35	32@35	32 1/2
1851		33@36	35@38	39@41	39@41	39@41	35@38	35@38	35@38	35@38	31@33	30@32	30@32	35 1/6
1852		30@32	30@32	30@32	30@32	26@27	26@27	26@27	31@34	31@34	40@42	36@38	36@38	32
1853		38@40	40@44	40@44	40@44	40@44	40@44	40@44	40@44	40@44	40@44	38@40	38@40	41
1854		38@40	36@38	36@38	36@38	36@38	33@35	30@33	28@30	27@30	25@28	25@28	25@28	32 1/3
1855		24@27	24@27	24@27	24@27	30@34	30@34	30@34	30@34	30@34	30@34	30@34	30@34	29 1/2
1856		30@34	30@34	30@34	33@38	33@38	33@38	30@36	30@36	30@34	30@34	31@37	31@37	33 1/3
1857		33@37	33@37	40@44	40@44	38@42	38@42	36@38	36@38	36@38	30@35	30@35	30@35	37
1858	24 p.c.	27@32	27@32	27@32	27@32	27@32	27@32	27@32	27@32	27@32	27@32	30@32	30@32	30
1859		36@40	36@40	36@40	42@45	42@45	34@38	34@38	35@38	35@38	35@38	35@38	38@40	38
1860		38@40	38@40	38@40	34@38	34@38	34@38	34@38	34@38	34@38	34@38	34@38	34@38	36 5/8
1861		30@34	30@34	30@34	33@34	33@34	33@34	28@30	22@25	28@30	28@30	28@42	43@45	32 1/3
1862	9 cts.	47	47	40@42	40@42	40@42	40@42	42@44	45@51	58@60	62@65	62@65	62@65	50
1863		62@65	65@70	75@80	75@80	70@73	65@67	65@67	62@63	62@63	62@63	65@67	68@70	67 5/8

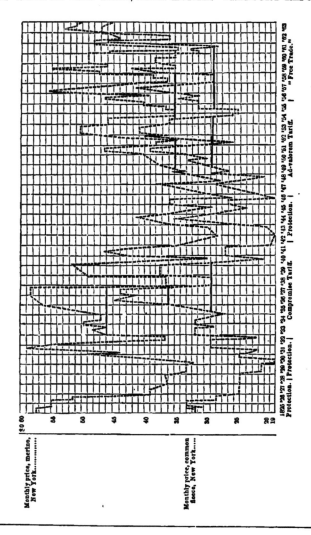

Highest price, merino, for two years, 1836–'37, 56 cents; five years, 1832–'37, 48 cents; twelve years, 1849–'61, 36 cents; common, two years, 1836–'37, 37 cents; five years, 1835–'39, thirty cents; six years, 1855–'61, twenty-nine and a half cents; six years, 1849–'54, twenty-six cents; seven and a half years, 1833–'39, twenty-eight cents.

WOOL—NEW-YORK QUOTATIONS REDUCED TO GOLD.

	1860.	1861.	1862.	1868.	1864.	1865.	1866.	1869.
Am. Sax'y fleece	54@58	45@48	46 @48	49½@53	42 @46	47 @50	41½@45	40½@44
full-bl'd meri'o	48@52	44@48	46 @48½	46 @47½	36 @41	44 @47	35 @39	38½@41½
Nat'e, ¼ & ½ bl.	34@46	38@44	48 @50	41½@45½	35½@39½	40½@44	30 @33½	33 @37
Extra pulled....	42@46	38@40	44 @46	46 @47½	44 @46	45 @47	35 @38	29½@33
Superfine "	37@40	36@40	43 @46	45 @46	35½@39½	44 @45	31½@32½	31 @34
No. 1 "	28@30	32@34	37 @38½	33 @36	31 @33	33½@37	23½@27	27 @29½
California,unw'd	24@32	27@32	29 @36	33 @34	24 @28½	25 @27	22 @27	17 @19½
" common, "	10@20	12	15½@25	26½@28	13 @22	13½@16	13 @16½	17½@20
S. A. Mestiza, "	16@25	16@20	19 @23	20 @21	22 @24	21½@25	21½@25	20 @24½
" common, "	10@13	14@17	14 @18	10 @13	13 @20	12 @15½	12 @15½	13 @15
Cordova	21@22	21@25	27 @31	25 @26½	28½@31	29 @32½	29 @32	20 @23
Valparaiso......	12@13	13@15	15½@18	14	16½@18½	17½@18	18 @20	15 @17½
African, washed.	16@28	20@30	31 @38½	26½@30	26 @44	23½@30	23½@30	27 @29½
African, unw'd..	9@18	16@20	21½@27	13 @23	18½@28½	10 @17	10 @16½	......
Mexican, "	11@14	12@14	19 @27	14½@15	18½	13 @17	13½@16½	12½@15
Smyrna, "	11@18	17@18	15½@21½	14½@18½	20	15 @17	14½@16½	......
" washed .	22@28	20@26	31 @35	26½@33	28½	23½@30	23½@30	......

The quotation for 1869 is that of September 11th; for the other years the prices of October 31st are given, taken from the *Chronicle*, New York.

PRICE OF WOOL.

YEAR.	NEW YORK.—AVERAGE OF MONTHLY RATES.			BOSTON.—G. LIVERMORE'S TABLE.		
	Common.	Merino.	Pulled.	Fine.	Middle.	Long.
1825...............	30@38	50@62	25@44	60	42	31
1826...............	28@30	35@75	18@33	42	38	32
1827...............	20@30	3 @45	15@28	40	42	26
1828...............	20@30	35@40	20@34	46	38	30
1829...............	18@25	32@36	18@33	41	34	29
1830...............	20@30	35@55	25@40	62	52	41
1831...............	25@35	45@70	*50@58	70	59	49
1832...............	25@30	40@45	37@40	53	43	33
1833...............	30@35	44@57	51@54	66	57	45
1834...............	25@30	44@52	40@42	61	51	40
1835...............	35@40	50@65	53@55	65	58	45
1836...............	40@50	50@68	52@58	69	59	49
1837...............	40@50	50@68	35@40	57	47	39
1838...............	28@32	37@40	36@38	51	44	35
1839...............	37@40	50@55	40@45	55	49	40
1840...............	20@23	35@37	27@28	48	40	35
1841...............	25@30	42@45	34@36	48	42	34
1842...............	18@20	28@30	26@28	42	37	30
1843...............	20@22	30@32	25@26	35	30	26
1844...............	32@34	40@42	34@35	46	38	31
1845...............	24@25	30@33	28@29	41	35	30
1846...............	20@21	27@28	22@23	40	33	27
1847...............	28@30	36@38	28@30	46	39	30
1848...............	20@22	27@30	25@26	36	32	26
1849...............	30@32	37@40	29@31	43	37	30
1850...............	32@35	39@42	34@35	45	38	32
1851...............	31@33	38@40	33@34	46	41	35
1852...............	40@42	44@46	35@36	49	43	37
1853...............	40@44	49@53	40@42	57	51	47
1854...............	25@28	35@37	25@28	45	40	34
1855...............	30@34	37@38	23@25	49	38	34
1856...............	30@34	32@45	30@35	57	48	41
1857...............	30@35	40@45	25@28	58	52	41
1858...............	27@32	37@41	25@27	50	41	35
1859...............	35@38	46@48	30@33	59	46	38
1860...............	34@38	48@52	28@30	50	45	39

* Pulled No. 1 from this point forward.

CHAPTER XIII.

IRON—HISTORY OF THE IRON MANUFACTURE PRIOR TO 1833.

WHAT is "the iron interest?" Is it confined to the taking of ore from the mountains; to the reduction of ore, by smelting, to raw iron, called pig-metal; or to the preparation of that metal, by further processes, for use as bar-iron, wrought-iron, or steel? Does it not include far more? Does not the whole business of casting iron into forms for use, and of manufacture of hardware, tools, cutlery, and wire, deserve consideration as part of "the iron interest?" Do not the making of nails and bolts, horseshoes, safes and locks, the shaping of sheet-iron into pipe, or the working of iron at the blacksmith's forge; the manufacture of agricultural implements, and of all forms of machinery, steam-engines especially included—do not all these deserve to be remembered whenever "the iron interest" is mentioned? Are not these, indeed, the very branches of that interest which most affect the welfare of the country?

To certain persons it seems otherwise, if we may judge by their words or acts. Whenever "the iron interest" is named, they seem to think only of pig-iron. To them, a large production and a high price of pig-iron seem to represent an approach to the millennium. Whenever protection is abroad in the land, it seizes upon the production of pig-iron as the tender infant which stands in greatest need of careful nursing. By these persons, the idea that an extravagant and unnatural price of pig may do injury to the iron interest as a whole is treated as the most absurd of all notions, and a suggestion that lower duties on pig-iron may benefit the iron interest as a whole is regarded as conclusive proof that its author has been " bought with British gold ! "

If some gardener, anxious to make his tree bear fine fruit, should dig up its roots and wrap them all closely in bandages to "protect" them from the soil and moisture, he would do a thing not more unreasonable than those are doing who make pig-iron costly, and call that " protecting the iron interest! "

In 1860, there were employed in all branches of iron manufacture 198,532 persons, and its aggregate product was valued at $256,137,736. In the mining and smelting of iron—the production of pig-metal—there were employed 19,133 persons, and their product was valued at $23,275,412. Less than one-tenth of the hands employed, less than one-eleventh of the product, belong to the making of pig. In forging and rolling iron, and making steel—in the preparation of iron—were then employed 22,903 persons, and the value of products was $38,417,099. As the production of pig employs 9½ per cent. of the hands, and yields 9 per cent. of the product of the whole iron interest, the preparation of iron employs 12 per cent. of the hands, and yields 15 per cent. of the product. Looking next to the branches which may more properly be termed manufactures of iron, we find that these are of two classes : those which are supposed to be sustained by protective duties ; and those which in the nature of things cannot be thus sustained because exposed to no competition, or which have been so developed in this country that they need no aid. In a classification of the iron interest (page 187) will be found the entries in the census-tables of 1860, arranged in four divisions : " Production," " Preparation," " Protected," and " Non-protected Branches." It will at once be granted that, if the non-protected branches cannot be aided by duties, they must be retarded or injured by any increase in the cost of iron. To these, therefore, if the classification is correct, the protective system can only do harm, if it increases the cost of the material. And these embrace more than half of the hands employed, and yield more than half of the product, of the whole iron interest.

Concerning the correctness of the classification, it may be remarked that in the making of all machinery our artisans are exposed to no competition ; that when, iron has been of moderate price, American locomotives have been shipped to Europe for use in England and Prussia ; that, sewing and other machines are even now largely exported to Europe ; that American fire-arms are not only of known excellence, but are made by machinery not equalled anywhere else for ingenuity and effectiveness ; that our agricultural implements have proved their superiority in European expositions, and the history presently to be reviewed will show that dependence upon foreign manufactures of this class was long ago prevented by the superiority of our products. The same fact will appear in regard to all cut nails—indeed, we export of them largely even when the raw iron is costly. The workers in sheet-iron are not separated in the census-tables, and in fact cannot be, from the workers in tin ; and while the making of sheet-iron can be protected, the shaping of it into pipe or other forms evidently cannot be exposed to any competition. Nor can the blacksmith be affected by duties except when they increase the cost of his tools and materials.

In general terms, then, it may be said that one-half of the iron interest cannot be aided by any form of protective duties on similar products, but must be injured if the cost of its material is increased.

Again, one-quarter of that interest, comprising those branches classed as "protected," must be injured if raw iron, bar or wrought iron, or steel, is rendered more costly.   Whether this injury can be compensated by duties on foreign manufactured products, must·be ascertained.

Again, one-eighth of the iron interest, engaged in the rolling and forging of iron, and the making of steel, must be injured if raw iron is rendered more costly, but its products may be correspondingly enhanced in price.

Finally, less than one-tenth of the iron interest—the production of pig-metal—if benefited at all in the increased price of its product—must be so benefited at the expense of injury to more than nine-tenths of the iron interest, and to a whole nation of consumers of iron and its products; or, stating it more exactly, the relation of the different classes, measured by number of hands and by value of aggregate product, is as follows :

	Hands.	Product.
Production (pig)................	9¼ per cent.	9 per cent.
Preparation (bar, etc.)............	12 "	15 "
Manufacture (protected)..........	24 " ·	25 "
Manufacture (not protected).......	54½ "	51 "
	100 "	100 "

This is "the iron interest," with pig for its roots, bar for its trunk, castings, etc., for its boughs, and the non-protected manufactures for its richest fruit, and our protecting gardeners have bandaged roots, trunk, and boughs, to make it bear more largely.   Has the experiment succeeded ?   In reviewing the history of this interest, it is important to keep in mind the relation of these classes to each other, and to inquire not only whether the production of pig alone, or of pig and bar iron, has been increased, but whether the production of wealth by the manufacture of iron in all forms has been increased by protective duties.

The fashioning of iron into shapes for use began in this country as early as 1646, when Joseph Jenks made the first castings in New England of which we find record.   In 1652 there were established in Massachusetts blast-furnaces, a bloomery, and forge-hammer; in 1655 there was granted to Jenks a patent for "an improved scythe," which, in every essential feature, was like the implement now in use ; in 1666 people skilled in wire-drawing were found, and in 1731 there were six furnaces for hollow ware in New England, nineteen forges, or bloomeries, one slitting-mill, and a nail-factory. Before the Revolutionary War, in Massachusetts, as in other colonies, there were made edge tools, augers, scythes, shovels, "better and cheaper than the English," nails, muskets, cannon, and almost every kind of domestic casting.

During all this time this industry, then really in its infancy, was exposed to the full force of a foreign competition, not only unchecked by any duties whatever, but even favored by British officials and British laws. If it grew so rapidly and vigorously, even then, can it be supposed that it would not now survive the removal of artificial aid? So rapid was its growth that the manufacturers of England became alarmed, and besought Parliament to protect *them* against the infant. By the act of 1750, England absolutely prohibited the erection of any slitting or rolling mills, plating-forges, or steel-furnaces, in the colonies, and prohibited the exportation from them of any manufactured products, but, with a greater wisdom than we have since shown, encouraged the exporting of pig and bar iron to England, that the British manufacturer might have his raw material both cheap and abundant. In fact, as early as 1718, raw iron had been exported to England from Maryland, and by 1730 the quantity exported from that colony, Virginia, and Pennsylvania, to England, was over 2,250 tons. In 1732–'33 we began to export bar-iron to England, and from that time until the Revolution a quantity of pig and bar was thus exported every year. Prior to 1750 the iron thus exported paid a duty of 3s. 9d. a ton, and, when it was proposed to repeal this impost, and admit American iron free, the iron-masters protested that their works at Sheffield and elsewhere, erected at great·expense, would be ruined, the laborers be rendered destitute, or forced to emigrate, and "the plenty and cheapness of wood would enable American iron to undersell the British, and thus ruin the trade, while the iron manufacture, rendered wholly dependent on so distant and precarious a source for material, would probably decay, and reduce thousands of workmen to want and misery!" How often have we since heard from American lips the same dismal prophecies! It is the old cry of a threatened monopoly, pleading anxious regard for the welfare of labor. Were these men honest? Every bit as honest as the men who say that American furnaces would now be closed by the repeal of duties on pig-iron!

The act of 1750 encouraged the importation of American bar, but prohibited the taking it ten miles from London. In 1756 the manufacturers petitioned for repeal of this prohibition, and, again, the owners of 109 forges in England and Wales represented that the American would compete with British iron, the making of which would be stopped, "and a great number of families, dependent thereon, be reduced to beggary." It was answered that a manufacture is much more valuable than the raw materials, and that, as these could not be produced at home in such quantity and at such a price as to sustain the manufacture, it was the duty of the legislature to encourage their free importation if it should arrest their production on the island; that progress of other nations made it more than ever necessary to obtain materials at a lower price, or lose the manufacture of fine articles of steel and iron; the only way to do this was to reduce the duty on foreign iron, " *or make it necessary for the iron-masters to reduce their price by raising up a rival in America.*" Is there not matter here which an American Congress to-day may well study ?

The prohibition was repealed, and the importation of American iron to England increased from 3,441 tons in 1755 to 5,303 tons in 1771, and then began to decrease. It is not necessary to add that this flood of foreign iron did not put out British furnace-fires; but, forcing British monopolists to put down the price of the material, it did build up in England a most powerful manufacture.

Not only before the war, but after the Revolution, and before the adoption of the Constitution or of any national tariff, our manufacture was exposed to the full force of British competition. The most abundant evidence exists that our industry was not only not crushed by this competition, but made very great and rapid progress. In the making of machinery our independence was thus early established; even then, before the invention of nail-machines, the making of nails was so extensively carried on, that there was a large surplus exported, both from Pennsylvania and New England; and, in making fire-arms and all forms of farming implements, American superiority was quickly demonstrated. Nor was the country prevented from commencing the higher branches of the manufacture. Before the adoption of the Constitution, the importations of steel had been materially reduced by the progress of our own industry, in spite of open competition with other countries. A single furnace in Pennsylvania was making 230 tons of steel in a year; and at that time we find it recorded that "a dangerous rivalry to British iron interests was apprehended in the American States—not only in the production of rough iron, from the cheapness of fuel and the quality of the iron, but also in articles of steel cutlery and other finished products, from the dexterity of the Americans in the manufacture of scythes, axes, nails, etc. In these they exceeded the French and most European nations, as well in the style and finish as in the quality of their articles, being made from the best iron." That the manufacture was not prostrated after the peace, Secretary Hamilton shows in his elaborate report of 1791, saying that iron-works were carried on more numerously and more advantageously than formerly, and the price of iron had risen because of the increase of the demand for the manufacture, from about $64, the average before the Revolution, to about $80. He particularly mentions that, in the manufacture of steel, several new enterprises on an extensive scale "had been lately set on foot." If this manufacture had here such natural advantages that in its very infancy it alarmed English manufacturers of the higher grades, and, though exposed to wholly unchecked competition with foreign industry, actually advanced with such vigor and rapidity, before the adoption of any tariff laws whatever, as to produce nails for exportation, machines unmatched in excellence, implements of acknowledged superiority, and scythes and axes equal to the best of European make, is it not the height of folly to say that it would never have existed, or could not now be sustained, without protective duties?

The first tariff framed by the founders of the government, though intended to give protection in some sense, imposed no higher duties than those upon iron, namely, 7½ per cent. on bar, bolt, and pig iron, one cent a pound on nails, and one-half cent a pound on steel. In 1792 the duty on steel was raised to $20 a ton, and on iron cables to $30 a ton; and in 1794 the tariff on rolled iron and steel was fixed at 15 per cent., on hardware 10 per cent., and on all other manufactures of iron at 15 per cent. These low rates were maintained until 1816, when protection of a very different character was demanded and granted.

From 1790 to 1800 the manufacture of iron steadily increased, though no accurate information of its progress is obtainable. Nor are there any records of the importations of iron at that time. But we find recorded the opening of twenty-one furnaces in Pennsylvania alone within that time, one of them yielding 2,800 tons per annum. It appears that in 1798 Lancaster County had 3 furnaces, 11 forges, and produced 1,200 tons of pig, and as much of bar; that Berks had 6 furnaces, and as many forges; that Chester had 6 forges, and produced 1,000 tons of bar-iron; and that, patents for nail-machines having been granted in 1794, there were three factories in operation in Philadelphia by 1797. In New Jersey also, in

1794, there were produced 1,200 tons of bar-iron, "besides hollow-ware and castings, and iron in pigs and bars was exported to a large amount. Only eight years later, the manufacture in that State had more than doubled. There were then produced 3,000 tons of bar-iron and 3,500 tons of pig, and four rolling and slitting mills were in operation. But in that same year, 1802, the citizens concerned in the manufacture petitioned Congress for increased duties on foreign products. We are not forced to look far for the explanation. It happens to be recorded that in 1789, before any duties had been imposed, the price of pig-iron was £6 10s., Pennsylvania money, equivalent to $17.33⅓, while in 1800 pig-metal was worth £10 a ton, or $26.67⅔. This enhanced price, whether caused in part by the duties, or altogether by increased demand for iron to be used in manufactures, had a double effect. First, it stimulated the building of those furnaces which we have seen starting up in every direction, and thus caused New Jersey to more than double its product of pig and bar iron in eight years. But, second, it rendered all manufacturers of iron less able to cope with foreign competition, for, the material costing more, they could no longer produce castings, nails, and other articles, as cheaply. Hence, a cry to the government for aid. Nor was it without excuse; for we find that in 1801 there were imported of nails 3,120,691 pounds, of spikes 280,237 pounds, and of steel 14,844 cwt. In 1790, as Secretary Hamilton stated in his report, there were imported only 1,800,000 pounds of nails, and he recommended a duty, "to put an end to this importation." It will be remembered, moreover, that a duty was granted, on nails one cent a pound, higher than on any other form of iron. And it will also be remembered that within the same decade the manufacture had been greatly improved by the invention of better machinery in this country than any other possessed. Yet, the importation had increased from 1,800,000 pounds to 3,120,691 pounds! Such was the effect of the first effort to "put an end to an importation" by duties! The iron had risen in price from $17 to $26 a ton, and bar-iron, protected now by duties of 15 per cent., had also risen in like proportion, and therefore the cost of domestic nails had risen more than the one cent a pound of protective duty, and the importation had increased. No better illustration can be desired of the workings of the tariff. Nor can it be supposed that other manufactures had fared better, for that of nails was justly regarded as most firmly established before the war.

Although the New Jersey men complained, and the manufacture was, no doubt, relatively retarded, it still continued to increase.

New works were opened; in 1805 there were 16 furnaces and 37 forges in Pennsylvania, and on the west side of the Alleghanies 11 forges and about the same number of furnaces; and 10 more furnaces, three forges, and a bloomery, were in that year erected in the State. In 1807 there were in Pittsburg four nail-factories, one making 100 tons of nails a year. And yet in that year the importation of nails was about as large as in 1801, being 3,072,238 pounds, and of spikes 284,742 pounds, and of steel 10,604 cwt. The importation of steel had decreased about one-third. In the next year, 1808, foreign trade was interrupted by the embargo, but in 1810 the foreign importations were about the same, except of nails, 2,112,223 pounds. At this point, Mr. Gallatin, Secretary of the Treasury, in a report on manufactures, classed that of iron as "firmly established," and estimated the quantity of bar-iron produced to be 40,000 tons, against about 9,000 imported. But he observes that a reduction of the duty on Russia iron was asked for by the rolling and slitting mills. The same difficulty of which the nail-makers had complained in 1802, namely, the cost of the raw material, had now, in 1810, extended to the rolling-mills. As to the nail business, he said that the use of machinery had extended throughout the country, and about 280 tons were already exported annually, but we still imported about 1,500 tons of wrought nails and spikes. The manufactures of iron were principally agricultural implements, blacksmith's-work, anchors, shovels, spades, axes, scythes, and other edge tools, saws, bits, and stirrups, and every sort of machine and other castings, and a great variety of coarser products, but cutlery and the finer hardware, and steel-work, were almost entirely imported. The value of iron imported was nearly four millions, and the value of iron produced and manufactured was from twelve to fifteen millions. To the important information of this report we have also added the census of that year, which stated the number of furnaces as 153, producing 53,908 tons of iron, and 4 steel-furnaces producing 917 tons of steel, whereas we imported only 550. In the same year, notwithstanding the duty, we imported 852,949 pounds of "anchors and sheet-iron," and 759,337 pounds of "sheet or hoop iron."

These statistics give a very fair idea of the condition of the iron manufacture before the war which soon followed. Until after the close of the war, neither duties nor importations affected our industry, but the great inflation and depreciation of our paper-money currency caused enormous prices, and prepared the way for inevitable disaster when the war ended.

High prices invite the seller, we reasoned in speaking of imports. This was forcibly illustrated after the War of 1812, when our industries, which had prospered before the war with little protection, were suddenly checked by importations of foreign products. Our people imagined that the whole world had conspired to ruin our industry by selling goods below cost. The truth was, that it cost less to produce in other countries, where lower prices prevailed. But, in the vain effort to arrest this influx of foreign products, the tariff of 1816 was adopted, with increased duties in 1818. The attempt failed. Nothing could stop the flood except a return to the natural level of prices, and that was precisely what people dreaded. In spite of the tariff, it came, and with it the prostration of manufactures in 1819 and 1820.

It is to be regretted that complete and reliable statistics do not exist of the immediate effect of foreign importations upon the iron business after the war, and prior to the tariff of 1816. It is said that 21,000 tons of British iron were imported in 1815, and a like amount in 1816, of which only 7,600 tons were bar-iron. It is not strange, for in 1816 Congress authorized a contract for 500 tons of iron for use in the navy, at a cost of $52,558, or $105 a ton. In 1818 iron had fallen at the seaports to about $100, but was still worth at Pittsburg $190 to 200, and at Cincinnati $200 to 220. In the latter city and at Zanesville castings and hollow-ware were worth $120 to 130. These facts show how the great depreciation of the currency affected our business. Where our industries were brought at once face to face with foreign prices, the evil was more quickly corrected, and it may be questioned whether, if that natural corrective had been left uninterrupted by legislation, the disasters which followed would not have been less severe and prolonged. It was inevitable that prices should fall before a healthy business could be done, and the great reduction which did follow—flour from $15 a barrel in 1817 to $5 in 1819; bar-iron from $140 to $80; pig-iron to $30, and castings to $75 a ton—was neither caused nor averted by any tariff. It appears, however, that the iron manufacture was by no means stopped by importations. New establishments, including some of great importance, went into operation in this very time of greatest depression. The census returns showed that thirty iron-works—fourteen blast-furnaces and sixteen bloomeries—had been built in Pennsylvania within ten years; new and important branches of the industry had been commenced, and the reduction of the price of pig and bar iron, and consequently of the profits of these branches, though depressing to them, was an encouragement to the manufacture of áll finished products.

The imports, in these years, were comparatively small. They included, in all, less than 8,200 tons of iron, against 21,634 in 1816. Of pig-iron there was imported only 329 tons—surely not enough to control the price! Of bar there was imported rolled 59,385 cwt. and hammered 389,797 cwt.; of castings only 6,202 cwt.; of anchors only 79,252 pounds—and yet it was said that excessive importations at this time stopped the manufacture of anchors at Baltimore—of sheet-iron only 12,520 cwt., of wire 127,866 pounds, of tacks and brads 23,506, of steel 7,802 cwt., and of nails only 220,682 pounds, and spikes 38,625 pounds. These figures do not indicate that the importation was heavy enough, or of such a character as, to prostrate the manufacture, and its depression must be referred to the general prostration of business, attending the contraction of currency and the return to a specie basis.

With reference to this period Mr. Henry C. Carey says:

In 1810, prior to our second war with England, our furnaces numbered 153, with an average yield of 36 tons, giving a total produce of 54,000 tons. Protection afforded by the war caused a considerable increase, but there exist no reliable statistics in regard thereto. Peace in 1815 was followed by the so-called revenue tariff of 1817, and that in turn, as is so well known, by the closing of factories and furnaces; by the ruin of manufacturers and merchants; by the discharge of workmen everywhere; by the stoppage of banks; by the bankruptcy of States; by the transfer under the sheriff's hammer of a large portion of the real estate of the Union; and by an impoverishment of our whole people general beyond all former precedent. The demand for iron had so far ceased that the manufacture was in a state of ruin so complete, that not only had it lost all that had it gained in time of war, but had, as was then believed, greatly retrograded. In placing it, as I now shall do, near the point to which, by aid of non-intercourse and embargo acts, it had been brought in 1810, I am, as I feel assured, doing it entire justice. *Such with little change continued to be the state of things until the passage of the semi-protective tariff of* 1824.

It is for readers to judge whether such a statement, wholly suppressing the vital fact of currency inflation and depreciation, and the destruction of paper-issuing banks, is a fair account of the events of this period. Mr. Carey surely was not ignorant of the fact that the enormous issues of paper during the war, and the creation of new banks, many of them financially worthless, had disordered the currency and increased prices most unnaturally; nor was he ignorant of the fact that the failure of such banks, the depreciation and ultimate abandonment of such a currency, its shrinkage from $110,000,000

13

in 1816 to $45,000,000 in 1819, and the return from fictitious
to legitimate prices, must in any case have produced severe revulsion, prostration of business, and embarrassment to all productive
industry.   If he knew these facts, it would surely have been more
candid, not to say honest, had he mentioned them as causes, in part
if not altogether, of the disaster described.   Nor are there known to
the writer any statistics which justify the statement that the manufacture "lost all that it had gained in time of war."   On the contrary, it appears that many new iron-works were established after
the war, and prior to the general failure of banks in 1819–'20,
among which may be mentioned a factory of steam and fire engines,
mill machinery and steamboat engines, in Cincinnati in 1817, and
another machine-factory in 1818, while another in operation at the
same time employed eighty hands.   The manufacture of chain cables,
by Cotton & Hill, was commenced at the same time at Boston;
and the Hunt Brothers, in Litchfield County, Conn., made anchors
of 8,000 and 9,000 pounds, and screws for the largest machinery,
while anchors were made at Baltimore for 8 and 9 cents a pound.
That there was great depression in the production of iron, caused by
decrease of prices, is stated, but the fact that new establishments
were started for the manufacture of iron accords with the reasonable
supposition that cheaper raw material would naturally stimulate
both manufacture and use.

Nor is it possible to reconcile the last-quoted statement of Mr.
Carey with recorded facts.   The iron production and manufacture
had both begun to revive before the year 1824.   This was in part
due, no doubt, to the opening of mines of anthracite coal, already
used in the working of iron to some extent, and the completion of
the Lehigh Canal, which forwarded to Philadelphia its first supply
of 365 tons in 1820, and in the year 1822 the canal brought its first
supply from the Schuylkill region, of 1,480 tons.   By the year 1824,
when the tariff was passed to which Mr. Carey ascribes all the subsequent progress, the quantity of coal forwarded from the Lehigh
region was 9,541 tons, and the whole amount was 11,108 tons.
This increase is a proof as it was a cause of rapid growth of the
manufacture of iron, which revived as soon as the currency had
reached a solid basis.   Numerous inventions in the production and
manufacture of iron were at that time made, as the patent records
show, prior to the change of tariff, and these contributed to the increased growth of that interest.   In 1822 Bishop records the first
extensive use of iron pipes for the water-works of Philadelphia, and

states that the iron-works in Brandon, Vermont, in that year produced a very superior quality of shovels, "said to be better and tougher than those imported," while "Mr. Conant's works, *recently* put in operation," made castings to the amount of 100 tons annually, including stoves so popular that the demand exceeded the supply.   Incidents like these do not indicate that the manufacture waited for the tariff before it revived.   Again, of 1823, Bishop says: "With the general revival of business about this time, the building of steamboats was resumed at Marietta," and "the business received a new impulse in the other river-towns."   In the same year the first railway act was passed, to give communication from Philadelphia to Lancaster County, of whose iron-works we have seen statistics. This does not indicate that all the furnaces there were idle, and waiting for the tariff!   In New Hampshire, in the same year, "fifty-four trip-hammers were at work, and a rolling and slitting mill and nail-works and machine-shops were in course of erection," *not* waiting for the tariff!   The first steam printing-press was put in operation in the same year ; a pin-machine was in operation in New York which would make thirty pins a minute, the best machines in London then making only fourteen, less perfectly ; and a cutler in New York used New Brunswick steel for penknife-blades, which he made superior to any of English blistered steel.   In the same year surveys were made for the Delaware and Raritan and Morris Canals, the latter giving access to the anthracite mines of Pennsylvania, and a cheap outlet for the iron of that region, which at that time had three furnaces and fifty-one forges, though many "had gone to decay in part from the scarcity of fuel and the increasing cost of transportation." And, in 1825, only a year after the tariff had passed, Pittsburg contained seven steam rolling-mills, eight air-furnaces, and a cupola furnace, a foundery, and six steam-engine factories, while there were five blast-furnaces north of the river supplying metal, besides several in Fayette, Westmoreland, Beaver, and Armstrong Counties. And Huntington County contained the next year eight furnaces and ten forges, one slitting-mill, and a nail-factory.   Not even Mr. Carey will claim that all these works were erected in a single year, or in two.   These incidents, among many which might be gathered from the records of that time, seem to prove conclusively that in all parts of the country the production and manufacture of iron had greatly revived, with the revival of other business, *before* the adoption of the tariff of 1824, to which Mr. Carey ascribes all the progress then made.   If this is true, it is not a candid statement to say that the prostration continued "until the passage of the semi-protective tariff of 1824." For the facts prove that it did not. It is of no small importance to ascertain whether Mr. Carey is right or wrong in this instance, for upon his authority rest many statements vital in the history of the iron interest. If it appears that in the statement quoted he has distorted or twisted, suppressed or misrepresented facts, we may be prepared to receive, not with absolute confidence, other statements by him in the same interest. Moreover, if the iron manufacture had actually revived, and begun to grow with vigor before the change of tariff, it is reasonable to conclude that its growth would have continued had there been no such change.

Some evidence of the real condition of the country in the years 1820–'24 may be drawn from the record of imports of iron. The duty being unchanged in those years, the great decrease of imports in 1821 marks the general prostration in business in that year, and the revival of imports in the years 1822 and 1823 marks a revival of business, and a renewed demand for iron, which benefited the domestic manufacturer more than the importer, for the quantity made here was several times as large as the quantity imported. From the Treasury reports we take the statistics of imports of iron from 1818 to 1844, which will be found at the close of chapter XIV.

It appears that the quantity of pig imported, less than 1,000 tons in 1821, increased to about 2,500 tons in 1823. This proves that an increased demand existed, while the quantity imported is still so small as to prove that domestic production was not perceptibly impeded by it. In like manner, the importation of hammered bar-iron increased from 17,000 tons in 1821, to 29,000 tons in 1823; and the importation of rolled bar from 2,000 tons in 1821, to 5,300 in 1823, and 5,790 in 1824. The whole amount of raw iron imported for manufacture was therefore 20,000 tons in 1821, and 36,800 tons in 1823. Now, Mr. Carey himself admits that there was produced as much as 53,000 tons, and it is known that furnaces existed for the production of at least 100,000 tons. The rapid increase of manufactories shows that a demand existed for the iron; is it likely that these furnaces remained idle? Is it not more probable that they shared with foreign producers the benefit of increased demand, and that the production grew as well as the manufacture? For, in the same time, the importation of nails and spikes *decreased*, from 1,072,000 lbs. in 1822, to 658,000 in 1823; and we remember that over 4,000,000 pounds had been imported in 1804, when the great part of the consumption was even then supplied by home products. The importation of manufactured wares paying ad-valorem duties, which was $2,767,757 in 1822, was $2,568,842 in 1823. Increasing imports of the material, and decreasing imports of finished products, with neither the one nor the other in such quantity as to overwhelm domestic production—these conditions surely indicate a growing demand and a growing manufacture. At all events, the statistics prove that the imports were not large enough to break down nor prevent the growth of the manufacture. Only $5,083,351 in value of iron of all kinds was imported in 1823, and $5,210,056 in 1822. But it will be remembered that, ten years before, the domestic product was over fourteen millions in value, and the importations four millions, the manufacture rapidly growing, and that the production had fully doubled before and during the war. It would be absurd to suppose that, after thirteen years of growth, an importation of five millions was enough to depress or check a manufacture which in half that time had doubled its productive power!

This is surely conclusive. We must dismiss Mr. Carey's special pleading at this point, with the conviction that, had he recognized two truths—first, that the iron interest had revived and begun to grow again before 1824; and second, that importations were not so great as to prevent a healthy progress—he would not, perhaps, have made out so great an apparent need for the tariff of 1824, but would have been more true to the recorded facts.

From 1824 onward, records bearing upon the iron interest are more complete. The tariff of that year did not increase the duty upon pig or rolled bar, and only raised the duty on hammered bar from 75 to 90 cents per cwt.; showing that the production of iron was not then thought to need much greater aid. Products before admitted under an ad-valorem duty of 20 per cent. now paid 25 per cent.; on castings the duty was raised from 75 cents per cwt. to 1 and 1¼ cent per pound; the duty on anchors, tacks, and brads, and on steel, was not changed; the duty on nails was raised from 4 to 5 cents per pound, but anvils, blacksmiths' hammers, cables and chains, muskets and rifles, braziers' rods, mill saws, cranks and irons, were taken from the ad-valorem list and placed under specific duties. This tariff lasted four years. In its first year it reduced the importations of iron to $4,518,134; in its second year they were higher than ever before, and in its last year, 1828, the importations of iron were $7,286,543. This attempt to protect does not seem to have protected.

Beginning with the raw material, we find that the imports increased as follows:

	1824.	1828.
Pig-iron (cwt.)	15,856	69,937
Rolled Bar, "	115,809	205,897
Hammered Bar (cwt.)...............	425,906	667,849
Total.........................	557,571	943,683

Thus the imports of the material increased from about 27,000 tons to about 47,000 tons. Mr. Carey asserts that the production of iron in the same time increased to 130,000 tons, "giving a duplication in the short period of four years." This is plainly an erroneous statement, for it has been shown that the product of 1824 was undoubtedly more than 100,000 tons, and the increase of production, not more than 30 per cent. in four years, was less than the increase of importations—which did nearly "duplicate in the short period of four years."

Notwithstanding a large share of articles had been taken from the ad-valorem list, the value of imports under that head was $2,486,164 in 1824, and $3,225,907 in 1828. Of the articles taken from that list for specific duties the imports increased as follows:

	1824.	1828.
Anvils (lbs.).....................	116,387	972,129
Blacksmiths' Hammers (lbs.)	10,144	58,855
Cables and Chains, "	210,550	847,655
Muskets and Rifles,................	2,142	7,097
Braziers' Rods (lbs.)	2,128	730,031
Wood Screws	$5,206	$87,100
Mill Saws.........................	$1,073	$2,758
Cranks	none.	$557

We certainly need not say that these attempts to protect singularly failed ! Other qualities of iron were also much more largely imported, thus:

	1824.	1828.
Steel (cwt.).....................	21,954	35,660
Sheet-iron (lbs.)...................	1,088,858	6,551,642
Nail-rods, "	2,307	985,909
Band-iron, "	6,832	97,909

Enough of these details ! How this tariff was ever called protective, or "semi-protective," unless on the principle "*lucus a non lucendo*," passes comprehension.

There is proof that during this period the production and manufacture increased, but the evidences of its progress are less numerous or conclusive than are those of progress in former periods.   The fact is noted that American hammered bar-iron had been enhanced in price, to $105 per ton, since the increased duty on foreign hammered bar, but pig and rolled bar, after a sudden and unnatural rise to enormous prices during the financial trouble in 1825 which affected England seriously, receded at once, and for the whole period slightly declined.   The increase of facilities for transporting iron was an important advantage gained at this time, which contributed more than all tariffs to the future growth of the iron interest, and this, as we have seen, began before the tariff of 1824.   The anthracite coal sent to market had increased to 77,516 tons, and the Delaware and Hudson Company had by this time completed its works, and began to deliver in 1829.

It was not the iron but the wool interest that demanded and obtained the tariff of 1828, but, to secure strength enough to carry the enormous duties desired by that interest, larger duties were also given to others.   The duty on pig-iron was raised to $12.50 per ton; on hammered bar to $22.44, or 67 per cent., and on rolled bar to $37 per ton, or 121 per cent.   Did this effort protect?   The importation of pig at first fell to 22,771 cwt., but then in two years rose to 203,025 cwt., far higher than ever before.   Rolled bar at first fell to 66,408 cwt., but after two years rose higher than ever before, reaching, in 1832, 427,745 cwt.   Hammered bar, in like manner, falling off to sixty-six million pounds, rose again to eighty-five million pounds. In 1828 we imported 47,000 tons of iron unmanufactured.   In 1832 we imported 74,000 tons, an increase of 57 per cent. in four years. Meanwhile, taking Mr. Carey's own statements, the domestic production of iron had increased from 130,000 to 200,000 tons, or in a ratio of 53 per cent.   Under this, the last effort of protection to shut out foreign products by extreme duties—by duties higher than ever before or since until recently—the imports of foreign iron had increased faster than the domestic production, so that actually a larger share of our consumption was supplied by imports in 1832, when this tariff was abandoned, than in 1828, when it was adopted.   No wonder it was abandoned!   No wonder men began to doubt whether protection really did protect!   Nor were the manufactures of iron more successfully shut out from foreign competition.   The duties imposed by the act of 1828 were very heavy, but the importations, though diminished in the first year or two, afterward became larger than ever:

	1828.	1832.
Nails, cwt.	.653,655	746,544
Steel, cwt.	35,660	54,929
Tacks, lbs.	21,859	32,885
Anchors, cwt.	55,640	78,921
Castings, lbs.	1,133,140	2,999,039
Anvils, lbs.	972,129	1,393,295
Chains, lbs.	847,655	2,454,360
Wood Screws.	$87,100	$133,698
Scythes, Spades, etc.	119,849	133,677
Axes and Adzes.	6,392	62,774
Bridle-Bits.	7,445	99,977
Steelyards.	3,804	67,613

In spite of the removal of many of these articles from the ad-valorem list by the tariff of 1828, the aggregate of those remaining was still larger in 1832 than the aggregate of the whole in 1828; the increase was from $3,225,907 to $3,894,298.   In face of these facts, it would be folly to expect that the manufacture had grown more rapidly than the production of iron.   In some branches it had made progress, but in all its real strength was undermined by teaching it to rely not upon skill but upon duties, and by enhancing the cost of the raw material, as compared with the cost in other countries.   This last expression needs especial consideration.

By reference to tables given at the close of chapter XV, it will be seen that the price of pig-iron here had slightly declined, from $38 in 1828, to $35 in 1832, and that the price of bar had also fallen from about $100 to $80 a ton.   Hence, it is said, the tariff did *not* enhance the cost of the raw material, and did not, therefore, retard the manufacture.   It is enough to point to the enormously increased importations of raw material.   These prove that the prices were relatively much higher here in 1832, as compared with other countries, than in 1828, otherwise this increased importation could not have taken place in the teeth of duties ranging from 60 to 120 per cent !   But we are not left to inference.   The facts are known.   The price of pig-iron in England in 1828 was from $31 to $39 a ton; in 1832 it was from $23 to $26 a ton.   The price of bar in Great Britain was in 1828 from $33 to $38, and in 1832 from $27 to $29.   The use of coke in smelting iron had for some time been rapidly increasing in England, while in this country our furnaces, carefully "protected" from any very serious competition, were content to get along in the old way, and even our vast supplies of anthracite were not used to smelt iron until sharp competition after 1837 forced new methods.

Hence the production in Great Britain had been so rapidly perfected that the cost of pig had been reduced from 25 to 30 per cent., while in this country it had scarcely been reduced at all. The natural tendency of the simpler manufactured products is to lower prices, as new inventions, and methods, and increased skill, are applied. "Protection" arrested that steady improvement here, by paying our iron-makers well for sticking to the old methods. It held up the price of iron, while in other countries it was being rapidly reduced. Hence the increased importations in spite of the increased duty. But other countries, having cheaper material, could sell manufactured products cheaper. Hence, in spite of increased duties, the finished products of iron came in from abroad more largely under the tariff of 1828 than before, and more largely in its last year than in its first.

At the time, this was well understood. The tariff which Mr. Carey and other gentlemen, who do not allow facts to bother them, so greatly admire, seemed to some of the iron-workers of that day a nuisance. Upward of three hundred mechanics of Philadelphia, employed in the various branches of the iron manufacture, petitioned Congress in 1831, representing that the high duties on bar-iron, imposed by the act of 1828, were extremely unfavorable to the manufacturing of hardware, blacksmiths'-work, and chain cables, "which last could now be imported cheaper than the rods out of which they were made," and a committee reported that relief could be afforded only by a reduction of the duties on raw iron. This little incident tells us the same story that the statistics have told— how the producers quietly went on in their old methods, and pocketed high prices, while the manufacturer, for want of raw material at reasonable rates, was forced to face a greatly-increased importation of foreign wares. And this was the glorious protective tariff of 1828!—the "thoroughly protective tariff," with its "marvellous prosperity," as Mr. Carey calls it! Truly, one must have a brilliant imagination to apply these phrases to such facts as we have reviewed.

Before we leave this brilliant period, one more fact must be fixed in mind. The building of railroads had now begun in earnest, and a demand was thus created for a large supply of iron in manufactured form. We had the iron, the coal, and the labor, and rolling-mills, but our glorious tariff had "protected" our industry against the stimulus of competition. Our furnaces were happy in the good old charcoal process, and while England was coking bituminous coal with which to master the world, and while our beds of anthracite were already yielding 363,871 tons a year, not a ton had been used in smelting iron. Consequently, England could supply rails cheaper, and when the Columbia and Pennsylvania road advertised for proposals to furnish iron in 1831, there were none for American iron, and the contracts were made in England for the whole quantity at £6 17s. 6d. per ton. Just here began England's mastery over us in the iron manufacture. Had our industry been in condition to meet this new demand, the future magnitude of which was not then foreseen, more than three million tons of manufactured iron, which we have since imported at a cost of one hundred and fifty million dollars, would have been made here. No one can estimate the power which this would have given to the iron manufacture thenceforward. But it was not in condition. It was indulging in the comfortable dream of protection against competition. When we were colonies, this unprotected manufacture had frightened England with its products. When we had learned to protect ourselves, England mastered our strongest and most natural industry. In its infancy, rugged and self-reliant, this industry exported pig and bar to England. After seventeen years of careful nursing and wrapping by the fireside of protection, this same industry looked helplessly on while England began to make rails for all our railroads. And this, the final and crushing blow, was the latest gift of the protective system to the infant manufacture! Ah, if, instead of so much shelter, we had given a little more stimulus; if, instead of so much coddling, we had subjected it to a few severe lessons in the rough practical world, how many millions we should have saved! Not a solitary American would to-day dream that a duty on any form of iron was needed, if in 1832 our industry had never been protected at all, and had preserved the rugged vigor and tireless invention of its colonial times.

THE IRON INTEREST.

	Entries Included.	Material.	Product.	Hands.	Net Product.
Iron, mining	....	439,562	2,405,292	3,206	....
Iron, pig	....	12,293,030	20,870,120	15,927	10,542,820
Iron, forged, rolled, and wrought	....	21,961,437	36,537,259	22,014	....
Steel	....	858,274	1,879,840	889	15,597,138
Castings (general)	....	15,524,619	36,678,073	26,961	....
Hardware	....	4,402,958	10,903,106	10,721	....
Forged	Anchors, chains, anvils, vices, axles	226,035	429,884	278	....
Wire, Cloth, and Rope	....	1,263,010	2,135,118	860	....
Cutlery and Tools *	....	3,671,247	9,151,893	7,284	....
Furnaces, etc	Furnaces, grates, japan'd-ware, tinned ironware, and sad-irons	642,668	1,689,148	812	35,316,685
Machinery	Includes machinist's tools	19,587,923	52,550,668	41,688	....
Locomotives	....	2,411,954	4,866,900	4,174	....
Sewing-Machines	Needles, shuttles, and cases	700,776	4,403,206	2,452	....
Other Machines †	....	1,059,622	4,040,692	2,937	....
Fire-arms	....	376,913	2,362,681	2,056	....
Safes and Locks	....	820,810	2,144,150	1,314	....
Agricultural Implements	Shovels, cotton-gins, machine-knives	7,004,162	20,944,004	17,094	....
Nails and Spikes	....	6,069,095	9,857,223	6,878	....
Bolts, Nuts, Scales	....	1,325,159	3,468,115	2,229	....
Horseshoes	Lightning-rods and fish-hooks	157,263	446,183	317	....
Sheet-Iron Workers	....	7,699,047	16,718,388	11,226	....
Blacksmith	Tools and c'riage-smiths'	3,421,410	11,655,843	15,733	82,823,864
Total	....	111,856,979	256,137,736	198,532	144,280,757

THE COTTON MANUFACTURE.

	Entries Included.	Material.	Product.	Hands.	Net Product.
Cotton Goods, etc ‡	....	57,309,387	115,785,931	122,202	....
Calico Printing	...	3,789,788	7,748,644	3,894	....
Bags, etc. §	....	2,420,124	3,522,152	1,766	....
Total	....	63,519,294	127,056,727	127,862	63,537,433

THE WOOLLEN MANUFACTURE.

	Entries Included.	Material.	Product.	Hands.	Net Product.
Woollen Goods	Goods, yarn, worsted, fulling, carding	41,975,917	69,739,469	45,357	....
Carpets	....	4,419,561	7,860,351	6,683	....
Hosiery		8,202,317	7,280,606	9,103	....
Shoddy, etc	Satinet printing, belting, dressing	336,487	667,960	427	....
Total	....	49,934,282	85,548,386	61,570	35,614,104

OTHER INTERESTS.

	Entries Included.	Material.	Product.	Hands.	Net Product.
Glass	....	2,914,303	8,775,155	9,016	5,860,852
Salt	....	1,054,780	2,289,504	2,213	1,234,724
Paper, etc	Bags, hanging, ruling, shades, and staining	12,786,662	23,449,702	12,281	10,663,040
Total, six protected interests		242,066,300	503,257,210	....	261,190,910

* Includes cutlery, carpenters', coopers', curriers', shoemakers', and stonecutters' tools, edge tools, and axes, saws, springs, and wired steel.

† Includes fire-engines, hoisting-machines, printing-presses, instruments, pumps, tinners' machines, jack-screws, and steam-heaters.

‡ Includes cotton-bags, batting, braid, cordage, coverlets, flannel goods, lamp-wick, mosquito-netting, and table-cloths.

§ Includes bags, bagging, flags, coach lace, etc.

CHAPTER XIV.

IRON.—THE COMPROMISE TARIFF.

THE history of the iron manufacture under the tariff of 1833 is full of interest. Passed with the avowed object of removing protection, and bringing back our industry to a self-supporting independence without sudden or violent changes, that act has been called the Carolina Compromise, and by Mr. Carey the free-trade tariff. As names do not fix facts, it is important to ascertain what changes of duty affecting the iron interest this tariff involved. The tariff approved July 14, 1832, added about two hundred articles to the free list, and largely reduced the duties on iron and most of its manufactured products, bringing them back substantially to the basis of the act of 1824. Thus the duty on pig was reduced from 62½ to 50 cents per cwt.; on bar hammered from $1.12 to 90 cents; on bar rolled from $1.85 to $1.50; on sheet from 3½ to 3 cents a pound; on nail-rods and band or slit, the same; on screws from 40 to 30 per cent., and the same on implements (scythes, sickles, spades, and shovels). But the compromise tariff, passed March 2, 1833, made still further reductions. It provided that after December 31, 1833, there should be deducted one-tenth of all excess above 20 per cent. duty, and that a like reduction of one-tenth should be made every second year thereafter, namely, December 31, 1835, 1837, 1839; and after December 31, 1841, one-half of the remaining excess should be deducted, and June 30, 1842, all duties should be reduced to 20 per cent. This progressive decrease caused the duties to vary thus:

	1832.	1833.	1834.	1836.	1838.	1840.	1842.
Pig-iron...	$12 50	$10 00	$9 47	$9 34	$8 59	$7 60	$5 31
Hammered Bar....	22 40	18 00	17 22	17 00	16 00	15 00	13 00
Rolled Bar.......	37 00	30 00	27 77	26 00	24 00	21 00	14 50

On manufactured articles the reduction of duty was in like proportion. It will be admitted that this tariff was very far from protective in its purposes. The manifest object was, to get rid of the whole protective system, without a violent shock to industries accustomed to unnatural conditions. What was the effect?

Under the "first completely protective tariff," as Mr. Carey styles that of 1828, imports of iron increased faster than domestic production. Under this system of rapid reduction of duties, smelting by the aid of anthracite was commenced, new iron-works sprang into existence in every year, the domestic production was increased 73½ per cent., and the imports of foreign iron were diminished.

In 1832, the last fiscal year of the protective tariff, 74,000 tons of pig and bar were imported. At the same time, according to the statistics upon which Mr. Carey relies, we were producing 200,000 tons of iron. Twenty-seven per cent. of the unmanufactured iron used therefore came from Europe. But in 1840, the last year under this tariff in which the production of iron is known, we produced 347,000 tons, an increase of 73½ per cent. in eight years. In the same year there were imported of pig 110,314 cwt., of bar rolled 656,574 cwt., and of bar hammered 576,381 cwt.; total 1,343,269 cwt., or 67,163 tons, a decrease in eight years of 6,603 tons, or 9½ per cent. In 1832, under protection, the entire consumption was 274,000 tons, of which 27 per cent. was imported. In 1840, under non-protection, we consumed 414,163 tons, of which only 16 per cent. was imported. These facts may astonish, as they will probably annoy, those who have maintained that the reduced duties of that period were fatal to the iron interest in this country; but they rest on no guess by any theorist—on no doubtful authority. The Treasury reports state the importations of iron, and the quantity produced in the two years is stated by all authorities, and by Mr. Carey himself, as just given. Eight years of reduced duties, then, increased domestic production 73½ per cent., and decreased importations 9½ per cent. Eight years of "British free trade," so called, reduced the proportion of foreign iron consumed by this country from 27 per cent. to 16 per cent.

It is true, the domestic production was less in 1841, if statements generally accepted are true. Concerning the production of that year and 1842 there is dispute. But no one questions the fact that the product of 1840 was 347,000 tons. Each year of census is a stumbling-block in the way of those who seek to shape facts to theories. Since the production of that year is undisputed, it affords the only sure and satisfactory test of the effect of this tariff. In spite of the panic of 1837, the disorder and contraction of the currency, the general disaster and bankruptcy which followed the suspension of the banks, the production of iron in 1840 was 73½ per cent. greater than in 1832, while the importations were 9½ per cent. less. The non-protective tariff, tested by statistics, proves to have given more real protection than the protective tariff.

Nor was this decreased importation of raw iron caused or balanced by an increased importation of manufactured iron.   In 1832, there were imported of iron manufactures, covered by specific duties by weight, an aggregate of 11,124 tons, and in 1840 there were imported of the same articles only 9,581 tons—a decrease of 1,543, or 14 per cent.   The tables following this chapter give the quantities of the leading articles.   It thus appears that the manufactured product was more thoroughly excluded by domestic production than the raw material.   According to the census of 1840, the value of the products of iron was $50,820,907, but, according to the Treasury records, the value of all iron imported was $7,241,407; the total consumption was, therefore, $58,062,314, and the imports were less than 13 per cent.   But in 1832, though the value of products of iron is not accurately known, it cannot reasonably be estimated at more than twenty-five millions, and the proportion of imports to consumption was about 27 per cent.   In eight years, we had progressed about half-way to absolute independence of all foreign nations, as to iron and its manufactures.

It does not shake this reasoning to observe that the importations of iron were much larger in the time of inflation.   The effect of an inflated currency is to increase importations, nor will it be forgotten that the duties in 1836 were higher than in 1840.   If high duties protect, why did not the higher duties of 1836 prevent an importation larger than that of 1840?   The truth is again illustrated, that importations depend not upon duties so much as upon prices.   In 1832, as has been shown, high duties had caused prices to stand still for years, while in other countries the price of iron was being reduced by great improvements.   Following this cause of high prices came another, the expansion of the currency.   The bank circulation rose from $61,323,898 in 1830, to $149,135,190 in 1837; and in that wild hour of speculation, when all things bore fictitious values, pig-iron sold for $52 a ton, and bar for $115 a ton.   It is not strange that sellers sought such a market for their wares.   Yet the excessive importations in 1836 and 1837 did not check domestic production.   To this fact, strangely enough, Mr. Carey testifies when he says, "The production of iron continued to increase in the three years which followed," "smelting by the aid of anthracite was first introduced here in 1837;" "by the close of 1841, six such furnaces had been put in blast."   Facts which Mr. Carey does not accidentally state may be added.   It was in 1836 that the first wrought-iron was used for gas and water pipes; in that year sixty-one steamers were built in Pittsburg, and, in the year 1837, wire factories in that town were supplying the whole Mississippi Valley, one using 600 tons of iron yearly. In 1838, Howe's solid-headed pin, and the Collins axes with punched eyes, were patented, as well as cast-iron car-wheels and improved ploughs; and, in 1839, Baldwin received from England application to build locomotives for English railways. In 1840, Griffiths was excluding foreign saws with his own; Sanford had pushed his skate-manufacture to success. At the same time other manufactures throve; the pin-machines at Derby amazed an English traveller, for each did the work of fifty-nine workmen; and our clocks began to travel over all Europe. In the same year an establishment in New York turned out fifty tons of horseshoes daily, and sold them ready for use at five cents a pound. The hardware manufactures, also, were noted as extending their enterprises rapidly, and, having sold their goods direct to the trade since 1837, were doing an increasing and paying business. Best proof of all—surest proof that the iron manufacture was vigorously growing—there were built, in 1837, 224 miles of railroad, and 416 in 1838, and 389 in 1839, and 516 in 1840, and 717 in 1841; so that, in the years 1840 and 1841, not less than 98,000 tons of iron were laid down in track and repairs, or used in engines and cars. Of this amount 52,000 tons were imported; the rest was of domestic manufacture. In the same years 141 new steamers were built, each requiring many tons of iron. These incidents prove that the production and manufacture of iron had not been checked by the large foreign importations, but that, when prostration of business and reduction of prices stopped importations, the domestic manufacture, still advancing, supplied the demand, and, as we have seen, excluded yearly a larger share of the foreign products. Such is the true history of the iron interest from 1832 to 1840, under the reduced duties. And, so inconvenient was it to explain, and so impossible was it to deny the increased production of iron until 1840, that Mr. Carey, in discussing the history of this period, absolutely ignores the crisis of 1837! It seems amazing that any writer addressing intelligent readers should venture upon such a step, but in his reply to Mr. Wells, in the second letter devoted to this period, there occurs not 'one word to indicate that the writer had ever heard of any disaster or disorder in that period prior to 1841! For, the quantity produced in 1840 being known, it was not possible to refer to the currency crisis preceding, without supplying to every reader a more reasonable explanation than Mr. Carey chooses to give of the reduction of prices in 1841 and 1842. Such treatment may be adroit and shrewd, but it is for candid readers to say whether it is worthy of any good cause.

The "Iron Manufacturer's Guide," a work prepared by the Iron Association with great labor, gives a record of furnaces, with the date of their erection. By examination of this list, it appears that one hundred and eighteen furnaces are recorded as having been built in the years 1833–'42, inclusive, as follows:

FURNACES BUILT.

	Pennsylvania.	Other States.		Pennsylvania.	Other States.
1833	3	7	1839	5	5
1834	2	7	1840	4	7
1835	7	8	1841	6	3
1836	6	8	1842	8	2
1837	5	13		—	—
1838	7	5		53	65

Other furnaces are mentioned, which appear to have been built during the same period, but the precise date is not stated. From this record it will be seen that the excessive importations of 1836 and 1837 did not prevent a rapid increase of domestic production in those years, and that the production continued to increase, in spite of the rapid removal of duties, and in spite of the panic and disorder of currency. Nor does this record show the whole number of furnaces then built, as we have stated; the number, indeed, does not match the known increase of production.

The tariff of reduced duties, during eight years to 1841, did not break down the iron manufacture, but so stimulated and strengthened it, that foreign iron had become less than 13 per cent. of the consumption. It remains to ascertain the cause of depression in 1841 and 1842.

The movement from a depreciated and worthless paper currency to specie values involves inevitable distress, and temporary disorder of business. In the year 1841, the banks moved toward specie payments, and resumption was reached in 1842. In the process, a large quantity of discredited paper, then in circulation, was thrown out, and the currency was severely contracted; prices fell, people stopped buying, specie was scarce, and for the time no sound currency sufficiently supplied its place. Distress was the unavoidable consequence, yet it was the sure sign of better days. A representative from Indiana, in the year 1844, described the change thus: "A return to a rigid system of economy was apparent everywhere; all men were trying to live within their means; there were fewer debts contracted in 1841 and 1842 than there had been during any twenty-four months for more than fifteen years past; the evils of the credit system were felt and acknowledged by every man, people everywhere were struggling to get out of debt, and limiting their expenditures to the least possible amount." Is this condition, so clearly described, one of disease and paralysis, or of returning health? Trade was greatly retarded for the time, but were the productive energies of the country destroyed or paralyzed by severe economy? Was this prostration of business caused by the tariff of 1833, or by the abandonment of a depreciated currency, and the return to specie payments? Mr. Carey says it was caused by the tariff. That his language may not be misunderstood, we quote: "With 1841 there came, however, as already shown, the fifth reduction of duty, under the Carolina nullification tariff of 1833." . . . . . "With each succeeding day, therefore, the societary movement became more completely paralyzed, until there was produced a state of things wholly without parallel in the country's history."

It is not directly asserted, but it is implied, that this fifth reduction of duty was the cause of all distress. Is it possible that Mr. Carey was so careless as not to observe that this same fifth reduction came, *not* "with 1841," but after December 31, 1841, and that the distress and prostration preceded it? When that prostration occurred, the duties were still the same that they were in 1840, when our mills and factories were active. Which is the more reasonable, to suppose that the expectation of a reduction of duty from $15 to $13 a ton on bar-iron caused people to stop making iron, or to suppose that the contraction of the banks, the refusal of depreciated currency, the change of prices from one currency to another, and the universal return to economy and patient industry, caused the prostration? May not the question be left to reasoning men, without argument?

Of a paper circulation of $107,290,204 in use, January 1, 1841, nearly fifty millions were virtually thrown out and discredited in a single year, and twenty-four millions were withdrawn altogether before January 1, 1842. To ignore such a fact as this, and to assign instead of it the prospect of a change of duty for eight years provided for by law as the cause of the prostration in 1841, is indeed a mode of reasoning in which its author can find few equals. The change of duty, when it came, did not cause an importation of iron as great as the average of the two years preceding, nor materially greater than that of ten years before, under the extreme protection of 1832. To ascribe to such importation the prostration of manufac-

14

tures would be absurd; but to ascribe the prostration to the mere apprehension of it, passes comment.

Mr. Carey studiously represents this period as one of absolute paralysis, and asserts—without an atom of proof—that the production of pig-iron fell to 220,000 tons in 1842.

A single fact shows whether "the societary movement" was "completely paralyzed." The record of produce moved by the Erie Canal to tide-water shows that the value of manufactured products—moved not from the sea to a consumer, be it observed, but from the interior to the sea—was $1,312,231 in 1840, and $2,159,832 in 1841, and $1,949,541 in 1842. That no difference of value may seem to account for this increase, it may be added that the quantity of manufactured products so moved to the sea in 1840 was 1,267 tons, and in 1841 it was 3,702 tons, and 2,659 in 1842. In 1843, after the tariff had taken effect, there was a reduction to 2,077, and in 1844 a startling decline to 853 tons. Is this a "paralysis of the societary movement, more complete with each succeeding day," when the quantity of manufactured products sent forward to market more than doubles in a single year? Or has Mr. Carey once more drawn upon his imagination for his facts?

In the year 1841, according to the records of the Iron Association, as already stated, six new furnaces went into operation in Pennsylvania, and four in other States; and in 1842 eight went into operation in Pennsylvania, and two in other States. Nor were the furnaces alone increased. In 1841 a nail-factory was built at Weymouth, Massachusetts; the Hecla rolling-mill at Pittsburg, and the Brady's Bend rolling-mill were built. In 1842 the Agawam rolling-mill of Massachusetts was rebuilt, the Fall River was built, the Cold Spring of Connecticut, the Heshborn and Crescent of Pennsylvania, and the Falcon of Ohio, were built. These facts appear in the statistics of the Iron Association. "With each succeeding day, therefore, the societary movement became more completely paralyzed," and the quantity of manufactured products sent to market doubled, ten new blast-furnaces were built each year, and several new rolling-mills!

Early in 1844, in an elaborate speech in favor of protective duties on iron, Mr. Bidlack, of Pennsylvania, made some statements deserving of notice, as follows: "It is now only about four years since the first successful experiment" (in smelting iron with anthracite coal) "was made, and there have already been erected no less than twenty furnaces on this principle, sixteen in Pennsylvania and four in New Jersey, and others are about to be erected. These furnaces are capable alone of producing 60,000 or 70,000 tons, being more than one-fifth of the whole production from charcoal in the United States."

Now, Mr. Carey himself states that there were six such anthracite furnaces in 1841, and we find twenty at the close of 1843. Are we to suppose that none of them were erected and put in operation in the year 1842? But Mr. Bidlack goes on to name "six furnaces in Columbia County," and two more near Danville; "these have been built within four years." Had these furnaces been built within one year (since the tariff), would he not have said so? Again, he tells us of a new and extensive rolling-mill just put in operation which "was commenced in 1841," and of another furnace and rolling-mill just starting, "after a suspension of about a year," and this was early in 1844. The suspension, then, must have taken place in 1843, after the tariff was passed. These are given as samples only of indications, which meet every reader of the records of those times, and they prove not that there was no depression, but that it was not a prostration of the whole iron interest, as some have represented, followed by a magical revival as soon as the tariff was passed. No one can read that new furnaces and mills were built, and new modes of manufacture adopted in the years 1841 and 1842, without realizing that the statements of Mr. Carey are not in strict accord with facts. People do not build new mills and put money into new furnaces, when half the furnaces in the country are idle. The larger furnaces would hold out longest; more than half the furnaces in the country must therefore have been idle in 1842, if, as Mr. Carey says, "there is the best reason for believing" the product of pig-iron was reduced from 347,000 tons, in 1840, to less than 200,000 tons. The production in the year 1840 was 347,000 tons, and in that year, and in 1841 and 1842, furnaces of the capacity of 44,000 tons more were built and put into operation, so that the productive power increased at the least to 376,000 or 387,000 tons before the adoption of the protective tariff, and yet Mr. Carey asserts that less than 200,000 tons were actually produced!

In this same period of alleged complete paralysis, we began to make railroad iron for our own railroads. The first rail-mill was built, it is stated, in 1841; but in the "Iron Manufacturer's Guide" it is stated that the Mount Savage, Md., was built in 1839, and the Cosalo, Pa., "in 1839 or 1840," and the Brady's Bend, Pa., in 1841. Once more Mr. Carey seems to be at war with facts, for he asserts that, after the passage of the tariff of 1842, the first rolling-mill for railroad iron "made its appearance on American soil." In this same period of "complete paralysis," American mechanics built locomotives to order for English railroads.   In 1842 it was stated in Congress that American locomotives were then rolling on railroads in England, Russia, Prussia, and Austria.   Under the system of protection, England began to supply our railroads with rails. But, under the system of protection, we began to supply England with railroad engines. To those who believe that the high wages of labor in this country make protection necessary, it may be difficult to explain how labor of the most costly kind can be put into a machine so expensive and ponderous for transportation, and that machine, shipped across the ocean, can be sold at a rate defying foreign competition, at a time when, Mr. Carey asserts, the pauper labor of England was prostrating our industry, and making it impossible for us to produce even the rudest and simplest form of iron!   In 1842, iron sold here for $25, and in England for $16.50 per ton; wages here were fully 20 per cent. higher than in England; yet our labor was so much more intelligent, and therefore efficient, that the more costly iron, worked up by more costly labor, was shipped to England in the form of locomotives.

What was the "prostration of the iron interest" in 1841–'42? A very simple explanation is consistent with all the reliable records. Though the price of iron had fallen to $25 a ton, the importation of pig-iron was only 18,694 tons—not enough to interfere in the least degree with our production.   But the whole people had begun to economize, and to consume as little as possible.   The production of iron had been pushed fully to the consuming power of the country. The fall in price had driven men to apply new methods, and the cheaper method of smelting with anthracite or coke began to be adopted.   In 1837 the first anthracite furnace was built; two more followed in 1839, two more in 1840, two in 1841, and three in 1842. These ten furnaces, producing perhaps thirty thousand tons—certainly far more than the whole quantity imported—were offering iron for sale at low rates in a market already stocked beyond the power of consumption.   The country was struggling out of debt, and reducing consumption, at the very time that the producing power was thus increased, not only by the building of anthracite furnaces, but by the opening of furnaces with coked bituminous coal, and the building of twenty-three new charcoal furnaces, mentioned in the "Iron Manufacturer's Guide" as erected in 1840–'42. These, no doubt, were in localities most favored by natural advantages, and able to supply the iron at low rates. With the market in such a condition, furnaces less advantageously situated, or adhering to more expensive methods, were forced to stop. Accordingly, it is stated in a record which appears in De Bow's "Industrial Resources," apparently taken from a memorial of the Pennsylvania iron manufacturers to Congress in 1849, that thirty-five iron works failed in Pennsylvania in the years 1840–'42, inclusive—though, according to the same table, a larger number were put in operation in the very same years. And this change, from old and expensive to new and cheaper methods, was the "complete paralysis" of the iron manufacture which Mr. Carey finds "the best reason for believing" reduced the production of pig-iron to less than 200,000 tons in the year 1842.

How long, it may be fairly asked, would our beds of anthracite have slept undisturbed, had protection sheltered our iron-makers from competition, and made it profitable to continue making iron in the most expensive locations and by the most wasteful processes? For twenty years England had been using mineral coal for fuel, and had so vastly increased her production, that at this very time her furnaces, by mutual agreement, stopped work for a time, to let the market relieve itself. The price in England had been reduced from about $40 a ton in 1828, to $16.50 in 1842, and to $20 in 1841. Yet, through all the era of protection, and through all the prosperity and extravagant prices of 1836, our furnaces continued to use old methods; and it was only when revulsion and trial came, that they began to use the anthracite that lay in masses beneath their feet. In the year of panic, 1837, the first furnace was built to test the anthracite; in the year of the second suspension, 1839, two such furnaces were built, and in the three years of "hard times" and low prices, 1840–'42, no less than seven anthracite furnaces were erected. At the same time, the use of this coal in working iron was more generally adopted. The production increased from 738,697 tons in 1838, to 818,402 in 1839, to 864,384 in 1840, and 959,972 in 1841, and to 1,108,418, rising for the first time above one million tons, in the very year when Mr. Carey represents that the paralysis was most complete! It is plain that the iron manufacture was greatly stimulated by the low cost of iron. It is equally plain that the making of iron, instead of being prostrated beyond all parallel, was simply changing its method from the old to the new, and preparing for a real and solid progress. This period, 1840 to 1842, may therefore be styled the new-birth of the iron manufacture. From the trials which forced it to better methods, dates its modern growth.

IMPORTS OF IRON.

By Quantities—(Treasury Report of 1845).

YEAR.	Pig.	Steel.	Bar, hammered.	Bar, rolled.	Nail-Rods.	Sheet.	Nails.	Anchors.	Castings.	Ad Valorem (Value).
	Cwt.	Cwt.	Cwt.	Cwt.	Lbs.	Cwt.	Lbs.	Lbs.	Cwt.	
1818......	3,970	11,343	298,438	53,979	....	17,856	1,087,899	118,857	15,915	....
1819......	6,034	8,461	324,933	51,290	....	18,315	864,563	205,370	19,099	....
1820......	6,584	7,802	389,797	59,385	....	12,520	220,082	79,252	6,202	....
1821......	18,856	11,570	343,094	48,094	....	24,122	673,554	72,580	7,037	$1,630,129
1822......	23,614	16,098	532,806	101,334	....	37,424	890,643	103,817	10,063	2,767,757
1823......	49,607	20,561	591,880	106,933	....	39,914	581,639	114,680	14,221	2,568,842
						Lbs.			Lbs.	
1824......	15,856	21,954	425,906	115,809	2,307	1,068,858	404,617	147,064	12,925	2,486,164
1825......	16,309	26,675	492,998	85,010	8,249	2,106,077	309,868	49,262	1,618,975	8,029,510
1826......	84,092	36,525	467,515	88,741	240	2,407,867	290,996	46,680	1,432,976	8,592†
1827......	35,118	25,012	440,200	162,052	840,986	4,419,732	502,457	67,371	1,103,113	8,202,058
1828......	69,987	35,660	687,849	205,897	985,909	6,551,642	653,655	55,640	1,133,140	8,225,907
			Lbs.							
1829......	22,771	24,000	66,089,460	66,408	7,232	2,441,024	532,407	54,023	1,248,157	2,725,480
1830......	22,499	24,472	68,752,943	138,981	32,848	2,836,796	613,704	22,672	1,157,256	2,906,978
1831......	198,967	34,208	52,232,102	304,918	227,160	5,672,779	814,748	54,771	1,174,510	3,735,010
1832......	203,025	54,929	85,450,104	427,745	126,542	6,391,578	746,544	78,921	2,999,089	3,894,298
			Cwt.							
1833......	196,001	42,629	722,496	560,566	214,240	7,505,246	686,228	322,904	6,080,156	2,831,715
1834......	222,265	48,623	635,608	577,927	1,553	4,960,516	610,883	294,763	6,831,109	3,470,543
1835......	245,917	52,116	630,584	568,204	3,702	4,508,005	1,068,733	222,152	2,077,088	4,110,104
1836......	170,822	57,570	658,752	983,514	24,925	8,115,800	1,261,654	235,419	2,025,054	5,870,240
1837......	292,571	61,234	626,512	956,792	1,064	11,293,703	619,165	183,708	3,016,026	4,405,852
1838......	243,830	39,145	426,399	723,466	3,191	5,079,706	337,661	195,252	2,190,588	2,035,894
1839......	250,154	59,174	711,153	1,205,697	80,404	7,412,382	1,650,534	201,728	2,921,877	4,049,612
1840......	110,314	44,506	576,381	656,574	1,108	5,529,585	715,191	154,227	3,694,488	2,204,311
1841......	245,353	51,270	562,108	1,261,118	30,360	8,166,550	939,899	251,867	3,981,002	8,455,907
1842......	373,881	55,428	390,236	1,231,965	40,269	8,001,941	773,996	196,594	2,769,095	2,617,601
1843......	77,461	16,624	125,081	*315,157	11,902	2,608,548	149,473	62,889	852,205	681,281
1844......	298,880	42,704	236,451	757,894	43,165	4,456,018	610,004	84,494	1,146,734	2,708,923
1845......	550,400		363,520	468,760	....	11,970,560				....
1846......	463,740	103,141	426,560	482,177	8,471	10,097,920	770,240	49,755	1,287,872	....

* Evidently a misprint, but copied from Treasury Report of 1845.

† Railroad bars separated in this year for different duty.

IMPORTS OF IRON.

By Quantities (Treasury Report of 1845)—Continued.

YEAR.	Anvils.	Blacksmiths' Hammers.	Cables and Chains.	Braziers' Rods.	Wood Screws.	* Implements.
	Lbs.	Lbs.	Lbs.	Lbs.	Values.	Values.
1824...........	116,387	10,144	210,550	2,128	$5,206	$6,095
1825...........	596,426	72,897	423,766	224,086	67,316	80,621
1826...	407,344	22,153	481,766	498,404	86,285	81,457
1827...........	1,011,412	41,003	388,893	771,944	112,790	105,329
1828...........	972,129	58,855	847,655	730,031	87,100	119,849
1829...........	699,836	65,896	810,372	169,531	61,967	77,262
1830...........	677,246	75,616	540,628	218,428	66,817	95,004
1831...........	1,253,450	116,166	1,004,540	487,013	112,545	118,743
1832...........	1,393,295	90,637	2,454,360	525,313	133,698	133,677
1833...........	943,203	63,418	4,216,261	506,447	110,343	97,071
1834...........	989,091	76,888	2,931,936	297,529	141,560	114,003
1835...........	1,386,293	120,328	2,023,332	254,665	150,963	97,626
1836...........	1,573,367	180,339	2,925,527	537,817	161,769	137,378
1837...........	1,177,735	93,931	2,330,878	450,817	145,565	133,949
1838...........	524,343	60,740	2,089,259	319,474	107,256	49,520
1839..........	1,026,497	116,271	3,486,810	852,695	166,570	88,126
1840...........	324,698	85,729	2,114,760	433,620	131,986	63,515
1841...........	558,237	36,150	3,825,038	367,090	138,527	60,035
1842...........	518,361	45,231	2,488,852	1,178,374	113,469	52,953
1843...........	266,452	19,307	884,259	378,415	7,551	10,602
1844...........	894,565	62,528	2,390,195	805,906	6,135	......
1845...........	......	......	......	......	......	......
1846...........	1,270,451	103,411	2,374,925	305,883	64,177 lbs.	......

* Includes Cutting-Knives, Scythes, Sickles, Reaping-Hooks, Spades, and Shovels.

IMPORTS OF IRON AND ITS PRODUCTS.

By Values (Treasury Report of 1845).

YEARS.	Pig.	Steel.	Scrap.	BAR.		Mt. Specific.	Ad Valorem.	Total Value.
				Rolled.	Hammered.			
1821......	......	$131,291	......	$1,213,041	....	$238,400	$1,630,129	$3,212,861
1822......	......	199,613	......	1,864,868	....	387,818	2,767,757	5,210,056
1823......	......	224,595	......	1,891,635	....	398,279	2,568,842	5,083,351
1824......	$3,444	236,405	......	962,897	$483,686	326,411	2,505,291	4,518,134
1825......	36,513	291,515	......	224,497	1,562,146	393,658	3,312,758	5,821,087
1826......	67,004	384,235	......	223,259	1,590,350	355,152	2,831,333	5,451,333
1827......	46,881	310,197	......	347,792	1,323,749	448,154	3,525,433	6,002,206
1828......	93,025	430,425	......	441,000	2,141,178	620,933	3,559,982	7,286,543
1829......	28,811	289,831	......	119,326	1,884,049	330,278	3,100,630	5,752,925
1830......	25,644	291,257	......	226,336	1,730,375	283,702	3,372,146	5,929,460
1831......	160,661	399,635	......	544,664	1,260,166	468,912	4,358,921	7,192,979
1832......	222,303	645,510	......	701,549	1,929,493	608,733	4,697,512	8,805,100
1833......	217,668	523,116	$24,085	1,002,750	1,837,473	773,855	3,361,582	7,740,479
1834......	270,325	554,150	33,243	1,187,236	1,748,883	656,000	4,090,621	8,534,458
1835......	289,770	576,988	11,609	1,050,152	1,641,359	524,155	4,827,461	8,921,503
1836......	272,978	686,141	28,224	2,131,828	1,891,214	879,465	7,001,404	12,891,254
1837......	422,929	804,817	18,391	2,573,367	2,017,346	1,038,382	5,488,311	12,363,543
1838......	319,099	487,334	7,567	1,825,121	1,166,196	543,779	3,069,507	7,418,603
1839......	285,300	771,804	10,161	3,181,180	2,054,094	922,447	5,585,063	12,810,049
1840......	114,562	528,716	15,749	1,707,649	1,689,831	609,671	2,575,229	7,241,407
1841......	236,228	609,301	10,537	2,172,278	1,614,619	827,820	3,428,140	8,885,823
1842......	295,284	597,317	8,207	2,053,453	1,041,410	652,583	2,919,498	7,567,752
1843......	48,251	201,772	2,743	511,282	327,550	277,349	734,737	2,103,684
1844......	200,522	487,462	43,396	1,065,562	583,065	531,659	2,782,137	5,693,823
1845......	506,291	775,675	119,740	1,691,748	872,157	908,043	4,169,745	9,043,399
1846.....	489,573	1,284,408	56,534	1,127,418	1,165,429	951,868	3,933,817	8,959,047

The figures for 1845 and 1846, as far as I can find them, are added to the tables from the report of 1845, which give none later than 1844.

ANTHRACITE COAL TRADE.

[FROM THE MINER'S JOURNAL.]

The following Table exhibits the Anthracite Coal sent to Market from the different regions in Pennsylvania, from the commencement of the Trade, in 1820, to 1868, inclusive, to which is appended the aggregate of Anthracite, Semi-Anthracite, and Bituminous Coal, moved toward the seaboard.

HARD ANTHRACITES.

Years.	SCHUYLKILL.					Sold on Line of Schuyl.	LEHIGH.			
	Canal.	R. Road.	Total.	Pine-Grove.	Little Schuyl.		Canal.	L. Valley Railroad.	Lehigh & Susq. Railroad.	Total.
1820.....	....	....	....	....	....	....	365	....	....	365
1821.....	....	....	....	....	....	....	1,073	....	....	1,073
1822.....	1,480	....	1,480	....	....	....	2,240	....	....	2,240
1823.....	1,128	....	1,128	....	....	....	5,823	....	....	5,823
1824.....	1,567	....	1,567	....	....	....	9,541	....	....	9,541
1825.....	6,500	....	6,500	....	....	....	28,393	....	....	28,393
1826.....	16,767	....	16,767	....	....	....	31,280	....	....	31,280
1827.....	31,360	....	31,360	....	....	....	32,074	....	....	32,074
1828.....	47,284	....	47,284	....	....	3,154	30,232	....	....	30,232
1829.....	79,973	....	79,973	....	....	3,832	25,110	....	....	25,110
	186,059	....	186,059	....	....	7,486	166,181	....	....	166,181
1830.....	89,984	....	89,984	....	....	5,321	41,750	....	....	41,750
1831.....	81,854	....	81,854	....	....	6,150	40,966	....	....	40,966
1832.....	209,271	....	209,271	....	14,000	10,048	70,000	....	....	70,000
1833.....	252,971	....	252,971	....	40,000	13,429	123,000	....	....	123,000
1834.....	226,692	....	226,692	....	34,000	19,429	106,244	....	....	106,244
1835.....	339,508	....	339,508	....	41,000	15,571	131,250	....	....	131,250
1836.....	432,045	....	432,045	....	35,000	17,863	148,211	....	....	146,211
1837.....	523,152	....	523,152	17,000	31,000	21,749	223,902	....	....	223,902
1838.....	433,875	....	433,875	13,000	13,000	28,775	213,615	....	....	213,615
1839.....	442,608	....	442,608	20,539	9,000	30,390	221,025	....	....	221,025
	3,031,960	....	3,031,960	50,539	217,000	171,725	1,319,963	....	....	1,319,963
1840.....	452,291	....	452,291	23,860	20,000	28,994	225,318	....	....	225,318
1841.....	584,692	850	585,542	17,653	40,000	41,293	143,037	....	....	143,037
1842.....	491,602	49,909	541,504	32,381	37,000	40,584	272,546	....	....	272,546
1843.....	447,058	230,254	677,312	22,905	31,000	34,619	267,793	....	....	267,793
1844.....	398,887	441,491	840,378	34,916	57,000	60,000	377,002	....	....	377,002
1845.....	263,587	820,237	1,083,796	47,926	74,000	90,000	429,453	....	....	429,453
1846.....	3,440	1,233,142	1,236,582	58,926	91,000	155,460	517,116	....	....	517,116
1847.....	222,693	1,360,681	1,583,374	67,457	106,401	226,610	633,507	....	....	633,507
1848.....	436,602	1,216,233	1,652,835	61,530	162,626	252,837	670,321	....	....	670,321
1849.....	489,208	1,115,918	1,605,126	78,299	174,753	239,290	781,656	....	....	781,656
	3,790,360	6,468,708	10,358,740	445,855	793,788	1,169,547	4,317,749	....	....	4,317,749
1850.....	288,030	1,423,977	1,712,007	70,919	211,960	207,863	690,456	....	....	690,456
1851.....	579,156	1,650,270	2,229,496	none.	310,307	312,367	964,294	....	....	964,294
1852.....	800,038	1,650,912	2,450,950	66,543	325,099	322,211	1,072,136	....	....	1,072,136
1853.....	888,695	1,582,248	2,470,943	80,660	389,295	394,078	1,054,309	....	....	1,054,309
1854.....	907,354	1,987,854	2,895,208	91,462	444,184	444,160	1,207,186	....	....	1,207,186
1855.....	1,105,263	2,213,292	3,318,555	119,213	426,208	471,861	1,275,050	9,063	....	1,284,113
1856.....	1,169,453	2,088,903	3,258,356	167,152	454,515	590,499	1,186,230	165,740	....	1,351,970
1857.....	1,275,989	1,709,552	2,985,541	145,012	346,877	511,977	900,314	418,235	....	1,318,541
1858.....	1,323,804	1,542,645	2,866,449	137,376	383,931	441,166	909,000	471,030	....	1,380,030
1859.....	1,372,021	1,632,932	3,004,953	125,262	366,343	554,774	1,050,659	577,652	....	1,628,311
	9,709,903	17,482,585	27,192,390	986,599	3,658,719	4,181,156	10,309,564	1,641,720	....	11,951,286
1860.....	1,356,688	1,878,156	3,270,516	152,957	323,136	608,877	1,091,032	730,642	....	1,821,674
1861.....	1,183,570	1,460,832	2,697,489	167,357	171,432	435,320	994,705	743,672	....	1,738,377
1862.....	981,729	2,305,606	2,890,598	183,985	249,451	545,916	398,927	882,573	....	1,351,054
1863.....	885,842	3,065,216	3,438,265	212,794	385,788	671,589	699,553	1,195,155	....	1,894,713
1864.....	1,000,500	3,065,577	3,642,218	211,216	537,488	748,448	758,087	1,295,419	....	2,054,669
1865.....	1,022,740	3,090,814	3,735,802	157,840	585,534	746,629	885,784	1,402,277	....	1,892,535
1866.....	1,297,047	3,714,644	4,633,487	167,833	617,278	1,010,905	1,066,308	1,730,475	....	2,128,867
1867.....	1,030,235	3,446,826	4,334,890	157,817	549,097	1,107,896	1,006,804	1,948,385	....	2,062,446
1868.....	987,628	3,574,874	4,414,256	163,633	389,994	1,268,573	989,947	2,603,103	1,058,054	2,507,582
	26,458,061	49,503,881	73,804,982	3,057,945	8,468,475	12,654,000	24,105,781	14,143,411	1,058,054	35,157,158

ANTHRACITE COAL TRADE—(*Continued*).

HARD ANTHRACITES.

| Years. | WYOMING REGION. | | | | | | | SHAMO-KIN. | AGGRE-GATE. | Annual Increase. | AGGRE-GATE OF ALL KINDS. |
	By Lehigh R.R.	Del. and Hudson Coal Co.	Penna. Coal Co.	By Canals.	G. Western R.R.	L. & B. R.R.	Total.				
1820..	....	....	....	....	....	....	....	....	365	....	365
1821..	....	....	....	....	....	....	....	....	1,073	708	23,195
1822..	....	....	....	....	....	....	....	....	3,790	2,647	38,243
1823..	...	....	....	....	....	....	....	....	6,951	3,231	37,384
1824..	....	....	....	....	....	....	....	....	11,108	4,157	18,236
1825..	....	....	....	....	....	....	....	....	34,893	23,785	60,533
1826..	....	....	....	....	....	....	....	....	48,047	13,154	83,712
1827..	....	....	....	....	....	....	....	....	63,434	15,387	108,691
1828..	....	....	....	....	....	....	....	....	77,516	14,082	109,618
1829..	....	7,000	....	....	....	....	7,000	....	112,083	34,567	157,476
		7,000					7,000	.	359,190		636,903
1830..	....	43,000	....	....	....	....	43,000	....	174,784	62,651	232,870
1831..	....	54,000	....	....	....	....	54,000	....	176,820	2,086	213,329
1832..	....	84,600	....	....	....	....	84,600	....	363,871	187,051	436,549
1833..	....	111,777	....	....	....	....	111,777	....	487,748	123,877	550,180
1834..	....	43,700	....	....	....	....	43,700	....	376,636	d111,112	448,262
1835..	....	90,000	....	....	....	....	90,000	....	560,758	184,122	610,727
1836..	....	103,861	....	....	....	....	103,861	....	684,117	123,359	792,549
1837..	....	115,387	....	....	....	....	115,387	....	879,444	195,327	1,032,894
1838..	....	78,207	....	....	....	....	78,207	....	738,697	140,747	867,780
1839..	....	122,300	....	....	....	....	122,300	11,930	818,402	79,805	999,953
		846,832					846,832	11,930	5,261,197		6,015,443
1840..	....	148,470	....	....	....	....	148,470	15,505	864,384	45,982	1,027,251
1841..	....	192,270	....	....	....	....	192,270	21,463	959,972	95,589	1,115,367
1842..	....	205,253	....	47,346	....	....	252,599	10,000	1,108,418	148,445	1,251,645
1843..	....	227,605	....	58,000	....	....	285,605	10,000	1,263,598	155,180	1,314,843
1844..	....	251,005	....	114,906	....	....	365,911	13,087	1,630,850	367,252	1,732,813
1845..	....	273,435	....	178,401	....	....	451,836	10,000	2,013,013	382,163	2,193,443
1846..	5,886	320,000	....	192,503	....	....	518,389	12,572	2,344,005	330,992	2,520,653
1847..	10,466	388,203	....	284,398	....	....	683,067	14,904	2,882,309	538,304	3,088,170
1848..	10,425	437,500	....	237,271	....	....	685,196	19,356	3,089,238	206,929	2,364,977
1849..	19,590	454,240	....	259,080	....	....	732,910	19,650	3,217,641	128,403	3,583,628
	46,361	2,897,981		1,371,905			4,216,253	146,537	19,373,429		21,109,575
1850..	32,156	441,403	111,014	243,250	....	....	827,823	19,921	3,321,136	103,495	3,786,186
1851..	25,072	479,078	316,017	336,000	....	....	1,156,167	24,899	3,829,530	1,008,394	4,876,163
1852..	41,890	497,105	426,164	319,341	....	....	1,284,500	25,846	4,899,975	570,445	5,510,664
1853..	26,235	494,327	512,659	442,511	....	....	1,475,732	15,500	5,097,144	197,169	5,959,639
1854..	39,232	440,944	496,648	492,689	133,965	....	1,603,478	63,500	5,831,834	734,690	6,903,498
1855..	50,209	565,460	504,803	464,039	187,000	....	1,771,511	116,117	6,486,097	654,263	7,556,030
1856..	44,270	499,650	512,500	510,631	305,530	....	1,972,581	137,406	6,751,542	256,445	7,858,969
1857..	37,959	480,699	536,008	407,914	490,023	....	1,952,603	155,806	6,431,378	d320,164	7,593,118
1858..	69,644	348,789	630,056	346,430	683,411	210,042	2,186,094	135,893	6,524,838	93,460	7,774,388
1859..	71,399	591,000	688,854	453,548	829,435	223,806	2,731,236	180,753	7,517,516	1,092,678	8,889,787
	438,066	4,836,455	4,834,723	4,016,353	2,629,364	433,848	12,961,725	875,641	56,954,864		66,169,401
1860..	100,277	499,568	701,523	435,306	1,080,327	519,177	2,941,817	210,108	8,143,938	626,422	9,629,455
1861..	111,073	726,644	629,657	316,765	1,104,319	848,399	3,055,140	241,451	7,621,354	d522,663	8,980,546
1862..	26,723	637,066	801,091	559,246	1,094,316	767,661	3,145,770	241,642	7,499,555	d121,799	9,015,504
1863..	....	828,150	662,904	662,721	1,223,165	964,753	3,759,610	274,936	9,427,619	1,937,064	11,580,356
1864..	9,314	852,136	759,544	630,142	1,302,457	929,374	3,960,836	333,478	9,998,046	564,388	11,747,984
1865..	250,694	759,575	877,494	358,463	1,007,074	674,744	3,256,858	457,162	9,272,157	d725,866	11,340,675
1866..	344,218	1,302,894	535,385	569,401	1,519,538	1,050,313	4,736,616	557,161	12,055,797	2,983,640	14,337,950
1867..	452,935	1,422,229	861,730	451,475	1,719,321	1,184,110	5,328,322	485,697	12,216,215	155,508	14,541,498
1868..	811,316	1,611,113	953,855	429,642	1,728,785	1,291,839	5,990,813	492,265	13,405,016	1,193,801	15,848,410
	2,590,983	17,229,658	11,111,905	9,803,569	14,408,565	8,464,818	58,107,921	4,627,008	171,578,026		201,362,074

In making up this table, the coal transported over all the railroads is given in full—but a large portion of the coal is transported over two or more roads from the same regions. In our tables the coal reported double is separated, deducted and credited to the different regions.

CHAPTER XV.

IRON.—THE TARIFF OF 1842.

THE protective tariff of 1842, passed in August of that year, restored high duties on iron, and imposed duties higher than ever before were imposed on steel, castings, anchors, anvils, screws, sad-irons, hinges, axle-trees, wrought iron, and wire, and the whole list of articles admitted under ad-valorem duties, such as axes, adzes, hatchets, knives, sickles, scythes, spades, shovels, saddlery, vices, chisels, etc. The importance of this tariff in the history of the iron interest justifies the following detailed statement, taken from the Treasury report of 1845, in which the duty and its equivalent proportion to the cost of the article is stated:

Pig Iron, duty—percentage	48.93	Castings, other	31.78
Scrap Iron	48.83	Blacksmith's Hammers	52.46
Rolled Iron	75.22	Anvils	45.09
Hammered Iron	35.56	Anchors	62.91
Steel, cast	11.65	Steam, Gas, or Water Pipes	29.20
" other	38.24	Mill and other Saws	38.03
Band Iron	70.47	Malleable Iron or Castings	46.22
Hoop Iron	115.98	Wrought Iron	88.03
Sheet Iron	60.20	Chains	101.02
Nail Rods	98.99	Chain Cables	87.20
Braziers' Rods	56.10	Spikes	168.14
Axle-trees	41.03	Nails, cut	39.00
Hinges	41.14	" wrought	58.31
Sad-Irons	87.54	Wood Screws	60.70
Glazed Hollow-ware	33.76	Tacks, Brads, Springs, etc	49.20
Castings, Vessels	51.31		

Pins and wire were classified, and bore duties, according to quality, from 18.42 per cent. to 70.31 per cent. This was the tariff of 1842, which continued in operation until December 1, 1846, and we have now to ascertain its effect. At the outset we must remember that the iron interest, when this tariff was passed, was just entering upon the great change spoken of already, from older methods to the general use of anthracite fuel. This change had been forced by the pressure of 1837 to 1842, and, as we have seen, it had increased the consumption of anthracite coal to 1,108,418 pounds in 1842, many mills having adopted the use of the mineral coal, while at least ten anthracite furnaces were in existence at the close of 1842. It need not be said that a change so important and advantageous, once begun, must have continued had there been no change of duty. The same tariff which caused it to be commenced would have caused its completion, and it may be doubted whether the change would not have been more rapid and thorough had the same conditions of necessity and sharp competition been maintained. By the tariff of 1842, foreign competition was checked during the year 1843, and part of 1844; but the change still went on, and in consequence the production of iron was still retarded, while old furnaces were being abandoned or modified. That this change actually took place, is proved by the record of consumption of anthracite, which increased 155,180 tons in 1843, in spite of the extreme depression, and 367,252 tons in 1844. In 1845 and 1846 it increased 382,163 tons and 330,990 tons, so that the consumption in 1846 was 2,344,005 tons, against 1,108,418 tons in 1842. This record is proof that the revolution which had commenced in the production and manufacture of iron was not entirely arrested, and the deliveries by the several lines of transportation show that the whole of this vast increase was supplied by improvements made before the tariff of 1842 went into effect. The Schuylkill and Lehigh Canals had been delivering since 1822 and 1820; the Schuylkill Railway began to deliver in 1841; the canals from the Wyoming region in 1842, and the Shamokin in 1839. Not a single new line was opened during the tariff period of 1842–'46, except the Lehigh Railway, which made its first delivery of 5,886 tons in 1846, the last year of that tariff.

Such a revolution in the iron manufacture having been commenced, due, as we have seen, not to the tariff of 1842, but to the conditions preceding its adoption, it must inevitably have resulted in large increase of the production of iron without corresponding increase of price as a stimulus—in other words, in a healthy growth. That this effect did, to some extent, follow independently of the tariff and in spite of its encouragement to iron-makers to adhere to less economical methods, is proved by the fact that after the tariff was removed, when the price, temporarily raised by the duties, had fallen much below the level of 1840—to little more than $20 a ton in 1849 and 1850—the production of pig-iron was 564,000 tons. This increase of over two hundred thousand tons in the decade, we may reasonably infer, is less than that which would have followed had no tariff intervened to check the general adoption of the most economical methods of manufacture.

But, it is said, the production under the high duties and high prices of 1844–'46 was far greater than that of 1850. Was it an advantage to the country, then, or to the iron manufacture as a whole if, by taxing the whole people, by enhancing the cost of the raw material of that manufacture, men were induced to continue to make iron in the least favorable localities and at the greatest waste of time and labor, when, without interference, they would have been driven to adopt better and more economical methods? Is the making of a great quantity of pig-iron in itself the chief end of man? Is a large product the greatest of all blessings, however much it may cost? Which is better, to keep an industry on stilts, or to push it to a healthy and vigorous progress?

It is at least certain that the tariff of 1842–'46 rendered iron much more costly. Before that tariff was passed, in June, July, and August, 1842, Scotch pig sold for about $25 a ton, and yet American makers at that very time were erecting new furnaces. After that tariff was repealed, pig-iron fell in 1848 to $25, in 1849 to $22.50, and in 1850 to $21 a ton, and even then American furnaces produced more than half a million tons. It is, therefore, plain that the actual cost of making pig-iron here, in localities reasonably favorable, and with proper facilities, was not greater than $21 a ton. But, while the tariff was in force, the price went so high that in one month, May, 1845, Scotch pig was sold for $50 and $52.50 a ton in New York, and during that year and the next was never quoted lower than $30. American iron sold at the furnace at prices varying from $30 a ton upward according to locality. The whole iron manufacture, then, was forced to pay about ten dollars a ton more than the real cost of its material, to enable certain men to continue the production in old modes, while others were adopting the new. Is this truly protecting the iron manufacture?

How greatly the production was thus increased is a matter of dispute. Mr. Carey, devoting to this point his utmost skill in the handling of facts, which, as we have seen, is not small, claims that the production in 1846 reached 758,000 tons, and that a still greater increase in 1847 and 1848 was caused by the tariff, which had then ceased to operate. But, while he claims to have for these statements authority in some "statistics of the Iron and Steel Association," to which the writer has not access, his language betrays the fact that these statistics, whatever they may be, do not absolutely establish any thing, even in his own estimation. Thus, speaking of the product in 1842, he says: "That it was under 200,000 tons, there is the best reason for believing, yet I have always placed it at 220,000." Of 1845 he says: "There exists no certain evidence thereto, and *I feel assured* that it" (the production) "must have exceeded half a million." That of which Mr. Carey "feels assured," with "no certain evidence" to sustain him, other people are at liberty to doubt. This language shows that his "statistics" are not derived from actual records, but rather evolved from his inner consciousness. And, again, of the product of 1848, which he asserts was 846,000 tons, he adds: "By no correction of the figures that can be even attempted will it be possible to reduce the quantity to 750,000. Admitting, however, that such a reduction be made," etc. This is not the language of one who has reliable records before him. And again, we find his inner consciousness called upon for statistical information: "That that presents more nearly than any other figure the quantity of iron actually produced in the closing years of that prosperous protective period *is my firm belief.*" This in regard to the year 1848, two years after the protective tariff had been repealed! And again, "As early as 1849, the product *was supposed* to have fallen off to 650,000." These phrases show that Mr. Carey is dealing not with statistical records of any kind, but with guesses. Yet in the same chapter he abuses Mr. Wells, because that official had not copied these guesses as established facts! It is proper to observe that in the report by Secretary Meredith, in 1849, there appears a statement as to the production of iron in Pennsylvania, prepared by S. J. Reeves from data obtained by a committee appointed in 1846, by the Iron Association; and from this statement it seems that the Association itself, in the year 1849, was obliged to rely almost wholly upon estimates, because it had been unable to obtain answers from the great majority of furnaces then in existence. The committee obtained answers from seventy-nine furnaces, which produced 84,885 tons in 1842, and guessed that a hundred and thirty-four others were in existence, and that their product was 67,000 tons, and the total production of Pennsylvania in 1842 was thus estimated at 151,885 tons. Yet, in this same year, Mr. Carey asserts that the production of the whole country was about 200,000 tons. By supposing that all the imaginary one hundred and thirty-four furnaces continued in existence, and were increased 25 per cent. in power, the Iron Association, in 1849, calculated that the quantity produced in Pennsylvania was 373,231 tons in 1846, and this guess, based upon such slender foundation, embodied the best information which the Iron Association could then obtain. But Mr. Reeves, writing in 1849, plainly admits that the production began to decrease in 1848: "The greatest production was during the last half of 1847 and the first half of 1848, when it must have been nearly 400,000 tons." Even this guess, based upon the supposed increase of power of imaginary furnaces, does not sustain the guess of Mr. Carey, for the iron-masters asserted that the production of Pennsylvania was then more than one-half of the whole production of the country. Nor does the statement of Mr. Reeves, as to the number of new furnaces built, correspond with that of Mr. Carey. It must be apparent that estimates so contradictory, and resting upon such slender foundation of facts, are not entitled to acceptance as indisputable records.

There is one test of the correctness of Mr. Carey's guesses which it may be well to apply at once. Of the production of anthracite coal, there are very complete and, apparently, very reliable records. Long before 1840, anthracite had been used very generally in the *manufacture* of iron, and, after 1840, it began to be much used in the smelting also. Every one will understand that the production of iron could not very greatly have increased, the manufacture requiring about five tons of coal to work up a ton of iron, also increasing in like proportion, without a corresponding increase in the production of anthracite. In the diagram appended are two lines, one showing the actual production of anthracite coal, and the other, the production of iron according to Mr. Carey's assertions. This contrast will, at least, warrant a little inquiry as to the facts, before we accept those assertions.

The only statements in the nature of fact which Mr. Carey gives are these, that eight new anthracite furnaces were blown in from 1841 to 1844, inclusive, and twenty-six charcoal furnaces in Pennsylvania; that eighteen new anthracite furnaces were blown in during 1845 and 1846, and (apparently) forty-one charcoal furnaces in Pennsylvania; and that eleven anthracite furnaces were blown in during 1847 and 1848, and eighteen charcoal furnaces in Pennsylvania. Mr. Carey infers that as many more charcoal furnaces were started in other States. He guesses that enlargements of old furnaces added 70,000 tons to the product. He asserts that the furnaces in existence in 1840, which actually produced 347,000 tons, could then have produced 430,000. Of these assertions there is not a particle of proof presented by him, or attainable by the writer. But it is by means of these data that he arrives at a production of 557,000 tons in 1844, and 846,000 in 1848. The assertions of a writer who does not know that there was a panic in 1837, are not statistics of unquestionable authority. Again, Mr. Carey asserts that the furnaces which, " in 1840, when pig had fallen to little more than half the price of 1837, had yielded but 347,000 tons, were now (1844) being driven to their utmost capacity, estimated at 450,000 tons." Mr.

IRON, COAL, AND RAILROADS.—MR. CAREY AND FACTS CONTRASTED.

The black line represents Mr. Carey's estimate of the production of pig-iron.
The medium dotted line, the recorded consumption of anthracite coal.
The fine dotted line, the number of miles of railroad built.

From 1844 to 1850, the dotted coarse line represents an estimate of the actual product of pig-iron, allowance being made for charcoal furnaces disused, and the consumption of 1848, other than for railroads, being supposed equal to that of 1850.

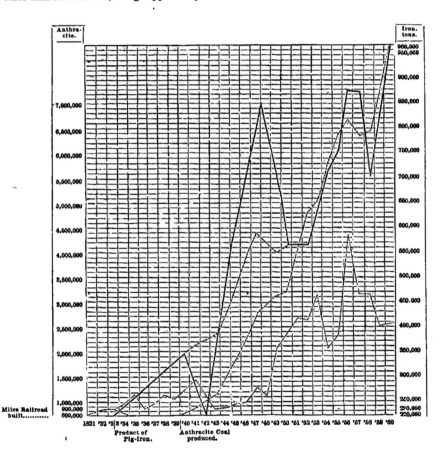

Carey wishes to have his readers believe that the low prices of 1840 caused these furnaces to produce little, and higher prices in 1844 to produce much; but in 1840, as the table elsewhere given from official sources will show, pig-iron did not sell in New York at any time below $32, and in 1844 it never rose as high as it did in 1840, and was quoted at $31 in January, and $30 in December. Such a witness clearly needs cross-examination.

In the diagram will be seen a dotted line, representing the number of miles of railroad built each year. If a vast quantity of iron was produced in the years 1843–'46, where was it consumed? Not in railroad-building, as a single glance will show. Yet in 1850 the quantity of iron used in building and repairing railroads alone must have been more than half as large as the whole quantity then produced. Without that demand, with scarcely any railroad-building until the tariff of 1846 was repealed, where did the country manage to consume the quantity which it is asserted was produced—vastly in excess of the known product of 1850? In the year 1848 only 397 miles of road were built, and, according to the statistics given in Bannon's work,* these averaged 86 tons of rail to the mile; adding for other iron used in building, and in cars, locomotives, and other equipment, the quantity of iron used in building and stocking is fully one hundred tons to the mile; hence there were thus used, in 1848, 39,700 tons of iron. But, upon the same basis, there were used in 1850, for 1,656 miles of road constructed, 165,600 tons of iron. Again, in 1848, there had been laid 4,633 miles of road, averaging 50 tons of rail to the mile, and 966 miles averaging nearly 90, making about 364,920 tons of rail then laid, to undergo yearly repairs. Bannon states that the average life of rails is 17⅔ years; if we suppose 20 years, 5 per cent. of the whole quantity laid must be allowed each year for renewals. Upon this basis, there were required for repairs in 1848 only 18,246 tons, and in 1850, on 523,860 tons of rail then laid, 26,193 tons. Thus there were used for all railroad purposes, in 1848, about 57,946 tons of iron, and in 1850 about 191,793 tons.

Other facts appear to prove, beyond possibility of dispute, that the entire demand for and consumption of iron were at least as great in 1850 as in 1848. In 1848 there were 175 steamers built, but in 1850 there were 259. Nor is there any evidence in the records of domestic commerce that the ordinary demand for iron was dimin-

---

* "Coal, Iron, and Oil."

15

ished, either by general prostration of industry and arrest of the societary circulation, or by especial disaster to manufactures. The
number of tons of manufactured products moved eastward on the
Erie Canal—*to* the sea, and not from the sea—was 5,560 in 1848,
and 7,858 in 1850. The number of tons of all products moved to
tide-water was 650,154 in 1848, and 850,239 in 1850. Tonnage on
the lakes increased from 160,250 in 1848 to 186,790 in 1850, and our
domestic exports to Canada were $6,399,959 in 1848, and $7,758,291
in 1850. Imports of lumber largely increased, showing increased
activity in building, and in every house iron is consumed. Our foreign tonnage increased from 1,360,887 tons in 1848, to 1,585,711 in
1850, and in every ship built there was needed a large quantity of
iron. Most conclusive proof that there was no general arrest of
trade or industry, the circulation of the banks increased—in Massachusetts from thirteen to seventeen millions, and, in the whole country, from one hundred and twenty-eight to one hundred and thirty-
one millions; the deposits in Massachusetts savings-banks grew
from twelve to thirteen and a half millions; the deposits in all banks
slightly increased, and, at the same time, as all know, the supply of
gold from California began to swell the circulation, and to give
greater life to all business. The coinage at the mint rose from less
than five millions in 1848 to over thirty-three millions in 1850. The
property assessed in Boston in 1848 was one hundred and sixty-
seven millions, and in 1850 it was one hundred and seventy-nine
millions; in Baltimore, 1848, it was seventy-four, and in 1850 it was
eighty millions; in New York, in 1848, it was two hundred and fifty-
four, and in 1850 it was two hundred and eighty-six millions. In
1848 the receipts for letter postage were three millions and a third,
and in 1850 over four millions and a half. The aggregate receipts
for taking produce from the West to the Atlantic cities on the New
York, Pennsylvania, Ohio, Indiana, and Illinois canals in 1848, were
$5,822,083, and in 1850 they were $6,018,340. The receipts for the
same kind of freight on the Erie, Little Miami, Michigan Central,
Georgia Central, Macon and Western, Philadelphia and Baltimore,
Reading, and Baltimore and Ohio Roads were in 1848, in the aggregate, $5,244,246, and in 1850, $6,219,582, every road showing an increase. The total tonnage arriving at tide-water on the Erie Canal
in 1848 was 1,447,905, and in 1850 it was 2,033,863. In short, this
volume would not suffice to contain the facts which could be presented to prove that the general business and industry of the country in all its main branches was more vigorous and active in 1850

than in 1848. But the facts presented surely suffice to prove that there was no such arrest of business and industry as to cause a decreased consumption of iron. Meanwhile, a few facts decisively prove that the manufacture of iron was itself not decreased. The consumption of anthracite coal in 1848 was 3,089,238 tons, but in 1850 it was 3,321,136 tons. The records of the Ohio and Miami Canals show the quantity of different products moved each year, and the number of pounds of iron, manufactured iron, and nails, moved by those canals * in the two years compares thus:

	1848.	1850.
From Cincinnati..	6,301,364	10,823,804
Total........	22,424,277	44,328,431

It needs but few facts like these to dispose of the assertion by Mr. Carey, that the demand for iron so decreased that the production in 1850 was " less than two-thirds of that of 1847–'48 !" One other fact must be added. It is recorded that in the year 1849 there were ten new iron establishments built in Pennsylvania alone, and twelve in other States, and in the year 1850 there were seven in Pennsylvania, and seven in other States.

Here, then, is a solid basis of ascertained fact: that the demand for and consumption of all iron in the aggregate, foreign and domestic, was at least as great in 1850 as in 1848. In the presence of abundant proof that it must have been greater, it will at least be conceded that it was as great. But it is easy to determine how this consumption was supplied. In 1850 the total supply was 887,600 tons, of which 180,789 tons were pig and bar imported, 142,036 tons were railroad iron, and 564,775 tons were of domestic production. From this deduct iron used for railroads, as already stated, 191,793 tons, and there remain, for consumption otherwise, 695,807 tons. But in 1848 the quantity used in railroads was 57,946 tons, and the quantity imported was 133,216 tons; the entire consumption, other

* IRON AND NAILS.

Pounds cleared on the Ohio and Miami Canals.

YEAR.	Cincinnati.	Total.	YEAR.	Cincinnati.	Total.
1841.....	2,389,306	13,172,295	1847....	4,945,800	15,674,326
1842.....	1,653,890	10,153,652	1848....	6,301,364	22,424,277
1843.....	1,930,318	10,363,223	1849....	8,781,467	28,449,934
1844.....	2,403,725	9,597,340	1850....	10,823,804	44,328,431
1845.....	3,026,385	11,049,652	1851....	19,345,053	63,136,687
1846.....	3,696,200	14,569,755			

than for railroads, of iron of domestic production, therefore, could not have been greater than 620,537 tons. For, had it been, the entire demand and consumption in 1848 must have been greater than in 1850.*

It is plain that Mr. Carey's estimates and guesses have in some way led him astray. Taking now the facts which he states, and leaving out of sight for the moment his guesses, we have a known production in 1840 of 347,000 tons, and, as the price was as high then as in 1844, we infer that the furnaces were worked as nearly at their full capacity. Mr. Carey states that eight anthracite furnaces were put in operation in 1841–'44, and 26 charcoal furnaces in Pennsylvania, and that their "estimated" capacity was 66,000 tons. The total capacity of furnaces in 1844 would then be 413,000 tons. Mr. Wells states that the actual product in 1845 was 486,000 tons. Again, Mr. Carey asserts that 18 anthracite, and 41† charcoal furnaces in Pennsylvania went into operation in 1845 and 1846, with estimated product of 125,000 tons. The capacity at the close of 1846 would therefore be 538,000 tons. Again, he states that 11 anthracite furnaces and 18 charcoal furnaces in Pennsylvania were opened in 1847 and 1848, with an estimated capacity of 72,000 tons;

---

* The following statement will make the reasoning more easily understood :

1850.

	Tons.	Tons.
Production (census)	564,775	
Imports, pig and bar	180,789	
Imports, railroad iron	142,036	
Total supply		887,600
Deduct for 1,656 miles of road	165,600	
Deduct for renewals	26,193	
Used in Railroads		191,793
Consumption other than for Railroads		695,807

1848.

	Tons.	Tons.
Consumption other than for Railroads		695,807
Add for 397 miles built		39,700
Add for renewals		18,246
Total consumption		753,753
Deduct imports, rails	29,489	
Deduct imports, pig	51,632	
Deduct imports, bar	52,095	
Total	133,216	133,216
Total domestic production,		620,537

† Mr. Carey estimates eighty-two charcoal furnaces in all, but I suppose that in this case, as in the others, he has taken double the number supposed by him to be opened in Pennsylvania alone.

adding for these, we have a production, at the close of 1848, of 610,000 tons. But by another method it has already been ascertained that the production in 1848 was less than 620,537 tons. This correspondence is so complete as to give strong reason to believe that these estimates are quite close to the truth. So perfect a coincidence of ascertained facts is at least worthy of some weight as against mere assertions.

Not only are the guesses and allowances of Mr. Carey evidently erroneous, but the truth seems to correspond very closely with the facts which he states without any estimated addition or allowance whatever. As to the year 1848, it is at least plain that the production was not greater than 620,537 tons; for, had it been, the total consumption in that year must have been greater than in 1850—and Mr. Carey, who estimates the product of 1848 at 846,000 tons, must, therefore, be in error by at least 226,537 tons!

Where, then, is the fault in Mr. Carey's reckoning? *He makes no allowance for furnaces disused or abandoned.* All charcoal furnaces after a time consume the available supply of wood around them, so that the abandonment of the furnace and the erection of a new one, near a fresh supply of wood, become necessary. But, apart from this, in the change from smelting by charcoal to the use of anthracite, many charcoal furnaces situated where supplies of coal were attainable were abandoned altogether, or rebuilt for the use of anthracite. In Mr. Carey's reckoning, furnaces built or rebuilt are noted, but he is careful not to mention the great number that were disused and abandoned. From 1850 to 1860, according to census reports, the whole number of furnaces in the United States decreased from 404 to 286, although the quantity of iron produced increased from 564,000 to 987,000 tons, because the anthracite furnaces yield several times more than the charcoal. There were 118 more furnaces abandoned than were built in this decade, though the product increased more than 400,000 tons. The change from charcoal to anthracite began in 1840, and, if the proportion of furnaces disused to the number built was as large in the decade 1840–'50 as in the following, there must have been sixty furnaces abandoned more than all that were put in operation. But, of all this, Mr. Carey makes no account or mention. In a memorial of the iron manufacturers of Pennsylvania in 1849 (quoted by De Bow, "Industrial Resources"), it was asserted that Pennsylvania then had doubled its production of iron, and made one-half of all the iron produced in the United States, and the article then gives, in support of the claim that the manufacturers were not sufficiently protected, a statement of the number of iron-works which had failed in that State since 1840, from which it appears that 28 failed in the three years of extreme depression, 1840–'42 inclusive; that 25 failed during the years 1843–'46, while the protective tariff was operative, and 61 more during the two years 1847 and 1848 which followed. Here is a statement, derived apparently from the iron manufacturers themselves, that 114 iron-works in Pennsylvania alone stopped operations during the very years 1840–'48, inclusive, during which Mr. Carey supposes that the production was increased by the full capacity of all furnaces built, without any allowance whatever for furnaces abandoned.

Not only does Mr. Carey omit this all-important item, but he allows 70,000 tons for enlargements, and supposes that as many charcoal furnaces were built in the other States as in Pennsylvania. But in 1840, according to the census, only 98,395 tons were produced in that State, and in 1850, according to the census, 285,702; increase in Pennsylvania alone, 187,307 tons, while the increase in the whole country was only 217,000 tons—from 347,000 to 564,000. Nearly the whole increase in that decade, therefore, was in the State of Pennsylvania; and, even if it be granted that the figures of the census of 1840 were about 30,000 tons below the actual product of Pennsylvania, the increase in that State would still be between two and three times as great as the increase in all the other States together. It is plain, therefore, that this allowance by Mr. Carey is entirely at variance with the facts.

There remains still another apparent error. Mr. Carey allows, for all anthracite furnaces built, an estimated product of about five thousand tons each. But the earlier anthracite furnaces produced much less. In a review of the history of the use of anthracite, in the census report of 1860, it is stated that there were in 1845 "nineteen furnaces with anthracite, four out of blast, and ten others erecting," and "they produced annually about 57,000 tons of pig metal." This is a product of three thousand tons each. Again, Mr. Carey allows 138,000 tons as the product of twenty-nine furnaces put in blast from 1845 to the close of 1848, which would make in all 195,000 tons of anthracite coal. But the same census report states that the product of anthracite coal in 1849 was only 115,000 tons, and the *Miner's Journal* states it at 118,664 tons, so that Mr. Carey seems to be in error to the extent of seventy-six thousand tons in this item alone. Indeed, the "Iron Manufacturer's Guide," issued by the association upon which Mr. Carey claims to depend largely for his facts, states that in 1856 the product of 121 furnaces was 394,509 tons of anthracite iron, which is but little more than three thousand tons to each furnace.

These most palpable errors certainly render Mr. Carey's calculations quite as valueless as his remarkable history of the panic period of 1837—with the panic of 1837 omitted. The reasonings already offered, based upon ascertained facts, assuredly have more weight than estimates confessedly based upon "firm convictions," and so grossly erroneous. The facts already observed certainly warrant the conclusion that the production of pig-iron in 1848 was less than 620,000 tons, the firm belief of Mr. Carey to the contrary notwithstanding.

The iron manufacturers of Pennsylvania, in their memorial in 1849, stated that there was produced in that State more than half of the pig-iron produced in the whole country, and in the next year the quantity actually produced, according to the census, was, in Pennsylvania, 285,702 tons, and in other States 279,053 tons. The increase during the decade had been mainly in Pennsylvania; if we suppose that its product in 1840 was fully 130,000, the increase in that State was 155,000, and in all other States only 62,000 tons. The table already referred to, apparently based upon the memorial of 1849, states that there were in Pennsylvania, in 1840, including those built in that year, 135 iron-works, of which six failed in that year; and the statement, evidently based upon guesses only as to the years 1842 and 1843, continues thus—(there are added to it a column showing the number of works remaining, if the account is correct, and another showing the number of anthracite furnaces built in Pennsylvania to the close of each year):

YEAR.	Opened.	Closed.	Remaining.	Anthracite.
1841	6	2	133	6
1842	20	20	133	8
1843	7	7	133	8
1844	21	11	143	13
1845	30	3	170	20
1846	53	4	219	27
1847	25	24	220	32
1848	17	37	200	37
1849	10	41	169	41

If this statement is correct, the whole number of iron-works remaining in operation at the beginning of 1850 was 169, of which

41 were anthracite furnaces. But the number actually reported in
1850, according to the census, was 168, so that the statement corresponds with the census. If it is correct, there were in operation
at the beginning of 1848 only 220 works, of which 32 were anthracite, and at the end of that year only 200, of which 37 were anthracite; the production, therefore, from an average of 35 anthracite,
and 176 charcoal works, could not have been greater than 281,000
tons in Pennsylvania, and, allowing 300,000 for other States, only
581,000 in the whole country. But, if this is the truth, Mr. Carey
is in error as to the production that year no less than 265,000 tons.

Again, the statistics of the Iron and Steel Association, to which
Mr. Carey so constantly refers as his authority, assert that the production of charcoal-iron in Pennsylvania, in 1847, was, hot blast
94,519, and cold blast 125,155; total, 219,674; and that the quantity produced then declined to 138,967 in 1849, and 113,282 in
1850. Now, the statement for 1847 is larger than is warranted by
any record of furnaces in existence which the writer can discover;
but, accepting it as correct, and adding 90,000 tons for the production of anthracite (from 27 furnaces at the beginning and 32 at the
end of the year), we have a production of pig-iron in Pennsylvania
of 309,674 in 1847, and, adding as much for other States, of 619,348
for the whole country. The quantity of charcoal-iron produced, the
statistics say, then declined, so that the aggregate production of
1848 cannot have been materially greater. But once more the figures correspond closely with the quantity, 620,000 tons, which it
was shown could not have been exceeded by the consumption of
1848. Finally, the record of furnaces given in the " Iron Manufacturer's Guide," if we include every furnace erected prior to and during 1848, and suppose them all to have been in operation during all
that year, at the rate of 3,000 tons for anthracite, and 1,000 for charcoal furnaces, thus making no allowance whatever for the furnaces
abandoned or disused from 1840 to 1848 inclusive, gives the following result :

Total number of anthracite furnaces built in Pennsylvania prior to and
    including 1848.. 37
Charcoal... 227
        Product....................................227,000+111,000= 338,000
Total number of anthracite furnaces built in other States prior to and
    including 1848.. 7
Charcoal... 268
        Product ....268,000+21,000= 289,000
                                                                ─────────
    Product of the whole country................................. 627,000

Since this result is reached with no allowance whatever for furnaces disused since 1840, and thus gives another and independent proof that the actual production in the year 1848 must have been less than 620,000 tons, it may be stated without hesitation that Mr. Carey is proved, by the statistics of the very association which he claims to quote, to be at least 226,000 tons out of the way as to the actual production of pig-iron in 1848.

By four distinct methods, each based upon records of fact, the same conclusion has been reached, that the actual production of pig-iron in 1848 was less than 620,000 tons. To reach a just estimate, a comparison of the records is necessary. The "Iron Manufacturer's Guide" gives the date of the building of furnaces, but rarely states when they were closed. The statement supposed to be based upon the memorial of 1849, if incorrect as to earlier years, is probably accurate as to the number of iron-works closed during the years 1844–'48, inclusive. The statistics of the production of charcoal-iron in 1847, 1849, and 1850, and of the quantity of anthracite-iron produced in 1845 and 1849, may also aid to reach the truth. The number of furnaces which are recorded in the "Iron Manufacturer's Guide" as built in the years 1840–'50, in Pennsylvania and in the other States, is given in the following table:

YEAR.	CHARCOAL.		ANTHRACITE.	
	Pennsylvania.	Other.	Pennsylvania.	Other.
1840.................	3	6	1	1
1841.................	4	3	2	..
1842.................	6	1	2	1
1843.................	6	3	..	1
1844.................	13	10	5	1
1845.................	20	15	7	1
1846.................	30	14	7	..
1847.................	13	21	5	1
1848.................	7	11	5	1
1849.................	2	12	4	..

The actual production in 1840 was 347,000, and it may fairly be supposed, for reasons already given, that the average production of anthracite furnaces, prior to 1850, did not exceed three thousand tons, and that the other furnaces averaged one thousand tons each. Upon this basis the productive power of all the furnaces in the country may be estimated, and we may thus reach the highest possible production for the years 1845 and 1846, thus:

YEAR.	PENNSYLVANIA.		OTHER STATES.		TOTAL.
	Increase.	Productive Power.	Increase.	Productive Power.	Productive Power.
1840.....................	6,000	130,000	9,000	217,000	347,000
1841.....................	10,000	140,000	3,000	220,000	360,000
1842.....................	12,000	152,000	4,000	224,000	376,000
1843.....................	6,000	156,000	6,000	230,000	386,000
1844.....................	28,000	184,000	13,000	243,000	427,000
1845.....................	41,000	225,000	18,000	261,000	486,000
1846.....................	51,000	276,000	14,000	275,000	551,000

So far, no deductions have been made for failures or abandonments of furnaces. It may, therefore, be assumed that the production of pig-iron in the last year of this tariff, 1846, cannot possibly have been greater than 551,000 tons, and was probably less. It will be observed that the result for 1845, thus arrived at by adding the product of all furnaces built, as recorded in the "Iron Manufacturer's Guide," happens to be precisely the estimate which Mr. Wells gave of the production in that year. The protective tariff of 1842, it appears, with the adoption of anthracite for fuel, increased the productive power of the iron furnaces from 376,000 to 551,000 tons, or 46 per cent.

In 1847, according to the statistical report of the Iron Association, the production of charcoal-iron in Pennsylvania was 219,674 tons, and it happens that the record prepared from the "Iron Manufacturer's Guide," adding all furnaces built since 1840, gives just 220 as the number of charcoal furnaces in Pennsylvania at the close of that year. But the production of anthracite-iron, which was 57,000 tons, in 1845, had been increased by the erection of seven furnaces at the beginning of 1847, and six more during that year, so that about 81,000 tons could be produced in Pennsylvania, and 96,000 at the end of the year. Probably the actual production was about 81,000 tons, which, with the charcoal-iron, gives 300,674 tons as the production of Pennsylvania in 1847. It happens that the aggregate power of production, adding for furnaces built according to the table, was 304,000, but it has also been stated that four establishments failed in 1846. The correspondence is sufficiently accurate, and, deducting also 2,000 tons from the aggregate power of production of other States, we have a production for 1847 of 597,674 tons.

This, however, makes no allowance for the twenty-four establishments stated to have failed in the year 1847, while all furnaces built in that year are added. The estimate, therefore, is probably larger than the actual product. Deducting now from the number of furnaces in Pennsylvania twenty-four for failures in 1847, and adding for furnaces built in the year 1848, it appears that the highest possible production of charcoal-iron in that year was 203,000, but, before the year closed, thirty-seven other works had stopped, reducing the productive power as to charcoal-iron to 166,000 tons. On the other hand, the anthracite furnaces increased from thirty-two to thirty-seven in that year, so that the productive power at the beginning of the year 1848 was 299,000, and at the end of the year 273,000 tons. The average, 281,000 tons, therefore, represents the utmost productive power of the furnaces in Pennsylvania in that year. Making deduction also from the productive power of furnaces in other States for less than half as many failures as occurred in Pennsylvania, namely, twelve in 1847 and sixteen in 1848, we reach an average production of 289,000 tons, making for the whole country 570,000 tons, as the product of the year 1848.

In the year 1849, two furnaces for charcoal were built in Pennsylvania, but forty-one stopped; the highest productive power in that year was therefore 168,000, and the lowest 127,000. The actual production of charcoal-iron is stated by the statistical report of the Iron Association at 138,967 tons, thus fully confirming the correctness of the computation for the year 1848. The production of all anthracite coal in 1849 is stated as 118,664 tons; if so, the production of Pennsylvania and anthracite furnaces outside of that State was 257,567 tons, and, with allowance for failure of twenty charcoal furnaces in other States—half the number of failures in Pennsylvania—the production of the whole country was 517,567 tons. But, if we allow for the whole number of anthracite furnaces in operation during the year, the product will be increased to 542,903 tons, which represents the productive power at the close of the year 1849.

Again, deducting from the number of charcoal furnaces in Pennsylvania for twenty-two failures in that year, the result is a productive power of 127,000 at the beginning and 105,000 at the end of the year 1850; but the actual product, according to the statistical report, was 113,282 tons, so that the estimates again are confirmed. But the production of anthracite-iron had increased, and the quantity of all iron produced in Pennsylvania, according to the census, was 285,702 tons. Meanwhile the records show that there were built in other States four charcoal and three anthracite furnaces, and the lowest production of the previous year—273,000 tons—thus in-

creased, amounts to 286,000 tons, or, with allowance for seven failures, to 279,053, the quantity produced according to the census.

This computation, then, accords at every point with the recorded
facts. Is it not absolutely impossible that estimates so fortified on
all hands by records of the Iron Association, by statistics of the date
of erection of furnaces, by records of the number of failures, and by
the census report of 1850, can be in error to the extent of 276,000
tons? Yet they must be, in regard to the year 1848, unless Mr.
Carey has been teaching his readers to believe that which is not the
truth.

Having now some basis of fact, we may inquire whether the
tariff of 1842 really aided the iron manufacture. Under its operation, the production of pig-iron increased from a known quantity
of 347,000 tons, in 1840, to not more than 551,000 tons in 1846,
but twenty-two anthracite furnaces had been opened, by which
66,000 tons of this increase were produced, and twenty-three
charcoal furnaces built in the years 1840–'42, inclusive, also swelled
the increase. Deducting these, we have 115,000 tons, the product
of furnaces other than anthracite, built under this tariff. But this
increase was at a cost of about ten dollars a ton to the manufacturer and consumer of iron. The increase by the use of anthracite,
it may fairly be reasoned, would have been at least as rapid if
iron-makers had not been tempted by high duties to continue
the use of old furnaces and less economical methods. The quantity of anthracite iron produced increased, after the repeal of
this tariff, from 118,000 tons in 1849 to 307,000 tons in 1854,
while under the tariff of 1842 only twenty-two anthracite furnaces
were built, producing about 60,000 tons. In the four years,
1853–'56 inclusive, 85 charcoal furnaces were also built, while 111
were built in the four years 1843–'46. It will be conceded, in the
presence of these facts, that a very large increase in the production
of iron would have followed the introduction of anthracite, whether
high duties had been imposed on foreign iron or not; and the question
may fairly be asked, whether the iron interest, as a whole, would not
have prospered quite as much in the end, had the production advanced
a little less rapidly in quantity of charcoal-iron produced, a little
more rapidly in quantity of anthracite-iron produced, and at less cost
of the raw material to the manufacturer.

Of the progress of the manufacture, no reliable statistics can be
given. It appears that in 1842, the last fiscal year preceding this
tariff, the imports of iron were $7,567,752, and in 1845 they were

$9,043,399, and in 1846 they were $8,959,047.   The quantity of bar
and pig iron imported in 1845 was 78,698 tons, about 16 per cent.
of the domestic production, but in the next year, and the last of the
tariff, it fell to 69,624 tons, or about 12 per cent.   Without question, the use of anthracite and the adoption of better modes of manufacture combined with the tariff to cause this reduction in the proportion of foreign raw iron consumed, but no statistics are attainable
for a like comparison as to manufactured products.

In 1840 we consumed 414,163 tons of iron, or 20½ tons to every
thousand of population, and 46 pounds per capita.   In 1846 we consumed about 620,000 tons, or 27 tons to the thousand, and about 60
pounds per capita.   But in 1854 we consumed 1,222,000 tons, or 47
tons to the thousand, and 105 pounds per capita.   The increase in
the consumption was therefore less rapid under the protective tariff
than after its repeal.   This appears to indicate that the natural increase in the use of iron was retarded by its cost.   It appears plainly
that the production itself, pushed fully to the power of the country
to consume at the ruling prices, might have been more rapidly increased had the prices been such as to invite the more rapid consumption which followed the repeal of duties.   But prices were not
reduced, because the making of iron by economical methods, and in
the most advantageous localities, had not been stimulated but retarded by the high duties.   Sooner or later, the business remaining
in this condition, there must have come general disaster to those
engaged in producing iron at a disadvantage in method or location,
and many establishments must have been driven to bankruptcy, if
not by the pressure of foreign competition and reduction of prices,
then by the excess of production over the power of the country to
consume, prices being maintained.   To this very cause are partly attributable the disasters and failures of 1847–'50.   The foreign importations were not then very large, nor was the price greatly reduced, but the pressure was sufficient to close a hundred and fifty
furnaces, mainly in Pennsylvania, where the anthracite-iron could be
more cheaply made, while in other parts of the country the production was but little reduced, new and improved furnaces almost supplying the places of those which were abandoned.   Was it well for
the country, then, that Pennsylvania was paid, at public cost, for
erecting so large a number of furnaces destined surely to be closed
and abandoned whenever the use of anthracite became more general?

Pointing to the wrecks scattered all over Pennsylvania, where
millions of money were lost by men who were tempted by the tariff

of 1842 into the making of iron at the public expense, the advocate of protection asks whether the country did not lose by the destruction of these works. It did lose, not by their destruction, but by their establishment. It lost by the investment of large sums of money and much energy and enterprise in a wasteful instead of a profitable manner. It lost money whenever a capitalist was led to invest his money in making iron where iron could not be profitably made except with protective duties and at the public cost. Each one of those blackened wrecks bears witness to the folly of teaching men to rely upon legislation rather than natural advantages and enterprise as a basis for their industry. The same blackened ruins would be seen to-day had the protective tariff never been repealed. Sooner or later, Pennsylvania would have learned to use her richest deposits of metal and fuel in a more economical manner, and then charcoal furnaces least advantageously situated or skilfully managed would have been abandoned or changed to the use of coke. Every wreck is eloquent. It teaches that a protective system, unavoidably transient and fluctuating, is not the safest basis for industry.

IMPORTS OF IRON—SINCE 1840.

YEAR.	Imports Pig-Iron.	Duty.	Imports Bar-Iron.	DUTY. Rolled.	DUTY. Ham'd.	Imports Railroad Iron.	Duty.	Value of all Iron Imported.
	Tons.		Tons.			Tons.		
1840	5,516	$7.60	61,647	$21.00	$15.00	29,092		$7,241,407
1841	12,267	7.60	92,661	21.00	15.00	23,253		8,885,823
1842	18,094	5.31	81,111	14.50	13.00	24,970		7,567,752
1843	3,882	9.00	22,011	25.00	17.00	9,654	$25.00	2,103,684
1844	14,944	9.00	49,713	25.00	17.00	15,577	25.00	5,693,828
1845	27,510	9.00	42,364	25.00	17.00	21,812	25.00	9,043,399
1846	24,187	9.00	45,437	25.00	17.00	5,897	25.00	8,959,047
				All Bar.				
1847	27,655	30 p. c.	*26,642	30 per cent.		13,536	30 per ct.	8,781,252
1848	51,632	30 "	52,095	"		29,489	"	12,526,854
1849	105,632	30 "	104,294	"		69,163	"	13,831,823
1850	74,874	30 "	105,915	"		142,036	"	16,333,145
1851	67,249	30 "	65,676	"		188,625	"	17,306,700
1852	91,873	30 "	45,761	"		245,625	"	18,957,993
1853	114,227	30 "	88,358	"		298,995	"	27,255,425
1854	160,483	30 "	45,551	"		282,866	"	29,341,775
1855	98,924	30 "	95,141	"		127,516	"	22,980,728
1856	59,011	30 "	91,579	"		155,495	"	22,041,939
1857	51,794	30 "	69,875	"		179,305	"	23,320,497
1858	41,985	24 "	52,657	"		75,745	24 per ct.	14,454,928
1859	72,517	24 "	81,902	"		69,965	"	15,000,866
1860	71,497	24 "	134,199	"		122,174	"	18,802,227
1861	110,025	24 "	77,968	"		74,490	"	....
				All Bar.				
1862	22,147	$6.00	24,250	$15.00		8,488	$12.00	....
1863	31,007	6.00	64,210	17.00		17,088	13.50	....
1864	102,223	6.00	96,380	22.40		118,714	13.50	....
1865	44,601	9.00	40,512	22.40		74,702	13.50	....
1866	101,261	9.00	54,904	22.40		73,510	13.50	....
1867	112,042	9.00	68,212	22.40		114,683	15.68	25,360,861
1868	112,133	9.00	59,270	22.40		203,819	15.68	23,496,835

PRICE OF PIG-IRON.

Average of Monthly Quotations in New York.—(From Treasury Report of 1863.)

YEAR.	Pig-Iron.	Bar-Iron.	Sheet-Iron.	YEAR.	Pig-Iron.	Bar-Iron.	Sheet-Iron.
	Average.	Average.	Average.		Average.	Average.	Average.
1825.	$57.08@63.12	$104 @ 108	$7.25@8.72	1845.	$37.16@38.79	$73.54@75.62	11¼@12¼ lb.
1826.	55.83@66.25	91.25@97.50	7.70@8.95	1846.	37.33@39 20	76.96@79.54	11 @12 "
1827.	50.00@53.00	82.91@87.95	7.08@8.00	1847.	33.96@34.92	71.46@73.12	11 @12 "
1828.	50.17@54.25	79.37@80.83	6.62@7.50	1848.	28.50@29.71	58.75@59.37	11¼@12¼ "
1829.	45.83@52.92	78.54@80.42	6.75@8.00	1849.	23.87@24.87	46.75@47.50	12⅓@13⅓ "
1830.	42.00@47.92	74.04@75.83	6.75@8.00	1850.	22.23	41.04@42.71	13 @14 "
1831.	40.00@46.66	71.50@73.75	6.75@8.00	1851.	20.77@21.85	36.04@36.95	13 @14 "
1832.	40.00@46.46	72.00@73.25	6.75@8.00	1852.	22.29@23.14	39.16@40.45	10⅓@11⅓ "
1833.	38.17@45.21	74.29@75.00	6.66@7.50	1853.	33.54@35.50	63.37@66.87	11 @11½ "
1834.	38.00@44.79	70.96@72.46	3.25@3.75	1854.	37.79@39.16	69.79@72.46	12½@12¾ "
1835.	38.00@42.50	68.33@70.41	....	1855.	28.25@29.25	57.50@60.00	14½@17 "
1836.	50.46@54.91	92.71@95.37	6.66@7.33	1856.	31.87@32.96	58.08@60.70	14½@16¼ "
1837.	49.79@54.16	94.79@96.66	7.00@7.50	1857.	30.54@31.71	55.62@56.66	12 @12 "
1838.	41.87@45.21	86.25@90.21	6 @ 7 lb.	1858.	23.91@25.04	50.83@52.95	11½@12½ "
1839.	38.33@40.91	87.71@89.17	6 @ 7 "	1859.	24.58@25.96	44.88@46.04	10½@11 "
1840.	33.66@36.71	74.17@77.08	6 @ 7 "	1860.	23.15@23.87	41.96@42.92	13 @13½ "
1841.	33.37@35.83	67.33@69.37	6 @ 7 "	1861.	21.54@22.96	43.04@44.75	16 @16½ "
1842.	27.95@29.37	56.04@58.12	13 @14 "	1862.	25.33@26.66	58.00@60.00	15 @16 "
1843.	25.46@26.79	56.46@57.50	11 @12 "	1863.	36.50@37.83	72.93@74.21	17 @18 "
1844.	32.04@33.08	60.37@62.29	11½@13⅓ "				

* From 1847 to 1865 this column includes only bar imported from Great Britain.

PRICE OF PIG-IRON.

From Treasury Report of 1863.

Year.	January.	February.	March.	April.	May.	June.	July.	August.	September.	October.	November.	December.
1825.	$35.00@50.00	$35.00@50.00	$35.00@50.00	$40.00@50.00	$40.00@50.00	$75.00	$75.00	$75.00	$70.00@72.50	$70.00	$70.00	$60.00@70.00
1826.	60.00@70.00	60.00@70.00	60.00@70.00	60.00@70.00	60.00@70.00	60.00@70.00	60.00@70.00	60.00@65.00	50.00@65.00	50.00@65.00	50.00@60.00	50.00
1827.	50.00	50.00	50.00@55.00	50.00@55.00	50.00@55.00	50.00@55.00	50.00@55.00	50.00@55.00	50.00@52.00	50.00@52.00	50.00@52.00	50.00@52.00
1828.	50.00@52.00	50.00@52.00	50.00@52.50	50.00@55.00	50.00@55.00	50.00@55.00	50.00@55.00	50.00@55.00	50.00@52.00	50.00@55.00	50.00@55.00	50.00@52.00
1829.	50.00@56.00	50.00@55.00	50.00@55.00	50.00@55.00	50.00@55.00	50.00@55.00	50.00@55.00	40.00@55.00	40.00@50.00	40.00@50.00	40.00@50.00	50.00@55.00
1830.	40.00@50.00	40.00@50.00	40.00@50.00	40.00@50.00	40.00@50.00	40.00@50.00	40.00@50.00	40.00@50.00	40.00@50.00	40.00@45.00	40.00@50.00	40.00@45.00
1831.	40.00@45.00	40.00@45.00	40.00@45.00	40.00@45.00	40.00@47.50	40.00@47.50	40.00@47.50	40.00@45.00	40.00@47.50	40.00@47.50	40.00@47.50	40.00@45.00
1832.	40.00@47.50	40.00@47.50	40.00@47.50	40.00@47.50	40.00@47.50	40.00@47.50	40.00@47.50	40.00@45.00	40.00@45.00	40.00@45.00	40.00@45.00	40.00@45.00
1833.	37.50@45.00	40.00@45.00	40.00@45.00	37.50@45.00	37.50@45.00	37.50@45.00	37.50@45.00	37.50@45.00	37.50@45.00	37.50@45.00	37.50@45.00	38.00@47.50
1834.	38.00@47.50	38.00@45.00	39.00@45.00	38.00@45.00	38.00@45.00	38.00@45.00	38.00@45.00	38.00@45.00	38.00@45.00	38.00@45.00	38.00@42.50	38.00@42.50
1835.	38.00@42.50	38.00@42.50	38.00@42.50	38.00@42.50	38.00@42.50	38.00@42.50	38.00@42.50	38.00@42.50	38.00@42.50	38.00@42.50	38.00@42.50	38.00@42.50
1836.	38.00@42.50	40.00@44.00	40.00@45.00	55.00@60.00	55.00@60.00	55.00@60.00	52.50@60.00	52.50@55.00	52.50@55.00	52.50@55.00	55.00@60.00	57.50@62.50
1837.	60.00@70.00	65.00@70.00	62.50@65.00	57.50@60.00	55.00@60.00	50.00@60.00	52.50@60.00	40.00@55.00	40.00@42.50	42.50@55.00	50.00@55.00	50.00@55.00
1838.	50.00@55.00	50.00@52.50	47.50@50.00	45.00@47.50	45.00@47.50	40.00@45.00	40.00@45.00	40.00@45.00	35.00@37.50	37.50@40.00	37.50@40.00	37.50@40.00
1839.	37.50@40.00	37.50@40.00	40.00@40.45	40.00@45.00	40.00@45.00	40.00@43.00	37.50@40.00	37.50@40.00	37.50@40.00	37.50@40.00	37.50@40.00	37.50@37.50
1840.	37.50@40.00	37.50@40.00	37.50@40.00	34.00@38.00	32.50@35.00	32.50@35.00	32.50@35.00	32.50@35.00	32.50@35.00	32.50@35.00	32.50@35.00	32.50@37.50
1841.	35.00@37.50	35.00@37.50	35.00@37.50	35.00@37.50	35.00@37.50	33.00@35.00	32.50@35.00	32.00@33.00	32.00@33.00	32.50@34.00	36.00@37.50	34.00@35.00
1842.	34.00@35.00	34.00@35.00	31.00@32.50	30.00@31.50	26.00@29.00	25.00@29.00	25.00@27.00	23.50@24.50	26.00@27.50	27.00@27.50	27.00@27.50	27.00@27.50
1843.	27.00@27.50	27.00@27.50	27.00@27.50	25.00@27.00	25.00@27.00	25.00@26.00	22.50@24.00	22.50@24.00	22.50@24.00	25.00@26.00	27.00@29.00	30.00@32.00
1844.	31.00@33.00	30.00@34.00	32.50	30.00@32.00	30.00@31.50	35.00	35.00	31.00@34.00	33.00@34.00	32.00@33.00	30.00@31.00	30.00@31.00
1845.	30.00@31.00	30.00@31.00	32.50@35.00	42.50@45.00	50.00@60.00	50.00@42.50	35.00	35.00@36.00	32.50@35.00	37.50	40.00@42.50	41.00@42.50
1846.	40.00@40.00	38.00@40.00	38.00@40.00	40.00@42.50	40.00@42.50	38.00@40.00	38.00@40.00	38.00@40.00	35.00@37.50	35.00@36.00	35.00@36.00	35.00@36.00
1847.	33.00@34.00	33.00@34.00	35.00	35.00	35.00	30.00	38.00@40.00	30.00	32.50@35.00	34.00@36.00	40.00@42.50	40.00@42.50
1848.	35.00@37.50	35.00@37.50	32.50	32.50	27.50@30.00	26.50@27.50	26.50@27.50	26.50@27.50	32.50@35.00	25.00@26.00	25.00@26.00	25.00@26.00
1849.	23.00@26.00	24.00@25.00	26.00@27.50	26.00@27.50	26.00@27.50	22.50@23.00	22.50@23.50	22.50@23.00	23.00@24.00	23.00@24.00	23.00@24.00	23.00@24.00
1850.	23.00@24.00	23.00@24.00	23.00@24.00	23.00@24.00	23.00@34.00	22.00@23.50	22.00@23.50	22.00@23.00	21.00@22.00	22.00@22.50	22.00@22.50	22.00@24.00
1851.	22.00@22.50	22.50@25.00	22.50@25.00	22.50@25.00	21.00@21.50	20.00@21.00	19.00@19.50	19.50@20.00	19.50@20.00	19.75@20.25	21.00@21.50	20.00@21.00
1852.	19.50@20.75	20.50@21.00	20.50@21.00	20.00@21.00	20.00@21.00	19.25@20.00	19.00@19.75	20.25@20.75	19.50@20.00	26.50@27.50	30.00@31.00	30.00@31.00
1853.	30.00@32.00	37.00@37.50	38.00@40.00	37.50@39.00	33.00@34.00	28.50@30.00	28.50@30.00	34.00@35.00	35.00@36.00	36.00@37.50	36.00@37.00	37.00@38.00
1854.	37.50@38.50	39.00@40.00	38.00@39.50	41.00@42.50	39.00@40.00	38.00@40.00	40.00@41.50	40.00@41.00	39.00@40.00	37.00@38.00	32.00@34.00	38.00@35.00
1855.	27.50@28.00	39.00@31.00	31.00@32.00	29.00@31.00	27.00@29.00	26.50@27.00	29.50@32.50	31.00@31.50	31.50@32.50	30.00@37.10	35.00@36.00	30.00@31.00
1856.	32.00@33.00	33.00@34.00	36.00@37.00	36.00@37.00	32.00@33.00	30.00@32.00	30.50@32.50	31.50@32.50	31.50@32.50	30.00@31.50	30.00@31.00	29.00@30.00
1857.	30.00@31.00	30.50@32.00	31.00@32.00	36.00@37.50	35.00@37.00	31.00@32.00	30.00@32.00	30.00@31.00	29.00	28.00@28.50	26.00@29.00	28.00@29.00
1858.	26.00@27.00	24.00@27.00	26.00@27.00	24.00@26.00	25.50@26.50	24.00@24.50	28.00@24.00	23.00@24.00	23.00@23.50	22.00@23.50	22.50@23.50	25.00@26.00
1859.	25.00@28.00	28.00@30.00	30.00@31.50	25.00@28.00	24.00@24.50	24.00@26.00	23.00@24.00	24.00@25.00	23.00@23.50	22.00@23.00	24.00@25.00	23.00@24.00
1860.	24.00@25.00	25.00@25.50	25.50@27.00	24.00@25.00	24.00@24.50	22.50@23.00	22.50@23.00	22.50@23.50	22.00@23.00	22.75@23.00	22.00@22.50	20.50@21.50
1861.	24.00@25.00	20.00@21.00	21.00@21.50	21.00@22.00	20.00@22.00	21.00@25.00	24.00@25.00	21.00@23.00	22.00@24.50	23.00@25.00	24.00@25.00	24.00@24.50
1862.	21.00@23.00	22.00@24.00	23.00@25.00	22.00@23.50	22.00@24.00	24.00@25.00	24.00@25.00	27.00@28.00	28.00@29.00	27.00@28.00	31.00@32.00	33.00@33.50
1863.	33.00	36.00@37.00	38.00@40.00	37.00@39.00	36.00	32.50@54.00	31.00@35.00	31.00@35.00	33.00@34.50	40.00@42.50	42.00@43.00	42.50@45.00

PIG IRON.—Price and Production.

The price is the lowest quotation each month at New York (Treasury Report, 1869). [The black line gives an estimate of the quantity of pig produced, and the dotted line represents the estimates of Mr. Carey.]

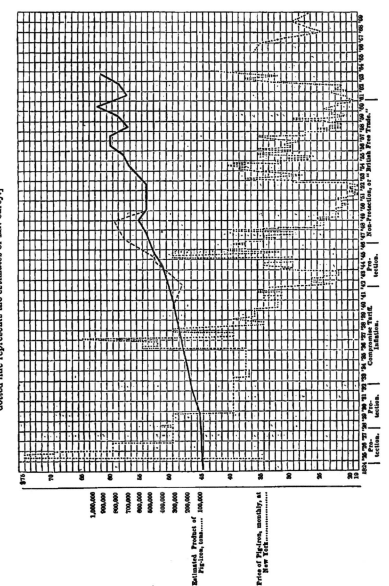

CHAPTER XVI.

IRON.—HISTORY SINCE 1846.

THE tariff of 1846—the free-trade tariff, as Mr. Carey has called it—went into effect December 1, 1846. As American iron-makers had been selling at artificial prices, the change of duty forced them to moderate their demands. The progress of the manufacture in England had greatly reduced the cost of iron; Scotch pig, which sold at Glasgow for $20 in 1845, fell to $11.10 in 1848, to $11.37 in 1849, to $11.15 in 1850, and to $10.02 in 1851. It was with such prices as these, and a vigor and skill of industry which made such prices profitable, that our furnaces were called to contend, habituated as they were to artificial prices, and to reliance upon government, rather than skill. The price of Scotch pig in New York, which had been $38 to $42.50 during the earlier part of 1846, fell to $35 to $36 December 1, to $33 to $34 January 1, 1847, and to $30 in June, July, and August of that year; and, after a rise during the winter, to $26.50 in June, 1848, and $25 to $26 in December, 1848; to $22.50 in June, 1849, and $22 in June, 1850.

In spite of the reduction of price, it is admitted by all that the production continued to increase in 1847, and Mr. Carey asserts that in 1848 it reached 846,000 tons. It is not worth while to inquire with what reason he ascribes this increase to a tariff which had then ceased to exist. The facts show that the maximum of production was reached in 1847, and that the building of new furnaces in that year and in 1848 nearly balanced the stoppage of the works run at the public cost in 1846. It appears also that, while the production of charcoal-iron in Pennsylvania decreased, it rapidly increased in other States—twenty-one furnaces being built in 1847, eleven in 1848, and twelve in 1849. In Pennsylvania the production had been overdone, and the removal of the duty and fall of price brought disaster, but in many other States the production continued to increase through all the years 1846–'50, and in all other States except Pennsylvania it was but 20,000 tons lower in 1850 than in 1848. Yet many furnaces, chiefly in Virginia, Maryland, and New Jersey, were driven, by competition of the growing anthracite production, to stop work or to adopt the use of coke or coal. Eight in New Jersey alone, and ten in Virginia, are mentioned as

having stopped work in consequence of the supply of cheaper anthracite coal, and it will at once be seen that, after deducting the
stoppages from this cause, in Pennsylvania, and the States adjacent
to the anthracite region, the aggregate production of charcoal-iron
in all the rest of the country must have been very much larger in
1850 than in 1848. Hence it appears that the charcoal furnaces
which had been artificially sustained at public cost in the region
which could be more cheaply supplied with anthracite-iron, hindered the growth of production in other States, and that, when
they were stopped, the production of charcoal-iron elsewhere increased.

What was the effect of the removal of protection, then? In
States beyond the immediate influence of the anthracite region, the
lower tariff did not prevent an increase, steady and quite rapid, in
the production of charcoal-iron. But within that circle, in the States
of Pennsylvania, Virginia, Maryland, and New Jersey, charcoal-iron
makers were prostrated, precisely as they must have been in any state
of tariff whenever the general use of anthracite began to force down
prices within that circle of supply. What, then, did the tariff do?
It simply fixed the time at which certain charcoal-iron furnaces within
that circle should stop operations. Had high duties been retained,
they might have continued work a little longer, but the cost of all
iron would have been greater. Had high duties been retained, they
must have failed before long, and the change of tariff simply short-
ened by a few years the life of furnaces which involved from the
outset a wasteful expenditure of capital and labor. Meanwhile, all
the rest of the country continued to increase its production of iron,
and the whole country obtained its iron at a lower cost.

The iron-makers in Pennsylvania and the adjacent States were
forced to consider whether they could make iron, not at the public
expense, but to the public profit. They were slow to adjust themselves to the new situation, and foreign iron flowed in largely—to
the value of $16,333,145 in 1850. The proportion of foreign raw
iron consumed rose to 24 per cent., and by far the greater part of it
was consumed in States near the Atlantic seaboard, which Pennsylvania had not yet learned to supply at a reasonable cost.

Then the question was fairly tested whether American industry
was equal to competition with British. The foreigner found our industry on crutches, habituated to false prices, wasteful methods, and
no competition, and he began to carry all before him, in that very
region which, being most richly endowed with materials for the cheap

production of iron, should have been best able to sustain the shock. While the manufacture in other States moved steadily forward, in Pennsylvania and the adjacent Eastern States it was prostrated. Then the healthful discipline of 1840–'42 found its value. Twenty-seven anthracite furnaces are mentioned as having been built in the years 1847–'50 inclusive, and the consumption of anthracite coal rose from 2,882,309 tons in 1847, and 2,344,005 tons in 1846, the last year of protection, to 3,321,136 tons in 1850, an increase of one million tons in four years, while under the protective tariff the increase had been from eleven to twenty-three hundred thousand tons. But the Pennsylvania iron-masters had not yet begun to work in earnest. In 1851 the consumption of anthracite coal suddenly rose to 4,329,530 tons, an increase of 1,008,394 in a single year—nearly as great in one year as had been the increase in four years of protection. In 1852 it rose again to 4,899,975 tons, a further increase of 570,445 tons; in 1853 it increased nearly 200,000 more, and in 1854 it increased three-quarters of a million, reaching 5,831,834 tons. The product of an-thracite iron was 118,664 tons in 1849, and it was 340,555 tons in 1854, according to statistics in the *Miners' Journal*, or 307,710 ac-cording to tables of the Iron Association, an increase of about 200 per cent., in five years. To this must be added 54,485 tons of iron produced with coke or raw bituminous coal in 1854, for many of the furnaces which had been forced to stop using charcoal, adopted better methods and cheaper fuel. In 1854 anthracite-iron was made in Pennsylvania at a cost of $15 a ton. Nor did the production stop in its increase, for in 1854 nineteen new anthracite furnaces were built, and in 1855 ten, and in 1856 ten more. The production of anthracite-iron rose to 444,012 tons in 1856 (according to the *Miners' Journal*, and 394,509 according to the Iron Association) and the production of coke-iron to 69,554 tons, so that the total production of that year was 874,428 tons.

While the iron interest in the anthracite region achieved this magnificent victory over foreign competition, the production of iron in other parts of the country, never seriously affected by changes of duty, moved steadily forward. In the Hanging Rock region (South-ern Ohio and Eastern Kentucky), thirty furnaces were erected since 1850, there being 59 in operation in 1856, and the product (nearly all charcoal) reached 92,116 tons in the latter year. In Northern Ohio, Western Tennessee, and Kentucky, Indiana, Illinois, and Missouri, the production of charcoal-iron was 71,934 in 1854, and 77,858 in 1856. In Michigan and Wisconsin splendid deposits were opened, and the production, only 990 tons in 1854, rose to 6,178 tons in 1856.

The panic of 1857 reduced production to 798,157 tons in that year, and to 705,094 tons in 1858, but the importations of foreign iron were at the same time reduced far more largely—from a value of twenty-three millions in the fiscal year 1857, to fourteen millions in the fiscal year 1858. As soon as the panic passed, the domestic production revived again; new furnaces were built; and in 1860, in spite of large importations caused by over-production and low prices in England, in spite of the fact that the price of iron here was lower than it ever had been, except in the years 1851 and 1852; the domestic production of iron was 913,774 tons according to the Iron Association, and 987,559 tons according to the census, which must be supposed the more reliable. In either case it was larger than it had ever been before. In that year, of raw iron (pig and bar) we imported 177,371 tons, and consumed 1,164,930 tons, so that only 15 per cent. of the unmanufactured iron used was imported. Yet the duties on iron were then lower than they had been at any time since 1816, and had been reduced from 30 to 24 per cent. in 1857.

In review of the history of the production of iron in this decade of non-protection, it may be said that it demonstrates most conclusively the fact that the production increases more rapidly and surely without protection than with it. From 1842, when the productive power of furnaces built was at least 376,000 tons, the actual production being unknown, to 1846 when the productive power was 551,000 tons, the increase was 46 per cent. But from 1852, when Mr. Carey states that the production was about the same as in 1850, namely, 564,000 tons, to 1856, when it was 874,428 tons, the increase was over 55 per cent. Under protection, the gain was effected by the wasteful expenditure of money and skill in continuing the production of charcoal-iron, within the region which could be and was destined surely to be more cheaply supplied with anthracite, and over one hundred companies were thus induced to devote their capital to certain destruction. But, under non-protection, a larger gain was effected by leaving men to adapt their industry to the natural resources of the country—to make anthracite-iron when that could be made most cheaply, and charcoal-iron where natural conditions favored. Under protection, a gain of 46 per cent. was effected, but under such circumstances that it was sure to be balanced by subsequent loss. Under non-protection, a gain of 55 per cent. was effected, and neither panic nor war has since broken down any considerable number of the establishments then opened.

Again, the history of this decade demonstrates conclusively that the country has now become so great, and its demand for iron so enormous, that it is no longer possible for foreign makers to control or seriously affect the market. In 1850 Great Britain found this industry disabled by its fall from the crutches of protection. English iron began to flood our market, but its cheapness invited an enormous consumption. We began to build railroads at the rate of two thousand miles a year. So vast was the demand, that it was impossible for England to supply it, and prices rose in 1852 in Glasgow to $11.37, and in New York to $30 a ton. In 1853 the average price at New York was $34.50, and in 1854 $38 a ton! In Great Britain, the same year, the average price was $17.05 per ton, a remarkable increase. The demand was, in fact, greater than Great Britain with all her energy could supply, and it forced up prices here almost as high as the protective tariff itself had done. But by 1852 our industry, no longer on crutches, but treading with firm foot the solid earth, was ready for the struggle. In the face of enormous importations, it made that wonderful progress which has been described, and by 1854 our domestic production began to force down the price of iron, which fell to $28.75 (average) in 1855, to $24.50 in 1858, and to $23.50 in 1860. Finding our industry prostrated in 1850, the British manufacturer, had it been within his power, would have kept it from recovering control of the market, and held prices so low as to prevent any increase of domestic production. But it was not in his power. The demand was too vast. The little colonies had grown to a great nation, needing iron in such quantities that the price in England was forced up by our demand in 1853 and 1854, and forced down by our production from that time until 1860. In a word, during the decade, 1850 to 1860, we achieved our independence of Great Britain in the production of iron. We won back that mastery of our own market which we enjoyed in colonial times, but of which, by a false system of protection, we had been so long almost deprived.

In the production of iron mining and smelting, the value of the product returned in 1850 was fourteen millions, but in 1860 it was twenty-three millions. In rolling or forging iron, a smaller number of establishments was engaged in 1860 than in 1850, but the number of hands employed had increased from eleven to twenty thousand, and the value of the product from sixteen to thirty-three millions. Including all branches of preparation and production, we find an increase of four thousand in the number of hands, and of twenty-six millions in the value of the product. Moreover, the average wages of hands employed both in mining and smelting, and in the rolling mills, increased materially from 1850 to 1860. This, then, was a healthy growth. Though the cost of iron to the consumer was about the same—in 1850 the average price was $22.33, and in 1860 $23.50—the aggregate value of the product had nearly doubled, and the wages of labor had increased. Of the branches of the manufacture proper, those classed as protected (see table of the iron interest), namely, the making of castings, forged iron, hardware, cutlery, tools of all kinds, and wire, increased in number of establishments from 2,290 in 1850, to 2,318, in number of hands from thirty-four to forty-seven thousand, and in value of product from thirty-seven to fifty-two millions. This is a gain far more rapid than the increase of population, and it proves that, even in those branches supposed to especially need protection, the manufacture moved forward magnificently under duties lower than have been in force at any other time since 1816. If, under this "free-trade tariff," as it has been called, the progress was so rapid, can it be said that protection is needed even for these branches? Finally, in the branches of manufacture not protected, namely, the making of machinery, nails, bolts, scales, agricultural implements, stoves, and sheet-iron articles, and in blacksmithing, there were employed, in 1850, about seventy-three, and in 1860 about one hundred thousand hands—an increase just proportioned to that of population. But the value of the product increased from sixty-seven millions in 1850, to one hundred and twenty-two millions in 1860. This vast increase in the efficiency of labor is one of the most striking features in the history of that period. In every branch of the manufacture there was wonderful progress; indeed, no better proof of the general prosperity of the manufacture can be asked than the fact that the consumption of anthracite coal mounted from 3,321,136 tons in 1850, to 7,517,816 tons in 1860. The product of steel was in value $172,080 in 1850, but it was $1,778,240 in 1860, a gain of nearly 900 per cent. The manufactures of steel produced in 1860 to the value of $9,151,893. The value of machinery produced in 1850 was $27,998,344, and in 1860 it was $46,644,586, a gain of 66.6 per cent. The forges and mills produced in 1850 to the value of $15,938,786, and in 1860 to the value of $31,888,705, a gain of about 100 per cent. The whole iron interest employed in 1850 about 142,534 hands, and in 1860 about 198,532 hands, while its aggregate product in 1850 was $135,672,171, and in 1860 it was $256,137,736. In this same year, 1860, under the lowest duties which have been imposed since 1816, the whole value of foreign iron and manufactures of iron imported was $18,812,227, or barely 7 per cent. of the value of all products of iron consumed.

Can it hereafter be said that low duties will destroy the iron interest ? The facts given show how splendid was the victory which American industry achieved, without protection, in its struggle with the iron manufacture of England. By them it is demonstrated that, since 1853, at least, the iron interest has been able not only to face, but to overpower all foreign competition. If the production of iron advanced, without protection, 55 per cent. in four years; if the manufacture advanced, without protection, from 60 to 100 per cent. in its different branches from 1850 to 1860; and if, at the close of that period, the proportion of foreign iron consumed in this country was barely seven per cent. ; what is the necessity of the protective duties which have since been imposed?

That the iron interest has made progress under protective duties, seems to some a proof that the duties have caused that progress. In the face of the marvellous victory achieved over competition during the last decade, this idea must be abandoned. It must be conceded that, unless the progress since 1860 has been greater than it was at any time under the non-protective duties, the country has simply been taxed by high duties on iron, without any benefit whatever. But if the progress has been greater than it was under non-protection, it remains to ask whether the acceleration in the growth of this industry has been such as to compensate the country for the increased cost of iron and its products.

The quantity of pig-iron produced in the year 1865 is stated at 931,582 tons. Five years of protection and war, it seems, had not only brought no increase, but an absolute decrease in the quantity. But since that time there has been a very large increase—to 1,350,943 tons, in 1866, to 1,461,626 tons in 1867, and to about 1,600,000 tons in 1868. The quantity now produced is known only by estimates and statements of the Iron Association, and these, as has been discovered in examination of the history of the years 1842–'48, are not always accurate. It is stated that the production for 1869 was 1,750,000 tons, but no facts are accessible to the writer which enable him to verify or correct the estimate. The quantity produced in 1868, stated by some as low as 1,550,000 tons, and by others as high as 1,650,000, was, undoubtedly, not greater than the latter estimate, and the increase in eight years since 1860 was, therefore, less than 66 per cent. But the increase under non-protection from 1832 to 1840 was 73½ per cent., and from 1852 to 1860 it was just 75 per cent. If the production in 1869 was 1,750,000 tons, as has been stated, the increase in nine years was 77 per cent., and it may then be said that the production of pig-iron has increased a very little more in nine years of protection than it did in eight years of non-protection. An increase in nine years, 3½ per cent. greater than in the eight years 1832 to 1840, or 2 per cent. greater than in the eight years 1852 to 1860, is certainly not a proof that the production of pig-iron has been remarkably increased by protective duties !

Yet there is reason to believe that without the tariff the increase would have been more rapid than at any former period. The war itself created an almost immeasurable demand for products of iron—in arms, projectiles, iron-clad vessels, and railroads, laid or repaired for military use, while nearly eighteen thousand miles of railroad have been built since 1860, government having given subsidies or grants to aid not less than four thousand, and about ten thousand miles of road at the South have been restored, repaired, and newly supplied. Not less than 2,800,000 tons of iron must have been used in building new roads or restoring those of the South, while the quantity yearly required for repair of track, at one-twentieth of the quantity laid, is now fully 240,000 tons, and in 1860 was only 150,000 tons. Yet, with all this enormous demand for iron, both during the war and since, the production has certainly increased little more in the nine years to June, 1869, than it increased in eight years under the "South Carolina nullification tariff," from 1832 to 1840, or in eight years under the "British free-trade tariff," from 1852 to 1860. If these names, which Mr. Carey so freely applies, have any meaning, it must appear that "British free trade" is more beneficial to the iron interest than the system called protective.

The importation of iron in 1860 was to the value of $18,802,227, and in 1869 the value imported was $29,443,917, and the increase was 56 per cent. But in ten years under low duties, from 1850 to 1860, the increase of importations was only 15 per cent., while the domestic production increased as largely as it has since the year 1860. It must therefore be conceded that, under protection, the country has not advanced in independence of foreign countries as rapidly as it did under non-protection.

Statistics cannot be obtained of the progress of other branches of the iron interest. But it is reasonable to infer that they have suffered, first, because the cost of iron has been greatly increased; second, because the importations of manufactured iron have largely increased; and third, because Congress is even now assailed with passionate appeals for still higher duties, to protect the true manufacturer, not against foreign nations, but against the exactions of those who produce the pig-metal.

The price of iron averaged $23.50 in 1860, and was only $20.09 in 1861, but was increased to $50.22 in 1864, to $48 in 1866, and during the year 1869 has averaged about $39. With gold at $1.27, near the close of the year, Scotch pig sold at New York for $31.50 in gold, and the same metal sold in 1860, at the close of the year, for about $21.50. Whatever progress has been made in the production, then, has been at a cost of about ten dollars a ton in gold to the consumer, and to that extent the raw material of the manufacturer has been rendered more costly. Indeed, the disadvantage has been still greater, for the better qualities of American iron have been enhanced in price much more than the Scotch pig, and the lower qualities which sell at nearly the same price. An increase of ten dollars in gold in the cost of the material is equivalent to a tariff of twelve dollars and a half in gold *against* the domestic maker of bar-iron.

In consequence, the value of railroad iron imported has increased from $3,700,000 in 1860 to $7,281,005 in 1869, and the imports of sheet, band, and other manufactured iron, have largely increased. At the same time the value of pig and scrap iron imported, which was $1,106,000 in 1859, has increased to over $4,700,000 in 1869. It is impossible to deny, what the iron manufacturers themselves indignantly assert, that the other branches of the iron interest suffer greatly from the cost of the material. But while they complain that " all the profits in the iron business go to the pig," and clamor for increased duties on iron manufactures and steel, the production of pig-iron increases less rapidly than the importation of pig and scrap, and not more than it increased during eight years under non-protective duties, when the manufacture also throve. It is known that the consumption of anthracite coal in manufacture bears so large a proportion to the whole consumption that the manufacture cannot have increased much more rapidly than the production of coal. But the quantity of anthracite sent to market in 1860 was 8,143,938 tons, and in 1868 it was 13,405,016, an increase of only 64 per cent. in eight years. It is not possible that the manufacture can have increased so much more rapidly as to equal the growth from 1850 to

1860, when the consumption of anthracite advanced from 3,321,136 to 8,143,938 tons, an increase of 146 per cent.

The manufacture of iron has therefore been retarded, the importation of foreign iron has been increased 56 per cent., and the production of pig-iron has advanced in nine years to June, 1869, scarcely more than it advanced without protection in eight years. What, then, is the effect of the protective system? Simply to put money into the pockets of those who smelt iron, to the disadvantage of all other iron-workers, and at the expense of the whole nation. Nineteen thousand men were employed in 1860 in producing ore and pig metal, and over 198,000 in all the branches of the iron manufacture. To enrich one-tenth at the expense of nine-tenths of this same iron interest, and at a cost of many millions to the nation—is this "protecting American industry?" Is it not, rather, taxing American industry for the benefit of a monopoly? In January, 1868, Mr. Hewitt, reporting upon the manufacture of iron as illustrated by the Paris Exposition, said:

In the Cleveland region (Great Britain), which is most favorably situated for the cheap production of iron, the cost of producing a ton of pig-iron is about forty shillings, which, at the average rate of wages paid around the blast-furnace, is equivalent to eleven days' labor—that is to say, the labor of eleven men for one day. It is possible that in one or two works this may be reduced to ten days, but in others it rises to twelve or thirteen. In the United States, the cheapest region for the manufacture of pig-iron, as yet extensively developed, is on the Lehigh River, in the State of Pennsylvania, where, taking coal and ore at their actual cost of mining, pig-iron is produced at an average cost of $24 a ton, which represents at the present rate of wages the labor of about thirteen days. But, when the iron business is established along the Great Valley which extends from Virginia to Alabama, the labor of bringing the coal and ore together will be considerably less than on the Lehigh River, and it is safe to say that then iron can be made in any required quantity, when the avenues of communication are sufficiently opened, with as little labor, to say the least, as it can.be produced in the Cleveland region.

The statement of Mr. Hewitt was made when gold was worth about 140; the average cost in gold, therefore, as stated by him, is $17.28. In 1854 the cost was not over $15; anthracite coal being $2 a ton. It requires now not more, but less, of human labor to make a ton of iron than it did it 1854; the mines are better developed, the facilities for transportation and for saving waste are more complete, and the construction and management of furnaces are much improved. If Mr. Hewitt's statement is correct, the protective system has increased the cost of production $2.28 in gold, partly by giving a monopoly to the coal-mines, and partly by the increased

cost of living, which necessitates higher wages for labor.   Pig-iron
has never sold below $10 a ton in England, and the cost of trans-
portation, twenty shillings, with insurance, interest, commissions,
and brokerage, about six shillings more at the least, increases the
cost of imported iron without duty, or any allowance whatever for
profits or transportation from shipboard to consumer, to at least
$16.50 in gold.   When iron could be made at a cost of $15 in gold,
the business prospered, and foreign iron, had there been no duty at
all, could not have been sold, even in the seaports, as low as the cost
of production here.   Not only was this true as regards anthracite-iron,
but charcoal-iron then cost, according to a statement by the manufacturers themselves at Constantia, New York, only $16.25 per ton—
the items being for 150 bushels charcoal at 5 cents, $7.50; for 2 tons
ore at $1.75, $3.50; for flux, 25 cents; for labor, $2, and for interest
and repairs, $3 a ton.   To get the imported iron to Constantia cost
$2 a ton freight from the seaport, and in proportion as furnaces are
located farther inland, the natural protection in cost of transportation becomes greater.   Prior to the war, therefore, iron could be
made, both with anthracite and charcoal, at lower cost than imported
iron, of inferior quality, could have been delivered at any seaport
free of duty.   But the actual cost in human labor is less now than
it was then.   If artificial burdens and prices have raised the cost of
production, as measured in gold, to $17.28, and in currency to $24 a
ton, they have to that extent rendered the country less independent
in its industry.   But Mr. Hewitt's statement is far below the figure
at which iron-makers now put the cost.   In memorials published,
makers in different parts of the country now assert that the actual
cost of making iron is from $29 to $32 in a currency now worth
about 80 cents.   They assert, therefore, that the cost of making
pig-iron is now $24 or $25 a ton in gold, whereas in 1854 it was $15
in gold, and in 1860 the average price of all the iron made in Pennsylvania, according to the census report, was only $19.41 per ton,
after yielding to makers a fair profit.   If their statements are truth-
ful, the system of artificial prices and burdens has simply increased
the cost of making a ton of pig-iron $9 a ton in gold, or 60 per
cent.   Evidently, then, the duty ought to be raised still higher,
because the poor iron-maker is actually worse off than he was in
1860!   By all means, let us have duties still heavier, so that the
cost of production may be still more increased, and our dependence
upon foreign countries may be rendered more complete!

The real cost of a ton of pig-iron, according to statements

recently published by Mr. Wells, is not more than $24 to $26 in currency, but in almost every part of the country it is claimed, apparently with truth, that furnaces favorably situated and well managed are making iron at a cost not exceeding $23. At Brazil, Indiana, it is asserted that the actual cost is $22.50, and that one furnace returned to the owners in seven months all the money invested. At Clarksville, Tennessee, according to a statement by Mr. George T. Lewis, iron can be made and delivered at Nashville at a cost of $19 a ton, currency. At Round Mountain, Alabama, works located upon the banks of the Coosa River can make iron at a cost of $16 to $20 a ton. At Youngstown, Ohio, the Mahoning works make iron, according to a statement of the proprietors, at a coast of about $25. At St. Louis, Missouri, the actual cost is believed to be less than $23. The following actual record of a week's work in the Carondelet furnace shows the items of cost:

	Quantity used.	Cost.	Per ton.
Coal.....................	163 tons.	$978.	$5.87
Coke....................	52 "	468.	2.81
Ore......................	222 "	1,276.50	7.66
Limestone..............	42 "	37.80	.22
Mill cinder.............	11 "	27.50	.16
Labor...................		738.18	4.43

166¼ tons produced ; cost, $3,525.98 ; per ton, $21.15

Allow for repairs $5,000 a year, which, the statement of one of the largest iron-makers in Pittsburg asserts, is sufficient to cover repairs and incidentals, and the cost will be $21.75. The furnace at Carondelet was an old charcoal furnace, height 40 feet, width of bosh 11 feet 3 inches, never suitable for smelting with raw coal, and very imperfectly repaired for the purpose of testing the Big Muddy coal. Its expense for repairs, therefore, is not properly included ; and in the above statement the actual weighings of material and payments for labor are given from the books of the company, but for coal $6 a ton is allowed, and for ore $5.75. But the ore actually costs at the mines $3.50 per ton, and for freight 74½ miles $1.90; total, with allowance of 5 per cent. for waste, $5.67. The coal costs at the mines $3.85 per ton ; freight to Carondelet 75 ; total $4.60, but the arrangements for transfer are so imperfect that it is claimed that 25 per cent. of the coal is wasted, and the cost of a ton weighed into the furnace is $5.75. Yet, with all these disadvantages and with allowance for more than the alleged waste, the cost of iron was only $21.15, or, allowing ordinary repairs, $21.75. In the same town two large and splendidly-equipped furnaces have been operated since July by the Kingsland Company, who state (January 1st) that they made 7,000 tons of metal, used 11,083 tons of ore, and 8,300 tons of coal. But the ore cost $5.40, and the coal $4.60: the cost per ton of metal made was therefore of ore $8.55, and of coal $5.45, and, supposing that the other expenses were the same as those of the other company, the cost was $21.62 per ton, or, allowing as before for repairs, $22.22.

These are estimates of the actual cost of making iron at present, when the coal costs $4.60 and the ore $5.40 per ton. But the cost of mining coal in 1860 was about 50 cents a ton, and it is now artificially increased. The cost of mining ore, accessible in inexhaustible quantities on the level of a railroad track, as at the Iron Mountain, should not be more than 50 cents a ton; in 1857 the Pilot Knob ore was delivered at the furnace at a cost of 20 cents. Adding freight, the cost of the coal at Carondelet would not necessarily be more than $1.25 a ton, and the ore $2.40 a ton. Where does the difference go? The greater part of it in profits to two monopolies, one of coal, and the other of iron. In like manner the cost of transportation of ore by railroad is increased, because there is but one road and it chooses to make somebody else pay for the increased cost of iron, rolling-stock, and machinery. The necessary cost of transportation is not more than $1 per ton of ore, and the necessary cost of the ore delivered is not more than $1.50 a ton. Allowing the same for other expenses as before, the necessary cost of making iron at Carondelet would be 11,083 tons ore, $16.624, or $2.37 per ton of iron; 8,300 tons coal $10.373 or $1.48 per ton of iron; flux, labor, coke, and repairs, $8.22 per ton; total cost, $12.07 per ton. The iron sells for $36 to $38 a ton. The difference goes in part to the owner of the coal-mine, in part to the owner of the iron-mine, in part to the owner of the railroad, in part in the increased cost of production caused by artificial burdens, and after paying all these charges there remains a profit of fourteen to sixteen dollars a ton to the makers of iron.

It is probable that iron can be made as cheaply in Missouri, or near the coal-fields in Illinois, as anywhere else in the country, and in quantity unlimited. But in other States, if the statements of Mr. Hewitt and Mr. Wells are correct, iron can be made at a cost below the lowest price at which foreign iron can be imported free of duty. It was made before the war at such cost as to defy competition, not only by Pennsylvania, but by other States. If the cost is greater now, to that extent has the system of protective duties deprived us of the industrial independence achieved before the war, and the plain remedy is to remove the artificial burdens which increase the cost of production. Take. away the duty, so that the owners of mines may be driven to consult their own interests, by selling a larger quantity of coal or ore at a smaller profit; so that railroad transportation may cost less; so that the making of iron may be increased in those regions where it can be made at reasonable cost. The duty on pig-iron is not merely unnecessary. It works great injury to the makers of bar and wrought iron and steel, to the makers of castings, hardware, and other products, in which competition is apprehended; to the manufacturers of all machines, agricultural implements, and nails, and to all blacksmiths and others included in the non-protected branches; to all other branches of manufacture in which machinery or tools are used; to all transporters by rail or steamer, and consumers of products transported, and finally— and mainly, for upon the producer all burdens at last must mainly fall—to the whole agricultural interest. If that duty were entirely removed, the whole iron interest would prosper. The rolling-mills could afford to reduce the price of railroad iron at least $12.50 in gold, and not a single ton of British rails could be imported at that price, while more railroads could be built, and transportation could be rendered less costly. It is a trifle in comparison with other benefits, that we should then keep at home $7,281,000 now sent abroad to pay for rails. Bar-iron could be likewise reduced in price, and the makers would not be forced, as many have been during the past year, to stop work or sell at a sacrifice. The makers of steel, who are now begging for higher duties, would be aided more by a reduction in the cost of the material than by an addition of $20 a ton to the duty on steel. Manufacturers of machinery of every kind could make better profits and pay better wages, and yet supply machines at less cost. Nails, which sold before the war at 3 cents and now sell at $4\frac{1}{2}$ cents, the mills even at that price losing money, could once more be reduced in cost, while the factories would become profitable. The founderies would prosper, and the poor man pay less for his stoves. Agricultural implements and machines would cost the farmer less, and the blacksmith, getting iron, and anvils, and hammers for less, could make more money, and work more cheaply. Thus the whole iron interest would prosper, and the increased demand for iron of all kinds would compel an increased production of pig-iron. American industry would thus be truly protected, and the benefits would be diffused, as the burdens are now, through the whole community.

Would the removal of the duty close the furnaces? Does not the history of the last decade answer the question? American stone-coal iron sells at about three dollars a ton more than Scotch pig, because of its superior quality. While anthracite sells for $38, charcoal mill iron sells for $42 to $44, and foundery-iron for $46 to $50. If the other qualities are so much more valuable that they command from $4 to $12 more per ton than the anthracite, it is plain that, if the anthracite-iron can meet foreign competition, no other need fear. But that iron is also worth more than the foreign. It sells for about $38, and the duty on the foreign iron is $9 in gold, or, when gold is at 130, $11.70 in currency. The price could not, therefore, be reduced by removal of the duty lower than $26.30. If the iron costs $24 a ton, as Mr. Hewitt states, the repeal of the duty would still leave a profit of $2.30 on every ton. But, if the actual cost is not greater than it was before the war, $15 in gold, or (at 130) $19.50 in currency, the profit on every ton would be $6.80. If the cost is greater, then protection has crippled our strongest industry, and the sooner we tear that industry from the lap of Delilah the better for the iron manufacture and for the country.

That the manufacture of iron suffers from the protective system, is confessed in frequent declarations like the following, from a letter published by W. H. Powell, superintendent of the Clifton Iron Works, Ohio:

It is, however, very true, as has been claimed by you in your issue of the 11th instant, that, at the present prices of pig-iron in the West, the entire rolling-mill, nail-factory, and foundery interests of the West, are completely paralyzed and rendered unremunerative, while the furnace interests *have beyond all possible contradiction* paid enormous dividends; and were it not for the fact that the production of pig-iron must, and will of necessity, in consequence of the largely-increased productive capacity, exceed the demand to the extent of a gradual decline, such as we have predicted, and which result will be reached in as short a period as could possibly be reached through Congressional legislation, we would earnestly and industriously advocate the change of the present tariff on pig-iron from $9 to $4 per ton, and an increase on bar-iron, etc., of $5 per ton. We are decidedly opposed to the frequent Congressional tampering with and changes in the laws that regulate the great industrial pursuits of our country.

The expectation that the price of domestic iron will in time be reduced (the tariff remaining), is not warranted by any incident in

17

our history.   For fifteen years under protection, from 1818 to 1832, the price was sustained, with scarcely any reduction.   During the last year of the tariff of 1842, when the production was over half a million tons, the price was over $38; though in the first year of that tariff, when the production was much smaller, the price was less than $26.   In 1860 we produced 987,000 tons, at a cost of little more than $22, and now it is claimed that the production has increased 77 per cent., but the price remains over $31 in gold—higher than in 1860, by just the amount of the duty.   The truth is, that there is really a monopoly in this branch of production, and as long as the iron-producers maintain their association, and prefer to stop work than to encourage the manufacture by lower prices, the experience of 1832 and 1846 is likely to be repeated.   But, if the statement of the iron-makers be accepted as truth, there is another reason for high prices.   They assert that the actual cost of production has been increased from $15 a ton in 1860 to $25 a ton in gold, or $30 currency.   If nine years of protection have so increased the cost, how many years more will be necessary to make it impossible to sell iron lower than $40 in gold without a sacrifice?   If nine years increased the cost 60 per cent., continued protection nine years longer, until 1878, would raise the cost of producing pig-iron above $41 in gold!

The country can no longer afford to garrote its most important branch of manufactures.   In the iron interest alone, we are strangling nine-tenths to protect one-tenth.   Nor does that protection accelerate the increase in the quantity of pig-iron produced, but it increases importations, increases the cost of production, and thus renders that industry permanently more feeble, more exposed to assault, and of less profit to the country.   At every point the system is wasteful.   Which is the true protection of American industry, to secure a profit of $17 a ton to the owners of a few hundred furnaces, or to secure prosperity to thirty millions of laborers; to secure more work and better wages to fifteen thousand blacksmiths, eleven thousand workers in sheet-iron, sixteen thousand makers of agricultural implements, forty-eight thousand makers of machinery, and to put sixty-seven thousand people engaged in the manufacture of iron beyond the reach of foreign assault?   Let that question be asked in Congress!   Let it be determined whether " protection to American industry " means a monopoly for the furnace-owner, or prosperity to the manufacturer, the machinist, the blacksmith, the transporter, the farmer, and the whole body of workmen of these United States.

PRICE OF IRON.

Average yearly, as stated in the Special Report of Commissioner Colwell, 1866.

YEAR.	PRICE OF PIG-IRON.		BAR-IRON.		RAIL'D BARS.	YEAR.	PRICE OF PIG-IRON.		BAR-IRON.		RAIL'D BARS.
	Great Britain.	United States.	Great Britain.	United States.	United States.		Great Britain.	United States.	Great Britain.	United States.	United States.
1810......	33@43	....	67@72		....	1838......	29@30	40	46@58	88.02	....
1811......	33@43	....	67@70		....	1839......	29	37	46@51	88.43	....
1812......	33@43	....	61@67		....	1840......	20	29.35	40@56	75	....
1813......	33@43	....	58@63		....	1841......	20	29.33	40@45	68.16	....
1814......	33@43	....	62@67		....	1842......	16.50	25.29	34	57.91	....
1815......	33@43	60	53@66		....	1843......	....	25.28	23.44	56.54	....
1816......	33@43	60	42@55		....	1844......	....	25.72	26.87	60.60	....
1817......	33@43	50@55	40@63		....	1845......	....	29.25	41.22	74.68	....
1818......	33@43	42@45	50@61		....	1846......	....	27.81	43.50	78.71	....
1819......	33@43	40@42	50@57		....	1847......	....	30.21	45.47	74.29	69.10
1820......	38@43	40	46@53		....	1848......	....	26.50	32.13	59.06	62.25
1821......	29@36	40	42@46		....	1849.	....	21.02	28.13	43.38	53.88
1822......	29@33	40	35@42		....	1850......	....	20.82	26.68	41.87	47.83
1823......	29@32	42	33@35		....	1851......	10.02	21.38	25.90	37.33	45.60
1824......	29@55	40	38@62		....	1852......	10.09	22.63	29.25	38.64	48.43
1825......	53@58	45	49@67	106.04		1853......	10.24	36.07	43.85	64.77	77.23
1826......	31@48	50	38@49	94.58		1854......	17.05	37.16	48.25	70.04	80.08
1827......	31@39	40	42@46	86.60		1855......	16.19	27.74	43.50	58.54	62.90
1828... ..	26@39	40	33@38	79.87		1856...:...	14.83	27.18	44.86	58.72	64.33
1829......	24@31	40@45	29@33	88.44		1857......	12.30	26.35	41.22	55.14	50
1830......	24	40	27@31	74.93		1858......	10.09	22.19	41.15	43.11	50
1831......	23@34	40	27@29	82.85		1859......	10.32	23.32	42	45.37	49.53
1832......	23@26	45	27@29	72.37		1860......	10.68	22.17	38.19	42.43	47.95
1833......	19@33	45	29@36	74.74		1861......	10	20.09	36.98	44.02	42.38
1834......	24@26	40@45	33@37	71.70		1862.:.....	10.56	23.92	37.18	59	41.73
1835......	24@26	40	33@38	69.04		1863......	11.25	35.24	39.61	73.57	76.84
1836......	30@38	48@50	38@56	94.02		1864......	11.13	59.22	37	....	126.02
1837......	23@31	55	37@53	95.06		1865......	10.64	46.25	....	....	98.62

By comparing this statement with the official record of actual quotations at New York (see pp. 221, 222), it will be seen that this table, which is supposed to be taken from "Statistics of the Iron and Steel Association," is often (and sometimes widely) in error in regard to American prices, and comparison with other records shows that it is entirely unreliable as to British prices. But it is, nevertheless, the only information obtained as to the price in certain years.

<hr />

CHAPTER XVII.

ARE MONOPOLIES BLESSINGS ?

THE three great manufacturing interests—iron, cotton, and wool—employing, with dependent branches, in 1860, not less than 387,964 hands, and yielding an aggregate product of $468,600,000, have now been considered. It has appeared that, of the iron interest, less than one-tenth is protected, to the injury of nine-tenths, and at the expense of the whole people, and that the single branch of industry thus favored—the making of pig-iron—has never by high duties been truly benefited, or stimulated permanently to greater production of wealth, but, by putting great profits in the pockets of a few men, the true progress of that industry has been retarded. It has appeared that the cotton manufacture has never needed protection, and, with or without it, has advanced in proportion to the increase of the cotton crop, but has been only retarded in a healthy growth by the protective system and the frequent changes therewith inseparably connected. It has appeared that the woollen manufacture has been repeatedly prostrated by the duties on wool, while those duties have never benefited, but uniformly injured, the wool-grower, and that this industry would now be stronger without the protective system and its fatal changes than with it.

Space does not permit a similar minute examination in regard to all other branches of manufacture. Nor is it necessary for the satisfaction of any candid inquirer. For it will surely be acknowledged that, if the system of protective duties has failed to strengthen or benefit these three great branches, which have been more assiduously guarded by legislators, and fenced about with higher duties than any others, then indeed no results more satisfactory can be expected from the less persistent and less careful protection which has been granted to other industries. No reasoner, whose object is the discovery of the truth, will pretend for a moment to defend the system of protective duties, unless it can be sustained in its application to these, the main objects of its care. No general tariff act, having protection in any degree for its object, has ever been passed in an American Congress, except at the urgent demand of one or more of these interests, and in the hope of aiding them. Take away the strength which those interests have in Congress, and there would not be left of the advocates of protection a force large enough to call the yeas and nays. Remove from the popular mind the feeling that those great branches of manufacture need artificial support, and can by such support be really aided, and there is not a State, from the Atlantic to the Pacific, in which persons, proposing to tax the people for the benefit of any other interest, would have strength enough to secure a hearing in any convention of any party. These three interests are the backbone of the whole protective policy; let it once be conceded that they cannot be aided, but have in fact been retarded by duties designed to aid them, and the policy of protection would, with almost absolute unanimity of opinion, be instantly and forever abandoned.

Neither is it necessary to the logical completeness of this inquiry, to trace the history of other branches of manufacture in detail. For it has been ascertained that the production of wealth by agriculture has been retarded by protective duties, and from agriculture come three-fourths of our annual product. Of those branches of industry from which the remaining fourth is derived, it was first ascertained that industries yielding two-thirds of that fourth were not aided by protection, and of the other third more than three-fourths are derived from the three great industries examined. The account stands thus:

SOURCES OF WEALTH.

Industry.	Effect.	Net Product.
Agriculture......................	Injured.	2,600,000,000
Natural Manufactures..............	"	478,100,000
Iron, Cotton, and Wool............	"	243,400,000
All other branches..............	Unknown.	80,900,000

So small in relative importance are the branches of industry remaining, that if every one of these had been absolutely created by protection, and had its entire product been due to that influence, it could not compensate for the actually ascertained injury to agriculture alone—namely, the loss of seven and a half per cent. in its yearly increase. Still less could it compensate for that injury and the further injury to the more important branches of manufacture already examined. It is therefore plain that the production of wealth, in the aggregate, has not been increased, but has been retarded in its natural progress, by the tariffs called protective. And, were logical completeness only desirable, this branch of the inquiry might here be dismissed. But it is also desirable to show, somewhat more fully, the effect of the protective system upon other branches of industry which produce necessaries of daily life, or the materials for such production. And, in glancing somewhat hastily at these, we shall find new illustrations and convincing proofs of the two principles which have already been so constantly traced, namely, that protection artificially increases the cost of production, and that security against competition prevents the surest and most rapid progress.

An important industry, and one formerly supposed to need protection, is the manufacture of paper, in which there were employed, in 1860, 10,911 hands, who produced to the value of $21,216,802.

At the first step in tracing its history there is found proof that, whatever it may once have needed, this industry does not now need artificial aid.   For, in 1850, the number of hands employed in this branch was 6,785, and its product was $10,187,177.   A manufacture which increased 110 per cent. in a decade of non-protective duties, the lowest since 1816, can scarcely be thought to need any extraneous assistance.   Indeed, this is *par excellence* the paper-making and paper-using nation of all the world ; we made more paper in 1860 than either England or France, and were believed to consume more than both together.   Those two countries produced in 1854 only 334,600,000 pounds of paper, while this country in that year produced 270,000,000 pounds, and the production of England and France was 4.55 pounds per capita, while that of the United States was 10.80 pounds per capita. As early as 1790, Alexander Hamilton classed the manufacture of paper among those which had arrived at the greatest maturity, and was most adequate to a national supply.   The census of 1810 showed that the consumption was supplied almost wholly by the domestic manufacture, and from that time to this rags have been largely imported to supply a lack of material.   After the war, among other manufactures which suffered from the competition stimulated by fictitious prices was that of paper, and duties were imposed in protective tariffs for its support, of 30 per cent. in 1816, specific from 3 to 20 cents a pound in 1824, and from 3 to 17 cents in 1842.   But in the general progress of manufactures in the period of the compromise tariff this branch became one of the most firmly established.   In 1830, just before protection ceased, the Fourdrinier machine was first manufactured here, and that and other greatly-improved mechanism were very generally adopted during the period from 1832 to 1840.   In 1836, when the importations of all articles were extravagantly large, we imported only $152,000 worth of paper of all kinds, and in the same year exported $44,857.   So insignificant were our imports of this article that in many Treasury reports of that date they are not specified at all, but our exports of paper and stationery became a regular item of consequence in the yearly account.   In 1847, we were exporting paper worth $88,731 ; in 1850, $99,696 ; in 1855, $185,637 ; and 1860, $285,798.   At no time have our imports of paper formed any appreciable share of our consumption ; thus in 1840 we made paper worth $5,641,499, and imported less than $100,000 ; in 1850 we made paper worth $10,187,177, and imported less than half a million ; and in 1860, when our product was over twenty-one millions, we imported writing-paper worth $300,000, wall-paper worth $144,000, and manufactures of paper amounting to about $200,000 more. In 1868, under the high duties, we imported about one million worth—more than before, but still not enough to be seriously compared with the domestic product. The truth is, that since the manufacture with the modern machinery became thoroughly established in this country, which had taken place by 1840, the paper manufacture has been absolutely independent—so independent, indeed, as to form at times, by combinations among makers, a most odious monopoly. The importation has been mainly confined to such products as the fancy or taste of consumers may prefer to the cheaper American article. From 1840 to 1850, with four years of protective duties, the manufacture increased 81 per cent. ; and from 1850 to 1860, without protective duties, 110 per cent. It would be a waste of time to consider this manufacture more at length, did not its recent history afford some instructive items.

When protection came as an epidemic in 1861, it attacked this interest among others, and gave it 35 per cent. duties upon foreign products, a tariff which still remains. Not long after, the war and other causes having induced a very rapid increase of consumption, the paper-makers found themselves in possession of a valuable monopoly, which they used remorselessly. Prices beyond all reason were demanded and obtained, and, all checks through foreign competition upon this plundering of the public being removed, the paper-manufacturers realized enormous incomes. In one collection district ninety-nine persons interested in this industry returned in 1865–'66 incomes of $948,988; one corporation an income of $178,000, and ten individuals an average of $31,430 each. In consequence, after the public had been fleeced in this way for three years, 1863–'65, the manufacture began to extend very rapidly ; and more paper-mills were put in operation in the years 1865–'66 than in a long period before. But the production had not been much less than the demand, and prices fell with great rapidity. The whole industry was prostrated more seriously than ever before; many men lost all their capital; many mills were sold at a great sacrifice ; and in the spring of 1869 the manufacturers in New England met in convention to discuss the propriety of " decreasing the production of paper." In October, 1869, a great storm helped them by destroying many mills and dams, and this providential interposition was regarded as a real relief. Was it for the good of the country to induce so many men to ruin themselves, in order to effect what foreign competition, if let alone, would have effected without injury to anybody —a reduction of the cost of paper? Can any system be a blessing to a country which needs a foreign war to give it a fair start, and an occasional earthquake or tornado as an antidote to its poison?

Yet is not this the very core of the protective theory—that withdrawal of foreign competition, by giving to an industry unnatural profits, will force it to a growth unnaturally rapid? It has been proved that this supposed law is not always sustained by facts; that in some cases the unnatural profits do not accelerate but really retard the growth of an industry. But in the history of the cotton manufacture, and now in that of the paper manufacture, it also appears that, in every case where the unnatural growth is produced, it is followed by a prostration correspondingly severe. That prostration cripples hundreds of the most enterprising men, sweeps away an enormous capital, and so crushes an industry that an earthquake or a tornado seems a blessing if it annihilates a property wasted in over-production, and then, with reduced energy and means, the industry begins once more the Sisyphus-labor of rolling the rock of protection up-hill!

If it be true—and facts prove that it is true—that these prostrations retard the progress of an industry more than the seasons of forced growth help it; that they undermine its vitality *by crushing not the worst but many of the best men engaged therein, whereas natural competition weeds out the poorer and strengthens the more competent manufacturers;* then does it not follow that the system of protection, even when its very best results are realized, and all its theories are answered by facts, simply retards real progress in the production of wealth? Does it not induce to wasteful employment of capital and energy, and sustain men for long series of years in such waste of means, when natural competition would quickly warn them of their error? Does it not in this way undermine and weaken even the most vigorous industry, and prepare it to need perpetual nursing in hospital, and shelter from that very competition which would have preserved its health? These surely are questions which go to the very root of the matter, and the records of the manufacturers of paper and cotton supply the answers. The protective system is a boomerang—a weapon fit only for barbarians to use, which, in civilized hands, is quite apt to knock the thrower on the head.

Paper-making employed 10,911 hands, printing employed 20,159, in 1860, and yielded a product of $31,063,898. Whenever high duties on paper increase its cost, they injure the larger industry of printing. Thus, during the years of extravagant prices already mentioned, the cost of paper forced hundreds of newspapers to suspend, while others, raising their price, checked the increase of their subscriptions. Hundreds of job-offices were broken down; and all, obliged to charge more for work, had less work to do. Many a book went unpublished which might have yielded a profit to publisher and author; many more which were published met with a sale limited by their enhanced cost, and resulted in loss instead of profit, because of the extravagant prices of paper. Thus the legislative boomerang not only came back with force upon the paper monopolists, who deserved it, but it damaged another industry far more important in the production of wealth, and incomparably more important in its bearing upon the education of the people.

But it is not true that, even at the expense of prostration, a monopoly always cures itself. The history of the pig-iron interest has proved that the monopoly sometimes perpetuates itself by checking consumption in time of high prices, and in the cotton and woollen manufacture it has appeared that over-production of a particular article is often relieved by working short time without a reduction of price. Perhaps the most striking illustration of this method of evading natural laws is found in the history of coal-mining.

In mining coal there were employed, in 1860, 36,486 persons, and the value of their product was $20,579,329. At that time there were mined 14,577,648 tons of coal, according to the census reports, and the number of hands employed had increased from 15,124 persons in 1850, or nearly 150 per cent., while the capital invested in this branch of industry had increased within the decade over twenty-one millions, or 253 per cent. It needs no other demonstration to show that this industry, as a whole, requires no protection whatever; and the least consideration of the cost of transporting a product so bulky in proportion to its value, will make it clear that any duties, however heavy, can have effect only within a short distance from the seaboard. In 1860 the cost of moving coal from the mines to market was declared by the census reports to be at least 50 per cent. on its cost at the mines, which was then $1.34 for bituminous, and $1.46 for anthracite coal. But the freight on coal from Port Carbon, Pennsylvania, to New York, in April, 1869, was $2.33 a ton, and in August, $4.08 a ton, while the price of coal in June was $3.75. One hundred per cent. on the cost is therefore charged for transportation 175 miles. It is plain that no foreign coal can be transported to this country, and then moved more than fifty miles inland, except in New England, without meeting a cheaper supply from our own mines; for our deposits of coal are scattered over the whole country, from tide-water in Pennsylvania to Monte Diablo in California, and foreign coal cannot possibly compete with our own, except in cities on the Atlantic coast and on the lakes, and in New England. The coal duty affects those localities only. In New England, Northern New York, and New-York City, foreign coal might be used in place of the American anthracite, if no duty hindered.

Coal is power. A vast manufacturing industry of New England and New York is by protection compelled to depend for its power upon supplies of coal from Pennsylvania. Anthracite-coal owners in the State of Pennsylvania tax all iron manufacturing in the Eastern States, and all other manufacturing which depends upon this coal for power. They are not slow to use the monopoly thus bestowed upon them by the aid of New-England votes in Congress; and, as long as they can persuade Eastern members to vote for protective duties, so long will Eastern constituents pay tribute to Pennsylvania. Millions of them, who use anthracite for fuel, have had occasion within the last year to thank their representatives for a tariff by which the cost of that fuel has been more than doubled. With them the burden and the remedy might be left, since their votes contribute to sustain the very system which plunders them, were it not instructive to see how a monopoly can be prolonged without benefit to anybody. For the anthracite mining is really a monopoly, controlled in part by the mining companies, and in part by the combination of miners themselves. Having within a narrow boundary the only considerable deposit of anthracite in the country, they control the price at their pleasure, and New York and New England, from which Nova-Scotia coal is practically excluded by the tariff, form their principal market.

Early in the year 1869 it was discovered, by no means for the first time, that the supply of anthracite coal exceeded the demand. When the same thing had occurred before, the mining companies, by agreeing among themselves to stop production, or by getting up strikes among their men, had repeatedly contrived to diminish the supply without permitting a reduction of the price. In 1869, the miners, who had learned the lesson thoroughly, took the matter into their own hands. Out of thirty thousand men employed in the entire anthracite region, over twenty-five thousand stopped work. The suspension continued for months. The price of coal rose to ten dollars a ton in New York, and the miners, in their negotiation with employers, formally demanded that it should be agreed that, whenever the price of coal should fall below five dollars a ton, all work should cease.   Before the strike, miners were paid about 90 cents a car, or 45 cents a ton, for mining, and at this price were making better wages than the very best mechanics, the lowest order of unskilled and newly-imported labor in the mines being paid $12 a week. After the strike the miners obtained $2.39 a car, or about $1.20 per ton for mining, and laborers received as much as $22 a week.   The object of the strike was to secure, first, such wages as these, and second, the agreement that work should stop whenever the price should fall so low as to make it impossible to pay such wages.

It is easy to see that, if the consumption is not checked, the price of coal can be kept as high as the miners please, and they can charge the public, if they like, a year's wages for doing only a day's work, provided all competition can be excluded.   But, if the coal of Nova Scotia were admitted free of duty, these monopolists could not plunder the public beyond that point at which it would be profitable to import.   No argument is needed to show that the production of wealth is retarded by this combination to keep up prices, and by the duty which makes it practicable.   The direct and avowed object of the combination is to prevent the natural increase in the production of. coal, and to compel other laborers to pay an unnatural price for their fuel, and other industries an unnatural price for their power. In a word, this is the protective system stripped bare of all disguises. Its object is to pay men for a wasteful application of capital and industry, either to the production of articles which can be more cheaply imported, or to the production by methods or in localities not the most advantageous and economical; and this it does by compelling other industries to pay the favored one an artificial price for its product.   When foreign competition is naturally excluded, by cost of transportation, from a large part of the country, and no duty whatever is necessary, the effect of the duty is, first, to plunder that part of the country which might otherwise supply itself more cheaply; and second, to create an absolute monopoly, like the mining of anthracite, with power to impose almost any tax it may please, and, by stopping production from time to time, to compel the consumer to pay more and not less, whenever over-production threatens to reduce the price.

Twenty-five thousand men idle for four months, and as many more idle because mills and factories could not afford to buy coal at $10 a ton—is this the road to wealth?   It is an absolute waste of the industry of two hundred thousand men for a month—of one-sixth of all the laborers engaged in non-agricultural production. But the same stoppage of production, to keep up prices, has been seen during the past year (1869), in the cotton and woollen manufacture, and in paper-making. Suppose a law should require that one-third of all laborers employed in manufacturing should lie idle every month, taking turns, and that those who work should pay the expenses of the idle third; would any one think that a wise and economical disposition of our industrial energies? Precisely the same in kind, if not in degree, is the effect of any law which, by securing artificial profits to any industry, prompts more persons to engage therein than the demand for its products will sustain, and enables them, by repeated seasons of idleness, to keep up prices in spite of the excess of production. High duties invite, in certain cases, an unnatural increase of the manufacture. Sometimes the result is a prostration, such as the paper manufacture has recently experienced. Sometimes, by perfect combination, the loss by wasteful over-production is thrown upon the consumer, as in the case of coal, and the country then pays three men for doing the work of two. The protectionist, when he interferes with natural laws, can never know with certainty which of these results will follow. But either of them involves a waste of energy, capital, and labor—a destruction of a certain share of the wealth-producing power of the country. If thirty thousand men, working eight months, can supply all the anthracite coal we need, twenty thousand, working the whole year, can do the same at two-thirds of the cost, and the remaining ten thousand ought to be forced, by natural competition, to go to work at some other industry, in which they could contribute to the national prosperity. But, the fact is, that the consumption is checked by the price. The work of thirty thousand, full time, is needed to give other industries cheaper power, so that the thirty thousand and all other laborers may have cheaper tools and clothing. And each man of them would get as much money in a year, with coal reduced in price and wages also reduced, as he now receives, working only two-thirds of a year. But a law has created a monopoly, and the miner tries to use it. The consequence is, that he must be idle one-third of the time, the country must pay him for doing nothing, his tools and clothing become more costly, and all the country is taxed and all industry embarrassed.

The manufacture of glass employed 9,016 persons in 1860, and yielded a product of $8,775,155. This is another industry which increased about 100 per cent. in the last decade of low duties; for in 1850 the number of hands was 5,668, and the product $4,641,766. And in this case also we observe a less rapid increase in the previous decade, during which the protective tariff of 1842–'46 occurred. For in 1840 the glass manufacture employed 3,236 persons, and produced to the value of $2,890,293. The history of this industry shows a natural and steady growth, not greatly affected at any time since 1820 by foreign competition. In 1791 it had hardly found a footing; but in 1810 Mr. Gallatin reported that the manufacture was firmly established, and the census showed a production of 4,967,000 square feet of window-glass, while only 27,000 boxes were imported. This was before the adoption of any protective tariff; thirty years afterward, after many years of high duties, the value of the entire product of glass-works was less than three millions, while the value of the window-glass alone produced in 1810 was over one million. The manufacture of window-glass and bottles for ordinary use had become, as Mr. Dallas stated in his report of 1816, so firmly and permanently established as to wholly or almost wholly supply the consumption; but the protective theory of that period seems to have been to place the heaviest duties on those articles the manufacture of which least needed aid, and accordingly heavy specific duties were placed on window-glass, while other glass was admitted at a revenue duty of 20 per cent. By 1818 it is mentioned that the New-England Glass Company was established, which made "every variety of fine, plain, and the richest cut-glass for domestic supply and exportation to the West Indies and South America;" and in 1823 ten glass establishments had been started in New York alone since 1818. The prostration of 1819 and 1820 severely affected the glass manufacture in Pittsburg, but with the revival of business it became more powerful than ever, and the New-England Company was in 1823 making 22,400 pounds of glass a week. In Pittsburg there were, in 1825, seven glass-works, producing 27,000 boxes annually, and about $100,000 worth of domestic glass was then exported. In 1827 the manufacture of stained glass, decanters, white, flint and green glass, rivalling any foreign glass in excellence, is mentioned, and among the many manufacturers who then appealed for more aid there were none of this branch. In 1829 the manufacture of watch-crystals by two establishments is mentioned, and in 1831 it was estimated that the manufacture employed 2,140 persons and yielded a product of three millions. Whether all this progress was due to the protective duties on window-glass, bottles, phials, and cut-glass imposed in 1824 and yet in force, we can judge from certain facts, namely: the manufacture had grown prior to the imposition of these duties

so as to become firmly established in 1816; it grew rapidly after the
prostration in 1819, and before the duties of 1824 were imposed;
and, when those duties were reduced in 1832 by the compromise
tariff, the price of American glass was affected very slightly. The
tables of prices at the close of this chapter show that the price per
50 feet had been absolutely unchanged during the whole period of
protection from 1824 to 1832, namely, $3.12, which shows that the
manufacture, sheltered against competition, either made no improvements or suffered no improvement to diminish the cost to consumers.
But in 1834 the price fell to $2.75, and in 1836 to $2.25 @ $2.37. In
that year the importation of foreign window-glass was only $190,000
—not enough to interfere with the manufacture in any degree. But
this competition simply proved that the domestic manufacturer could
afford the ordinary qualities cheaper than the foreign glass could be
imported.   From that time the price was steadily reduced to $1.87
@ $2.67 in 1842, and to $1.83 @ $2.62 in 1843, according to the
statement of Philadelphia sales.   In 1840 the importation had fallen
to $56,000, and was almost wholly of plate-glass.

While the manufacture of window-glass, by far the most important branch of this industry, thus proved its independence, the
domestic manufacture was pushed by competition, after the change
of tariff in 1832, to that invention which has given it in this country
a peculiar success.   In 1834 the invention of pressed glass is first
mentioned as having been adopted in this country, and it caused a
complete revolution in the manufacture, enabling it to produce a
great variety of articles at prices much below those attained by
methods formerly in use.   This invention, though borrowed from us
by England, helped to put this industry beyond the reach of danger,
and the importation was reduced from $618,107 in 1836 to $360,847
in 1840, while the number of hands employed increased from 2,140
in 1831 to 3,236 in 1840.   With such an increase of the manufacture, and importations decreased so largely in spite of reduced
duties, and so trifling in comparison with the domestic production,
this industry may certainly be considered in little need of the protection given by the tariff of 1842.   At least, that tariff did not
diminish the trifling importation, but increased it to $519,210 worth
of window and plate, and $167,019 of other glass in the closing year,
1846.   It is, perhaps, a suggestive fact that the years 1845 and 1846
are the only ones, prior to 1860, in which English crown-glass is
quoted in the tables of prices published in the Treasury report of
1863.   In those years English glass is quoted at $3.50 to $4, and

American glass, which before the tariff had sold at $1.87 @ $2.67, rose in 1846 to $2.06 @ $2.81, according to the Philadelphia tables. But after the expiration of that tariff the price fell to $1.65 @ $2.16. These facts appear to indicate that prices of American glass were so high in 1846 under protection that the English glass began to be considerably imported. For ordinary use, however, the American glass completely excluded the foreign, both before and after this protective period, and the importation then and since has been mainly of the finer qualities and larger sizes of plate and of silvered glass. In 1860 these items amounted to $1,630,000, while all other imported glass was valued at about $500,000. Importations not greater than these it will not be supposed could have retarded the manufacture, and it has been shown that the increase during the decade of low duties was 100 per cent. During the same non-protective period we increased our exports of glass more than 200 per cent.; from $90,860 in 1846, the closing year of protection, to $136,682 in 1850, and $277,948 in 1860.

The high protective duties recently imposed have not prevented an importation of glass nearly double that of 1860. For in that year the value of glass imported was $2,175,000, and in 1869 it was $4,194,881. No facts are accessible to the writer which indicate that the domestic manufacture has grown with equal rapidity, though it has been much extended. Several times, within the past few years, the price has been put up, strikes of workmen being alleged as the cause, and recently the workmen seem to have learned, like the coal-miners, to manage the matter for themselves, and the rates now paid are extravagantly high. Meanwhile the importation has increased most largely of those very qualities which we long ago demonstrated our ability to exclude by domestic production. In 1868 the cast polished plate imported, silvered or not, amounted to $712,608. But the "cylinder, crown or common window glass" was imported to the value of $1,238,239. Of this quality there was imported in 1860 only 18,827,897 square feet, and in 1868 not less than 29,325,991 *pounds!* The importation of 1869 was very much larger; in seven months in 1868 the quantity imported was less than 15,000,000 pounds, and in the same seven months in 1869 the quantity was 24,301,262 pounds. How much longer must this "protection" continue, before it brings into absolute peril that very manufacture of window-glass which, far back in 1810, was officially declared to be permanently established, and which under the low duties in 1840 had excluded all foreign window-glass except to the value of

$56,746 ? Truly, if this is the effect of protection as compared with non-protection, the glass manufacture may well pray to be protected against its protectors !

PRICE OF WINDOW-GLASS.

From 1835 to 1849, at Philadelphia.—(*Statement by Hay and Coffin, Treasury Report,* 1849.)

YEARS.	8 x 10.	10 x 12.	10 x 14.	12 x 18.	YEARS.	8 x 10.	10 x 12.	10 x 14.	12 x 18.
1835........	$2 37	$2 37	$3 09	$3 56	1843.....	$1 83	$1 92	$2 36	$2 62
1836........	2 49	2 49	3 09	3 56	1844.....	1 80	1 90	2 30	2 57
1837........	2 36	2 48	2 93	3 37	1845.....	1 70	1 79	2 19	2 44
1838........	2 23	2 46	2 90	3 35	1846.....	2 06	2 25	2 44	2 81
1839........	2 22	2 35	2 87	3 19	1847.....	1 92	2 10	2 28	2 63
1840........	2 23	2 35	2 87	3 19	1848.....	1 79	1 95	2 11	2 44
1841........	2 05	2 26	2 76	3 07	1849.....	1 65	1 80	1 87	2 16
1842........	1 87	1 96	2 40	2 67					

PRICE OF AMERICAN GLASS AT NEW YORK.

From Treasury Report, 1863.

YEARS.	Per Box.	YEAR.	Per Box.	YEAR.	Per Box.
1825..........	$3 12	1838..........	$2 75@3 00	1851..........	$2 62@3 50
1826..........	3 12@3 25	1839..........	2 75@3 00	1852..........	2 62@3 50
1827..........	3 12	1840..........	2 75@3 00	1853..........	2 50@3 25
1828..........	3 12	1841..........	2 75@3 00	1854..........	2 50@3 25
1829..........	3 12	1842..........	2 75@3 90	1855..........	2 50@3 25
1830..........	3 12	1843..........	2 75@3 00	1856..........	2 50@3 25
1831..........	3 12	1844..........	2 75@3 00	1857..........	2 75@3 50
1832..........	3 12	1845*.........	3 50@4 00	1858..........	3 00@3 75
1833..........	3 12	1846*.........	3 50@4 00	1859..........	2 75@3 50
1834..........	2 75@3 00	1847..........	2 62@3 50	1860..........	2 75@3 50
1835..........	2 50@2 75	1848..........	2 62@3 50	1861..........	2 75@3 50
1836..........	2 25@2 37	1849..........	2 62@3 50	1862..........	2 75@3 50
1837..........	2 75@3 00	1850..........	2 62@3 50	1863..........	3 25@4 50

CHAPTER XVIII.

THE SALT MANUFACTURE.

LONG ago, when Albany was a frontier town, the Indians used to bring salt from Onondaga to Albany with their furs. The manufacture which these savages were able to continue, though having to carry their product hundreds of miles on foot, now demands a duty of 130 per cent. to keep it alive !

In 1629, the fishermen of Cape Cod brought back from the seashore good salt, spontaneously produced by the evaporation of the

---

* For these two years the Treasury table gives no quotation of American glass, but gives " English crown " instead.

water left upon marshes and rocks. Then it was first learned that our warmth and dryness of climate are peculiarly adapted to the manufacture of salt. But the work which the sun did spontaneously for the fishermen of 1648—of whom Plantagenet writes that "without boiling, only in pans with the sun, each laborer may make six bushels a day"—that work their descendants cannot do without a duty of 130 per cent. to protect them!

In 1787, the Oneida Indians ceded to New York the Onondaga salt-lands, and in 1797 the State first legislated on the subject; and the product of the springs was 25,474 bushels. Sixty miles westward, this salt could then be sold for half a dollar a bushel, or $2.50 a barrel; in 1867, its price at Syracuse was $2.35 per barrel, and at Buffalo, $2.50; but in New-York City the patriotic owners, after paying 37½ cents a barrel for transportation, could afford to sell it for $1.75, and in Canada they are selling it even now at $1.35 a barrel, in gold.

These wells yield a bushel of salt for every 30 to 50 gallons of brine evaporated, and the actual cost per bushel in 1858 was not more than 6 cents. If the cost was doubled in 1867—and it was not—the Onondaga Company realized on every barrel of five bushels, costing 60 cents, a profit of $1.75, at the Syracuse price—not quite 300 per cent. An industry so needy and deserving as this surely should be carefully protected by every statesman!

In the War of 1812, the salt-wells on the Alleghany were opened, and before the close of the century salt was made and sold at moderate prices in Kentucky, Tennessee, on the Illinois and Wabash, and west of the Mississippi; and the Wabash salines had been used for more than half a century by the Indians for the manufacture of salt, before the Americans came into possession. In 1809 these supplied 130,000 bushels of salt, and many other works at the West so reduced the price that during the war with England salt averaged only 87½ cents a bushel at the West, while worth from three to six dollars at the seaboard. Yet Mr. Greeley thinks we must put on high duties to prevent the West being forced to pay too large prices. There are a great many people at the West, at this moment, who would be pleased to get foreign salt at the cost of importation, so remorseless have the monopolists learned to be under protective duties.

In 1789 Congress imposed a duty of six cents a bushel, and in 1790 we imported 2,337,920 bushels. But, finding that a then far more important industry would suffer in consequence, Congress authorized a drawback on salt intended for the fisheries, and, when

18

the duty was increased in 1797 to 20 cents a bushel, an increased drawback was authorized. But, in 1806, convinced that the whole duty was onerous and worse than useless, Congress repealed it, in spite of protests. The product of the Onondaga salt-works in this year was 165,448 bushels, and by 1809, or within three years after the duty was repealed, it had increased to 300,000 bushels. The importation was neither materially increased nor diminished, but for six years ending 1807 had averaged about 3,000,000 bushels, exclusive of the quantity used in fishery and for exported meats. During the next ten years after the repeal of the duty, extensive works were erected, and the domestic production greatly increased. By 1810, works in North Carolina, covering 275,000 square feet, had been erected, and the Western States supplied about 300,000 bushels. The census of 1810 reported 62 salt-works, producing 1,238,365 bushels.

During the war our foreign trade was greatly interrupted, first by hostilities, and second by another blessing—in the estimation of protectionists—enormous duties. A duty of 20 cents a bushel on salt, with the interruption of trade, caused the price to rise, in 1814, at New York, to $3 a bushel. The production was rapidly increased, but could not supply the demand, and in spite of the duty, after hostilities ceased, imports became larger than ever. In 1826 it was stated, in documents laid before the Senate, that the quantity of salt made in the United States was 4,113,000 bushels. If this estimate be accepted as correct, it enables us to make a comparison of domestic production with imports. For in that year, notwithstanding the duty of 180 per cent. on the first cost, the imports of salt for consumption were 4,534,040 bushels; total consumption, 8,647,000 bushels, of which 47 per cent. was of domestic production. At that time the price was 50 cents in New York, although Turk's Island salt cost at the island eleven cents, and New-York salt was not claimed to cost the producer more than 20 cents. In 1829, three years after, a report to the New-York Legislature recommended a bounty, in addition to the enormous duties, to still further stimulate this needy manufacture. Yet this same report admitted that salt was made at the works at a cost of 12½ cents a bushel with fair profit to the makers, though it sold in New-York City at about 50 cents. Meanwhile the cost of Turk's Island salt had been somewhat reduced, and the importations had increased to 5,945,547 bushels, while the domestic production had increased to 4,444,929 bushels. Thus, in three years, the proportion of domestic salt to the whole consumption fell from 47 per cent. in 1826, to 44 per cent. in 1829.

Very sensibly, Congress reduced the duty to 15 cents in 1830, and to 10 cents after that year, but in 1831 a committee reported that the poor manufacturer would be ruined unless the duty was restored. The same report stated that the average price at the West was then 62½ cents a bushel, and yet the manufacturer who could produce at a cost of 12½ cents a bushel could not live! Under the reduction of duty the price fell in 1831 to 42 cents in New York, and to 38 cents in 1833. In that year Baltimore merchants petitioned for a further reduction of duty, stating that a factory in Maine was able to sell rock-salt at 25 cents a bushel, and cleared $100,000 a year. But, although the manufacturers had declared that they would be ruined by the reduction of duty, it appears that the product of New York State increased from one million bushels in 1829, to 2,209,867 in 1834—a gain of more than 120 per cent. in five years. Thenceforward, with duties reduced under the compromise act to almost nothing, the manufacture rapidly increased, so that in 1840 the domestic production was 6,179,174 bushels, while the price at New York fell to 32 cents in 1840, and to 26 cents in 1841. But the admission of foreign salt at lower duty did not materially increase the importation, for in 1829 the quantity imported was 5,945,547 bushels, and in 1842 it was 6,127,439 bushels; in 1834 the value of salt imported was $839,315, and in 1842 it was $841,572.

Contrast now the two periods, protective ending in 1830, and non-protective ending in 1840. The protective period held up the price of salt to 50 cents, though it actually cost only 12½ cents, and increased production from 4,010,569 bushels in 1820, to 4,444,929 bushels in 1830—an increase of 10 per cent. in ten years. Meanwhile, the importation of salt had increased from 4,200,000 bushels to 5,945,547 bushels, or 42 per cent. But the non-protective period lowered the price of salt from 50 to 30 cents, increased domestic production from 4,444,929 bushels to 6,179,174 bushels, or 42 per cent. in ten years, while the importation increased scarcely any. Is it not plain that the non-protective period, increasing the production of salt 40 per cent., and lowering the price to consumers 40 per cent. without increasing imports, was really of greater benefit to the country at large, and more truly beneficial to the salt manufacture itself, than the protective period, which increased production 10 per cent., kept up the price, and permitted an increase of imports of 40 per cent.?

This contrast ought to be forced upon the attention of every man who claims that high duties must reduce prices, and at the same time check imports, and increase domestic production. The same principles which govern one branch of industry, also govern others. If these theories, the pet arguments of those who defend monopoly, are conclusively proved to be false in one case, they are unworthy of reliance in every case.

The tariff of 1842 imposed a duty of about 75 per cent. on foreign salt, and the domestic production increased from 6,100,000 in 1840 to 6,500,000 in 1845. (The production in 1846 the writer has been unable to ascertain.) But in the same time the value of imports had increased from $841,572 in 1842 to $911,512 in 1844, and $898,663 in 1845, and the quantity of salt imported from 6,127,439 bushels to 8,543,527 bushels in 1845.

The tariff of 1846 reduced the duty to about two cents a bushel, and the production of salt at once rose from 6,500,000 in 1845 to 9,763,849 bushels in 1850, a gain of 50 per cent. in five years. Yet salt sold for 35 cents in New York, in 1845, and for 40 cents in 1846, and it fell in 1850 to 21 cents. Here was a gain of 50 per cent. in the quantity manufactured, and a gain of nearly 50 per cent. in the cost to the consumer. During the same time, imports had increased only to 11,224,185 bushels—barely 30 per cent.

Here is the same contrast again. Protection increased the domestic production 6 per cent., at a cost of 5 to 10 cents a bushel, imports meanwhile increasing 40 per cent. Non-protection increased domestic production 50 per cent., and lowered the price 14 to 19 cents, imports meanwhile increasing 30 per cent. The two periods were each of five years, and each began with a year of contrary character—the protective period with the year 1841, non-protective; and the non-protective period with the year 1846, protective. Is it not time for some advocate of high duties to reconcile these oft-recurring contrasts, so striking and so impressive, with the theories upon which all protective tariffs are based? Does it seem strange that high duties check production? It is not strange at all. They create a monopoly, increase the cost of production, keep up prices, and pay people for adhering to wasteful methods. Meanwhile, prices elsewhere being reduced, partly because our duties force foreigners to cheaper production or smaller profits, importations increase more rapidly than domestic production. But low duties and low prices increase consumption, invite competition, and compel our industry to strengthen itself against that of other countries by better methods or development of greater natural advantages.

The duty on salt was reduced still further, to 1½ cents a bushel, by the tariff of 1857, and the production of salt, during this entire period of low tariff, increased more rapidly than population. It is noteworthy that this increase was not only in that locality which has the greatest natural resources then developed. The New York product increased from 3,838,851 bushels in 1846, to 7,521,335 bushels in 1860—a gain of about 100 per cent. But the product of the whole country increased from 6,500,000 to 12,717,200 bushels—a nearly equal gain. The average value of the product for the whole country was about 18 cents a bushel in 1860, and that of New York about 17 cents. In 1846 salt sold in New York for 40 cents, and in 1850 for 21; it rose during the years 1853, 1854, and 1855, but fell again to 26 cents in 1856, to 20 cents in 1857, to 16 cents in 1858, and was sold at 17 in 1859 and 1860, and as low as 15 in 1861. Under these low prices the consumption rose enormously, and while Great Britain consumed only 25 pounds of salt per capita, and France only 21½ pounds, our whole consumption in this country in 1860 was 26,811,427 bushels, or nearly a bushel per capita, and our domestic product alone was 22½ pounds per capita, or more than the whole consumption of France. Thus do low duties stimulate consumption, create an enormous demand, and consequently invite and sustain a great increase of the producing industry.

Because this manufacture had not absolutely excluded foreign salt, and though it had grown in New York and in the whole country 100 per cent. under low duties, there was still more salt imported than was produced, our legislators imposed duties designed to be prohibitory. By records of actual importations, Mr. Wells has proved that these duties range from 115 to 170 per cent. on the cost of the article. The price in other countries has not yet been so much reduced as to entirely overcome this obstacle, and the importations for 1868 were 636,041,262 pounds, or, at 56 pounds to the bushel, about 11,358,000 bushels—a reduction of 2,700,000 bushels. The quantity actually produced in the country is not known to the writer, but the price is so largely increased that it may well be supposed that consumption has been checked. The same salt which sold as low as 15 cents in 1861, and 17 cents in 1860, at New York, now sells at 48 to 50 cents, while Onondaga salt sells at Buffalo at $2.45 a barrel; salt made on the Ohio River sells at Cincinnati for 46 to 48 cents, and the price at New Orleans is about 50 cents.

If we have increased the domestic production of salt, we have done it at the expense of an increase of price from 17 cents in 1860 to 37 cents (gold) in 1868-'69, so that, if consumption is as large in proportion to population as it then was, we are paying a tax of seven millions and a quarter in gold, in increased cost of the salt which we use, and of that tax precisely $1,136,225.76 is paid to the government. Over six millions a year in gold is paid in the shape of bounty, and those who wish to know where it has gone, may read the testimony of the secretary of the Onondaga monopoly, who states that the company has increased stock worth $160,000 in 1860 to not less than $4,498,969 in 1867. The letter of Duncan Stewart, president of the Saginaw Salt Association, who declares "the present high tariff simply an outrage on the best interests of the country," and the pertinent facts presented by Mr. Wells in his reports, must surely convince any man that the protective duty on salt is not now necessary for the support of that industry; and the facts here given prove that it never has been of any service, but has simply retarded the growth of this manufacture. Let the facts be remembered:

		Protection.		Product to consumption
YEAR.	Domestic product.	Imported.	Consumed.	per cent.
1820......	$4,010,569	$4,200,000	$8,210,569	48
1826......	4,113,000	4,534,040	8,647,040	47
1829......	4,444,929	5,945,547	10,390,476	44

Average price, 50 cents a bushel.
Increase of product, 10 per cent.
Increase of imports, 42 per cent.

Non-protection.

1842......	$6,179,174*	$6,127,439	$12,306,613	50

Price reduced from 50 to 30 cents.
Increase of product, 40 per cent.
Increase of imports, 3 per cent.

Protection.

1845......	$6,500,000	$8,543,527	$15,043,527	43

Price increased to 35 and 40 cents.
Increase of production, 6 per cent.
Increase of imports, 40 per cent.

Non-protection.

1850......	$9,763,849	$11,224,185	$20,988,034	46$\frac{1}{2}$
1860......	12,717,200	14,094,227	26,811,427	47$\frac{1}{2}$

Price reduced to 17 cents.
Increase of production, 95 per cent.
Increase of imports, 65 per cent.

---

* The product of 1840 is given instead of that of 1842, which is not known, but supposed to be at least as great. The figures for 1846, the last year of the second protective period, are not known to the writer.

Readers will ask with surprise two questions: "How does it come to pass that any American Congressman can suppose a duty on salt necessary or useful for protection?" "How does it happen that duties of more than 100 per cent. have not checked the importation of this article?" The first question can be answered only by Congress itself. The second is within the understanding of the ordinary human intellect.

Twenty-five years ago it was declared that "provisions packed with ordinary domestic salt suffer a depreciation in value, not only in foreign but in our own markets." There is a chemical difference between the salt spontaneously produced under a tropical sun and any which has yet been manufactured by any process, dear or cheap, in more northern latitudes, and the salt of the West Indies is therefore superior for use in packing meats, fish, and provisions, to any which this country produces. When we import Turk's Island salt, we are importing so much tropical sunlight, as the raw material of our packing industry—and the attempt to shut it out is simply an endeavor to deny to our provision-packers the benefit of that tropical sunlight, and to "light the world with gas!"

No wonder it is impossible to exclude this necessary material of an industry so important! In 1860 the packing of provisions employed 7,479 persons, and yielded a product of over $31,000,000. The salt manufacture employed 2,213 persons, and yielded a product of two millions and a quarter. But under the name of protecting American industry we are taxing, prostrating, and driving out of the country, an industry worth thirty millions a year, in a futile attempt to help, which in fact only injures, an industry worth two millions a year! The number of hogs packed at the West, under the protective tariff, when salt cost from 30 to 40 cents a bushel, was 1,079,082 in 1844, 781,372 in 1845, and 1,087,862 in 1846; but when the duty was reduced to 20 per cent., and the cost of salt to 21 to 24 cents in 1850, the number of hogs packed increased to 1,652,220, to 2,201,116 in 1853, and 2,350,822 in 1860, when salt cost 18 cents. In this industry there was an increase under low duties, from 1846 to 1860, of more than 120 per cent., and, were statistics accessible, it would probably appear that the whole packing business of the country increased, if not quite as largely, at least more largely than the importation of foreign salt. When this industry is retarded, a part of the loss falls upon the farmer. In 1826, when the duty on salt was 20 cents, and salt cost over 50 cents in New York, the price of hogs in Cincinnati was $2 per cwt. In 1835, when the duty was about seven cents, and salt sold in New York from 30 to 40 cents, the price of hogs in Cincinnati was $3.12 per cwt. In 1846, when the duty was eight cents a bushel, and the cost of salt about the same as in 1835, the price of hogs was $3 per cwt. But, after the reduction of the duty to 20 per cent., the price of salt fell to 20 cents in 1852, and 26 cents in 1853, and to 17 to 18 cents in 1859–'60, and the price of hogs at Cincinnati rose to $4 per cwt. in 1853, and to $6.21 in 1860.

Two facts prove at once the uselessness of the present duty for protection, and the evil effect of that duty upon other industries. From Mr. Wells's report it appears that the salt company in New York not only can, but actually does, send the salt to New England seaport towns, and there sell it to the fishermen, who are by law privileged to use foreign salt free of duty, at as low a rate as that foreign salt can thus be obtained. At the same time, we annually export to the British possessions over half a million bushels of American salt, which can there be sold at lower rates than foreign salt can be obtained. The Toronto *Globe* states that the Onondaga Salt Company (December, 1869) are offering salt in that city at $1.35 a barrel, and at the same time the very same salt cannot be bought on this side of Lake Ontario for less than $2.45, currency, or $1.94, gold. Nothing can more forcibly illustrate the character of the shameless and soulless monopoly, built up and sustained by the protective duty, than these facts. The company can afford to sell, and actually do sell, their salt in Toronto, after paying the cost of transportation to and across the lake, at 27 cents a bushel, and as transportation costs probably 10 cents a bushel, they make a satisfactory profit, even now selling their salt for 17 cents—just what it was worth in 1861. But on this side of the lake, having a comfortable monopoly, they refuse to sell for less than $1.94, gold, a barrel, or about 39 cents in gold a bushel. With satisfactory profit at 17 cents, they are permitted, under the name of "protection to Amercan industry," to force every American wool-grower to pay 22 cents more in gold—$1.10 gold, or $1.43 currency per hundred sheep—for his salt; to force every American pork-packer to pay $110, gold, or $143, currency, more than a fair price for every hundred barrels of salt used; to force the whole people to pay, upon perhaps 35,000,000 bushels consumed, not less than $7,250,000 in gold, or over $9,000,000 in currency, *more* than their salt actually costs. The duty robs the whole people. It plunders the farmer and the provision-packer. It does not even increase the production of salt, but, as statistics have proved, only retards the growth of that industry, and places it at a disadvantage compared with foreign competition. Whom, then, does it benefit? The salt monopolists. The men who have been able to realize a profit of $4,338,969 in seven years on an investment of $160,000.

This same duty is driving a more important manufacture to Canada. The Toronto *Globe*, already quoted, shows that American beef and pork can be packed more cheaply in that country, with foreign or even with American salt, than in this country within the clutches of the monopoly. As a matter of fact, therefore, seventeen millions of pounds of salt passed across this country in bond, imported and then exported, in 1868, to supply packing-establishments in another land where industry is not so marvellously benefited by legislation. Large packing-establishments have already been removed to Canada, and American beef and pork, there put up, already are exported from Canada to Liverpool. In 1860 there were 2,350,822 hogs packed at the West; in 1868–'69, for a population increased from thirty-one to thirty-eight millions, there were packed only 2,781,084 hogs, and the statistics thus far published indicate that the number for the season 1869–'70 will be still smaller. Thus, to enrich a monopoly, we retard the salt industry, worth $2,500,000 yearly, tax the wool industry, rob the people of ten million dollars, and drive the packing industry, worth over thirty millions yearly, to cross the border. How long shall we do this thing, and call it "protecting American industry?"

PRICE OF TURK'S ISLAND SALT AT NEW YORK.

From Report of Secretary of the Treasury, 1863.

YEAR.	Jan.	Feb.	March.	April.	May.	June.	July.	August.	Sept.	Oct.	Nov.	Dec.
1825	48	48	40	51	52	53	50	51	50	53	56	58
1826	53	50	50	50	53	50	52	49	48	48	49	49
1827	50	50	54	60	62	60	..	55	..	58	58	58
1828	53	50	..	50	48	48	48	47	46	48	52	53
1829	47	45	48	48	51	51	51	47	48	50	49	45
1830	45	45	40	44	46	48	45	45	45	..	56	55
1831	..	42	45	47	50	54	48	49	52	56	62	..
1832	45	42	46	50	50	45	48	48	46	53	53	51
1833	45	41	40	46	42	38	44	46	46	50	45	42
1834	38	35	36	40	..	40	39	38	38	38	42	37
1835	39	30	35	37	40	40	35	35	35	35	41	35
1836	34	32	32	35	40	40	38	38	33	37	41	45
1837	40	40	40	43	40	31	33	34	35	40	41	37
1838	35	35	35	35	33	33	42	41	38	45	48	47
1839	36	35	35	..	41	41	38	37	38	40	36	32
1840	32	..	..	..	36	34	34	34	..	35	..	35
1841	30	31	30	30	31	30	..	..	30	26	27	28
1842	..	..	..	..	..	..	..	..	..	..	..	..
1843	28	22	25	27	31	31	29	26	24	26	31	30
1844	..	..	..	..	..	..	..	..	..	..	..	..
1845	24	..	..	26	25	25	24	27	..	30	33	35
1846	28	20	45	40	25	20	26	28	29	32	31	32
1847	25	24	..	34	31	28	30	32	30	32	33	28
1848	26	..	25	27	26	26	25	23	24	26	20	22
1849	21	..	24	..	..	20	25	22	23	24	25	24
1850	23	..	..	..	21	..	23	24	27	28	23	21
1851	22	..	..	..	25	..	22	..	..	..	21	20
1852	20	..	19	20	21	..	23	..	..	22	21	21
1853	27	26	26	..	35	30	40	32	31	32	50	49
1854	45	..	42	45	47	46	45	50	48	53	50	47
1855	50	..	..	48	..	30	32	37	40	56	45	40
1856	..	..	..	..	27	27	29	30	34	33	31	26
1857	22	20	24	26	..	23	23	21	22	22	19	19
1858	16	18	18	..	17	18	22	19	19	..	17	18
1859	17	..	18	20	20	..	18	17	..	16	19	20
1860	19	18	17	18	18	19	19	..	18	20	21	19
1861	17	15	15	19	20	21	19	20	23	24	23	21
1862	20	30	30	24	24	27	30	31	30	31	36	32
1863	31	34	36	37	38	40	42	40	42	44	49	50

CHAPTER XIX.

SKILLED LABOR PROTECTS ITSELF.

NEITHER space nor accessible statistics permit a detailed examination of the history of minor branches of manufacture; yet there are many which illustrate, with peculiar force, principles already deduced from the history of those branches which are recognized as of chief importance, and which have been most zealously protected. Nor can any reasoning person escape the conclusion that, if high tariffs have been unnecessary to sustain those industries which require the largest capital, they have also been unnecessary to sustain others. If high tariffs have increased, in those industries, the cost of production in this country as compared with that in others, and have thus tended to defeat themselves, the same effect must have extended to minor branches of manufacture; and if high tariffs, interrupting the natural effect of competition, have checked real progress, the minor branches must also have been deprived of a healthy and natural growth, in proportion as they have been interfered with by legislation.

It must at least be conceded that if tariff discriminations have really given stimulus to any industry—if protection has been real, and not a sham—those branches which have received especial aid must have increased more rapidly than those which have been less favored, or which have received no artificial aid whatever. But, if the principles just stated are correct, those industries which have been left to the operation of natural laws, or but little considered in schemes of protection, must have progressed the more surely and rapidly. A comparison is possible. The principal manufactures which protection has been designed to stimulate have been those already examined, namely, of iron, cotton, wool, paper, glass, and salt. The following table, prepared from the census returns for 1840, 1850, and 1860, will show whether the increase in these branches of industry has been more rapid than the increase in other branches of manufacture, which have been in a less degree or not at all objects of protective care:

YEAR.	SIX BRANCHES. PROTECTED.		UNPROTECTED.	
	Hands.	Product.	Hands.	Product.
1840...................	152,413	$127,759,260	303,256	$112,076,964
1850...................	342,748	309,904,014	614,311	709,202,602
1860...................	411,474	503,257,210	899,772	1,381,016,320
Increase, 1840–50.........	....	144 per cent.	....	533 per cent.
" 1850–60.........	....	63 per cent.	....	94 per cent.

The greater completeness of the census in 1850 than in 1840 explains the apparent increase in that decade, both in the protected and the unprotected branches. But in both decades the unprotected —those branches of manufacture which have been in a less degree or not at all the objects of legislative aid—have grown more rapidly than those already considered in detail, which have been most assiduously cared for by legislation. No just comparison between the two decades can be instituted, because the returns of 1840 embrace only the leading branches of manufacture in each class, thus: the only entries for iron in 1840 are cast, rolled, hardware, and machinery, which yielded in 1850 less than seventy millions out of a total of one hundred and thirty-six millions produced by the whole iron interest. In like manner, more than half of the industries classed as unprotected were omitted from the account of manufactures altogether in 1840, so that the increase in that decade is apparent and not real. But the differences in the returns do not account for the fact that in each decade the product of the six industries chiefly protected increased less rapidly than the product of others not so favored. It should also be observed that during these decades, and all other decades in our history, whether we have had high duties or low, the country has increased more rapidly in manufactures than in population, and, regardless of all changes of tariff or in spite of them, we are steadily progressing toward a healthy and natural diversification of industry.

It is argued, by the advocates of protective duties, that such duties are needed because of the higher rate of wages in this than in other countries. To this it is enough to reply, that Continental nations are trying in vain to fence in their industries against British competition, although wages in England are higher than in any of those countries. Mr. Wells, in his report of 1869, presents this fact clearly and forcibly, and from his statistics we find that the wages in Belgium are actually lower, as compared with those of Great Britain, than are those of Great Britain as compared with the United States. Yet England floods Belgium even more than this country with her manufactured goods. It is also argued that the higher rate of interest in this country than in England places us at a disadvantage in manufacturing. Yet tables of the rate of interest in England and France for every month since 1830, published in "Bigelow on the Tariff" (p. 204), show that the rate during by far the greater part of thirty years has been higher in England than in France. It is a well-known fact that the rate is higher in England than in Germany, or in other Continental countries. Yet British manufacturers overpower those of all Continental nations, in spite of the higher rate of interest and the higher wages of labor. With what reason, then, can it be claimed that the difference in these respects would be fatal to our manufacturers if unprotected?

The rate of wages measures the value of labor. The rate of interest measures the value of money. In countries where labor is valuable, because ample opportunities exist for its profitable employment, wages are high. In countries where money is valuable, because opportunities for profitable investment are numerous, the rate of interest is high.   Other things being equal, then, high wages and high rates of interest in this, as compared with other countries, simply prove that labor and capital can be more profitably employed here than in other countries.   Now, if labor and capital can be more profitably employed here than elsewhere, so much the less need of "protection," or artificial remuneration for either.   It must be remembered that wages may be nominally when they are not really high, because the purchasing power of money is temporarily diminished, and that currency may command high rates of interest, simply because the interest itself is to be paid in depreciated currency ; that whenever prices are artificially swollen, whether by depreciation of currency, or by tariffs interfering with free exchange, the high rate of interest or of wages is imaginary rather than real.   But, these causes of disturbance aside, if the rate of wages or interest is higher here than in other countries, it only proves that labor or money can be more profitably employed here than there, and hence stands in the less need of any artificial reward.

But facts test the truth of these theories.   Pig-iron, wheat, salt, coal, lumber, are products in which comparatively a small amount of labor and capital is invested.   A steam-engine, a gold watch, a sewing-machine, are products requiring not only the labor of many men, but the most costly and skilled labor, and the employment of large capital.   These products this country either exports largely now, or did export before an artificial cost of production interrupted the trade. In 1842, American locomotives were rolling on British railroads. The labor put into those machines was the dearest labor in any country, because it was the best, and because in this country were the best opportunities for its employment.   The labor and capital invested in those engines were dearer than labor and capital in England, but we could export these machines requiring for their production large capital, and much labor of the costliest, while we could not export to that country a ton of pig-iron or a bushel of salt, requiring far less capital, and far less labor, as well as labor of less skill.   To-day, in spite of our artificial prices, and in spite of the extravagant cost of iron, we can send our agricultural and sewing machines to Europe, why ?   *Because* the production requires a higher-priced labor than England possesses.   Yet these machines are in every part finished products of skilled labor, and they require far more capital to produce them than the ton of pig-iron or the bushel of salt.   In spite of the fact that England has cheaper iron, we can send her these machines, but we cannot send her the iron or the salt. Must England "protect" herself against the skilled labor and inventive genius of this country, just as we protect ourselves against her "pauper labor?" Certainly, if all "protection" is not a blunder and a failure! If England pleases to deny herself the use of our machines, as we try in vain to deny ourselves the use of her worsteds and of the salt of the tropics, will anybody imagine that English labor is "protected," because English farmers still have to use the sickle, and English sewing-girls still sing Hood's "Song of the Shirt," while ours do not?

One other illustration must suffice. No other article of general use embodies so much money or so much labor as the watch. If high rates of interest and of wages render our manufacturers incapable of competing with those of Europe, then, surely, of all manufactured products, the watch must be the very one which we can least afford to produce without aid. If pig-iron needs a duty of 50 per cent., if salt needs a duty of 130 per cent., to secure high wages to American labor and interest to American capital, then the watch, embodying more money, more labor, and the most costly kind of labor, must require a duty of 1,000 per cent. Yet we are to-day exporting American watches to London and to Paris! Unaided by any duty, but greatly embarrassed by the almost prohibitory duties on the fine steel springs and some other materials required, the American watchmaker nevertheless has contrived, by the help of a labor more intelligent and skilful, and therefore better paid than that of other countries, to import the springs paying the enormous duty, to import other materials, and then to send back the finished American watch to the very country from which the materials were brought, there to be sold at a lower price than any foreign watch of like quality. Will some advocate of protective duties explain how this branch of manufactures has contrived to conquer foreign competition, in spite of the rate of interest and the high wages of labor?

If those branches of industry which require the largest proportion of labor and capital need no protection, but conquer foreign competition on foreign soil, and with all the advantages against them; and if unprotected industries thrive better and grow faster, both under low and under high duties, than those which we have weakened by a fruitless and unwise attempt to shelter them from competition, must it not be admitted that "protection" does not protect?

We are now prepared to give definite answer to the question,

Have high duties on imports increased the production of wealth by domestic industry? We have ascertained that the progress in the production of wealth by agriculture was less in periods of high duties than in periods of low duties. We have ascertained that the production of wealth, by the six great branches of manufacture which duties have been especially designed to protect, has not increased under high duties as rapidly as under low duties. We have ascertained that, in attempting to aid these, we inevitably embarrass other branches of manufacture more important both in number of persons employed and in value of product. We have ascertained that other branches of manufacture which have not been protected at all, or have at most received but slight attention, have progressed more rapidly in the production of wealth than those with which legislation has most interfered. We have ascertained that the production of wealth by manufactures, therefore, has, on the whole, been retarded by high duties, and most greatly increased under low revenue tariffs, while industries not protected at all have proved themselves strongest in open competition with those of other countries.

It follows that the production of wealth has been retarded by high duties, and has been most accelerated by non-interference with the natural laws of trade and industry.

Nor is it difficult now to understand why the growth of agriculture has been retarded by high duties. Three causes will occur to any who have studied the facts already presented: The demand for agricultural products for export has been checked. The increase of facilities for transportation has been checked. The cost of implements and machines, of clothing and furniture, and, finally, of labor, has been artificially increased, while the value of farming products has been reduced. These causes, operating together, though in different degrees in different localities, have placed agriculture at a disadvantage in times of high duties, and have retarded the production of wealth by agricultural labor.

CHAPTER XX.

SHALL OUR LABOR BECOME PAUPER LABOR?

If high duties do not benefit a country in its exchanges with other countries, and if they do not increase the production of wealth within the country itself, in what way can they benefit it?

The advocate of protection, driven from point to point by facts, finds in his reply to this question his "last ditch." He answers: "The aggregate production of wealth may not be increased by protection, but its distribution is changed. There are better things for a country than the mere accumulation of wealth. If the rich grow rapidly richer, while the poor do not advance in condition, or become poorer, the nation may get rich at the expense of the laboring classes; it may coin wealth from the sufferings of the poor. This, we maintain, is the fact under free trade, while protection, by enabling the employer to pay higher wages, improves the condition of the laborer, and increases the proportion of the aggregate increase of wealth which falls to his share." And we then listen to eloquent words upon the necessity of securing high wages and comforts to the laboring people in this country, because here they are invested with the responsibilities of freemen. This reasoning has proved more effective than all others to reconcile Americans to the burdens of high tariffs.

An argument addressed to popular feeling must be met with facts. Theories, though never so sound, do no good. The political economist may prove, ever so conclusively, that the tariff system only gives greater power to the capitalist; that the distribution of wealth cannot be changed to the advantage of the laborer by taxing a whole community to secure large profits to a few manufacturers, or to build up an unnatural industry by artificial prices for its products; and these reasonings cannot be controverted; but they do not meet the necessity. The laborer points to his weekly receipts, and replies: "I used to get six dollars a week. Now I get nine. Protection to American industry is a good thing!" Intelligent men may, indeed, see that the nine dollars in currency is worth not quite seven dollars in specie; that the actual increase of wages is therefore not more than 16 per cent., and that the increase of the cost of living, reduced to gold prices, has been in much greater ratio. But, to the great body of laborers, it is a very satisfactory fact that they now receive nine dollars where they formerly received only six.

In any attempt to meet this reasoning, we are brought face to face with the whole problem of wages and prices—one of the most intricate and difficult of all the questions which political economy presents. It is in the last degree intricate, because in all times the wages of different kinds of labor vary considerably, and the wages of the same kind of labor vary in different places at the same time; while there is a still greater diversity in the mode of living of different families in the same place and the same or in different employments, or of families in the same employment, but in different localities. The question becomes still more complicated because both wages and prices are affected in different degrees by fluctuations of the currency. These complications render necessary to any complete investigation of the subject a mass of detailed information, as to wages of different classes of laborers, at different localities, and for a series of years, and as to prices of many articles, at different periods, and in different localities. Such information it is extremely difficult to obtain.

Efforts have recently been made to contrast the condition of laborers in this country at different times, or of laborers in this and other countries, by selecting certain articles and comparing the prices of these articles with the wages of laborers. Thus we are told that the wages of one week's labor in a particular employment will buy in England of felt carpets 133¾ yards, while in Hartford, Connecticut, near the great carpet manufactory, the higher wages of the laborers in the same employment will buy only 113¾ yards of the same kind of carpet. A thousand such illustrations are current, and they have truth to give them force. But they scarcely convince the inquirer. Human beings do not live altogether on carpets, on woollen blankets, on Irish poplins, on pig-iron, or on common salt. While the prices of these and other articles may be extravagantly high, the prices of some other articles of necessity or common use are lower in this country than in England, and the illustration leaves upon the candid mind a sense of incompleteness. Most men know that carpets, blankets, and salt, are greatly enhanced in price by extravagant duties, and the question at once suggests itself whether these articles are not chosen for illustration because they are extravagantly high. The advocate of protection has at hand a very conclusive reply to all comparison of prices and wages in this country and in Europe: "How does it happen that people fly from Europe, where wages are relatively high and prices relatively low, to this country, where the laborer is so badly off?" It does not answer to say that political freedom attracts them. That is indeed true, but all men know that the material condition of immigrants is also improved, and that they come to this country in part because they know that they can improve their condition.

Sophistries do not pay in argument. Candid men are repelled by them. It is a sophistry to reason that the high price of blankets and pig-iron renders the laborer, on the whole, worse off in this coun-

19

try than in Europe. It is no less a sophistry to reason that the laborer is in better condition here than in Europe because of protective tariffs. Labor is generally better paid in this country than in others, because it is more valuable—can be employed more profitably. And this is because in this country cheap and rich land is accessible to every one; because facilities exist for transportation of products to a market; because mines the richest in the world, and other resources almost boundless, lie yet undeveloped; because in many branches manufacturing has not yet attained its natural growth; because the rapid growth of the country constantly opens a new demand for labor of all kinds, and renders speedily remunerative enterprises which, in an older and more fully-settled country, would wait for years or generations before attaining a solid success. In a word, labor is profitable here because this is a new country, of extraordinary natural resources, in which the political institutions, and the character of the people, stimulate enterprise to the utmost vigor. These causes exist independently of changes of tariff. No tariff causes the ore to burst from the earth in mountains of iron. No tariff has overlaid vast tracts of earth with the rich, black loam of Western bottoms and prairies. No tariff has caused immense forests of splendid timber to grow, or the broad and navigable streams to flow which bear their products to the sea. We have proved that high tariffs have not accelerated, but have absolutely retarded the development of these natural resources, especially by checking the increase of facilities for transportation, by enhancing the cost of production and consequently of development, and by interrupting the natural demand for our products for export to other countries. If the natural development of the country has been retarded, the natural demand for labor must have been checked. It follows, therefore, as a logical result of the facts already established, that in consequence of high duties the demand for labor in this country must, on the whole, have been checked, and its remuneration diminished, although in some branches of industry the demand may have been increased by the protective duties.

This is the true question to be considered. We have no reason to maintain that at any time the general demand for labor here has been less than in Europe, or that at any time the general condition of the laborer has been worse. In some branches of industry it has been true at other times, or may be true now, that the laborer in Europe is actually better paid, considering the purchasing power of wages, than the same class of laborers in this country. But this, if it were true, would not be conclusive as to the general effect of high duties, for labor of other kinds may have been at those periods in an equal or greater degree benefited. The question is, whether the laborers of this country, *in the aggregate,* have been benefited, or the contrary, by the protective system. For the discussion of that question, we may suppose that labor in the aggregate has at all times been better paid here than in Europe. The sole question is, whether it has been better paid under one system of duties than under another.

The reasoning already offered will to many minds be conclusive. If the development of the country has, on the whole, been retarded in times of high duty, and if the production of wealth has, on the whole, been checked in its natural increase, it follows, as an inevitable consequence, that the demand for labor in the aggregate must have been checked, and that its remuneration, on the whole, must have been diminished. But to the majority of readers one fact appeals more strongly than a thousand syllogisms. Therefore, let us ascertain facts. At all times the majority of American laborers have been employed in agriculture. According to the census of 1860, out of 7,259,155 persons enumerated as employed in different forms of non-professional labor, 3,375,141 were in agriculture—and the slave-laborers, mainly engaged in agriculture, do not appear to have been included. There are also enumerated as "laborers," not otherwise classified, 969,301; and, while many of these were engaged in building railroads, digging canals, or in various occupations in cities or towns, no small portion were probably employed, partially or entirely, in agriculture. In trade and transportation there were enumerated as employed 800,575 persons, and in mechanic arts, mining, fisheries, or manufacturing, 2,114,138 persons. But, of the persons enumerated as employed in manufactures and the mechanic arts, there were many women and children. The tables of manufactures show that more than one-fourth of the whole number were females, and a considerable number of the males were children—how many the census does not state. In agriculture both women and children are actively engaged in contributing to production of wealth on every farm, but they are not included in the record of occupations. Allowing for this difference, and for the omission of slave-laborers, it may be presumed that at least two-thirds of all our labor was engaged in agriculture. The census of 1840, less minute in its information regarding the mechanic arts, appears to have been somewhat more precise in regard to occupations; for, according to that census, there were employed in agriculture 3,717,756 persons, and in all other employments 1,078,661, divided thus: Manufactures and trades, 791,545; mining, 15,203; commerce, 117,575; ocean navigation, 56,025; internal navigation, 33,067; professions, 65,236. Here fully three-quarters appear to have been engaged in agriculture. In 1820 the proportion was still greater; in agriculture 2,070,646 persons, and in commerce, manufactures, and trades, only 421,999. The natural progress in diversification of industry appears in these statistics somewhat greater than it really has been, since it is probable that the records of 1820 and 1840 were less complete than those of 1860 in enumeration of the persons employed in non-agricultural industry. But it is apparent that more than two-thirds of our labor has at all times been employed in cultivation of the earth.

If the wages of labor employed in agriculture have at any time been decreased, as compared with prices of products by farmers purchased and consumed, fully two-thirds of all American laborers have been injured, while less than one-third can have been benefited. In that case, to maintain the aggregate remuneration of American labor, the few must have gained per capita more than twice as much as the many lost per capita.

Of labor employed in agriculture, a large proportion obtains its only remuneration through the sale of farm products. The very large majority of farming laborers either own or hire the land which they cultivate, or are the sons of farmers, and their labor is paid precisely in proportion to the price of farm products sold, as compared with the price of articles bought for use and consumption. The farmer and his sons have no other wages, can in no way get any other remuneration for their labor, than by the excess of the price of farm products sold, over the price of articles of food, clothing, and convenience, and implements and machines purchased and consumed. The rise in the value of land, by reason of the labor expended in fencing and reducing it to cultivation, or by reason of the settlement of the country, and the increased facilities for transportation, though a most important part of the remuneration of the farmer, may better be considered as the profit on his investment of capital, for every farmer who owns or rents land is at once capitalist and laborer. These profits of his investment can be realized only when he chooses to sell or leave the farm. As a laborer, his condition must be measured by the comforts which he can afford to enjoy, and the money which he can save or apply to objects of desire. And these depend upon the price which he receives for farm products, as compared with the price which he pays for articles purchased.

The wages of agricultural laborers hired by the year, month, or day, we shall find, will depend closely, though not absolutely, upon the same conditions. On one side of the equation, the conditions affect both alike; both have to purchase clothing and comforts, and the purchasing power of wages depends upon the prices of clothes, hats, boots, and other articles of use. To both, board is ordinarily the same, and, if high prices of articles of food prevent their use, the laborer equally with the farmer is forced to deny himself. The wages paid in money vary, generally, with the prices obtained for agricultural products, but not in every fluctuation nor to the full extent. But, since cheap land is always to be had, high prices for agricultural products, operating as an inducement to every laborer to seek land for himself, unless balanced by increase of wages, will soon diminish the supply of laborers and thus compel higher wages. In general, therefore, the money paid for wages to hired laborers will vary with the price of agricultural products as compared with the cost of articles which the farmer has to buy, and the purchasing power of the money also varies with the prices of articles of necessity or consumption, so that the hired laborer does well when the farmer does well, and his condition deteriorates when that of the farmer deteriorates. But the number of persons so employed is not large compared with that of owners or lessees of land and their sons. In 1860 it was less than one-fourth. We may, therefore, safely assume that the wages of farming labor, that is, of two-thirds of all American labor, depend upon the prices of agricultural products as compared with the prices of articles of necessity or comfort.

We have already traced year by year the prices of some most important articles of agricultural production, namely, cotton, wool, and flour, and in each case have found that statistics establish the rule that, in time of high duties, the price has been lower than in time of low duties. The price of flour, it need not be said, depends upon and indicates the price of wheat. And these three products, wheat, wool, and cotton, constitute in value about one-third of our entire agricultural product.

But, since this point is of vital importance, and the advocate of protective duties rests every thing upon the oft-repeated assertion that high tariffs will, in some way, secure to the farmer a better market and higher prices for his products, a few stubborn facts may be presented.

The tables which follow are prepared from the tables of monthly quotations of prices, given in the official report of the Secretary of the Treasury for 1863. Only the average of the monthly quotations in each year is given, but, as these quotations cover the highest and lowest prices, and the averages for each month in the year, the comparison is as perfect as can be made. The average prices are also given for six periods, first, the years covered by the protective tariff of 1824 and the higher protective tariff of 1828; second, the ten years covered by the compromise non-protective tariff, 1833–'42 inclusive; third, the protective tariff of 1843–'46; fourth, the four years which followed under non-protection; fifth, the succeeding four years; and, finally, the remaining years of that decade of non-protection. Similar figures for recent years are not given, first, because no official record presents the data; and, second, because it may be supposed that fluctuations of gold have unfavorably affected the price of agricultural products since 1860. It is a well-known fact that the prices of nearly all products of the farm are now lower than they were in 1860, except those of the Southern States, but the fact is commonly ascribed to other causes than to the effect of a tariff upon the producing and consuming power of the community. But, if it shall appear that articles of farm production, whether those which are largely exported, or those which are consumed almost wholly at home, have commanded a higher average price in every period of low duties than under the preceding or following protective tariff, and that this same rule holds good in every case for thirty-five years, in spite of changes of currency, short crops or large crops, or other causes tending to affect the price, then, indeed, it must be admitted, even by the most obstinate advocate of protective theories, that high tariffs do not benefit the farmer, but in some way deprive him of a fair price for his products. Let the facts testify :

PROTECTION—1825–'32.

YEAR.	Wheat.	Cotton.	Corn.	Rye.	Oats.	Butter.	Cheese.
1825	92	18¼	55	54	31½	15	7½
1826	94	11	76½	70½	47½	15½	8
1827	99	9¾	61	68	40½	17	7½
1828	122	10	52½	53½	29½	15½	6
1829	124½	9	56½	66	35½	13½	6
1830	107	10	56	65	28½	13½	6¾
1831	118½	9	69½	78	37½	15	6
1832	126	9½	68	83	45½	15½	6
Average	110½	10¾	62	67	37	15¼	6¾

COMPROMISE TARIFF.

YEAR.	Wheat.	Cotton.	Corn.	Rye.	Oats.	Butter.	Cheese.
1833	119½	12½	73½	80	40½	16	7
1834	106	12½	66	66	35½	14½	7½
1835	121½	16¾	90½	91	48½	17½	7¼
1836	178	16½	92	104	53	19½	9
1837	177	12	104½	112½	52½	18	9½
1838	192	10¾	84	104½	39½	20	8
1839	124½	13	86	97	47	19	9¼
1840	104½	8¾	57	59½	34	17½	7
1841	118½	10	62½	64	44	12	5¾
1842	114	8	59½	65½	86½	12	7
Average	135	12	77½	84½	43	16½	7¾

PROTECTION—1843-'46.

YEAR.	Wheat.	Cotton.	Corn.	Rye.	Oats.	Butter.	Cheese.
1843	98¼	6½	55	62	29	8½	4¾
1844	97½	6½	50	67½	31½	10	4¾
1845	104	6¼	55	68½	38	13½	6¾
1846	108½	7¼	68	74½	39½	13	6¾
Average	102	6½	57	68	34½	11¼	5¾

NON-PROTECTION.
FIRST PERIOD.

YEAR.	Wheat.	Cotton.	Corn.	Rye.	Oats.	Butter.	Cheese.
1847	136½	10¼	85½	99	49	16	7
1848	116½	6	63½	73½	41½	16	6¾
1849	124	8	63	60	39	15	6
1850	127½	12	62½	65	43	15	6¼
Average	126	9	68½	74½	43	15½	6½

SECOND PERIOD.

YEAR.	Wheat.	Cotton.	Corn.	Rye.	Oats.	Butter.	Cheese.
1851	107½	10	71	73	43½	14½	5¾
1852	110½	9	62	81½	43	19	7
1853	139	10½	67½	92	47½	18	8½
1854	219	9	84½	119½	54	19½	9½
Average	144	9½	71½	91½	47	17¾	7½

THIRD PERIOD.

YEAR.	Wheat.	Cotton.	Corn.	Rye.	Oats.	Butter.	Cheese.
1855	243½	9¼	99	133½	59½	22	9½
1856	175	10½	70½	96	43	21½	8½
1857	167½	14	81	94	53	21½	9½
1858	132½	13	80½	72	45	18½	7
1859	143½	11½	86½	85½	48	19	8½
1860	150	10½	74	82½	42	16½	10
Average	169	11½	81½	94	48½	19½	8½

RECAPITULATION.

YEAR.	Wheat.	Cotton.	Corn.	Rye.	Oats.	Butter.	Cheese.
1825–'32..........	110½	10¾	62	67	37	15¼	6¾
1833–'42..........	135½	12	77½	84½	43	16½	7¾
1843–'46..........	102	6½	57	68	34½	11¼	5¾
1847–'50..........	126	9	68½	74½	43	15½	6½
1850–'54..........	144	9½	71½	91½	47	17¾	7½
1855–'60..........	169	10½	81½	94	48½	19½	8½

During eight years of protection, 1825–'32, the average price of wheat ranged from 92 cents to 126 cents, and the average for the period was $1.10½. But the ten years of non-protection which followed gave an average price of $1.35; and, although the crop had increased in quantity 73½ per cent., and the three years of "hard times" were years of low prices, the farmer even then received more for his wheat than the average price during the whole protective period preceding. The average price of cotton during eight years of protection was 10¾ cents; but, during ten years of non-protection, though the crop had been enormously increased, from less than one million bales in 1832, to over two million three hundred thousand in 1842, the average price was 12 cents. The average price of corn during the protective period was 62 cents; but, during the non-protective period, it was 77½ cents. But these, it may be said, are crops whose price is governed by the export demand. The price of rye, oats, butter, and cheese, certainly was not so governed; the quantity of these articles exported was then too small to affect the price at all. But the price of rye under protection was 67 cents, and under non-protection 84½ cents; the price of oats, under protection, was 37 cents, and under non-protection, 43 cents; the price of butter was 15¼ cents under protection, and 16½ cents under non-protection; and the price of cheese was 6¾ cents under protection, and 7¾ cents under non-protection. The export theory does not account for these facts. If protection creates a home market, how does it happen that eight years of protection reduced the price of cheese from 7½ to 6 cents, while ten years of non-protection raised it to 7 cents? If non-protection destroys manufactures, and drives people into agriculture for a living, how does it happen that ten years of non-protection raised the average price of every one of these products, and caused crops of wheat three-fourths larger than were raised in 1830 to be consumed at higher prices? Does it not follow that there were more consumers, or a greater ability to purchase and consume, even in the hard time of 1840–'42, than in the whole protective period?

But it may be supposed that the inflation of the currency in 1836 and 1837 accounts for these facts. Let it be observed, then, that the average price of every article except rye, during the whole protective tariff which followed, was not only lower than the average price for the period of low duties, but was lower than the price during the years of extreme contraction of the currency and "hard times," 1840 –'42! Wheat was worth 118½ in 1841, and 114 in 1842; but, during the protective tariff, it never rose for either year above 108½, and averaged 102. Cotton was worth 10 cents in 1841, and 8 cents in 1842; but it averaged, under protection, only 6½. Corn was worth 59½ to 62½, and it averaged under protection only 57. Rye averaged lower, under protection, than it did during the previous period, but not lower than during the years of "hard times," and it is the only exception. Cheese, which the home market, if one had been created by the tariff, would surely have consumed at a fair price, never rose as high in any year as it was in 1842, the last year of low duties.

Still more conclusive is the proof, when it is observed how the price of every article bounded upward when the burden upon agriculture was removed. During the four years of non-protection which followed, wheat averaged $1.26, or 24 cents higher than it had under protection; cotton 9 cents, or 3½ cents higher; corn 68½ cents, or 11½ cents higher; rye 74½ cents, or 6½ cents higher; oats 43 cents, or 8½ cents higher; butter 15½ cents, or 4 cents higher; and cheese 6½ cents, or ¾ of a cent higher. Was this change caused by the famine in Europe and the export demand? Then let it be observed that the next four years gave a still further increase of price, on every article—those which we consumed at home as well as those which we exported. Surely no demonstration can be more convincing. Of all the articles named, not one ever fell again for a single year lower than the average price for the whole protective tariff of 1842–'46, and only one, cheese, fell in a single year as low as that average.

Facts have already been given showing the enormous increase in quantity of agricultural crops during the decade of uninterrupted non-interference, and it is interesting to remember those facts in connection with this record of prices. An increase of nearly three millions of bales, over 100 per cent. in the cotton crop, had lowered the price only 1½ cent as compared with 1850, and the price in 1860 was higher than the average of the years 1849–'51. An increase of seventy-three million bushels of wheat had occurred, but a crop three-quarters larger was consumed at a price 23 cents higher by a people more prosperous, because they had been let alone in their industry. A crop of corn two hundred and forty million bushels larger was consumed at a price 11½ cents higher. A crop of rye 50 per cent. larger was consumed at a price 17½ cents higher. A crop of oats twenty-six million bushels larger was consumed at a price only one cent lower. In 1850, the farmers made 313,247,014 pounds of butter, worth in New York 15 cents a pound, but in 1860 they made 459,681,372 pounds, worth in New York 16½ cents a pound. In 1850 they made one hundred and five million pounds of cheese, worth, at 6¼ cents a pound, $6,560,000; and in 1860 they made one hundred and three million pounds, worth, at 10 cents a pound, $10,366,392.

Need these comparisons be pursued further to convince every doubter that low duties enable the farmer to get high prices for his products, while high duties force him to sell at lower rates? The fact being proved, it is not necessary to propose any theory in explanation of it. To variation in the demand for export it cannot be wholly or mainly due, because the same effect extends to crops produced for a home market. Can there be more than one rational explanation? Is it not plain that, under high duties, the consumers of agricultural products are as a whole unable to consume largely at high prices, while, under non-protective duties, all trades and arts and manufactures so thrive that a larger body of more prosperous consumers is enabled to consume larger crops at prices more profitable to the farmer? Do not the facts force this conclusion upon every reasoning mind?

But, if so, high tariffs are not only robbery to the farmer, but injury to the manufacturer and the mechanic. No other conclusion is possible.

It is at least established that the farmer receives lower prices for his products under the system miscalled protective, than under low duties and non-interference. To that extent, therefore, two-thirds of American laborers have been injured by high duties, unless in times of high duties the prices of articles used and consumed by the farmer have been in equal measure reduced.

The prices of pig and bar iron, of woollen and cotton goods, of glass and salt, have been traced, and we have seen that these have been higher in every period of high duties than in the following periods of low duties. Upon the price of iron depends in a measure the cost of stoves and utensils, of farm implements, of wagons, blacksmith's-work, horseshoes, of all machinery, of tools used in every trade, and of all transportation. The cost of clothing and household goods is affected by the price of woollen and cotton fabrics, and the cost of all mechanical work is also affected by the price which workmen have to pay for clothing and for tools. In like manner every other increase of prices which a tariff on imported articles may cause is passed on from importer to retail dealer, from dealer to consumer, from consumer to those for whom he performs any service, and thus all are diffused through the whole community, falling at last, in large proportion, upon the farmers, who are two-thirds of the productive laborers of the country. If a tariff increases the cost of pig-iron from $20 to $40 a ton, which for two million tons consumed would be a tax of forty millions yearly, that tax ultimately goes back to the producers of wealth, and the farmers, being two-thirds of the purchasers, pay twenty-six millions of the forty. Does any one ask in what form? A little in every stove and iron utensil for the household, in every chain, crowbar, shovel, plough, fork, hoe, or other implement; a little in every wagon, or job of repairs; a little in every work which a carpenter, blacksmith, or other mechanic, may do for him; a little in every pound of nails used in house or barn, and a great deal in increased cost of transporting to him all articles used, or from him to market all products of his farm. Sooner or later, it all comes back to the producers, and, of all taxes which the producers have to pay, the farmers pay two-thirds.

Here the advocate of high tariffs will reply that the cost of stoves and nails, implements and machines, is not affected by the duty on such articles, which is in part true. That is not the tax which the farmer pays. He pays the tax by which *the iron* is enhanced in price. If the iron out of which his stoves were made had not cost the foundery more than $20 a ton, he would have had his stove for less money than he now pays.

"But, some articles made of iron cost less now than they did years ago, when iron was cheaper!" Very true, and they ought to cost still less. Such improvements in the manufacture have been effected, that the machine can now be made out of iron, at $40, at less cost than it could once out of iron at $20. But the cost of iron, nevertheless, increases the cost of the machine; for, if with the new inventions it can now be made for any given price, it could be made for less if the iron had cost but half as much.

The favorite device of protectionists is to point to articles which have absolutely fallen in price, and ascribe that fall to the tariff. They know that there is a constant tendency to lower prices for all manufactured products, as increased skill and new inventions diminish the actual cost of production. That decrease should be steady, and, when no arbitrary laws interfere to check it, is sure. It is part of the blessings which science, art, and progressing civilization, bestow upon the human race, and we are all entitled to a share in it. The farmer has a right to his share as much as the mechanic; the laborer of this country has a right to his share as well as the laborer of England. Whenever arbitrary laws in this country arrest the downward progress of the price of any article, while in other countries the natural decrease continues, the tax is just the same as if the cost of the article had been increased to the same amount. For ten years ending in 1832, the price of glass in this country, being arrested by protective duties, stood unchanged, while the price in England and on the Continent was falling. If the difference in 1832 was fifty cents a box—and it proved to be nearly as much—then the tariff in that year taxed the consumer just fifty cents a box, as truly as if it had raised the price, while in other countries it remained stationary. The farmer, who wants glass for his new house, has a right to his share of the benefits which science has conferred by the cheaper manufacture of glass. But the tariff steps in, arrests the price, robs him of fifty cents a box, and the advocate of protection then says: "You have not been taxed at all, for glass is no higher now than it was twenty years ago!" Yet the farmer was robbed nevertheless. He had a right to buy for less.

So when prices have decreased, we are told that this is the effect of the tariff. The introduction of the power-loom and other improvements, with the low price of cotton, reduced the cost of shirtings from twenty to seven cents a yard, and the protectionist pointed to the fact in 1845, as proof that the high tariff was a good thing. He forgot to mention that the same goods had sold in 1842, before the tariff was imposed, for $6\frac{1}{2}$ cents, and that, instead of rising, they should have declined still further, had no law interfered. Other goods were being steadily reduced in cost under the low duties, and yet, as we have seen, the manufacture of wool and cotton, iron, and other products, was increasing. Just then the tariff arrested the natural decline, and the prices of those goods either increased, remained unchanged, or declined but little until its removal.* The instant competition was readmitted, it was seen that prices in other countries had been still further reduced. The manufacturers cried "Fraud!" and there was fraud! They had defrauded the consumer of

* Facts, showing in detail the effects of the tariff of 1842 upon prices, are given in the next chapter.

that natural decrease of price, and yet had pointed to some slight re-
ductions here as proof that the tariff had been a blessing.

These considerations show how easy it is for the advocate of high
tariffs to find facts which, disingenuously or dishonestly used, seem
to sustain him in the theory that "a high tariff does not usually enhance the cost of manufactured products." If they have declined in
price, he claims a victory, and conceals the fact that in other countries they have declined still more, and that the difference is a tax
caused by the tariff. If they have remained stationary in price, he
declares that there has been no tax; and, as before, conceals the difference in price between other countries and this.

But when the raw materials of industry are increased in price,
then no sophistry can evade the conclusion that the manufactured
products have been artificially made more costly—either more
costly absolutely, as compared with the former price; or more costly
relatively, as compared with prices in other countries; or, in a third
case, of which some examples may be seen, more costly than they
naturally would have been, although both absolutely and relatively
decreased in price. As an example, we may take the sewing-machine. It was an American invention, and has been so skilfully
manufactured here that it can be profitably exported from this to
other countries where iron costs much less. It has decreased in
price, sharp competition between makers pushing all to the lowest
rates. And yet the tariff makes every sewing-machine more costly
than it ought to be, though cheaper now than it was, and cheaper
both now and then than in other countries. For, if the iron of
which it is made cost less, and if the steel cost less, the machines
could be furnished for less money, and competition would push the
manufacturers to do so. Have not the sewing-girls of this country
a right to every advantage over foreign labor which the skill and
inventive genius of their own countrymen can give them? Yet,
they are robbed of part of that advantage, by a tariff which forces
them to pay more for the machine which earns their bread! The
poor wife, whose "best friend" helps her through the toil of caring
for a family, is robbed by the tariff when she pays five dollars, or
one dollar, or one cent, more for that blessing than it should naturally have cost. Who pockets the money? Not the government!
Remember the figures—one million goes to the Treasury, and at
least twenty millions to the pockets of those who own iron-furnaces,
and clear 100 per cent. profit in seven months!

This illustration will make it clear how the farmer is also taxed in the increased cost of every implement, utensil, and machine, he uses, even though the machine may in some cases cost less to-day than it did ten years ago, the manufacture having been improved, and less now than in any other country.   The farmer, also, has a right to his full share of the blessing which the skill and genius of his countrymen bestow. 'He has a right to the machine, not only lower than it was formerly, not only lower than it is in Europe; but lower than it is here and now!   For the iron of which it is made is artificially increased in cost, and the machine therefore costs more than it naturally would.

But the manufactured articles which are cheaper to-day than they were in 1860, are few in number.   In one or the other of the three ways described, all are enhanced in cost, but the great majority not only cost more now than they do in other countries, but cost more now than they did here in 1860.   What, then, is the truth?

The farmer receives less for his products than he did under low duties.

The farmer pays more for manufactured products used and consumed, for clothing, buildings, implements, machines, and transportation, than he would have to pay if no duties interfered.

Therefore the farmer is injured at both ends of the exchange; his products sell for less, and the purchasing power of the price paid is less than it should be.   He is plundered when he sells, and plundered when he buys.   Two-thirds of American laborers, therefore, are robbed by the high-tariff system, both in their wages and in the cost of their living; a part of their earnings are taken, and they are forced to spend more for the necessaries and comforts which they buy.   If two-thirds of American laborers have been injured, what has been the result to the remaining third?

It may appear that if the cost of agricultural products has been less, in times of high tariffs, this, though a disadvantage to the farmer, has been a benefit to the mechanic, manufacturer, miner, and other laborers; while, if the price of any manufactured products has been increased, this, though a disadvantage to the farmer, has been a benefit to the laborer by whom those articles were produced, since it has enabled his employer to pay him more liberally.

To some extent these positions are both true.   Reduced cost of agricultural products does benefit other classes in the community in some degree.   Increased price of manufactured products does sometimes enable the manufacturer to pay better wages.   Just as far as these things are true, the protective system does benefit other laborers at the expense of the farmer—plunders two-thirds of American labor for the benefit of some part of one-third.

But in the end this benefit is usually more than balanced, and the one-third, in the aggregate, remain worse off than if no attempt had been made to aid them. This occurs in several ways. Either by reduced consumption or increased cost of manufactured products, the benefit derived from increased price of products may be neutralized to the manufacturer. By increased cost of preparation for use, of transportation from producer to consumer, or increased friction and waste in exchanges, the benefit of cheap agricultural products may be absorbed before they reach the consumer. When the farmer finds himself pinched, and restricts his purchases, the manufacturer finds a surplus left on his hands, and must either sustain a loss, or reduce production by working short time. If he loses, wages cannot be increased; if work is suspended, wages are in effect reduced.

But the manufacturing laborer must also suffer from any increase in cost of manufactured products of necessary use. Not more than one-half of the expense of living, even to operatives in manufacturing establishments, is for articles of food, and of these not all are products of this country. After extended investigation, Commissioner Wells stated that the average expenditure of families in manufacturing towns in 1868, for articles of food, was, for parents and one child, $6.39; parents and two children, $8.15. In the same tables it appears that the other expenses were from nine to eleven dollars. In larger families a larger proportion is required for food, but in such families older children often assist by their work or earnings. Of the expenses of unmarried workmen the proportion for food is still less. Taking all workmen employed in manufactures together, it is probable, therefore, that the cost of food forms about one-third of their expenses, and it is certainly less than half. But of the expense for food, a part is for articles not produced in this country. In the estimate by Mr. Wells, of the $6.39 allowed as the average weekly expenditure for food, there are 73 cents for sugar and molasses, 26 cents for tea, 20 cents for coffee, and 9 cents for spices and salt, and none of these articles are agricultural products of this country, except the sugar and molasses, of which the quantity produced here is insignificant compared with the quantity consumed. Not less than $1.28 is spent for these articles, not produced by our own agriculture, out of $6.39 expended for food. More than two-thirds of the entire cost of living, and, taking the whole working-class together, probably three-fourths of the whole, is for articles other than the products of our farms. If agricultural products have been made cheaper to the consumer—and it does not yet appear that they have —he has, nevertheless, been worse off on the whole, wages remaining the same, if other articles of necessity, such as clothing and household goods, have been rendered in like proportion more costly. If rents have also been increased as much in proportion as the cost of food has decreased, the balance is decidedly against the laborer.

With these facts in mind, to assist us in judging how far a general increase in the cost of manufactured products, or in the cost of agricultural products, has affected the cost of living in the aggregate, we may now search for facts to show in what manner wages on the one hand, or the cost of living on the other, have been affected by different forms of the tariff.

——— •◆• ———

CHAPTER XXI.

WAGES AND PRICES IN 1845.

OF documents accessible to the writer, the earliest reliable data throwing light upon the wages and expenses of laborers of different classes, are supplied by the investigation of the Secretary of the Treasury in 1845. By that officer, inquiries were addressed to a great number of persons in all parts of the country, and, though a large proportion of the manufacturers declined to answer his most important questions, enough replied, of manufacturers, merchants, farmers, and others, to give valuable information. This, it will be remembered, was at the close of the third year of the protective tariff of 1842, and the inquiries invited information as to the condition, not only at that time and during the three years under that tariff, but during the ten years of low duties which had preceded. The replies given conflict on many points, but as to certain essential facts there is very general agreement.

First, as to wages of agricultural labor, it appears that there had been no material change for years in the Eastern States, until the decade 1832–'42, during which wages rose a little—on an average, perhaps, from $9 to $10 a month and board. In some States, as Connecticut, the price rose to $14. But at the West it reached $17 a month. There is no room for dispute as to the effect of the tariff of 1842. From every quarter came detailed statements of the decreased price of agricultural products since the protective system was adopted, and the strongest advocates of that system referred to the fact as an evidence in their favor. Even in the New-England States, New York, and Pennsylvania, where growth of manufactures had supplied that "home market" upon which the farmers now are asked to rely, the same general and marked decrease in the price of agricultural products was stated by one party and admitted by the other. In Maine, wheat had fallen from $1 to 90 cents, corn from 75 to 70 cents, wool from 42 to 31 cents, potatoes from 30 to 25 cents; in New Hampshire, wool from 45 to 35 cents; in Massachusetts, wool from 43 to 35 cents—in Berkshire and Hampshire counties "its price is so seriously depressed as to induce a disposal or slaughter of very many sheep this fall;" in Rhode Island, where surely a "home market" existed if anywhere, hay had fallen from $15 a ton to $12, corn from 92 to 70 cents, rye from $1 to 87 cents, potatoes from 33 to 30 cents, onions from 37 to 25 cents; beef from 6 to 4 cents a pound, butter from 12 to 10 cents, and cheese from 8 to 6 cents. In New York, Henry S. Randall, the well-known wool-grower, gave several tables showing that "wool averaged higher under the compromise tariff than under that enacted in 1842," and was higher even in the years of greatest prostration and contraction just before the tariff than since its passage; that wheat from 1832 to 1842 averaged $1.33½, and from 1842 to 1845 only 92¼ cents; that corn had fallen from 60 cents in 1840 to 50 cents in 1845; barley from 45 to 40; buckwheat from 38 to 31; peas from 50 to 40; pork from $4.50 to $3.50 per cwt.; beef from $6 to $4.50; and wages of agricultural labor from $12 a month to $10.

These records are conclusive for the Eastern States, but the Western farmers had suffered still more severely. In Ohio, wheat had sold before 1842 on the lake-shore at $1 a bushel, and since had fallen to 70 cents, while pig-iron had advanced at the same point from $18 to $25 a ton. At Massillon, before the tariff, wheat averaged $1, and, after it, had fallen to 65 cents. In Indiana, hogs, the principal product, had ranged from $4 to $7 per 100 pounds, but since the tariff had fallen $2 to $3. In Illinois, wheat ranged before the tariff from 75 cents to $1 a bushel, and corn from 25 to 40 cents. In 1844 wheat was 50 cents, and in 1845, 40 cents, and corn had fallen to 12½ cents a bushel. No wonder that wages had fallen from $12 and $15 per month to $7 and even to $5 per month!

Further quotations are needless; no fact can be more indisputably proved than this, that the prices of agricultural products, and the wages of agricultural labor, were reduced, under the protective tariff of 1842, from 20 to 50 per cent. Did the prices of articles which farmers have to buy decrease in like proportion?

20

Among the questions asked by the Secretary were these: of the manufacturer, "At what prices have the manufactures been sold since the establishment?" and of others, "Whether the average prices of what are called the protected articles have been as low in proportion to the average prices of the staples for the last three years as in the preceding ten?" Of the manufacturers who sent replies to any of the questions, very few stated the prices at which their goods had been sold in different years. On the other hand, almost every person of other employment stated that the cost of manufactured articles had been generally greater since the tariff was adopted than before, and proceeded to explain the fact according to his individual opinions: if opposed to the tariff, ascribing the increased cost to the duties; and, if in favor of it, either ascribing the fact to other causes, or arguing that temporary high prices, "if they should lead to a large increase of the manufacture, sufficient, within a reasonable time, to supply the wants of the country at a price not much above the cost of the same articles if brought from foreign countries free of duty, would in the long-run be beneficial." What the effect has actually been upon the manufacture, we have seen. We are now seeking to ascertain whether prices have been increased by high duties, and the concurrent testimony of advocates and opponents in 1845 was, that the prices of manufactured articles had at that time been generally increased. Let it be here well understood that the duty did not in all cases, and does not always, enhance the price to the full amount of the duty. No fallacy has been more conclusively refuted by facts than this. On the contrary, we shall see that many articles were actually lower in price after the duty was imposed than before, because the materials were cheaper, or the manufacture had been improved; that others remained unchanged in price, though the materials were cheaper; and that, while very many were enhanced in price, in many cases the increase was not equal to the duty imposed. But it is maintained, and the facts prove, that there was an increase in the price of manufactured articles generally, and that, when there was no absolute increase, the cost of the manufactured article had in nearly every case been reduced less than the cost of materials and of manufacturing, so that the consumer paid for the article more than its natural price.

Of the manufacturers who did reply, a few were frank enough to give precise statements, but these were generally manufacturers of coarse cottons, who stated that they needed no protection, that the duty did not benefit them, that they were exporting of their products to other countries, and that a reduction of price had been effected by improvements which had reduced the cost of manufacture from 33 cents a pound in 1828 to 14½ cents a pound in 1840, and to 11 cents a pound in 1845, and, by a decrease in the cost of the raw material from 12.84 cents in 1830, to 7 cents in 1845. In consequence, the price of prints had been reduced in 1841 to 5.85 cents, and in 1842 shirtings No. 30 sold at 6.75 cents, printings at 4.75 cents, and sheetings No. 14 at 5.50 cents. But since that time prices had slightly risen, though the cost of manufacture had been reduced from 14½ cents a pound to 11 cents a pound, and the cost of the raw material from about 11 to 7 cents a pound. In 1845 the prices were, for shirtings No. 30, 7 cents; for printings No. 30, 6 cents; for sheetings No. 14, 6 cents. These are the figures given by the Great Falls Manufacturing Company. The Hamilton and Appleton Companies of Lowell stated that scarcely any foreign goods of similar descriptions to those of their make were imported, and "some would not be in any state of duty, as they appear to be made cheaper here than in any other part of the world; the others are made nearly as cheap here as anywhere." Though neither these nor any other manufacturers reported prices at which their products sold as plainly as did the company above mentioned, we can understand that the markets were the same for all, and that the same causes—improvement of manufacture and reduced cost of cotton—had affected the cost of producing other classes of cotton goods.

Other evidence, however, is accessible, to prove that cotton goods were generally increased in price under this tariff. The Treasury report of 1849, a very elaborate work in the interest of the protective system, gives detailed statements of the prices of many articles which had been reduced in price from 1835 to 1849 by the progress of the home manufacture. The argument which these selected facts were designed to sustain was, that the cost of the articles named had been reduced in consequence of the tariff of 1842, it being quietly taken for granted that the domestic manufacture would not have existed, or would have made no progress, had not that tariff been enacted! At this day not a word need be said in refutation of an assumption so contrary to the history of our industries, and it is amazing that any Secretary of the Treasury ever resorted to such a sophistry in a labored report. It is plain, too, that the facts presented in the report were carefully selected for the purpose, for out of thousands of articles of domestic make, not one was given the history of which conflicted with the Secretary's peculiar theory, and only those were selected which had most steadily declined in price. Taken by itself, therefore, the report of 1849 was only calculated to create a false impression; it kept out of sight the great multitude of articles which had been most enhanced in price, and gave elaborate records of those only which had been reduced in price with enough of regularity to sustain the reasoning of the Secretary. But the facts which this report presented, taken in connection with others which it suppressed, are of great value. Its statistics of the prices of certain cotton goods from 1835 to 1849 show most conclusively that the progress of the manufacture from 1835 to 1843 caused a very rapid reduction in the cost of every article; that the tariff of 1842 simply arrested that reduction, and in a great majority of cases caused higher prices in 1846, the last year of that tariff, than in 1842, the last year preceding its adoption, although the raw cotton cost less in 1846 than in 1842. This will appear from the accompanying table, in which those statistics of the report of 1849 are condensed which show the prices of cotton goods of certain qualities from 1835 to 1849.

This table shows a very great reduction in the price of all goods from 1835 to 1842 inclusive, under the non-protective duties, and in 1843, the raw material having fallen nearly two cents a pound, prices of goods fell still lower. But in 1844 every article quoted, except one, increased again, many of them 30 to 50 per cent., in a single year; in 1845, notwithstanding a fall of cotton to the lowest price then ever reached, the price of goods remained about the same; and in 1846, cotton selling for $2\frac{1}{2}$ cents less than its price in 1841, and for a lower price than it commanded in 1842, the prices of goods were with very few exceptions higher than in 1842. Of sixty-six articles and qualities quoted in the table, only nine were slightly lower in price in 1846 than in 1842, and only five remained unchanged, while forty-seven had increased in price. Not only was the natural reduction of price arrested—that reduction caused by progress in manufacture which had enabled the makers to sell sheetings for 6 cents, shirtings for $6\frac{1}{4}$ cents, drillings for $7\frac{1}{2}$ cents, duck for $12\frac{1}{2}$, calicoes for 5.70, and cotton yarn for 19 cents—not only was the consumer deprived of all benefit from a reduction in the price of cotton from 8.1 cents in 1842 to 5.9 cents in 1845, and 7.8 cents in 1846, but there was an actual increase of price, of sheetings to $6\frac{3}{4}$ cents; of shirtings to $6\frac{1}{2}$ cents, of drillings to $7\frac{3}{4}$ cents, of duck to $13\frac{1}{4}$ cents, of calicoes to 5.83, and of cotton yarn to $19\frac{3}{4}$ cents. The cotton bought in 1841 at 10 cents a pound, and worked up by the

PRICE OF COTTON GOODS.—(*From Treasury Report of* 1849.)

Mill.	Location.	Goods.	Width.	Yards to Pound.	1835.	1836.	1837.	1838.	1839.	1840.	1841.	1842.	1843.	1844.	1845.	1846.	1847.	1848.	1849.
Lowell	Lowell, Mass.	Plain Osnaburgs	30	2.20	14½	14½	12	11½	11½	10	10	8	8½	9	8¼	8¼	9¼	7½	7½
"	"	" "	36	1.90	17½	17	14	13½	13½	12	11½	10	10½	11	9¾	10	11¼	9½	9½
"	"	Twilled "	30	1.70	18½	18	16	15	16	14	13	11½	12½	13	11	11	12¼	10½	10¼
Lawrence	"	Stout Brown Sheetings	37	2.85	12	12	11½	10½	10¼	8¾	7¾	7	7¾	7⅛	7¾	7¾	8½	6¾	7
Jackson	"	" "	37	2.85	12	12½	11½	10	10¼	8½	7¾	7¼	7¾	8	7¾	7¾	8½	6¾	7
Tremont	"	" "	37	3.20	10½	11¼	9½	9	9¼	7½	6¾	6	6½	7¼	6½	6¾	7¼	5¾	6
Jackson	"	" Shirtings	30	3.50	10	10½	9¼	8	8½	7½	7	6¼	5¾	6½	6¼	6½	6¾	5¾	5⅝
Lawrence	"	Fine Brown "	37	4.20	13	13½	11	11	11¼	9½	9	8¼	8	8¾	9	9	8½	6¾	6¾
Boott	"	Stout " Drillings	30	2.80	..	14	12¼	11	10¾	9½	9	8	7	8⅝	8¼	8	8	7	7
Tremont	"	Brown Shirtings	28½	4.50	8	8½	6¾	6¼	7	5¾	5½	5	4½	5¼	5½	5½	5½	4	4
Suffolk	"	" Drillings	30	2.83	13	14	11½	10	10	9	8¾	7½	7	8¾	8½	7¾	8¼	6¾	6½
Stark	Manchester, N. H.	" "	30	2.83	13	14	11½	10	10	9	8¾	7½	7	8¾	8½	7¾	8¼	6¾	6½
Appleton	Lowell, Mass.	" Sheetings	37	2.90	12½	12½	10½	9¾	10	7¾	7¾	7	7¼	7½	7¾	7½	8½	6¾	6¾
Stark	Manchester, N. H.	" "	37	2.90	12½	12½	10½	9¾	10	7¾	7¾	7	7¼	7½	7¾	7¼	8½	6¾	6¾
Appleton	Lowell, Mass	" Shirtings	30	3.55	10	10½	8½	7½	8¾	6¼	6	5½	5½	6½	6¼	6	6¾	5½	5¾
Newmarket	Newmarket, N. H.	R. Brown Shirtings	..	3.	..	..	12	10¾	11	9½	9½	8½	8¼	8½	8	8¾	9	7¾	7½
"	" "	A. " "	..	4.10	..	..	13	11½	11½	10	9¾	8½	8¼	8½	9	9	8	6¾	6½
"	" "	H. " "	..	4.60	..	..	11½	10½	10½	9½	8¼	7½	7	7	8	8½	7½	5½	6
Bartlett	Newburyport, Mass.	Wissacumcon Long Cloth	31	..	..	..	..	..	..	12	12	10½	10¼	11½	11½	10½	10	8	8½
"	" "	" "	33	..	..	..	..	..	..	13	13½	11½	11¼	12½	12½	11	10½	9½	10
"	" "	" "	36	..	..	..	..	..	..	15	16½	12½	12¼	14	13½	13	12	11	11½
"	" "	" "	40	..	..	..	..	..	..	..	18	14½	12½	15	14½	14	12½	11½	12
"	" "	" "	46	..	..	..	..	..	..	..	21	15½	13½	17	18	17	16	13	14
Palmer	Palmer, Mass.	Printing Cloth	..	..	10	11½	10½	9½	9½	7	7¾	6¼	6¼	7	8	7	6¼	5¼	5¼
Nashua	Nashua, N. H.	No. 1 Brown Shirting	30	3.73	9.62	10.20	8.35	7.28	8.25	6.50	6.64	5.55	5.24	6.29	5.93	6.45	6.46	5.57	5.12
"	"	No. 3 " "	37	2.96	11.84	11.84	12.25	10.19	10.85	8.48	8.15	7.39	6.50	8.03	6.81	7.93	8	6.41	6.34
Dedham	Dedham, Mass.	Printing Cloth	..	..	..	9½	6½	7½	7½	7	7	4¾	5	6	6½	5¼	5½	4½	4¼
Great Falls	Great Falls, N. H.	"	28	5.	..	..	..	..	..	6½	7	5	5¼	6½	6¾	6¼	6	5	4½
Perkins	" "		30	6.	..	..	..	8¼	9	7	8	6¼	6½	7½	7½	7¼	6¾	5	5½
Dwight	" "	Bleached Shirtings	33	4.52	..	..	..	..	..	..	11	9	9¼	10½	10¼	10¾	9½	8	8
Chicopee	Cabotville, Mass.	Printing Cloths	28	5.07	8	8½	7½	6¾	7	6	6	5	4¾	6¼	6¾	5¼	5¼	4¼	4¼
"	" "	Brown Sheetings	37	2.09	11¼	12	11	10	10¼	7	8½	7½	7¼	7½	7½	7½	8	6¾	6¾
Great Falls	Great Falls, N. H.	Bleached Shirtings	31	..	..	..	..	..	..	8¾	8½	7¾	7½	8½	8½	8¾	7½	6¾	6¾
"	" "	Brown "	33	4.65	..	..	..	..	..	8¼	7¾	7¾	6¾	8	8	8¼	7¼	6¼	6½
"	" "	" Sheetings	37	3.20	..	..	..	..	..	7½	7½	6½	6¾	7	7	7¼	7½	6½	6¼
	Providence, R. I.	Printing Cloth	28	..	..	..	7⅜	7⅛	7½	6⅞	6½	5¼	7⅞	6¾	6½	5¾	6¾	4¼	4⅜
Gladding	" "	Brown Sheetings	4-4	1.	..	..	..	..	..	..	8½	7¾	7⅝	8¼	8	8½	8⅛	6¼	6⅛
Richmond	" "	"	..	..	..	..	..	..	..	..	7¾	6¾	..	7⅞	6⅝	..	7¼	6	5⅝
"	" "	Printing Cottons	..	..	..	..	..	..	7.54	6.14	6.50	5.50	4⅞	6¾	6.47	5.72	5.22	4.22	4.31
Chicopee	Cabotville, Mass.	Brown Sheetings	4-4	3.	11.80	12.55	11.66	10.69	11	9	8.58	7.08	7.37	8.16	7.67	8	8.10	6.62	6.90
Suffolk	Lowell, Mass.	Blue Drillings	27	2.83	15	16	13½	12	12	10½	10¼	9	8½	10¼	9¾	9¼	9¾	8¼	8
Merrimack	"	Calicoes, N. M. C.	27	5.46	..	17.83	17	14.39	15.98	13.78	13.25	11.91	10.56	11.60	11.50	10.82	11.05	9.89	9.28
Hamilton	"	Denims	30	2.70	15	18	18½	16	18	15	14½	13	11	14	12½	13¼	13	10½	11
"	"	Tickings	30	2.60	15	16	18	14½	15	10¾		11	9	11¼	10¾	11¼	11	9½	9¼
"	"	Shirting Stripes	30	2.70	14½	16	17	14	15	12	11½	11	9	10½	10¾	11	10⅞	9½	9¾
Amoskeag	Manchester, N. H.	Tickings, A. C. A.	31	2.05	22	25	24½	22	21½	17	17½	14½	13¼	15½	15	15	16¾	14¾	14
"	" "	" A.	31½	2.25	20½	24	23½	21	19¾	16	15¾	13¾	11¼	13½	12¼	12¼	13	11¾	11
"	" "	" B.	29½	2.40	19	23	22½	20	17¾	15	..	11	9¾	12	11¼	11¼	11¼	9½	9¼
Dorchester	Dorchester, Mass.	" A. A.	30	2.	20	23	19	18	17½	15	15	12	12½	14	13½	13½	14	12½	13
York	Saco, Maine	Blue Denims	27	2.50	..	..	16	16	16½	15	14	12	12	13½	13	12¾	12½	11	12
"	"	Blue Stripe Shirtings	27	3.	..	..	15	13	14	12	11½	10	10	11	11	11	10¼	9	9¾
"	"	Blue Tickings	27	2.60	..	..	14	14	14½	12	11½	10	10	11	11	11	10¼	9	9¾
Nashua	Nashua, N. H.	Calicoes	28	5.50	8.86	8.75	9.30	6.75	7.31	5.62	6.96	5.70	4	5.65	6.40	5.83	5.17	3.63	3.95
Cocheco	Dover, "	"	..	..	..	..	14.14	11.79	14.41	11.40	11.15	10	7.73	10.76	10.89	10.88	10.06	10	8.62
Methuen	Methuen, Mass.	Tickings	31	2.35	..	..	..	..	..	15.50	15½	13½	12½	14½	14½	14½	14	12	12½
"	"	Duck	31	2.	..	..	..	..	..	14	14	12½	11½	14	13½	13½	13½	11½	11½
"	"	Denims	28	2.30	..	..	..	..	..	17	17	14½	12	14½	15	14	14	11½	11½
Lancaster	Clintonville, Mass.	Ginghams	..	..	..	..	..	..	..	..	..	..	..	..	..	..	..	..	..
Merrimack	Lowell, Mass.	Blue Prints	..	..	..	..	..	..	16½	14¾	13¾	12¼	10¾	11¼	11¾	10¼	10⅞	10½	9¼
David Mlhs & Son	Philadelphia, Pa.	Checks, No. 10	..	..	..	..	..	..	15¾	13⅞	13½	12½	11¾	13¼	13¼	12¼	13¼	12½	12
Woodward & Brinckle	"	Cotton Yarn, No. 5—26 lbs.	..	..	..	..	..	..	24½	21¾	23	19	20	20¾	21	19¾	23¼	18¼	17
Average price of raw cotton			..	..	16.8	16.8	14.2	10.3	14.8	8.5	10.2	8.1	6.2	8.1	5.9	7.8	10.3	7.6	6.4
Pounds of cotton consumed per capita			..	..	5.31	5.73	5.33	5.74	6.36	6.68	6.08	5.85	7.11	7.42	8.15	8.54	8.87	11.99	12.75

manufacturer at a cost of 11 or 12 cents a pound, he sold in 1842 at small profits in goods at the prices quoted, but the cotton bought in 1845 at 6 cents, if worked up at the same cost, he sold, in 1846, at a profit of more than 4 cents a pound if his goods were unchanged in price since 1842—a profit of more than 60 per cent. in sheetings and shirtings. The consumer was taxed just as truly as if the price in 1846 had been 60 per cent. higher than in 1842.

That all consumers were thus taxed appears still more conclusively from the great reduction in prices from 1847 to 1849, on calicoes from 5.83 to 3.95 cents; on shirtings, from 9 and 8½ to 6½ and 6 cents; on sheetings, from 7¼ to 6¼, and from 8 cents to 6.90 cents; on duck, 2 cents a yard, and on yarn, 2¾ cents a pound. The price of cotton was higher in 1849 than in 1845, and in 1848 than in 1846, and yet the consumer gained in price just as he had lost under the protective tariff. It is only necessary to remember that the consumption per capita suddenly increased from 8.54 under protection to 12.75 under low duties in 1849. The manufacturer, content with smaller profits, found a larger market, and was able to extend his business fully 50 per cent. in three years.

Under the protective tariff, therefore, the consumer was taxed fully 60 per cent. on his cotton goods. The grower received less for his cotton. The manufacture was extended much less rapidly in four years under protection than in three years after the protection had been removed. And it will presently appear that the wages of operatives were lower in 1845 than they had been in 1839, or than they were in 1849. Who, then, was benefited? The capitalist, and nobody else. In 1845 all companies reported profits, ranging from 10 to 30 per cent., and some reported profits even during the worst years, 1841 and 1842—the York Company, in Maine, reporting a profit in 1840 of 14¾ per cent.; in 1841, of 13½ per cent.; in 1842, of 5 per cent.; in 1843, of 9 per cent.; and in 1844, of 20½ per cent.

We have not yet traced the effect of the tariff to the consumer. A statement of the prices actually paid at Charleston, South Carolina, for goods there most used, enables us to realize better how the tariff operated. Common calicoes, costing the manufacturer 4½ cents a yard, were selling to consumers at 9 to 16 cents. The transporters and middle-men were evidently transferring their share of all the burdens to the consumers. Cheap cambrics were selling at 18 to 20 cents; fine and checked cambrics, from 25 to 30 cents; white dimity, from 15 to 22; coarse counterpanes, for $1 to $4 each; medium quality, from $2 to $4; blue and white checks, for 10 to 12½ cents;

plain negro cloth, for 40 to 55 cents; and cotton thread, not on spools, for 40 to 75 cents.

If the cotton manufacture, which needed no protection, at least for coarser qualities, because the goods "are manufactured here cheaper than anywhere else in the world"—if this manufacture was thus affected by the high duties, so that the price of its products actually increased, though the cost of those products was reduced, and if the consumer was then forced to pay in some localities several times that increased price, what shall we expect of other manufactures less favorably situated?

The price of leather was not especially increased, as the manufacturers state, because we "can manufacture for less than any other nation." Yet, while the price of some qualities of boots and shoes and other manufactures of leather was reduced, the price of others was increased, not so much because the shoemaker needed protection, as because, having control of the market, and having a tax to pay, he chose to make somebody else pay it. The duty on hides was 5 per cent., and on leather 6 and 8 cents per pound. The manufacture of tobacco was also independent of duties, but the prices, though lower than the imported articles, allowed large profits. Lumber and its manufactures had somewhat increased in price in States near the Canada border; in Maine, Washington County, pine sold for $9.50; spruce, for $6.50; and laths, for 85 cents. Plaster, like almost every thing else, was cheaper than it was during the inflation of 1836, but still sold for $1 for ground, and $1.62½ to $1.75 for calcined, while the product from Canada could still be imported to some extent in spite of the duty, so much lower were prices there. White lead (ground in oil), with a duty of four cents a pound, had risen to $7 per cwt., or about 20 per cent., and a manufacturer reports that a much lower duty would be ample. Soap and candles were not affected, "as the raw materials are lower here than in Europe." Printing-paper, which had sold for 12½ cents a pound in the highest inflation of 1837, was only reduced to 10 cents. It may be easily inferred that the consumer paid an unnatural price, and the manufacturer realized an unnatural profit, although the paper was still sold within the price at which dutiable paper could be imported. Salt, which sold for 22 cents a bushel in New York in 1842, cost 35 cents in 1845, and 45 cents early in 1846, and in the interior was still higher.

The wool manufacture presented a curious phenomenon. We have seen that wool at this time was very cheap—so low was the price, indeed, that actual exportation to Europe proved that the English manufacturer was at a disadvantage of 5 per cent. in the cost of material. Nevertheless, imports of almost every kind of woollen goods increased, to the value of over one million in the aggregate, while the wool was so low that great numbers of sheep were being slaughtered. The broadcloth experiment, sustained, as Mr. Randall showed, by a supply of cheap wool from South America, not only made some progress, but encouraged the growing of fine wool to some extent, yet the importation of foreign cloths was increased, which shows that the price was much higher here than elsewhere. Other goods, of a quality likely to be imported, were increased in price, while goods never imported, if decreased in price at all, were reduced less than the cost of the material. Thus, goods which sold for 68 cents in 1839, when wool cost 40 cents a pound, were reduced in 1844 to 53 cents, when wool cost only 27 cents at that factory. But flannels increased in price more than 30 per cent. in 1844, and satinets 25 per cent.; low-priced cassimeres, which cost in England 1s. 4d. to 2s., were sold here in cities on the coast for from 50 to 90 cents; cheap overcoat pilot-cloth, costing 1s. 4d. to 1s. 6d. in England, sold here for 50 to 65 cents. This occurred while the material was actually cheaper by 5 per cent. to our manufacturers than to the English. It was not pretended by any manufacturer that the price of goods had been generally reduced, but nearly every one acknowledged that improvements in machinery and greater skill had caused large profits. It is very plain, then, that these improvements had not resulted in benefit to the consumers; that the low price of his wool did not secure the farmer correspondingly cheaper cloths, and that, with an actual advantage over the English in cost of material, our manufacturers sold at rates so high as to encourage importations actually larger than those of 1840, when the wool cost much more here, and when some of the improvements in machinery had not been made. Nor can it be said that the natural increase of consumption was wholly unchecked by the high prices; for, in reports from the farming States, it is recorded that a great many people had been obliged to discontinue the use of woollen cloths, other than those made on the farm. And we shall see that the manufacturers, with all their admitted profits, allowed no increase of wages, but were paying men 87½ cents a day, women from 40 to 50 cents, and children from 20 to 37½ cents. While agriculture was depressed, and wages were reduced from $17 to " even $5 a month " in Illinois, the labor thus forced to seek employment from manufactures gained no increase of wages from protection, though large profits were realized.

PRICES OF WOOLLEN GOODS.

Compiled from Treasury Report of 1849.

ARTICLES.	Width.	1835.	1836.	1837.	1838.	1839.	1840.	1841.	1842.	1843.	1844.	1845.	1846.	1847.	1848.	1849.
		$	$	$	$	$	$	$	$	$	$	$	$	$	$	$
Hamilton, Southbridge, Mass.—1st qual. Broadcl'h.	6-4	4 25	4 50	4 25	4 00	4 25	4 00	4 00	3 25	3 00	3 50	3 50	3 50	3 00	2 12½	2 00
" " " 2d " "	6-4	4 12	4 25	4 00	3 75	4 00	3 50	3 62½	3 00	2 75	3 00	2 87½	2 87½	2 50	1 90	1 87½
" " " 3d " "	6-4	3 75	4 00	3 73	3 50	3 75	3 25	3 12½	2 62½	2 62½	2 87½	2 75	2 62½	2 37½	1 87½	1 75
" " " 4th " "	6-4	3 50	3 50	3 50	3 00	3 50	3 00	2 75	2 50	2 25	2 35	2 37½	2 25	2 12½	1 62½	1 60
" " " 5th " "	6-4	3 12	3 25	3 25	2 75	3 00	2 50	2 50	2 25	2 12½	2 25	2 12½	2 00	2 00	1 56¼	1 45
" " " 6th " "	6-4	2 50	3 00	2 75	2 50	2 75	2 12½	2 25	1 87½	1 87½	2 00	2 00	1 70	1 62½	1 40	1 37½
Northampton, Northampton, Mass.—Broadcloth...	6-4	..	..	3 37½	3 75	3 50	3 00	3 00	2 75	3 00	3 00	3 00	3 00	3 00	2 37	2 00
Middlesex, Lowell, Mass.—Black Cassimeres.......	3-4	..	2 00	1 87½	1 87½	1 70	1 80	1 70	1 50	1 50	1 40	1 35	1 30	1 30	90	1 00
Monson, Monson, Mass.—Blue Satinets............	3-4	..	..	..	..	95	85	75	65	50	65	75	65	55	57½	50
Andover, Andover, Mass.—Scarlet Flannel.........	28 in.	38	40	35	35	37½	30	27	20	23	30	26	24	24	21	21
Lowell, Lowell, Mass.—White Linseys............	30 in.	28	31	25	23½	24	22	22	20	20	24	21	17	16	16	17
" " " White and Black Linseys...	30 in.	28	31	25	23½	24	22	.22	20	22	24	22	16	15½	15	15
" " " Fancy Linseys............	30 in.	28	31	25	23½	24	22	22	20	23	27½	22	17	17	16	17
" " " Superfine Carpets..........	4-4	1 10	1 15	1 12½	1 05	1 07½	97½	90	80	70	80	80	77½	77½	77½	70
" " " Fine "	4-4	95	1 00	97½	90	92½	80	70	65	62½	67½	65	65	65	65	60
Henderson's, Merrimack, N. H.—Superfine Carpets	4-4	..	..	..	..	..	..	..	76¾	77½	77½	75	75	75	75	71½
Henderson & Anderson's, S. Wrentham, Ms.—Fine.	4-4	..	..	..	..	..	..	..	62½	62½	67	66¼	60	61¼	61¼	58¼
Adams, Canton, Mass.—Common Carpets..........	4-4	..	..	..	..	..	..	..	53¾	55	56¼	53¾	51¾	48¾	47½	46¼
Ballard Vale, Andover, Mass.—Flannels...........	4-4	..	66½	58¾	55	65	55	50	40	32½	47½	45	47½	47½	40	45
Salisbury, Salisbury, Mass.— " No. XVI....	36 in.	38	43	38¾	36	36	29	. 29	28	24	26	26½	26½	27	34½	31
" " " " No. XVII...	38 in.	44	50	44¾	40	39½	33	33	32	28	28½	30	30	30½	38½	35
Blanket—Twilled Blankets........................	10-4	..	..	..	5 25	5 50	4 25	4 25	4 00	4 00	4 50	4 50	4 50	4 50	4 00	4 12½
" " "	11-4	..	..	..	6 00	6 50	4 75	4 75	4 50	4 75	5 25	5 50	5 25	5 25	5 00	4 87½
" " "	12-4	..	..	..	8 25	8 75	7 25	7 25	7 00	7 00	7 75	7 75	7 50	7 50	7 25	7 12½
Price of Wool at New York—Merino..............	..	37½	59	59	38½	52½	36	43½	29	31	41	31½	27½	37	28½	38½
Common............	..	37½	45	45	30	38½	21½	27½	19	21	33	24½	20½	29	21	31
Pulled No. 1.........	..	54	55	37½	37	42½	27½	35	27	25½	34½	28½	22½	29	25½	30

But was the consumer taxed? Once more the statistics of the report of 1849, although giving only selected facts, and those the most favorable that could be ascertained, help to a correct decision. The preceding table presents prices of woollen goods, as stated in that report, for the years 1835 to 1849, and the prices of merino, common and pulled wool, at New York, as recorded in the Treasury report of 1863. Again, there is apparent a very considerable reduction of prices from 1835 to 1843, caused in part by the low price of wool in 1842 and 1843, but in part by the improvements in manufacture. Broadcloth had been reduced in cost about one dollar a yard; cassimere, fifty cents; flannels, 18 cents, or 50 per cent.; linseys, 8 cents, nearly 30 per cent.; carpets from 95 cents to 65 cents a yard. Blankets had also been reduced in cost since 1838 about $1.25 a pair. The low prices of 1843 were followed, after the tariff began to have effect, by an increase of price in almost every article. In 1846, with wool actually lower than in 1842, and far lower than in 1841, when the wool was purchased for goods made and sold in 1842, the prices of the goods selected by the Secretary show scarcely any decrease in price, while some of them were higher. A cloth requiring $2\frac{1}{4}$ pounds of wool to the yard, made from merino wool bought in 1841 at the average price for that year in New York, would have cost for raw material alone $94\frac{1}{2}$ cents, but the same raw material bought in 1845 would have cost $68\frac{1}{4}$ cents to the yard; and from this cause alone the price of such cloth could have been reduced 26 cents a yard, but no quality of cloth was reduced in price in that proportion from 1842 to 1846, while the average price of the Lowell black cassimeres was precisely the same, the price of satinets was 4 cents higher, the price of Northampton broadcloths was 25 cents higher, linseys of Lowell were 3 or 4 cents lower, and carpets were some $2\frac{1}{2}$ cents lower, and some as high; flannels were also about the same in price, and blankets were 50 and 75 cents per pair higher in 1846 than in 1842, and 25 to 50 cents higher in that year, or in 1845, than in 1841 or 1840. In view of the fact that those prices were doubtless reported to the Secretary for publication which would best sustain the protective policy, it is impossible to doubt that consumers of woollen goods were generally taxed, not only by depriving them of the advantage in the price of wool, but in the majority of cases by an actual increase in the price of their goods. Not only was the wool-grower deprived of a part of the value of his wool, but he was obliged to pay more for his cloth. The consumer was taxed. Even the hands employed in woollen manufacture gained nothing in wages, but had to pay more of their wages for clothing. For whom was the whole community thus taxed? For the manufacturers, whose profits were so large that in 1845 nearly all refused to report them.

All iron-makers admitted that the cost of making pig-iron had decreased since 1840, and was still decreasing. It was shown that the actual cost of anthracite pig-iron was, in some cases, not over $15 a ton. Yet the price of pig-iron had increased from $25 a ton in New York, and $20 a ton at some of the furnaces, to $37 to $39 in New York, and from $30 to $35 at the furnaces, for cash. With such enormous increase of profits, we shall see the manufacturer had not granted any corresponding increase of wages; at many furnaces the workmen were paid an average of 87½ cents. While the raw material was thus being reduced in cost and increased in price, is it strange that the true manufacturers of iron complained? A maker of castings reported that his product had increased in price because of the increased cost of iron, and that he needed a reduction of the duty on pig. Another reported that he sold castings at $70 in 1844, when pig-iron cost $30, and then made a profit of 10 per cent. only; and another stated that his castings sold in 1845 for $80 a ton; that in 1842 they cost only $50 a ton; and during the inflation of 1836 sold for $100. A manufacturer of stoves reported no increase in wages, but an increase in the cost of his products. A maker of mechanics' tools and agricultural implements speaks of " the high price we are enabled to obtain," and adds: "Without the protection at present afforded by the government, we could not successfully compete with the foreign manufacturer." This is a confession, first, that the consumers were taxed, both farmers and mechanics, and that heavily; second, that the price of pig-iron had brought this very manufacture, which in colonial times had taught England how to make scythes and shovels, into such a predicament that duties were necessary to keep out foreign implements. In Cincinnati, rolled bar cost $55 a ton in 1842, and $70 a ton in 1845, and the effect on manufacturers who used that material can be easily inferred. Nevertheless, such were the improvements in manufacture, not only during the existence of this tariff, but before and after it, that many articles, the manufacture of which needed no protection, and in which the raw material consumed caused but a small proportion of the cost, were reduced in price during the tariff of 1842, as they had been before its adoption, and were after its repeal. These instances were paraded with great spirit by the advocates of the tariff as proofs that it had decreased the cost of manufactured articles. Thus in the report of

1849, different tables give the accompanying statement of the prices of certain articles of iron, but it is to be observed that nearly all of them are products in which the raw material is not an element of chief cost, and nearly all are articles which were successfully made in this country at an early day.

The fact that of these selected articles all except four had been reduced in price prior to the adoption of the tariff, while every one, without exception, was greatly reduced in price after the removal of the tariff, and nearly all far more within the three years 1847–1849, inclusive, than they had been within the four years 1843–1846, inclusive, effectually disposes of the idea that any reduction of the price which took place under the operation of the tariff was attributable to its influence. On the contrary, eight of these articles were sold at the same price in 1842 or 1843 as in 1846, the last year of the tariff, and nine were sold at a higher price in 1846 than in 1842 or 1843, while nine were slightly lower in price. Only three articles in the list were reduced in price as much from 1843 to 1846 as from 1846 to 1849. These very statistics, then, prepared in support of the tariff, to prove that domestic competition had reduced the price of some articles, show very forcibly that the natural decline in cost by reason of improvements was, in almost every instance, retarded, and, in most instances, arrested, by the protective duties, while of these articles about one-third were rendered more costly by the tariff. Taken in connection with the fact that these are but a few articles selected from a great number of products of iron, and they are generally articles in which the raw material used is comparatively a minor element of cost, the table will satisfy the mind that the great majority of products of iron were actually raised in price by the tariff; that, as to almost all, the natural reduction of price was arrested; and that there were very few indeed which were reduced in price as rapidly during the operation of the tariff as before its adoption, or after its repeal. But the consumer was taxed upon all articles of which iron is a material. If the improvements in manufacture enabled the maker to reduce the price of hoes from $3.25 in 1842 to $2.37 in 1846, it will not be denied that he could have reduced the price to $2.25, as he did in 1849, if the iron had cost less money. If nails made of iron costing $40 a ton could be sold in 1845 for 4¾ cents a pound, the same quality could undoubtedly have been sold for 4 cents, as they were in 1849, if the iron had not been made costly. Thus every consumer was really taxed, if not by the duty on nails or hoes, or other finished products needing no protection, then by the duty on pig-iron.

PRICES OF IRON ARTICLES.

Compiled from Treasury Report of 1849.

	1835.	1836.	1837.	1838.	1839.	1840.	1841.	1842.	1843.	1844.	1845.	1846.	1847.	1848.	1849.
Cut Nails, lb.	6	6	6	6	6⅛	5½	5¼	4¾	4¼	4½	4¾	4½	4½	4¼	4
Axes, doz.	15@16	15@16	15@16	13@15¾	13@15¼	13@14	12@14	11@14	11@12	11@11½	10½@11	10@11	9½@10½	8@10	8@10
Iron Pipes, ton	$55	$55	$60	$55	$55	$50	$50	$48	$45	$45	$42	$42	$42	$40	$40
Hollow-ware, ton	..	..	..	75	70@75	70@75	70@75	60@65	60@65	60@65	55@60	55@60	55@60	52½@57½	50@55
Hoes, doz.	..	4@5	4½@5	3½@5	3½@5	3½@4	3¼@4	3@3½	2½@ 3½	2½@3	2¼@2½	2¼@2½	2¼@ 2½	2¼@ 2½	2@ 2½
Sad-Irons, lb.	..	..	..	....	....	..	5¼	5	4	3½@4	3½@4½	3½@4	3¼@ 3½	3 @ 3½	3@ 3¼
1 inch, No. 14 Wood-Screws., gross, English	..	..	..	....	....	..	38	38	38	38½	37	35	29	29	29
1 inch, No. 14 Wood-Screws, gross. American	..	..	..	....	....	..	40	37	33½	30½	36	36	29	27	22½
Narrow 3-inch cast-iron Butt Hinges, English, doz.	..	..	..	....	....	..	58	58	....	55	62	58	58	52	52
Narrow 3-inch cast-iron Butt Hinges, American, doz.	..	..	..	....	....	..	....	..	....	67	62	58@59	50	46	42
Files, 12-in. flat bastard, doz.	2 87	3 33	3 83	3 83	3 33	3 33	3 13	3 13	3 13	3 13	3 35	3 35	3 20	3 30	3 13
Closet Locks, 4-inch, doz.	1 17	2 04	..	1 36	1 56	1 36	1 26	1 17	1 04	1 53	1 53	1 56	1 56	1 26	1 17
Vices, bright standing, doz.	..	..	..	....	5¼	5¼	5¼	5¼	5¼	5¼	....	5¾	5⅜	5¼	5¼
6-inch Bed-Screws, doz.	1 89	3 19	..	....	2 44	..	1 89	1 78	1 44	1 47	2 03	2 27	2 22	1 78	1 67
No. 3 Polished Trace-Chains, pair	..	63	60	55	....	..	38	37	32	36	38	43	42	40	33
Tinned Saucepans, No. 4	..	52	..	43	40	35	38	35	37	37	43	37	37	35	35
4-quart sheet-iron Tea-Kettles	90	1 24	..	....	77	72	69	63	63	69	63	69	69	58	63
Shingling-Hatchets, doz.	..	..	..	....	....	..	5@6½	..	5@6	....	....	4@5½	....	....	3@5
Scythes, best, doz.	..	..	..	....	....	..	13 00	..	12 00	....	....	12 00	....	....	10 00
Shovels and Spades, best, doz	..	..	..	....	....	..	5 50	..	5 00	....	....	5 00	....	....	4 50
Mortise Locks, cheapest, doz	..	..	..	....	....	..	18 00	..	12 00	....	....	12 00	....	....	7 25
Rim Locks, 6-inch, doz.	..	..	..	....	....	..	....	..	13 50	....	....	13 50	....	....	10 00
Gimlets, lowest, gross	..	..	..	....	....	..	3 50	..	2 75	....	....	2 50	....	....	2 25
Nail-Hammers, best, doz.	..	..	..	....	....	..	10 00	..	8 00	....	....	8 00	....	....	7 00
Augers, doz.	..	..	..	....	....	..	6@7c.*	..	4 50@5 50	....	....	4 50@5 50	....	....	*3¼@4½
Carriage-Springs, lb.	..	..	..	....	....	..	12@15	..	10½	....	....	9½@10	....	....	9@9½
Cotton and Wool Cards, doz.	..	..	..	....	....	..	4 50 & 3	..	4 & 2 50	....	....	4 & 2 50	....	....	2 75@1 75

* Per ¼ inch diameter.

It will not be overlooked that the prices of cotton and wool cards, $4 and $2.50 per dozen in 1843, were not reduced until the repeal of the tariff, but were then quickly and materially cheapened. In this and other methods the duty on iron simply embarrassed other manufacturers, by making it impossible for them to cut down the cost of production as rapidly as manufacturers elsewhere were enabled to do. It does not seem possible to doubt that by this tariff agriculture was doubly retarded, by reduction of the price of agricultural products and the wages of agricultural labor, and by a general increase in the cost of manufactured articles. While many articles were not affected in price, implements, clothing, and a large proportion of articles used by the farmer, were rendered more costly at the place of production or in wholesale markets, while neither internal navigation nor railroad facilities increased at the natural rate, and the cost of transportation was enhanced. Agricultural labor, then three-fourths of all American industry, if the census of 1840 was reliable, was injured by this tariff, both in its receipts and its expenditures.

Injury to agriculture involves injury to the mechanic, the tradesman, the merchant, the professional man; for all these classes depend upon the farmers, the majority of the population, for support. Nor can it be supposed that the transporting interest was helped by duties which made iron cost from $35 to $40 a ton, and increased the cost of hemp, timber, and tools. There is no evidence known to the writer that the tariff of 1842 resulted in any increase of wages or profits to these classes or either of them, while every one can understand that, when a maker of mechanics' tools boasted of the high price which he was enabled to charge for them, the mechanic must have regarded the matter quite differently. That hatters needed no aid is plain from the fact that in 1840, under extreme low duties, there were imported of "hats, leather, wool, and fur," only $7,000 worth, while there were exported $103,000 worth, and in 1846 the value of fur hats alone imported was over $12,000. In 1841 we imported of boots and shoes of all kinds only $17,166, and exported $100,725, while in 1846 we imported $37,572. In 1840–'42, inclusive, the three years of lowest duties preceding the protective tariff, there were imported only $28,000 of ready-made clothing, an average of $9,000 a year. The tailors surely did not need protection against a competition amounting to less than 10 cents a year per tailor! But the protective tariff so enhanced the cost of cloth that, though the tailors were also "protected" by duties of 33 to 50 per cent. on clothing, people began to import ready-made clothing instead of cloth, and in 1845 there was imported about $200,000 worth—an increase of more than 2,000 per cent. in four years. It is not only plain that the tailors were not benefited—it is plain that the cost of clothing to consumers was increased generally from 33 to 50 per cent. in the cost of material alone. This tax, like that involved in the cost of iron, bears upon all classes, and to the farmers and mechanics, and persons employed in non-protected manufactures, at least, it was in no wise compensated.

There remain less than one-twentieth of the whole force of laborers—the number then employed in manufactures supposed to be aided by protection. If these were greatly benefited, if their wages were increased tenfold, did it profit the country to inflict injury upon three-fourths of its laborers, the farmers, and to embarrass or tax all others, simply to benefit one-twentieth? Is this " protecting American industry ?"

But was the one-twentieth of American laborers benefited? Upon them, as upon all others, fell the burden of increased cost of clothing and of many other manufactured articles. Were their wages increased? Upon this point the proof is singularly conclusive.

The returns from manufacturers who answered the inquiries of the Secretary must be accepted as at least as favorable to the protective tariff as the facts would permit. If the manufacturers strained the truth at all, they certainly did not do so to the disadvantage of the system intended to secure them large profits. Those who did not reply at all would certainly have done so if the facts had enabled them to make a more favorable showing for the system than others could make. The vital importance of the inquiry in regard to wages was perfectly understood by every one ; and if any manufacturers were paying wages above the average of those in the same business, we may be sure that they would have been the most prompt to state the fact. Accepting the statements actually made as a fair presentation of the best phase of the facts, we must conclude that the average of all wages in any employment was certainly not higher than the average paid by those who made returns.

In the cotton manufacture, over twenty establishments in New England made returns, and the wages paid by these averaged, for men, $1.17 a day ; for women, 50 cents, and for boys and children, 32 cents. The wages of men were ordinarily $1 a day, or $10 a month with board, but skilled mechanics and experienced hands were sometimes paid $1.50 or even $2. The wages of women ranged from 75 cents a day, the highest, to 30 cents, the lowest; and of children, from 50 cents to 19 cents. But the vital question is, whether these wages, however small, were an increase upon those paid in earlier years. On this point there can be no doubt. Not a single one of these establishments claimed to have increased the wages paid; but, while some were paying "the same as for twenty years past," others admitted that they reduced wages in 1842. The Saco establishment, indeed, stated that it paid two per cent. higher wages in 1844 than it did in 1834; but did not give any figures for 1836 to 1842, when other establishments increased or decreased. The Hamilton mill, at Lowell, which gave more detailed information than any other, said: "The number of persons employed is as follows: Men 245, average wages $1.03 per day; women 669, average wages 53 cents per day; boys 34, average wages 44 cents per day. . . . In 1842, when there were hardly any dividends, and when this company made none at all, there was a reduction of wages, but it was small in proportion." Of all these companies, five worked ten hours a day, two worked eleven hours, five worked eleven and a half hours, ten worked twelve hours, one worked fourteen, and the rest did not state the number. In New York, fourteen cotton-mills reported, not one of them paying a higher average to men than $1.25, and the average of all was, men $1.15, women 42 cents, children 30 cents, all boarding themselves, and all the mills working twelve hours. Four of these state that wages have not materially varied; but three, all paying the highest wages reported, frankly ascribe their prosperity in part to "diminished wages paid;" a "small percentage of reduction," or a "decline of labor."

It may, therefore, be held established, from the statement of the manufacturers themselves, that the tariff of 1842, which caused some increase in the price of cotton goods, notwithstanding a decrease in cost of cotton, did not cause any improvement in wages, but that, on the contrary, less wages were paid in the majority of establishments in 1845 under protection than in 1840 under "free trade." Yet the profits of the manufacturers, according to their own statements, had greatly increased, many admitting that they made 25 per cent., and the great majority declining to state how much they did realize. It is quite noteworthy that the Lowell company, looking back over years of extreme low duties and financial prostration, refers to one year, 1842, as "the year in which few dividends were made, and in which this company did not make any." From this single remark we can judge whether the whole period of low duties was absolutely fatal!

It must be admitted, then, that in the cotton business high duties had not increased, if indeed they had not really decreased wages, to the year 1845.

The iron interest was not more liberal to labor. Of seventeen establishments in New England, New York, and Pennsylvania, not one reported paying to ordinary men more than $1, while two paid only $5 a week, and one 87½ cents a day. To skilled mechanics higher wages were paid—in one establishment as high as $1.75, and one other reported as high as $2.50. The other establishments, except two in Alabama, which reported high wages, paid in no case higher than $2, and the average of them was $5 to $6 a week for ordinary hands. The average for the whole country, including all classes, was about $1.12½. But the labor paid over $1 a day was in the machine-shops or founderies. The pig-iron establishments, as far as reported, paid an average of only 87½ cents a day, and they made larger profits than others. Of all the iron establishments of all kinds, not one claimed to have granted an increase of wages, while some said that wages had not materially varied, and one acknowledged that there had been a reduction.

Returns from plaster, lumber, cordage, tobacco, flour, paper, and pottery establishments, all gave the rate of wages as $1 a day, and not one claimed that there had been any increase. Of leather establishments one was paying $18 a month; of ashes and wines one each was paying $15 a month. In a soap establishment wages had been decreased, and were on an average only 69 cents a day, though the profits were 15 per cent. In one salt establishment the average sum paid was only $8 a month, though the duty on foreign salt was over 100 per cent.

Finally, we take the woollen-mills, of which twelve reported in the Eastern and Middle States. Of these, several were paying as high as $1 a day to men, others 90 cents, others 88 cents, while two paid only an average of 75 cents to men, one only 65, and one paid only 55¼ cents on the average to men and women. The average for all the establishments reported was 89 cents for men, and 30 cents for boys. One establishment paid $3.50 a week to women, four others 50 cents per day, some 40 cents, and three as low as 37½ cents. The average was about 45 cents. Again, we have to observe that not one of these establishments claimed that there was any increase of wages; but, while several said that wages had not increased—were "the same as ever"—one, paying 75 cents a day to men, stated that wages had decreased. Another, paying the highest wages reported —over one dollar to men, and $3.50 a week to women, claimed to be

21

paying "the same as ever." If this, the highest return in 1845, was the average in former years, the decrease of wages in the woollen manufacture must have been considerable. But all the mills report profits, due to improved machinery and the low price of wool. While the farmer was injured, then, nobody was benefited except the capitalist, whose profits the tariff increased.

We have been thus minute in examining these returns, because they furnish conclusive proofs as to the working of the only protective tariff since the development of manufactures by modern methods, and prior to the war. The results now ascertained cannot be ascribed to any fluctuation of the currency or of the banking credits, for the amount of currency in circulation during the latter part of 1845, and through 1846 and 1847, was almost precisely the same as the amount in circulation in 1840 and 1841, prior to the resumption of the banks, while the line of deposits was somewhat larger, January, 1845, than in either of the years 1840 and 1841. Neither can it be said that the condition of labor in this year was exceptionally unfavorable, for the country had recovered from the prostration which followed the return to the specie basis, and was in that condition which all advocates of protection have been accustomed to mention as "marvellously prosperous." The records of this year, as it happens, are a fairer test of the effect of the tariff, than those of the following year, the last of its operation; for, in 1846, a demand for breadstuffs from England began to revive agriculture, and the prospect of a change of the tariff gave hope to all who were straitened by its operation. What, then, is the result?

The evidence is conclusive that the tariff of 1842 did depress the agricultural interest, reduce the price of its products and the wages of agricultural labor, and at the same time increase the cost of many articles of necessity to the farmer, or of universal use, particularly clothing, salt, glass, and the products of iron.

The evidence is conclusive that the wages of labor employed in manufactures were not increased, but in many cases had been reduced since 1840, particularly in those very branches of manufacture which were most favored by duties, and which, owing to cheap materials and great improvements in method or machinery, were making the largest profits.

It is conclusively proved, then, that American labor in the aggregate received less wages under the tariff of high duties in 1845, than it had under the tariff of low duties. in 1840, and that the cost of many necessities and comforts of general use was increased.

To whom was this tariff a benefit? Not to the farmer—it robbed him. Not to the operative—it did not increase his wages, and did increase his expenses. It was a benefit to those capitalists who, under it, were able to charge people higher prices for goods than the cost of production warranted, and who were blessed with large profits. To enrich them, the labor of the whole country was taxed.

CHAPTER XXII.

PROTECTION AND NON-PROTECTION CONTRASTED.

THE conclusions arrived at in regard to the effect of the tariff of 1842 are singularly confirmed by statistics given in one of the most elaborate works in defence of the system—"The Tariff Question"—by Hon. E. B. Bigelow. In that work, for the purpose of proving that laborers in England are paid less than laborers here, he gives statistics of wages paid by manufacturing establishments at Lowell, in the years 1839, 1849, and 1859. As these statistics are derived from the records of the companies, and have the authority of a gentleman of high reputation, we may accept them unhesitatingly, and advocates of the tariff system will be sure that one of its most sincere defenders has not distorted the record to its disadvantage.

Mr. Bigelow seeks to prove that labor is dearer here than elsewhere, and therefore needs protection. This error has already been exposed. Labor is dearer here because it can be more profitably employed, and therefore does *not* need protection. The contrast between the wages paid in England and in Belgium or France conclusively proves that the higher-priced labor is not the less effective, but the more effective; does not give more costly products, but cheaper products. The world over, it is the "pauper labor" that needs protection most.

Mr. Bigelow himself has contributed largely to the demonstration of this truth. To him we owe many inventions more ingenious and wonderful than any of like object in use in other countries, and the weaving of the Brussels carpet, especially, has been revolutionized by the loom of his invention. One who has contributed so much to make American labor more effective, should surely have considered the fact that its inventive talent and its superior intelligence are a better protection against the world than any that laws can give.

Though useless for the purpose for which they were collected, the statistics given by Mr. Bigelow happen to be of great use in another quarter. It boots nothing to prove that our laborers get better wages than those of England; we all know the fact, and they would surely need protection if they did not. But it is of vital importance to ascertain whether our labor is better paid under the protective system than under a non-protective tariff. That is the question of questions, and Mr. Bigelow helps to settle it. The years selected by him happen to be years just preceding the tariff of 1842, just after its close, and just preceding the protective period of 1861 –'69. Neither of them illustrates by itself the working of the protective system. But, contrasted with the facts already given, by which the record of 1845 is quite clearly presented, they are of value. As to the manufacture of textile fabrics, the record of Lowell will be accepted as the best test, for that manufacture is there most extensive and successful. Fortunately, two of the most important establishments at Lowell made full and detailed returns in 1845, which we can compare with the record of wages in 1839, before the tariff, in 1849, after the tariff, and in 1859, after thirteen years of low duties.

In 1845, the Lowell companies stated that they were paying to men, on an average, $1.03 and $1.05 a day—the work being twelve hours a day. In 1839, as we learn from Mr. Bigelow's statistics, the Lowell companies were paying to fifty-two different classes of male hands, from overseer down to the common laborer, in all branches of the cotton manufacture, $411.30 a week, or an average of $7.91 a week, and $1.32 a day. The hours of labor were the same. The conclusion already arrived at, that there was a reduction of wages from 1840 to 1845, is therefore confirmed.

The tariff was changed by an act passed in August, 1846. If any increase of wages had occurred prior to the change, no record of it is known to the writer. But in 1849, three years after the change of tariff, what were the wages? The same Lowell companies were paying, to men in fifty-two different classes of labor in the cotton manufacture, an aggregate of $407.07, or an average of $7.82 a week, and $1.30 a day. This is not quite as high as was paid in 1839, but it is higher than the companies reported in 1845. And in 1845, when the average of wages was $1.05 for men, the work was for twelve hours a day; in 1849, when the average of wages was $1.30 a day for men, the work was for only eleven hours a day. Under the non-protective tariff, therefore, the men were actually paid higher wages for one hour daily less work than they were paid in 1845 under the protective system.

In the woollen manufacture, wages were also lower in 1845 than in 1839. As we have seen, some of the mills were paying only 75 cents a day for men, and 40 cents for women, in 1845, and only one reported paying "from $5 to $8 a week for men, and from $3.50 to $5 for women"—the highest wages then reported by any company in the country. The average was 89 cents for men, and 45 cents for women. Now, in 1839, according to Mr. Bigelow's statistics, the average wages of men of all classes employed in the woollen manufacture was $5.63 a week, or about 94 cents a day. There had therefore been some reduction of wages from 1839 to 1845. After the high duties were removed, in 1849, the same statistics show that the average wages paid for eleven hours' work was $5.02 a week to men; which, considering the time, is about the same as was paid in 1845. As we shall see, the rate subsequently increased under the non-protective system. Meanwhile, both woollen and cotton goods were much cheaper in 1849 than in 1845, although the wages paid were not reduced.

With the aid of Mr. Bigelow's statistics, we now proceed to compare the wages in 1845, under protection, and in 1849, shortly after its removal, with those paid in 1859, near the close of the longest period of low duties. Beginning with cotton, it appears that the hands who were paid for fifty-two different classes of labor in 1849 an aggregate of $407.07 weekly, were paid in 1859 an aggregate of $446.85 weekly. In 1849 the average was $7.82 a week for eleven hours' work. In 1859 it was $8.59 for eleven hours' work. The fact is thus established that, during the long period of non-protective duties, the laborers were not "ground down" to poverty, as it has been asserted must be the case under that system, but actually gained in their wages in the aggregate nearly forty dollars for fifty-two persons, and in the average, each 77 cents a week. Nor does the woollen manufacture show a different result. The same classes which were paid in 1849 an average of $5.02 a week for eleven hours' work, were paid in 1859 an average of $5.43 for eleven hours' work. Mr. Bigelow also gives the wages for 1849 and 1859 in the manufacture of ingrain carpets, in which, in 1849, there was paid, to twenty-seven persons of the different classes of labor, $232.23 a week, and to the same persons in 1859 there was paid $246.42 a week. In 1849 the average was $8.60 a week, and in 1859 it was $9.12. In brief, the result of this comparison of records, the data being furnished in every case by the manufacturers themselves, is as follows :

WAGES AT LOWELL.

	"Free Trade."	"Protection."	"Free Trade."	
	1839.	1845.	1849.	1859.
Cotton, 52 classes..........	$411.30	....	$407.07	$446.85
Average weekly............	7.91	$6.30	7.82	8.59
" daily...............	1.32	1.05	1.30	1.43
Hours of work............	12	12	11	11
Woollen, 11 classes.........	61.96	....	55.22	59.70
Average weekly............	5.63	5.34	5.02	5.43
" daily...............	.94	.89	.84	.90½
Hours of work............	12	11 to 12	11	11

In 1845, the hours in the different establishments were not the same, and the wages of women are not given by Mr. Bigelow by the day or week, but by the job. They show the same increase from 1849 to 1859, but cannot be satisfactorily compared with the wages reported by the day or week in 1845.

If these statistics are reliable—and they are all taken from the statements of manufacturers themselves—we have conclusively established :

1. A reduction of wages from 1839 to 1845, in cotton and woollen manufactures both, the hours of work remaining in nearly all cases the same.

2. An increase of wages from 1845 to 1849—from "protection" to "free trade"—in the cotton manufacture, of $1.52, in the average weekly wages, the hours of work being reduced from twelve to eleven. In the woollen manufacture, the wages were changed from 89 cents, average for eleven and twelve hours, to 84 cents, average for eleven hours.

3. An increase of wages from 1849 to 1859—during ten years of "free trade"—the hours of work remaining the same, in the cotton manufacture, from $7.82, weekly average, to $8.59, weekly average; in the manufacture of woollen goods, from $5.02 weekly, to $5.43 weekly; and in the manufacture of carpets, from $8.60 to $9.12.

The increase of wages from 1845 to 1860 was not confined to the two branches of manufacture just mentioned. By comparing the statistics gathered by the Secretary of the Treasury in 1845 with the records of wages in 1860, prepared by Mr. Wells, we find that the same increase extended to other kinds of manufacture, and particularly to the iron manufacture in all its branches. In the manufacture of edge tools in 1845, the wages were from $4 to $12 a week, and averaged about $7.50; but, in 1860, the wages of all the different classes of workmen averaged $10.70 a week. In 1845, the wages of men employed in hardware establishments averaged $1.25 a day. But in 1860, according to Mr. Wells's statistics, the wages paid to thirty-three different classes of laborers were, in the aggregate, $307.61 a week, the females and boys being omitted, and the average was $9.32 weekly, or $1.55 daily. In founderies and furnaces, in 1845, the wages paid to men ranged from 87½ cents to $1.75 a day, and the average paid by all the establishments was not over $1.22 a day. But in 1860 the average was $9.07 weekly, or $1.51 a day. In the manufacture of leather in 1845, the wages were one dollar a day, or $18 a month with board, but in 1860 the wages were $8 a week. In the paper-mills, in 1845, one dollar a day was the average; but in 1860 the average for all classes of males was $7.38 weekly, or $1.23 daily.

It is placed beyond dispute that the wages of men in manufacturing establishments of all the leading branches increased quite perceptibly from 1845, under protection, to 1860, the close of the period of " free trade."

The wages of agricultural labor increased still more largely. In 1845, we have seen, farming wages had fallen to $10 a month, at the highest, and as low as $5 a month in Illinois. Nowhere was there reported for that year any higher rate than $10, and the average for the free States was probably less than $9. But in 1859, according to tables published in *Hunt's Merchants' Magazine*, the wages paid in eight localities in New England averaged $15 a month; in ten localities in New York, $13.30; in Pennsylvania and New Jersey, $12.50 and $13; in Ohio, $13.50; in Illinois, from $13 to $18; and in Iowa, from $15 upward. The average for the free States must have been about $14, a gain of more than 50 per cent. since American industry had ceased to be mis-" protected." But, since the large majority of farmers own or rent the farms on which they work, it is much more important to determine whether the prices of agricultural products had improved. The price of wheat and of flour, of wool and of cotton, as we have already seen, was somewhat higher during the period of low duties than it had been under protection. Taking New-York wholesale prices, the lowest quoted, for the 1st of August, we have the following comparison :

LOWEST PRICES, AUGUST 1ST, AT NEW YORK.

		1845.	1860.
Flour.......................per bbl.		$4 31	$5 05
Rye..........................." "		2 87	3 50
Corn-meal....................." "		2 31	3 40
Wheat..................per bush.		90	1 40
Rye........................." "		68	81
Oats........................." "		42	40
Corn ...." "		51	64
Lard......................per lb.		7	12
Butter......................." "		15–16	10–19
Cheese......................." "		5	7
Rice......................per cwt.		3 50	4 50
Seeds, clover................per bush.		6	8
Sugar, New Orleans...........per lb.		5	6
Tallow ...." "		7	10
Tobacco, Kentucky............." "		2– 7	3–12
Wool, common................." "		24–26	34–38
" merino ...." "		32–34	48–52
" pulled, No. 1............" "		28–30	28–30

Yet these figures by no means show the full value of the period of low duties to the farmer. These are New-York wholesale prices, but the prices actually paid to the farmer are in the main governed by New-York prices and the cost of transportation from the farm to New York, or some other market. During the years 1845–'60, greater reduction was made in the cost of transportation than during all other years of our whole history. Twenty-four thousand miles of railroad were built, for low duties on foreign iron enabled us to build roads with unexampled rapidity. Also, 3,512 steamboats were built, for iron was cheap. Vast progress was made in the system of canal transportation. By these great changes, the cost of getting his produce to a market was so greatly reduced that the farmer actually received much larger prices, in proportion to the wholesale rates in New York, than he received in 1845. It is impossible to estimate the value of these changes to the agricultural interest in the increased prices received for products, and it is equally impossible to estimate their effect in the increased value of farms. It would not be rash to say that the entire value of farming land in the Northern States was increased fully 50 per cent. by the railroads alone that were built during this period of low duties.

It only remains, regarding the period of low duties, to notice that the cost of many manufactured products was reduced. Receiving more for his crops, the farmer, in common with all other consumers, paid less for his iron, his glass, his salt, his clothing, his boots, and his implements and machines. In the year 1845 pig-iron ranged from $30 to $50 a ton; in the year 1860 it ranged from $20.50 to $27 a ton. In 1845 the average price was about $38, and in 1860 the average price was $23.50. A difference of $15 a ton in the price of iron involves a material difference in the cost of nails and implements, tools and machines. In the year 1845 salt sold at an average of 37½ cents in New York; in the year 1860 it sold at an average of 18½ cents a bushel. Nails were 4½ cents in 1845, and 3 cents in 1860. Linseed-oil, the important element in the cost of all paints, was 73½ cents a gallon in 1845, and 58 cents in 1860. Boots (men's heavy), which cost $3.50 in 1845, cost $2.90 in Rhode Island, and an average of $3.30 in the Eastern and Middle States in 1860.

The fact will be observed that the wages of labor at Lowell have kept pace closely with the price of wheat. The comparison is note-worthy:

	1839.	1845.	1849.	1859.
Wages at Lowell.......	$1 32	$1 05	$1 30	$1 43
Price of Wheat........	1 24¼	1 04	1 24	1 48½

Is there not some law of economy underlying this singular parallelism? To all manufacturers the farmers are the consumers. If the farmers are able to purchase largely, the demand for products and the demand for the labor of operatives increase, and the rate of wages rises. But, if the farmers are rendered unable to purchase liberally by the low price of their products, the demand for manufactured goods and for labor in manufactures must decrease, and the rate of wages must fall.

Generally, then, the rate of wages in manufactures must rise or fall with the price of agricultural products.

So far, the cost of living and the wages of labor keep pace with each other. The laborer, benefited by higher wages, has also to pay in like proportion more for his food. But the cost of food produced by domestic agriculture is not more than one-third of the whole cost of living. Other articles, if controlled in price not by the natural law of demand, but in part by an artificial law, may be costly when the price of farm products is low, and when the rate of wages is low.

Whenever that occurs, all labor, agricultural and manufacturing, has its cost of living increased in proportion to its consumption of the article so enhanced in cost. And this increase, being without any corresponding increase of wages or of the price of farm products, is a burden upon farmer and manufacturing operative—a tax which can in no way be compensated.

The cost of iron and of other articles, products of protected industry, has in fact been artificially increased, at a time when both agricultural prices and the wages of all labor have been reduced. As illustrations, take iron, the material of all tools, implements, and machinery; salt, which is an element in the cost of all packed meats and fish; nails, and linseed-oil, a material of importance in the cost of paints:

	1839.	1845.	1849.	1859.
Price of Wheat........	$1 24½	$1 04	$1 24	$1 43½
Wages, Lowell.........	1 32	1 05	1 30	1 43
Pig-Iron, per ton.......	39 00	38 00	24 37	25 00
Nails, cut, per lb........	06¼	04½	04	03
Linseed-Oil, per gallon..	75¼	74	63½	60½
Salt, per bushel........	37	37½	24¼	18½

Because prices of manufactured articles were not lower in 1845 than in 1839, in proportion to the decrease in agricultural prices or in the wages of operatives, all classes were taxed, and all labor burdened. The cost of living was not in all its elements reduced in proportion to the reduction of wages. But, when the protective tariff had been repealed, wages of labor and agricultural prices rose, but prices of all the manufactured products declined. The cost of living did not increase, then, in proportion to the increase of wages or the remuneration of the farmer, but, as affected by the important articles mentioned, it declined. And during the succeeding ten years of non-protection, while the wages of labor and the price of agricultural products materially advanced, the cost of living, as affected by the price of the manufactured products named, either decreased still further or increased but slightly.

It is not necessary to show that prices of all other manufactured products have corresponded with the prices of those given, nor are statistics for that purpose accessible. The conclusion is unavoidable that, if important elements in the cost of living have been artificially increased by duties, at a time when prices of agricultural products, cost of domestic food, and wages of labor, were reduced in correspondence, then all labor has been taxed, and all industry burdened by interference with the natural laws of exchange. Capital has pocketed profits. But labor has been taxed to pay them.

CHAPTER XXIII.

THE PRESENT SITUATION.

THE conclusions justified by experience in former times are peculiarly valuable now, when all acknowledge that the condition of the country is most unsatisfactory, but for the admitted fact different causes are assigned. Knowing how other protective tariffs have affected farming and other labor, we can judge more confidently whether existing evils are due entirely to a depreciation of currency, or to a mistaken interference with natural exchanges.

Tables given at the close of this chapter show that, during the war, the price of farm-products was very low—hardly higher in the average, measured in gold, than the rates of the panic period, January, 1858. During this time manufacturing was also seriously retarded, but all disorders were ascribed to the war. In 1865 the crop of wheat was short, and for two years thereafter a continued deficiency of supply lifted the price of wheat above that of 1860, although corn sold for very little more, and hay and some other products for much less than was realized before the war. By the high price of wheat the farmer was barely paid for a short crop, but, though in other respects worse off, he continued to hope. The crop of 1868 was ample, and a sudden and serious fall of prices was the result. Those who had ascribed the partial good fortune of 1866 and 1867 to the tariff, began to be undeceived.

Meanwhile, the condition of laborers in manufacturing and mechanical employments was by no means enviable. In the report of 1869, Mr. Wells, Special Commissioner of the Revenue, presented, in a very strong light, the contrast between the condition of such labor in 1860 and its condition in 1867–'68, and the mass of statistics gathered by him proved that the average increase of wages in manufacturing establishments was "for unskilled labor" 50 per cent., and for "skilled labor" 60 per cent., while "the increase of all the elements which constitute the food, clothing, and shelter of a family had been about 78 per cent., as compared with the standard prices in 1860–'61." The material part of these tables is copied at the close of this chapter, and no inquiry by private individuals can add weight to these official statements, nor has any private citizen at command the facilities for a more extended investigation than that of the commissioner. The fact which the commissioner also records, that wages in the cotton-mills were reduced in 1868, and that the prices for puddling and rolling iron declined in that year, so that the increase since 1860 was about 67 per cent., though the cost of making iron was still about 75 per cent. greater than in that year, will be noticed in due season, for this reduction accompanied the sudden fall in the price of agricultural products in 1868. When the tables were prepared, wheat was selling for $2 in gold, and yet the average increase in the wages of agricultural labor was only 50 per cent., little more than the difference at that time between currency and gold values. The tables of wages, contrasted with those of retail prices, in the manufacturing towns of New England, New York, Pennsylvania, New Jersey, and Delaware, leave no room to dispute the conclusion that at that time wages had increased since 1860 less than the cost of living, and the workmen in mechanical and manufacturing employments were actually worse off than they were before the war. Reducing the results to gold values, at the rate of 1867–'68, we find that the average increase of wages in gold was for unskilled labor 7, and for skilled labor 14 per cent., but the average increase in the cost of living in gold was about 27 per cent. The skilled workman who received $100 a month in 1860, and expended $90 for his living, in 1868 received wages worth $114 in gold, but the cost of living, if he purchased the same quantity of the same articles as in 1860, was increased to $114 in gold, and, though he could save $10 a month in 1860, he could save nothing from larger wages in 1868. Nor was his case in any way improved by calling his wages $160 in currency, for the cost of living, reckoned in currency, had increased to $160 also. While the workmen in manufacturing employments were thus circumstanced, the wages of agricultural labor had increased only 7 per cent. in gold. But not more than one-third of the cost of living is for the products of domestic agriculture, and these products, as the tables show, had not increased in cost more than manufactured or imported articles. If the cost of living to other laborers was about 27 per cent. higher in gold than it was in 1860, the cost to farming laborers, after deducting all products of agriculture in this country, must still have been increased more than 13½ per cent. Counting as nothing the products of the farm consumed in supporting its laborers, the cost of their living had still been increased at least twice as much in gold as their wages had been increased in gold.

At that time, high prices of some farm-products were balanced, as they were caused, by short crops. Having calculated to raise one thousand bushels, and expended in seed and labor enough to raise that quantity, the farmer found that his crop was from five to eight hundred bushels only, and, even at the high prices then obtained, it returned to him little more than his outlay. Hay, however, was lower than in 1860, and wool also. Had the cost of living been no greater than it was before the war, both farmer and mechanic would have prospered, but the actual increase was far more than the increase in wages, or in the profits of farming.

In the year 1868 the crops were ample, and the price of wheat fell nearly a dollar a bushel. The first fair crop in several years was consumed at a price scarcely higher in gold than the farmer had obtained in 1860. With an increase of population from thirty-one to thirty-seven millions, the number of farmers and of persons depending upon agriculture for support must have increased one-fifth, and, to yield them as fair wages as were received in 1860, the value of crops produced should also have increased one-fifth. But the actual increase in the gold value of Northern crops, as has been shown in the examination of the progress of agriculture, was from $1,079,000,000 in 1860 to $1,113,000,000 in 1868, while the gold value of all crops, cotton and tobacco included, was less in 1868 than in 1860. The return to each farmer or laborer per capita was, therefore, materially diminished; there were about six laborers in 1868 to divide returns not greater in gold than were divided by five persons in 1860. But the cost of production and the cost of living had been affected also. Receiving less per capita for products sold, the farmers were compelled to pay more for articles imported or manufactured; for clothing, boots and shoes, blankets, household goods, tea, coffee, and sugar, and for implements. It need not be said that the farmers generally suffered. Within the year ending June 30, 1869, in some of the agricultural counties of Ohio, it has been stated, more mortgages were effected than in any preceding year for a long period. Wool declined so rapidly in price that the slaughter of millions of sheep began. Yet the farmer continued to pay, to purchase, and to hope. One more good crop, he trusted, would relieve him. It came—the excellent crop of 1869. All know the result. Prices have fallen still lower. Michigan wheat sold in New York, January 1, 1869, for $2.12½, and January 1, 1870, for $1.55; No. 1, spring, declined from $1.70 to $1.30 a bushel; wheat-flour from $6.60 to $4.85; rye-flour from $7 to $5; rye from $1.50 to $1.02; oats from 78 to 65 cents; hay from 90 to 85 cents. These are New-York prices. At Chicago, January 1, 1869, wheat was worth $1.13, and January 1, 1870, only 78 @ 79 cents; oats had declined from 46½ to 41½ cents; rye from $1.12 @ 66 cents; barley from $1.48 to 77½ cents; beans from $3 @ $4.25 to $2 @ $3 per bushel; and hay from $19.50 to $14 per ton. At Cincinnati the fall in flour was from $7.75 per barrel to $5.50; in wheat, No. 1, from $1.75 to $1.14; in rye from 1.35 to 93 cents; in barley from $2.35 to $1.35; in clover-seed from 15 to 13½ cents; in butter from 38 to 30 cents; apples from $4.50 to $3.50 per barrel; potatoes from $2.50 to $1.50 per barrel. Nor do these prices at the principal Western markets present to the mind the full extent of the loss to the farmer. Thousands of bushels of wheat were bought in Iowa for 40 cents a bushel during the closing months of 1869. No farmer can afford to produce wheat at such prices. In plain terms, the farmers of the country have quite generally failed to realize the actual cost of their products. They begin to restrict their purchases. The merchants in the country find it hard to remit to the city; and the whole system of exchange is clogged. The load borne by two-thirds of American laborers has proved too heavy. They have been taxed too long to support enormous monopolies, and blunders in national economy more fatal to industry than the hungriest monopoly, and their misfortunes must now be shared by others.

No other branch of industry can long continue to prosper, after the farmer has been forced to economize. Accordingly, in spite of a reduction in the cost of living as far as that is affected by the price of agricultural products, the condition of laborers in mechanical and manufacturing employments has not on the whole improved. Bad as it was in 1868, it is now even worse, and the fact has been forced upon the attention in all parts of the country by strikes of unusual number and magnitude. Many of these have been unable to resist a reduction of wages. In one article, treating of the condition of labor in the metropolis and neighboring cities, the New-York *Times* mentions thirty strikes, and adds, "of these a few only were successful." The painters had 1,300 men idle for more than three months; the iron-moulders of Williamsburgh were idle for three months; the potters of Trenton were on strike for five months, with serious loss to employers and employed. Carpet-weavers about Philadelphia were on strike for some time, but finally accepted reduced wages. In Pittsburg the wages of plasterers in 1869 were 11 per cent. lower than in 1865; of masons 20 per cent., of blacksmiths 21 per cent., of carpenters 20 per cent., of painters 20 per cent., and of machinists 20 per cent. Mr. Wells records the fact that in 1868 the wages of iron-moulders were reduced, and it is elsewhere stated that the reduction was for puddlers 25 per cent., rollers 40 per cent., and laborers 25 per cent.

Nor is this the only form in which wages have been reduced during the past two years. Thousands of establishments have been forced to reduce the number of their hands. In Chicago alone, on the 1st of January, 1869, it was estimated that over twenty thousand persons were out of employment. In every part of the country, the number of hands employed in mechanical occupations has been diminished, in consequence of the embarrassment of farmers. The country blacksmith, carpenter, or shoemaker, finds little money coming in when the farmers in his neighborhood are pinched, and he is compelled, not only to economize in his own purchases, but to discharge some of his hands. Thousands of mechanics and workingmen are drifting to cities, from country towns where they have been employed, and seeking work at such wages as any employer may choose to offer.

Even where the larger manufacturing establishments have neither reduced the number of hands nor the rate of wages, they have in very many cases reduced the aggregate sum paid in wages during the year by stopping work for a time. In many different branches of manufacture this expedient has been resorted to, because it was found that the markets were overstocked, production having increased, while the increase of consumption has been suddenly arrested. Many cotton-mills have worked short time; yet the quantity of cotton manufactured has been scarcely greater, and actually less in proportion to population, than the quantity manufactured in 1860. Woollen and carpet establishments in considerable numbers have temporarily stopped work during the year. The paper-manufacturers have held a convention to agree to diminish production. The *American Workman*, organ of the Shoemakers' Union, states that the men employed in that branch of industry have had work only ten months out of the twelve. Out of thirty thousand anthracite-coal miners, twenty-five thousand stopped work for months, demanding a formal agreement that production should never be continued when the price of coal should fall below five dollars a ton. Tailors in New York, working less than full time, found their wages insufficient, and demanded larger. Iron establishments throughout the West have been greatly embarrassed, few working full time; and notices in the newspapers indicate that many Eastern establishments have also been working below their full force. The hat-manufacture complains of extreme depression, the domestic consumption having been reduced, within the past three years, fully twenty-five per cent., while the large demand for export, which for many years before the war sustained fully one-seventh of the production, has almost wholly ceased, our manufacturers for the first time in many years being unable to supply foreign markets as cheaply as can England, Germany, and France. The copper mining and manufacture are as seriously depressed as ever before; and though large establishments, engaged in smelting foreign ores at Boston and Baltimore, have been broken up by the duties imposed by the act of 1869, the consumption has been so much more largely reduced, that the price of the domestic products has fallen four cents—from 26–27 to 22–23 cents—since the passage of that act. Manufacturers of paper-hangings, because of the duty imposed by the act of 1869 upon "Dutch metal," have been obliged to raise the price of their products from five to twenty-five cents a roll, according to the quantity of leaf used on each roll, and testify to a general falling off in sales, "owing to the high price and the difficulty of making the consumer understand the reason why we charge more." It does not occur to these gentlemen that the consumer, though he should understand perfectly well, might still be limited in his purchases by his ability to pay. The number of hogs packed at the West, according to statements recently published, will fall short of the number packed in 1868–'69. Lumber-dealers and brick-makers, in important centres, have been driven to reduce their operations. Of several of the large Western cities, in which records are published of the number of houses built each year, all except one show a decrease in 1869 as compared with 1868. While these facts appear in regard to the most important branches of industry, there is no reason to doubt that the same causes have in like manner affected minor interests, whose complaints attract less attention in public journals and documents.

These facts only accord with the reasoning that, whenever the farmers are pinched, the consumption of products of other industry must be checked, the demand for labor in other industry must be reduced, and the wages of such labor in the aggregate must be diminished. During the two years 1868 and 1869, wages in mechanical and manufacturing employments have in many cases been reduced in rate; in other cases, the rate being unchanged, there has been a virtual reduction by temporary stoppage of work; and, in others still, the aggregate paid in wages has been reduced by the discharge of hands. It is beyond question, therefore, that the rate of wages is on the whole lower than it was in 1867–'68, when Mr. Wells's inquiries were made; and, if the thousands of laborers now out of employment be taken into account, the aggregate paid in wages to non-agricultural labor must be quite materially reduced. But in 1868 the average increase since 1860 was only 14 per cent. in gold for skilled and 7 per cent. for unskilled labor. The accompanying table of prices, January 1, 1860, and January 1, 1870, shows that the cost of living, measured in gold, has been increased far more largely:

PRICES IN 1860 AND 1870.
Manufactured Products and Imported Articles.

	1860.	1870—Currency.	1870—Gold.	Inc. or Dec. p.c.
Ashes, pots, 100 lbs.	$5 12½	$7 50	$6 22	+ 21
Candles—Adamant, lb.	17	20½	16½	— 3
" Sperm, lb.	39	51½	42½	+ 8
Coal—Anthracite, ton.	5 50	7 75	6 43	+ 18
" Liverpool, ton.	10 50	15 00	12 45	+ 20
Copper Sheathing.	25½	32	26½	+ 4
Fish—Orleans, lb.	11¾	26	21	+ 90
" Dry Cod, quintal.	4 50	7 50	6 22	+ 38
" No. 1 Mackerel, bbl.	16 00	27 50	22 88	+ 42
Fruits—Raisins, box.	2 35	4 20	3 48	+ 49
" Currants, lb.	6	13½	11	+ 68
Hemp—Manila, lb.	6¼	....	14¼	+130
Indigo—Manila, lb.	60	....	80	+ 33
Iron—American Pig,* ton.	22 17	37 50	31 12	+ 40
" English Bar, ton.	42 25	86 25	71 58	+ 70
" Nails, cut,* lb.	3	5	4½	+ 41
Leather—Hemlock Sole, lb.	20	30	25	+ 25
" Oak Sole, lb.	30	42	35	+ 16
Lime—Rockland, bbl.	75	1 50	1 24½	+ 66
Liquors—Brandy, gallon.	3 00	....	6 00	+100
" Whiskey, gallon.	26	98	82	+200
Molasses—No. —, gallon.	53	78	64	+ 20
" Cuba, clayed, gallon.	24	35	29	+ 20
Oils—Whale, gallon.	50	85	70½	+ 34
" Linseed, gallon.	57	90	74¾	+ 30
Provisions—Pork, Mess, bbl.	16 37½	29 75	24 69	+ 50
" " Prime, bbl.	11 75	24 50	20 33	+ 73
" Beef, plain West., bbl.	9 50	14 00	11 62	+ 22
" " prime Mess, tce..	9 00	27 00	22 41	+149
" " Hams, extra, bbl.	14 50	33 00	27 39	+ 88
" Hams, pickled, lb.	9¼	15	12½	+ 33
" Shoulders, lb.	6½	12	10	+ 54
" Lard, Western, lb.	10½	17¼	14½	+ 40
" Butter, Western, lb.	16	30	25	+ 50
" " State, lb.	20	42	35	+ 75
" Cheese, factory, lb.	9	17½	14½	+ 24
Salt—Turk's Island,* bushel.	19½	48	40	+110
" Liverpool, ground, sack.	1 15	1 70	1 41	+ 23
" Domestic,* bbl.	90	1 50	1 24	+ 37
Soap—Brown,* lb.	5	10	8	+ 60
" Castile,* lb.	8½	13	10¾	+ 26
Tea—Young Hyson,* lb.	25	70	58	+132
" Oolong,* lb.	35	87½	72½	+117
Tobacco—Manuf'd, No. 1,* lb.	21	45	37	+ 79
Whalebone, lb.	79	....	87	+ 10
Sugar—Cuba, raw, lb.	7¾	10¾	9	+ 16
" " refined, lb.	10	14½	11¾	+ 17
Coffee—Rio,* lb.	11½	....	15½	+ 36
Laths,* M.	2 00	2 55	2 11	+ 5
Paints—Red Lead,* lb.	6	10½	8½	+ 40
Collins Axes,† doz.	9 00	12 00	9 96	+ 10
Lowell Ingrain 2-ply Carpets,†	75	1 30	1 08	+ 44
Blankets, 10-4,† pair.	3 50	5 50	4 56	+ 30
Men's ordinary Boots,† dozen.	21 50	43 00	35 69	+ 67
Wax-legged Boots,† pair.	4 50	6 83	5 67	+ 26
Black Alpaca,† yard.	24	40	33	+ 37
Steel—Sheffield C.† lb.	14	19	16	+ 14
Stoves, 5 holes †.	6 00	9 50	7 88	+ 31

* Prices thus marked are taken from the Treasury Report of 1863, and newspaper quotations of January 1, 1870, mostly from the New York *Tribune*.
† Prices thus marked are given in the report of Commissioner Wells as the prices for 1859 and 1869.
All other prices given are from tables published by the *Journal of Commerce*. For American pig-iron, however, the price given for 1860 is the average for that year, as stated by Mr. Colwell, report of Revenue Commission, 1865–'66.

22

PRICES IN 1860 AND 1870.
Agricultural Products.

	1860.	1870—Currency.	1870—Gold.	Inc. or Dec. p.c.
Wheat-Flour—State, bbl...........	$5 30	$5 85	$4 44	— 16
" " Western, bbl........	5 29	4 85	4 02	— 24
Rye-Flour, bbl......................	4 00	5 00	4 15	+ 4
Corn-Meal (Brandywine), bbl......	3 90	5 00	4 15	+ 6
Wheat—Michigan, bushel...........	1 50	1 55	1 28	— 14
" No. 1 Spring, bushel... ...	1 18	1 30	1 07	— 10
Rye, Western, bushel...............	92	1 02	84	— 7
Oats—State, bushel.................	46½	65	54	+ 16
" Western, bushel...........	45½	62	51	+ 12
Corn—Western, bushel.............	90	1 10	90	=
" Southern, bushel...........	88	1 02	84	— 4
Hay, Shipping, 100 lb...............	1 10	85	70½	— 36
Hops, lb...........................	16	25	20¾	+ 25
Seeds—Clover, lb..................	8½	13	10¾	+ 25
Potatoes, bushel *.................	1 35	1 50	1 24	— 8
Hides—B. A., lb..................	24½	....	22½	— 10
Tobacco—Kentucky, lb.............	12	13	10¾	— 10
Wool—Saxony †..................	54–58	46–55	38–45	— 26
" Merino, ¾ and blood.......	48–52	43–50	35–41	— 24
" Common and ½ blood......	34–46	40–50	33–40	— 9
" Extra pulled...............	42–46	39–45	32–37	— 21
" No. 1 pulled...............	28–30	24–29	20–24	— 24
Cotton—Middling Upland, lb.......	11	....	21	+ 90
Rice, 100 lbs......................	4 20	.... —	7 25	+ 74

In all the long list of articles quoted, excepting the leading agricultural crops, there are scarcely half a dozen which have not increased in price since 1860 more than the average of wages of skilled labor had increased in 1867–'68, both being reduced to the gold standard, while many of the most important have increased from 20 to 200 per cent. in gold. Prepared meats and other packed or prepared food have increased in cost remarkably. Plain Western beef, which has increased only 22 per cent., and factory cheese, 24 per cent., are the lowest, but beef hams cost 88 per cent. more in gold, and mess beef 149 per cent. more in gold, than they cost in 1860; Turk's Island salt costs 110 per cent. more in gold; fish from 40 to 90 per cent; raisins 49 per cent., currants 68 per cent., tea over 100 per cent., and manufactured tobacco about 80 per cent. more in gold than the same article cost ten years ago, January 1st, as quoted in the same paper, the New-York *Journal of Commerce*, from which these quotations are taken. The contrast between the prices of farm crops· and manufactured products will strike every reader. While wheat, flour, rye, corn, tobacco, potatoes, hides, tallow, wool,

---

* Not having New York price of potatoes in 1860, I have given Cincinnati prices for December 31, 1860, and December 31, 1869.

† Wool prices for 1860 are from tables in the New York *Chronicle*, and for October 31; for 1870, January 1st, "Walter Brown's Circular."

All other prices are from the tables in the Treasury report of 1863, or from the New York *Journal of Commerce*.

and hay, sell for less money in gold than in 1860, and oats and hops for little more, and the only agricultural crops of considerable importance which command higher prices are cotton and rice, the price of nearly every manufactured or imported article in the list is much higher. To the quotations from the *Journal of Commerce* are added, from other papers, statements of the prices of leading articles January 1, 1870, and statements by Mr. Wells of the price of a few manufactured goods in 1859 and in 1869.

It is creditable to the cotton manufacture that its products are not now enhanced in price, in view of the greatly-increased cost of raw material, and it may be added that from this manufacture, which has thus given evidence of real vigor and enterprise, there come none of those clamors for yet higher protective duties with which Congress is assailed. Indeed, some of the ablest and most conspicuous cotton manufacturers are earnestly and openly advocating the repeal of the protective system. The prices of blankets and carpets may fairly be taken as indicating the change of price in a large class of woollen goods of which the domestic manufacture does not fully supply the demand, and in which the protective system gives a virtual monopoly. But tables already given show that some other woollen goods sell for about the same in gold as in 1860, though, wool being cheaper, they should sell for less. It may fairly be presumed that products of iron generally have not increased in cost less than stoves and cut nails.

These, however, are wholesale prices, but the cost of living depends upon retail prices. The statistics presented by Mr. Wells show that the difference between wholesale prices at the principal markets and retail prices paid by consumers in Eastern manufacturing towns was much wider in 1868 than it was in 1860.

In 1860 the wholesale price of Western flour at New York was $5.30, but the average price to consumers in Eastern towns, as shown by the elaborate investigations of Mr. Wells, was $7.48, and the difference, which may be called the cost of exchange, was then $2.18 in gold. In 1867–'68 the wholesale price of the same grade at New York was $9.55 in currency, or $6.87½ in gold, but the average retail price of flour in the same towns as before was $10.39 in gold, and the difference, or cost of exchange, was $3.52 in gold. The gap between the retail price of flour and the wholesale price at New York had therefore enlarged from $2.18 to $3.52 in gold, or about 64 per cent. In 1860, the Western wheat from which this flour was made sold at Chicago for 95 cents to $1 a bushel, but in January, 1868, the same grades sold for $1.25 to $1.30 in gold, and the increase in the cost of the wheat was, therefore, about 30 per cent. But the increase in the retail price of the flour to Eastern consumers was from $7.48 to $10.39 in gold, or about 40 per cent. In 1860, the price of live hogs in St. Louis was about $6 per cwt., and in Cincinnati $6.20, and at that time the retail price of smoked hams to Eastern consumers was 12.36 per pound. But in 1867–'68 the price of live hogs at St. Louis ranged from $5.50 to $7.25 in currency—never higher than $5.21 gold. Yet consumers in the same Eastern towns were paying for smoked hams $22.21 in currency, or $15.86 per cwt., in gold. The retail prices of pork in Eastern towns compare with the price of live hogs at St. Louis, all reduced to gold, thus:

	1860.	1868.	
Pork, fresh........................	$9.54	$12.	Increase.
" corned or salted	10.39	12.56	"
" bacon........................	10.28	12.6	"
" hams smoked	12.36	15.86	"
" shoulders....................	9.46	12.20	"
Live hogs, St. Louis	6.00	5.21	Decrease.

A part of this difference is explained by the fact that in 1860 Turk's Island salt for packing cost at St. Louis and Cincinnati about 30 cents a bushel, and in 1868 about 65 cents. A part of it is explained by the fact that, in moving from the Mississippi River to the great centres of manufacturing industry in Eastern States, products roll over about one thousand miles of rail, which cost in 1860 $47.95 a ton (American), and which now cost about $75 a ton. At one hundred tons to the mile, each line of railroad has to pay nearly $3,000 per mile more for its iron alone than it paid in 1860, and every barrel of flour, every bushel of wheat, every barrel of meat, or head of cattle, sent to market over these railroads, must help to pay for the increased cost of building and maintaining them. A part of the difference, moreover, is explained by the fact that in 1860 the wholesale price of hams in New York was $9.25, while the average retail price in Eastern towns was $12.36; difference, $3.11 per cwt.; but in 1868 the wholesale price in New York was 12 cents currency, or $8.64 in gold, while the average retail price in Eastern towns was $15.86 in gold; difference, $7.22 per cwt. In 1860, lard cost at wholesale in New York 10½ cents, and the average retail price in that State was 12 cents; the difference was, therefore, $1.50 per cwt. But, in 1868, lard cost at wholesale in New York 12¾ cents, and the average retail price in towns in that State was $18.36;

difference, $5.61 per cwt. In 1860, dry codfish cost per quintal at New York $4.50, and the average retail price in towns in that State was 5 cents; difference, 50 cents per cwt. But in 1868 dry cod sold in New York for $5.50, and the average retail price in towns in that State was 9 cents; difference, $4.50 per cwt.

These comparisons might be almost indefinitely extended. But they show quite clearly that the cost of preparing and transporting food has been increased, and that the gap between retail and wholesale prices has been greatly widened. They reveal an increased waste and friction in the whole system of exchanges, by which it comes to pass that the consumer at the East does not get the full benefit of low prices of agricultural products, while the farmer at the West, receiving less than he did in 1860 for his products, is compelled to pay not only high prices for manufactured products consumed, but greatly increased charges for transportation and exchange. Nor is this strange. The dealer and transporter have to meet increased expenses, and they have both the power and the will to pass the burden over to the producers. If a pair of shoes actually costs 5 cents more than it did in 1860, the dealer finds his excuse for charging 10 cents more. If the cost of making or moving a barrel of pork, or of flour, is increased 20 cents, the dealer has his excuse for increasing his price 50 cents. If one article of woollen cloth is doubled in cost, the dealer knows that few customers will understand that other similar articles are not equally affected, and, if any customer complains at any increase of price whatever, the high tariff affords him an unfailing excuse. At all points, the friction of "the societary movement" is increased. Everybody is charged a little more for every thing, and, having a burden to bear, feels that he must also charge everybody a little more. Thus it happens, first, that the increase in wholesale prices of manufactured products is multiplied in retail prices to consumers, and, second, that the reduction in wholesale prices of agricultural products does not result in a proportionate reduction of retail prices to consumers. Much of the advantage to consumers resulting from the low price of crops is neutralized by increased cost of transportation and exchange. But the disadvantage resulting from increased cost of manufactured products is multiplied, to all consumers, by the same increase of friction.

The price of manufactured products, it would naturally be supposed, must be reduced in consequence of the arrest of consumption already described. But a reduction to the natural level is prevented by the increased cost of production. Many illustrations have already

been given of the effect of the protective system in that respect, and
the table of prices affords others. In 1860, 100 bushels of Western
corn at the New-York price would buy 23 barrels of corn-meal, but
in 1870 only 22 barrels; of Southern corn, in 1860, 100 bushels would
buy 22⅔ barrels, but in 1870 only 20½ barrels. In 1860, 100 pounds
of ingot copper would buy 88 pounds of copper sheathing, but in
1870 only 64 pounds. In 1860, 100 pounds of South American hides
would buy 122½ pounds of hemlock sole-leather,* but in 1870 the
same weight of foreign hides would buy only 55 pounds of that
leather. In 1860, 100 pounds of hides would buy of men's ordinary
boots 13½ pair, but in 1870 the same quantity of hides would buy of
the same quality of boots only 6⅓ pairs. In 1860, 100 pounds of Kentucky tobacco would buy of " manufactured tobacco No. 1 " 50 pounds,
but in 1870 only 22 pounds. In 1860, 100 bushels of corn would
buy of mess pork 5½ barrels, but in 1870 only 3⅓ barrels. It has
been observed that all prepared meats, fish, and provisions, are increased in price, and this change is not fully explained by the cost
of live animals and of salt. The farmer, in 1860, who had for sale 100
pounds New-York Saxony fleece, could obtain 56 cents a pound in
gold, and could buy 37⅓ yards of Harris cassimere; but in 1870 the
same farmer, selling 100 pounds of the same fleece at 48 cents
currency, could buy only 24 yards of the same cloth. Having 100
pounds of full blood merino fleece in 1860, he could sell at 50 cents
in gold, and could buy 14⅓ pairs of Holland 10-4 all-wool blankets;
but in 1870, with the same fleece selling at 45 cents in currency, he
could buy only 8⅓ pairs of the same quality of blankets. His common wool selling in 1860 at 46 cents, the farmer could with 100
pounds buy 61⅓ yards of Lowell ingrain two-ply carpeting; but in
1870, 100 pounds of the same common fleece, bringing only 46 cents
in currency, will buy only 35⅓ yards of the same quality of carpet.
Illustrations of this kind need not be multiplied. It is enough to
call attention to the fact that in almost every branch of industry the
cost of production has been materially and in some cases very greatly
increased. Every step from the rudest products of unskilled labor
toward the fashioning of any thing for use or for food seems to cost
more, not in currency merely, but in proportion to the original cost
of the material, than the same process did in 1860.

It should not be overlooked that the materials of house-building

---

* January 1, 1860, according to price tables in the Treasury report of 1863,
Buenos Ayres hides sold for 24½, but the *Journal of Commerce* table states the price
of hemlock sole-leather, January 1, 1860, as 20 cents a pound.

are all increased in cost, not in currency alone, but in gold. Lumber is higher, lath cost a little more, lime costs 66 per cent. more in gold, nails cost 41 per cent. more in gold, glass of the cheapest quality was quoted in 1860 at $2.75 and is now quoted at $6; linseed-oil, the main element in paints, is 30 per cent. higher in gold, and red lead 40 per cent. higher; and English bar-iron is. 70 per cent. higher. It is not strange, then, that rents are much higher. Mr. Wells stated that the increase in rents in New York and other large cities has been from ·90 to 100 per cent., in small towns in New Jersey 111 per cent., and in small manufacturing towns of Pennsylvania 81 per cent. The *Pittsburg Commercial*, indeed, states that " within the past *five* years houses containing two, twelve, and fourteen rooms have doubled; houses containing six, seven, and eight rooms, have advanced 150 per cent., while three, four, and five room tenement-houses have in a majority of cases trebled. These are the homes of the working-classes." This change, it will be observed, is within five years—since the war-prices had culminated. The increase since 1860 must therefore have been even greater in that city.

Paying such rents, buying provisions costing from 22 to 88 per cent. in gold more than in 1860, buying clothing, boots, carpets, blankets, stoves, salt, tea, coffee, and tobacco, thus increased in cost, and paying an increased tax for every step in the preparation of food and clothing for use, how can the laborer live without a large increase of wages? It is clearly impossible. But the higher wages themselves increase the cost of producing other articles of use or necessity. The prices of manufactured articles cannot be reduced in proportion to the prices of agricultural products until wages and the cost of production can be reduced; but these, again, cannot be lowered until the cost of living can be reduced. Hence the manufacturer, unable to make or to sell at such rates as to stimulate purchases, burdened with a stock of goods left on his hands by arrested consumption, and finding the outlet for this surplus in the export trade artificially clogged, if not plugged up entirely, is forced to reduce production by discharging hands or working short time. If he proposes a reduction of wages, his hands protest, and with truth assert that they are worse off to-day, with wages nominally high, than they were in 1860 with wages and prices both at a natural level. If he discharges men, the country loses their industry, but must still pay in one form or another for their living. If he works short time, the effect is worse than a reduction of wages. A payment of thirty dollars a week each to fifty hands, while fifty men are idle, is far worse for industry than fifteen dollars a week, the whole number being employed. Twelve dollars a week, if the factory stops work two months in the year, is not better pay for the operative than ten dollars a week and full time. The country loses two months of industry; prices must be increased to compensate for the loss. The production of wealth and the aggregate wages of labor are reduced, but the cost of living and the cost of production do not correspondingly decrease.

It cannot be denied, in view of the facts presented, that other labor, as well as agricultural, has suffered in consequence of interference with the natural system of exchanges. The farmer has been driven into debt, and consumption of manufactured products has been arrested. The manufacturer finds himself loaded down with a stock of goods unnaturally costly in production, larger than the home market will consume, and too high priced for exportation. The operatives find their wages decreased, either in the sum paid weekly, or by suspension of work. Yet the cost of clothing, houses, food, and necessaries of life, cannot be properly reduced, because of the cost of production, and all classes are compelled to pay heavier charges for exchanges and transportation. The whole community is taxed. The greater part of the tax is passed to the producers. Of these the farmer bears the largest share of the burden, but his embarrassment inevitably recoils upon the laborer employed in manufactures. Nor can the phenomena be reasonably ascribed to any other cause than a tariff which artificially lifts the prices of manufactured products. For the very same sequence of events—low prices of agricultural products and disaster to manufacturers—followed the protective tariff in 1829-'30, when the currency was neither depreciated, inflated, nor fluctuating in value. The very same extraordinary depression in prices of agricultural products followed the protective tariff in 1843-'44, when the currency was neither depreciated, inflated, nor fluctuating. The same increase in cost of manufactured products, in cost of production, and of exchange, accompanied by low wages of labor, in proportion to the cost of living, has appeared under every other protective tariff as far as statistics have enabled us to examine them. The secret of the disorder is the break between the remuneration of capital and labor applied to agriculture, and capital and labor applied to manufactures, and that break is caused by the artificial increase of the price of manufactured products, while it is not possible for any tariff to secure an equal advantage to the farmer. The gulf thus artificially created, as long as a tariff continues to widen it, can only be temporarily bridged by short crops, to the disadvantage and loss of all, or filled up by a general collapse of industry, to the utter ruin of many.

"True, the cost of production has increased; but that is because the labor is better paid," say the advocates of protection. Labor does, indeed, receive more money than in 1860. But, in that which money will buy, labor is paid less than it was then. The cost of labor has increased, but far less than the prices of manufactured products. The increase of wages in gold, in the iron-mills, according to Mr. Wells's report for 1868, was only 20 per cent. since 1860; but the increase in the cost of bar-iron was 70 per cent. in gold. Since that time wages have been reduced, but bar-iron still sells at $85 a ton, as it did in 1868. With an increase of only 15 per cent. in gold in wages in the founderies, the cost of stoves has increased 31, and of nails over 40 per cent. The cost of labor per ton, in making pig-iron in Pennsylvania, was not less than $2.30 in gold; and, in 1868, it was stated by the manufacturers to be $4 in currency, increase in gold 58 cents, or about twenty-five per cent.; but the cost of pig-iron, though lower now than then, is still 35 per cent. higher than it was in 1860. The wages of men employed in cutlery works were increased, from 1860 to 1868, only $3\frac{7}{10}$ per cent. in gold; but the price of Collins's axes had increased $10\frac{6}{10}$ per cent. in gold. The wages in sugar-refineries had increased, in gold, 14 per cent.; but the cost of refined sugar had increased 20 per cent. in gold. The wages in glass-works had increased 17 per cent. in gold, but the New-York quotations of the cheapest glass had increased over 50 per cent. in gold. The rate of wages in leather establishments had increased in gold 22 per cent.; but, though hides were 10 per cent. lower in gold, the price of hemlock sole-leather had increased 25 per cent. in gold. The wages of hands in the woollen-factories had increased less than 16 per cent. in gold; but, though wool cost less in gold in 1868 than in 1860, the cost of blankets had increased 30 per cent. in gold, and the cost of ingrain carpets 44 per cent. in gold. These comparisons, also, might be indefinitely extended. Because manufactured products have increased in cost more than the wages of the labor employed in making those very same products, and manufactured products generally have increased in cost more than the wages of labor employed in manufactures, the laborer, though receiving more money, actually receives less pay than he did before the war. Where, then, is the leak? Labor has gained nothing; the products which it consumes are en hanced in cost more than the increase of its wages. The people gain nothing; the goods which they buy cost more in proportion to the cost of raw materials. The farmer gains nothing; his wheat buys less iron; his hides buy less leather; his wool buys less cloth. Has manufacturing capital gained, while all labor and all the rest of the community has lost? In certain monopolies this is true. But, in the majority of cases, the manufacturer is embarrassed by the cost of production, by a restricted market, and by arrest of the natural increase of consumption. In the long-run and in the aggregate, manufacturing capital also must realize smaller profits than if let alone. Nature's laws will be avenged. Men are tempted to wasteful employment of capital, to adherence to wasteful methods, by the expectation of unnatural profits. The capital and the labor, if let alone, would be more economically and profitably employed. Everybody must be taxed to make up for this diversion of industry from the most remunerative employments and methods. The burden is diffused over the whole people, and it falls upon the manufacturer himself as well. He must pay more for his machinery, in order that somebody may make iron in Pennsylvania, when it could be more cheaply made elsewhere. He must pay more for his buildings, in order that somebody may cut down our own rapidly-wasting forests, instead of using the timber of Canada also, and in order that somebody else may realize profits in making linseed-oil and paints, and in order that somebody else may get rich, in making glass, faster than he did before the war. He must pay more for his labor, because his workmen have to pay somebody for making their blankets and carpets, their clothing and boots, an unnatural price, and must pay in every pound of prepared meat or fish they consume a part of the bounty to the salt monopoly. When all these taxes have been met, the manufacturer often finds that the cost of production has so increased as to eat up his expected profits. Meanwhile, the laborer is taxed more than his wages are increased; the community is embarrassed in all its exchanges; the farmer sells his sheep for cloth really worth one-half the value of the wool on the sheep's back. Everybody is taxed, and nobody permanently and really benefited— nobody, save those whose monopolies are sucking up the life-blood of the country.

RETAIL PRICES IN 1860-'61, AND IN 1867-'68.

In towns in New York State, and the average in the States of Maine, New Hampshire, Vermont, Massachusetts, Connecticut, Rhode Island, New York, New Jersey, Pennsylvania, and Delaware, with percentage of increase, and prices of 1867-'68 reduced to gold values.

From the Report of Commissioner Wells for 1868.

ARTICLES.	NEW YORK. 1860-'61.	1867-'68.	Percent'ge of incr'se.	GENERAL AVERAGE. 1860-'61.	1867-'68.	Percent'ge of incr'se.	Prices in '67 red'd to gold†
PROVISIONS.							
Flour, wheat, superfine, bbl..	$7 02	$13 32	90	$7 48	$14 55	94.53	$10 39
" " " ℔....	3.86	7.03	82	3.99	7.71	93.21	5.51
Flour, rye, bbl.............	4 86	9 00	85	4 44	8 11	78.62	5.79
Corn-meal, bbl	2 94	5 47	86	3 13	5 33	70.3	3 81
Beef, fresh, roasting-pieces, ℔	10.25	20.5	100	11.46	22.66	97.73	16.19
soup-pieces, ℔...	5.25	10.33	96	5.78	11.06	91.33	7.9
rump-steaks, ℔...	10.33	20.10	94	12.25	24.4	99.38	17.5
corned, ℔..........	7.67	14.22	85	8.46	15.95	109.6	11.4
Veal, fore-quarters, ℔.......	7.25	14.11	95	8.06	14.54	80.41	10.4
hind-quarters, ℔......	9.14	17.38	90	10.27	18.48	89.95	13.2
cutlets, ℔.............	11.43	22	92	12.92	22.16	71.54	15.83
Mutton, fore-quarters. ℔.....	8.8	11.75	34	8.02	14.59	81.92	10.42
legs, ℔........	9.63	16.67	73	10.29	19.01	84.75	13.58
chops, ℔.....	10.14	18	77	11.39	19.79	73.69	14.14
Pork, fresh, ℔..............	9.75	15.11	55	9.54	16.79	76.10	12
corned, or salted, ℔....	10.25	16	56	10.39	17.59	69.31	12.56
bacon, ℔............	10.75	17.5	64	10.28	17.63	71.53	12.6
hams, smoked, ℔.....	11.25	20.17	79	12.36	22.21	79.09	15.86
shoulders, ℔.........	9	16.5	87	9.46	17.08	80.54	12.20
sausages, ℔..........	11	18.33	66	11.6	19.67	69.6	14.05
Lard, ℔...................	12	18.36	52	12.47	17.88	46.84	12.72
Codfish, dry, ℔............	5	9	80	4.87	8.72	79.31	6.24
Mackerel, pickled, ℔........	9.18	13.45	47	8.01	13.59	69.51	9.71
Butter, ℔..................	18	35	94	19.7	37.72	91.48	26.95
Cheese, ℔.................	10.7	17.7	65	11.38	19.61	72.27	14
Potatoes, bushel...	46	90	96	55.34	98.94	78.79	70.67
Rice, ℔...................	6	13.27	110	6.09	13.31	118.73	9.51
Beans, quart..............	6.36	11.18	76	6.96	13.37	92.05	9.55
Milk, quart...............	4.25	7.50	76	4.64	7.49	61.45	5.35
GROCERIES, ETC.							
Tea, Oolong, or good Black, ℔	63	1 44	128	67.72	1 34.88	99.19	96.34
Coffee, Rio, green, ℔........	15.4	32.7	112	14.96	33.19	121.82	23.71
roasted.....	20	40.44	102	18.26	38.67	111.74	27.62
Sugar, good brown, ℔.......	8.20	14.10	72	8.34	14.65	75.67	10.46
yellow C, ℔..........	9.50	16.20	70	9.02	15.80	75.13	11.29
Molasses, New Orleans, gall..	48	1 00	108	49.74	1 02.22	105.49	73.02
Porto Rico, gall....	45.54	93.63	105	44.1	88.87	115.14	63.48
Syrup, gall................	63	1 22.4	91	9.79	1 15.75	65.85	82.68
Soap, common, ℔...........	8.63	12.36	43	7.86	12.72	61.82	9.09
Starch, ℔.................	10.73	14 68	39	9.91	14.9	50.39	10.64
Fuel, coal, ton.............	5 62	7 48.33	34	5 58	8 11	45.53	5 80
wood, hard, cord.......	4 50	6 94	54	4 44	7 14	60.87	5 10
pine, cord.......	3 41	5 25	55	3 28	5 31	64.44	3 78
Oil, coal, gallon..........	87.5	62.5	(*	87.05	64.28	35*	45.92
DOMESTIC DRY-GOODS, ETC.							
Shirtings, brown, 4-4, stand'd quality, yard..............	9.63	20	107	9.62	19.39	101.56	13.85
Shirtings, bleached, 4-4, do...	13	25	94	11.79	23.31	97.71	16.65
Sheetings, brown, 9-8, ..do...	10.25	22	115	11.15	23.16	107.68	16.54
bleached, 9-8, do...	12	24	100	13.56	26.79	97.59	19.14
Cotton Flan'l, "Hamilton," yd	13.33	31.8	138	13.14	28.09	113.68	20.06
Tickings, good quality, yard.	19.50	37	90	18.57	39.83	111.78	28.1
Prints, Merrimack, yard.....	11.3	18	60	11.59	18.37	58.48	13.12
Mousseline de Laine, dom., yd	18.5	25.3	36	18.02	25.33	40.56	18.10
Crash, domestic, yard........	11.33	18.75	67	10.24	17.79	73.75	12.71
Satinet, medium quality, yard	61.20	98	60	56.43	84.81	50.30	60.58
Boots, men's heavy, pair.....	3 47	5 05	46	3 80	5 31	60.61	3 79
HOUSE-RENT.							
Four-roomed tenements, m'th	4 20	6 85	51	4 44	7 39	66.31	5 28
Six-roomed tenements, month	5 78	9 37	62	6 02	9 83	63.32	7 02
BOARD.							
For men, week..............	3 15	4 75	51	2 75	4 69	70.63	3 85
For women, week............	2 53	4 00	58	1 86	3 38	81.47	2 41

* Decrease.　　　　　　　　　　　† Calculated at $1.40.

THE RATE OF WAGES IN 1860-'61 AND IN 1867-'68 COMPARED, WITH THE PERCENTAGE OF INCREASE.

From the Report of Commissioner Wells, for 1868.

COTTON-MILLS.

Table showing the average rates of wages paid to persons employed in the cotton-mills of the United States in the respective years 1860–'61, and 1867 ; also the percentage of increase in the latter year.

OCCUPATION.	AVERAGE RATES OF WAGES OR EARNINGS PER WEEK.								Percentage of Increase.
	In Massachusetts.		In New England.		In the Middle States.		Average in the United States.		
	In 1860 -1861.	In 1867.	In 1860 -1861.	In 1867.	In 1860 -1861.	In 1867.	In 1860 -1861.	In 1867.	
CARDING.									
Overseer	$17 18	$20 00	$12 90	$17 61	$9 58	$16 30	$12 66	$17 60	39
Second hand	9 18	13 33	7 36	11 25	6 26	10 55	7 23	11 14	54
Picker tenders	5 00	7 42	4 77	8 22	4 78	8 84	5 13	8 18	59
Railway tenders	2 83	4 70	2 80	4 51	3 67	5 75	2 83	4 61	63
Drawing-frame tenders	2 87	5 02	3 00	5 00	2 81	4 16	2 93	4 82	64
Speeder tenders	3 61	6 26	3 54	5 96	3 07	5 16	3 54	5 81	64
Picker-boy	....	....	....	....	2 92	4 50	2 92	4 50	54
Grinders	5 78	9 80	5 85	9 37	....	....	5 85	9 37	60
Strippers	5 17	7 18	4 54	7 86	5 12	7 50	4 74	7 41	56
SPINNING.									
Overseer	16 65	20 60	11 88	16 98	9 80	16 72	11 71	16 90	44
Second hand	8 85	13 21	6 93	10 90	5 55	10 04	6 46	10 27	59
Mule spinners	5 93	11 16	6 10	10 18	6 25	11 18	5 80	10 14	74
Mule backside piecers	1 64	3 17	1 83	3 14	1 72	3 46	1 69	3 09	81
Frame spinners	3 33	6 05	2 83	5 18	2 13	4 50	2 64	4 76	80
DRESSING.									
Overseer	15 15	21 44	12 19	18 09	8 75	16 50	12 02	17 70	48
Second hand	8 30	13 45	7 70	12 42	5 76	13 00	7 44	12 53	68
Third hand	6 50	10 75	5 57	9 18	....	13 50	5 71	10 11	77
Spoolers	3 40	6 49	3 12	4 71	2 48	3 99	2 85	5 03	76
Warpers	3 96	6 81	3 59	6 09	4 13	5 87	3 62	6 00	64
Drawers and twisters	3 72	6 75	3 75	6 41	4 15	6 66	4 10	6 77	65
Dressers	5 10	9 89	7 03	11 40	7 22	13 17	7 64	11 66	52
WEAVING.									
Overseer	15 94	21 11	12 73	17 84	10 31	16 08	12 18	17 36	42
Second hand	8 83	14 23	7 08	11 42	6 66	11 17	6 95	11 50	65
Third hand	7 12	11 83	5 89	9 10	6 25	9 50	5 60	9 40	67
Weavers	4 50	9 06	4 63	7 80	4 75	6 85	5 24	8 48	62
Drawing-in hands	3 45	6 02	4 07	6 65	4 50	8 00	4 10	7 21	76
REPAIR-SHOP, ENGINE-ROOM, ETC.									
Foreman or overseer	14 89	19 20	12 65	18 11	11 65	17 25	12 60	17 77	41
Iron-workers	8 82	13 75	8 71	13 65	7 92	13 20	8 60	13 95	62
Wood-workers	9 09	13 83	8 70	13 66	9 39	14 13	8 78	13 76	57
Engineer	....	14 00	6 42	10 78	11 50	18 00	7 24	11 61	60
Laborers	6 15	9 17	5 98	9 09	6 00	9 38	5 96	9 14	53
CLOTH-ROOM, ETC.									
Overseer	13 31	17 09	11 31	14 41	7 32	11 19	9 75	13 22	35
Second hand	7 46	10 54	6 77	9 77	4 83	9 00	5 93	9 25	56
Other hands—males	5 85	8 92	5 95	8 97	....	....	5 90	8 96	52
Females	3 57	5 50	3 21	5 14	2 44	4 23	2 82	4 68	66

Hours of labor per week.. 66
Apparent average increase of wages in 1867 over those in 1860-'61, per cent...... 56
True average, per cent... 63

WOOLLEN-MILLS.

Table showing the average rates of wages paid to persons employed in the woollen-mills of the United States in the respective years 1860-'61 and 1867-'68, with the percentage of increase in the latter year; also the rates paid in England, with the percentage of excess in the rates paid in the United States over that country.

OCCUPATION.	AVERAGE WEEKLY WAGES OR EARNINGS.										
	In New England.		In New York State.		General average in New England and New York.		Percentage of increase.	Rate of 1867-'68 in gold (at 140).	In England.		Percentage of advance in U. States over England.
	In 1860-'61.	In 1867-'68.	In 1860-'61.	In 1867-'68.	In 1860-'61.	In 1867-'68.			Sixty hours per week.	Adding 10 per to equal 66 hours.	
PREPARING.											
Wool-sorters	$8 05	$12 35	$7 53	$11 00	$7 84	$11 86	51.28	$8 47	$6 00	$6 60	28.33
Wool-washers	5 65	9 46	5 13	8 31	5 42	9 00	66.05	6 43	4 85	5 34	20.41
Dyers	6 13	10 13	4 80	8 22	5 46	9 17	68.32	6 56	5 00	5 50	19.27
Overseers	12 00	19 13	12 38	22 00	12 19	20 56	68.66	14 69	10 00	11 00	33.55
Assistants	8 50	11 50	7 75	11 00	8 13	11 25	38.38	8 04	....	....	....
CARD'G AND SPIN'G.											
Pickers	5 25	8 03	4 90	8 63	5 11	8 25	61.45	5 89	4 60	5 06	16.40
Carders	4 15	5 96	4 00	6 35	4 08	6 12	50.00	4 37	3 50	3 85	13.50
Spinners	6 74	11 34	7 00	11 25	6 84	11 30	65.20	8 07	5 50	6 05	33.38
Warp's & Beamers	5 48	9 04	5 00	11 00	5 27	9 88	87.48	7 06	5 12	5 63	25.40
Reelers	2 90	4 62	2 50	3 67	2 73	4 21	54.21	3 01	2 50	2 75	9.46
Overseers	11 50	18 43	12 38	23 25	11 85	20 27	71.06	14 48	10 00	11 00	31.64
Assistants	7 50	11 10	7 88	13 13	7 69	12 00	56.04	8 57	....	....	....
WEAVING.											
Weavers	4 44	7 73	4 88	8 38	4 66	8 02	72.10	5 73	4 25	4 67	22.70
Burlers	3 14	5 34	2 69	4 50	2 92	4 95	69.52	3 04	2 25	2 48	22.58
Overseers	11 70	17 75	13 13	24 75	12 33	20 55	66.67	14 68	10 00	11 00	33.45
DRESSING AND FINISHING.											
Fullers	6 00	8 88	5 88	10 69	5 93	9 78	64.92	6 99	5 25	5 77	21.14
Dressers or Giggers	5 00	8 81	4 50	7 88	4 77	8 34	74.84	5 96	5 00	5 50	8.36
Finishers	6 50	9 00	4 13	8 50	5 55	8 80	59.45	6 29	5 50	6 05	4.00
Press Tenders	6 50	9 00	5 38	8 75	6 05	8 90	47.10	6 36	5 25	5 78	10.04
Drawers	4 50	9 00	3 75	7 50	4 12	8 25	100.00	5 89	3 75	4 13	42.15
Brushers	2 25	3 50	6 00	9 00	3 50	5 33	52.28	3 81	2 50	2 75	38.55
Packers	5 00	7 50	4 50	8 25	4 75	7 75	63.15	5 54	5 00	5 50	00.73
Overseers	7 88	14 25	11 75	17 25	11 12	18 62	68.34	13 30	10 00	11 00	21.00
Assistants	7 50	12 00	8 03	11 00	8 06	11 00	48.88	8 57	....	....	....
ENGINE-ROOM, ETC.											
Engineers	9 62	14 00	10 50	20 75	9 97	16 70	67.50	11 93	7 50	8 25	44.61
Mechanics	9 31	15 98	8 84	16 00	10 54	15 98	51.61	11 41	7 50	8 25	38.30
Laborers, W'hmen, and Yard Hands	6 13	10 50	5 83	7 50	6 00	9 64	60.66	6 84	4 50	4 95	38.18
Foremen	13 50	18 00	....	....	13 50	18 00	33.33	12 86	7 50	8 25	55.88

NOTE.—General average hours of labor per week in New England and New York, for 1860-'61, 71; and for 1867-'68, 66; in England, 60; adding 10 per cent., 66. Average increase in rates of wages in 1867-'68 over those of 1860-'61, 60.65 per cent. Average advance in rates of wages paid in the United States over those of England (both in gold), 24.63 per cent.

LEATHER MANUFACTORIES.

Table showing the average weekly wages paid to persons employed in manufactories of leather in the United States in 1860-'61 and in 1867 ; also the rates paid in Scotland in 1866, as compared with those in the United States in 1867.

OCCUPATION.	AVERAGE WEEKLY EARNINGS IN—					
	United States, 1860-'61.	United States, 1867-'68.	Percentage of increase in '67.	Wages in 1867 in gold.	Edinburgh, Scotland, in 1866.	Percent. of exc. in U. S. over Scotland.
Tanners...........	$7 00	$15 00	114	$10 71	$6 25	4.46
Curriers.........	9 00	15 00	67	10 71	8 50	2.21
Dressers....	9 00	15 00	67	10 71	8 50	2.21
Beam-men	10 00	18 00	80	12 86	6 25	6.61
Shed-men	7 00	10 00	43	7 14	6 25	0.89
Tanners' labor's.	6 00	9 00	50	6 43	3 75	2.68

Average increase of wages in 1867 over 1860-'61, 71 per cent. Average advance of rates in the United States in 1867 over those of Scotland in 1866, 48 per cent.

GLASS-WORKS.

Table showing the average earnings of persons employed in glass-works of the United States in the years 1860-'61 and 1867-'68, with the percentage of increase in the latter year ; also the earnings in glass-works of England in 1866, compared with those in the United States in 1867.

OCCUPATION.	Av. weekly earnings in the U. S.		Percentage of increase.	Earnings of '67 in gold.	Earn'gs in England in 1866.	Percentage of excess in U. S. over England.
	1860-'61.	1867-'68.				
Glass-blowers....	$14 00	$22 73	62.36	$16 23	$12 00	35
Phial-blowers....	12 00	18 00	50.00	12 86	10 50	22
Assistants......	6 00	10 00	65.67	7 14	5 41	32
Batch-mixers....	8 50	14 25	67.65	10 18	6 25	63
Master-teasers...	12 00	18 00	50.00	12 86	....	..
Assistant " ...	6 50	13 00	100.00	9 28	6 25	48
Potmakers.......	11 50	19 00	65.22	13 57	....	..
Assist't "	7 00	12 00	71.43	8 57	....	..
Packers..... :...	7 50	14 50	93.33	10 35	6 25	65
Blacksmiths.....	13 00	17 50	42.31	12 50	7 50	53
Carpenters......	8 50	14 25	67.65	10 18	7 00	45
Demijohn-cover's	8 05	14 00	75.00	10 00	....	..
Skilled boys....	3.25	6 00	84.61	4 28	....	..
Engineers	10 25	15 00	46.34	10 71	....	..
Laborers.........	5 50	9 32	69.45	6 66	....	..
Apprentices.....	2 50	4 25	70.00	3 03	....	..
Foremen........	13 50	19 50	44.44	13 93	....	..

Average increase of earnings in 1867 over 1860-'61, 63 per cent. Average excess in United States over England, 45 per cent.

PAPER-MILLS.

Table showing the average weekly wages paid to persons employed in paper-mills in the United States in the respective years 1860-'61 and 1867-'68, with the percentage of increase in the latter year ; also the rates paid in Scotland in 1866, with the percentage of advance in the United States.

OCCUPATION.	Av. weekly earnings in the U. S.		Percentage of inc. in 1867-'68.	United States in 1867 (gold).	Edinburgh and vicinity in '66.	Percent. in adv. in U. S. o'r Sc'd
	1860-'61.	1867-'68.				
Machine-tenders.	$9 67	$15 67	62	$11 19	$5 50	103
Assistant "	4 50	9 00	100	6 43	....	..
Rag-cutters,mal's	7 17	12 17	70	8 69	4 00	117
" females	3 67	6 00	60	4 29	....	..
Loft-men or dry's	6 17	10 83	75	7 74	4 00	93
Callender-men...	8 75	14 25	63	10 18	....	..
Finishers........	7 50	12 67	69	9 05	4 50	101
Engine-men......	7 50	12 00	60	8 57	5 00	71
Helpers on Eng's	4 75	8 50	79	6 07	....	..
Bleachers........	7 00	11 00	57	7 86	4 50	75
Sizers	4 50	10 25	127	7 32	4 44	65
Millwrights......	10 50	19 00	81	13 57	7 00	94
Masons..........	10 00	20 00	100	14 29	6 25	128
Carpenters......	9 50	16 50	73	11 78	6 25	88
Blacksmiths.....	9 00	14 00	55	10 00	5 75	74
Laborers, etc....	5 92	8 92	50	6 37	3 75	69
Apprentices.....	4 00	6 00	50	4 29	....	..
Firemen..... ...	9 00	14 00	55	10 00	4 50	122

Average increase of wages in 1867-'68 over 1860-'61, 84 per cent. Average advance in rates paid in the United States in 1867 over Scotland in 1866, 93 per cent.

IRON-ROLLING MILLS.

Table showing the average weekly earnings of workmen in the iron-rolling mills of the United States in the respective years 1860–'61 and 1867–'68, with the percentage of increase in the latter year ; also the earnings in England in the year 1867, with a comparison of the earnings in the two countries.

OCCUPATION.	AVERAGE WEEKLY EARNINGS.		Percentage of increase in 1867 over 1860.	Earnings in 1867, in gold.	Earnings in England in 1867.	Percentage of excess in U. States over Engl'd.
	In 1860–'61.	In Sept., '67.				
Puddlers......................	$13 37	$23 17	73.30	$16 54	$8 75	89.03
Puddlers' Helpers...........	7 27	13 46	85.14	9 61	4 50	113.55
Shinglers....................	12 06	22 27	84.66	15 90	11 25	41.33
Shinglers' Helpers..........	5 33	9 50	78.24	6 79	6 75	....
Puddle-Mill Rollers.........	9 77	19 02	94.68	13 58	11 25	20.71
Top and Bottom Rollers....	10 75	25 06	133.12	17 90	15 00	19.33
Forge Rollers...............	10 25	21 25	107.32	15 18	11 25	44.93
Merchant-Mill Finishers....	18 50	35 00	99.31	18 50	13 75	35.57
Rail-Mill Rollers............	27 00	37 69	39.60	26 92	12 00	124.33
Sheet and Plate Rollers.....	12 00	20 67	72.25	14 76	20 00	dec. 26.20
Second Rollers..............	8 97	16 41	82.94	11 72	6 00	inc. 95.33
Third Rollers...............	8 75	13 87	58.51	9 90	4 50	120.00
Fur'e-men or Heaters' H'lps.	7 39	11 91	61.16	8 51	6 00	41.83
Shearmen...................	9 04	14 98	65.71	10 70	6 00	78.33
Catchers....................	6 71	14 80	120.57	10 57	6 00	76.16
Roughers...................	8 67	20 24	133.45	14 46	8 00	80.75
Heaters....................	14 83	25 36	71.00	18 11	12 50	44.88
Foremen or Superintend'ts..	14 87	24 90	67.45	17 78	12 00	48.17
Machinists.................	12 08	18 11	49.92	13 64	7 50	81.86
Engineers..................	9 64	14 28	48.13	10 20	7 50	36.00
Carpenters.................	8 44	15 46	82.70	11 01	7 00	57.28
Blacksmiths................	8 07	14 66	81.66	10 47	7 50	39.60
Laborers, etc..............	5 34	9 10	70.41	6 50	4 00	62.50
Teamsters..................	6 00	10 25	70.83	7 32	4 00	83.00
Apprentices and Boys......	2 80	4 34	55.00	3 10	2 50	24.00

Average increase of wages in 1867 over the rates in 1860–'61, 76 per cent.

Average price of puddling in the New England and Middle States in 1867, $6.63 per ton; in 1868, $6 per ton.

The prices for puddling, rolling, etc., having declined in 1868, the average increase of 1868 over 1860 is thereby reduced to about 67 per cent. But, although the cost of labor has advanced but 67 per cent., the real advance over 1860, in the cost of making iron, is believed to be about 75 per cent.

The average advance in the earnings of the workmen employed in the rolling-mills of the United States over those of Great Britain (both in gold) is 48.34 per cent.

STEEL-WORKS.

Table showing the average weekly earnings of workmen employed in the steel-works of Pittsburg, United States, in 1867–'68, as compared with those in Sheffield, England, in 1866–'67.

OCCUPATION.	Av. weekly earnings in Pittsburg, '67–'68.		Av. weekly earnings in Sheffield, '66–'67.	Percent. of excess in Pittsburg in '67–'68.
	Currency.	Gold.		
Converter.................	$19 50	$13 93	$10 00	3.93
Converters' Laborer.......	12 00	8 57	5 25	3.32
Common Laborers........	9 00	6 43	4 50	1.93
Melter....................	32 50	23 21	11 25	11.96
Puller-out................	16 25	11 61	8 00	3.61
Moulders.................	12 00	8 57	5 00	3.57
Cokers....................	12 00	8 57	5 00	3.57
Forgeman and Tilter......	30 00	21 43	12 50	8.93
Forgeman's Heater.... ..	12 00	8 57	6 00	2.57
Roller....................	38 00	27 14	18 00	9.14
Roller Furnace-man.......	18 00	12 85	7 50	5.35

Average advance of wages in the steel-works of Pittsburg over those of Sheffield, 62.23 per ct.

IRON-FOUNDERIES AND MACHINE-SHOPS.

Table showing the average weekly wages paid to persons employed in the iron-founderies and machine-shops of the United States, in the respective years 1860–'61 and 1867, with the percentage of increase in the latter year; also the wages paid in England in 1866, and the percentage of advance in the rates paid in the United States over those of England.

OCCUPATION.	AVERAGE WEEKLY WAGES OR EARNINGS.											PERCENT-AGE.
	In New England.			In Middle States.			General Average in United States.			In United States 1867, in gold.	In England. 1866.	Ex. wages in U. Stat's over England.
	1860–'61.	1867.	Perc'ge of in. '67 over '60.	1860–'61.	1867.	Perc'ge of in. '67 over '60.	1860–'61.	1867.	Percent'ge of increase			
Moulders	$10 00	$15 68	56.80	$10 19	$16 51	69.02	$10 08	$16 13	60.02	$11 52	*$8 00	44.00
Machinists, best	11 29	17 60	55.89	11 58	18 80	62.35	11 54	18 19	57.62	12 99	8 50	52.83
" second	10 67	16 29	52.67	9 39	16 00	70.40	10 21	16 15	58.17	11 54	7 00	64.86
" ordinary	8 73	13 10	50.06	8 98	14 89	66.90	8 76	13 83	57.88	9 87	6 50	51.85
" inferior	6 89	10 50	52.40	7 00	12 19	74.14	6 92	11 13	60.84	7 95	5 00	59.00
" helpers	5 85	9 19	57.10	5 99	9 86	64.61	5 92	9 54	61.15	6 81	4 50	51.33
Blacksmiths	10 92	19 08	74.72	10 03	15 41	53.64	10 47	17 25	64.76	12 33	*7 12	73.03
" helpers	7 00	10 67	52.43	6 94	10 04	69.02	6 57	10 35	57.63	7 39	4 50	64.22
Riveters	10 00	15 48	54.80	10 25	10 61	62.05	10 15	16 14	59.01	11 53	7 50	53.73
Holders-on	6 50	10 10	55.38	6 68	10 85	62.42	6 60	10 50	59.09	7 50	5 00	50.00
Boiler-makers	10 96	17 80	62.50	10 71	17 55	63.87	10 70	17 70	65.42	12 64	*7 50	68.53
" helpers	6 20	10 52	69.68	6 52	10 69	63.90	6 39	10 63	66.20	7 59	4 50	68.67
Flangers	12 95	21 60	66.80	13 00	20 71	59.31	12 80	21 30	65.63	15 14	7 50	101.87
" helpers	6 35	10 63	67.24	6 81	11 35	66.67	6 60	11 02	66.97	7 87	4 50	74.89
Engineers	9 19	15 90	73.01	9 84	15 87	61.28	9 50	15 96	68.00	11 40	6 25	82.40
Pattern-makers and Carpenters	9 00	18 62	105.78	10 38	17 37	67.34	9 81	18 00	83.48	12 86	*8 50	51.29
" assistants	9 00	13 58	50.89	6 88	10 95	71.63	8 05	18 77	68.63	9 12	7 50	21.60
Laborers, Carters, etc.	6 07	9 90	63.10	5 98	9 68	61.87	6 02	9 84	63.45	7 08	*4 50	56.22
Apprentices	3 81	5 58	46.46	3 08	5 21	71.95	3 50	5 46	56.17	3 90	*2 50	64.00
Brass-Founders	11 00	19 00	72.73	11 00	11 75	61.36	11 00	18 28	66.17	13 06	7 50	74.13
Brass-Fitters and Turners	10 33	16 50	59.74	10 20	15 57	52.64	10 26	16 97	55.65	11 41	6 50	75.54
Millwrights	12 75	19 50	52.94	10 25	16 70	62.93	11 50	18 10	57.39	12 93	7 50	72.40
" assistants	9 00	15 00	66.67	....	....	....	9 00	15 00	66.67	10 71	6 50	64.77
Painters, first class	9 17	13 83	50.82	....	....	....	9 17	13 88	50.82	9 88	7 00	41.14
" second class	8 00	13 50	68.75	....	....	....	8 00	13 50	68.75	9 64	6 00	60.67

Hours of labor per week.................. 60.
Average increase of wages paid in 1867 over 1860.............. 60.45 p. c.

Average increase of wages paid in 1867 over 1860........both in gold......14.61 p. c.
Average advance of wages in the U. States in 1867 over England in 1866, 57.72 p. c.

* The rates of wages given in this column were those paid in Sheffield, Hull, and other manufacturing towns of England. In Glasgow the rates were lower, being as follows: Moulder, $7.25; black-smith, $6; boiler-makers and machinists, $6.26; engineers, $4.75; pattern-makers, $5.75; carters, $4.50; and common laborers, $3.74.

HARDWARE MANUFACTORIES.

Table showing the average weekly wages of persons employed in the hardware manufactories of the United States in 1860–'61 and 1867, with the percentage of increase in the latter year; also the rates in similar establishments in Great Britain in 1866, compared with those of the United States in 1866.

OCCUPATION.	AVERAGE WEEKLY WAGES OR EARNINGS.					
	In 1860–'61.	In 1867.	Percentage of increase 1867 over 1860.	Rates of 1867 in gold.	Wages in England in 1866.	Percentage of excess in United States over England.
Moulders	$7 95	$13 18	65.79	$9 41	$7 50	25.46
Cupola-tenders	7 15	10 65	48.95	7 61	....	....
Annealing-furnace Tenders	7 06	11 02	56.09	7 87	....	....
Filers	7 57	11 21	48.09	8 02	6 25	28.32
Japanners	7 33	11 58	57.98	8 27	....	....
Forgers	11 03	17 25	56.39	12 32	8 50	45.00
Helpers	6 61	10 18	54.01	7 27	5 00	45.40
Grinders	8 87	12 16	37.09	8 69	6 50	33.69
Polishers	8 11	11 58	42.79	8 27	6 75	22.51
Turners	7 92	11 50	45.20	8 21	7 50	9.46
Lock-makers	12 00	15 00	25.00	10 71	7 50	42.80
Machinists	11 48	18 18	58.36	12 99	7 50	73.20
Engineers	10 70	16 50	54.21	11 79	7 50	57.27
Laborers	6 00	9 60	60.00	6 86	5 25	30.60
Packers	7 29	12 00	64.61	8 57	....	....
" Females	3 88	5 85	50.77	4 18	2 50	67.20
Diemakers	13 00	20 40	56.92	14 57	10 00	45.70
Press-workmen	8 34	11 79	41.37	8 42	....	....
" Females	3 75	6 00	60.00	4 29	....	....
Rollers	10 50	15 00	42.86	10 71	....	....
Welders	10 50	15 00	42.86	10 71	....	....
Jointers	9 00	14 25	58.33	10 18	....	....
Stampers	12 00	15 00	25.00	10 71	....	....
Graduators	12 00	13 50	12.50	9 64	....	....
Finishers	9 19	13 94	51.69	9 96	6 75	47.85
Pattern-makers	11 50	17 86	55.30	12 76	8 50	50.00
Carpenters	9 64	16 52	71.37	11 80	7 00	68.57
Trip-hammer Men	11 10	16 20	45.95	11 57	10 00	15.70
Crimpers	10 50	16 50	57.14	11 79	....	....
Twisters	10 50	18 00	71.43	12 86	....	....
Fitters up	7 75	10 50	35.48	7 50	....	...
Screw-cutters	6 26	10 10	61.34	7 21	....	....
Blacksmiths	9 22	14 53	57.59	10 38	7 50	38.40
Helpers	6 48	9 50	46.60	6 79	5 00	35.80
Foremen	13 06	19 87	52.14	14 19	10 00	41.90
Apprentices or Boys	3 59	5 64	57.10	4 03	3 12	22.75

Hours of labor per week 60
Average increase in rates of wages in 1867 over 1860–'61 .... per cent.. 50
Excess of rates of wages in United States in 1867 over those of England in 1866..do..... 40

23

MANUFACTORIES OF EDGE TOOLS.

Table showing the average weekly earnings of persons employed in manufactories of edge tools in the United States in 1860–'61 and in 1867, with the percentages of increase in the latter year; also the comparative rates in similar establishments in Sheffield, England, in 1866–'67.

OCCUPATION.	AVERAGE WEEKLY EARNINGS.					
	In the United States, 1860–'61.	In the United States, 1867.	Percentage of increase of 1867 over 1860.	Earnings in 1867, in gold.	In Sheffield, England, 1866–'67.	Percentage of excess in U. S. over England.
Forgers....................	$13 50	$17 50	29.63	$12 50	$8 50	47.
Helpers...................	10 50	13 50	28.57	9 64	5 00	92.
Temperers...	10 50	15 00	42.86	10 71	6 50	65.
Grinders..................	12 00	18 00	50.00	12 86	9 25	39.
Polishers.................	10 50	14 50	38.10	10 36	6 75	53.
Laborers.............. ..	6 00	10 25	70.83	7 32	5 50	33.
Carpenters...............	10 50	16 50	57.14	11 79	7 50	57.
Foremen..................	11 00	17 25	56.82	12 32	10 00	23.
Apprentices or Boys.....	6 00	8 00	33.33	5 71	3 75	52.
Machinists	12 00	18 00	50.00	12 86	7 50	71.
Trip-hammer Men.........	15 00	21 00	40.00	15 00	10 00	50.

Hours of labor per week... 60
Average increase of earnings in 1867 over 1860–'61.....................per cent.. 44
Average excess of earnings in the United States over England............do.... 50

MANUFACTORIES OF AGRICULTURAL IMPLEMENTS.

Table showing the average rate of wages paid to persons employed in manufactories of agricultural implements in the United States in the respective years 1860–'61 and 1867–'68, with the percentage of increase in the latter year.

OCCUPATION.	Aver'ge weekly earnings		Percentage of increase.
	In 1860–'61.	In 1867–'68.	
Moulders	$10 97	$17 29	57.61
Machinists...................	8 68	15 69	80.76
Blacksmiths..................	8 50	15 57	80.32
Blacksmiths' Helpers........	5 75	8 90	54.78
Wood-workers...............	8 75	14 61	66.90
Painters.....................	7 77	12 23	57.40
Plough-makers...............	9 00	15 00	66.67
Teamsters...................	6 82	10 52	54.25
Grinders.....................	7 87	12 05	53.11
Pattern-makers..............	9 08	17 25	89.97
Watchmen...................	8 97	12 69	41.47
Clerks	18 22	31 96	75.96
Engineers....................	9 00	15 00	66.67
Laborers and unskilled Workmen......	5 33	9 92	86.12
Apprentices or Boys..........	2 62	4 53	72.90
Foremen or Overseers...........	13 12	23 54	79.42

Hours of labor per week... 60
Average increase of wages in 1867 over 1860–'61........................per cent.. 68

CHAPTER XXIV.

THE LABOR BAROMETER.

WITH good reason, the movement of population from one country to another has been regarded by all writers as a very conclusive indication of the relative condition of the laboring classes in those countries. Other causes besides suffering in one country or hope of wealth in another do indeed prompt men to migrate, but the effect of these is comparatively slight, and can readily be traced. But it is a rule of almost universal application that, when men remove in large numbers from one land to another, the great majority of them do so in the hope of bettering their condition. A famine or a revolution at home may drive them away, but the world is wide, and, if they select one country rather than another for their future abode, the great majority do so because they expect there to earn better wages and to live more comfortably than elsewhere. Hence, whenever opponents of the system of protection have endeavored to show that it renders certain workmen of this country less able than similar workmen in other countries to purchase articles of common use, the advocates of protection have answered, with convincing effect, " Yet the laborers do come in great numbers from the land where you say their burdens are light, to the land where you say their burdens are heavy!" There the argument must needs end. Everybody understands that laborers do not knowingly and intentionally migrate from comfort into poverty. When Moses would lead the children of Israel out of a grievous bondage, he promised them not freedom, but " a land flowing with milk and honey," and from that day to this nothing less than the hope of material gain has been potent enough to uproot large bodies of men from their native soil and transplant them in other lands.

The protectionist is right; there never has been a time, since the second war with England, when the general condition of the laboring classes in this country was not better than their condition in the older countries of Europe. But that is merely an adroit evasion of the real question; granting that the laborer at all times, and under all forms of duty and taxation, has been on the whole in better condition here than in older countries, the real question is, whether his condition has been better here under one system of taxation than under another.

The great richness of this land, its vast resources still undeveloped,

and the enterprise, energy, and rapidity of growth, which free institutions favor, have made the demand for labor greater here, at all
times, than in any country of Europe. But at what times has that
demand been greatest? Our natural and political advantages have
rendered this country, at all times, more attractive to the industrious
laborer than other new countries, but under what system has that
superiority over other new countries been greatest? If under protective duties a larger number of immigrants have come to this country from Europe, and a larger proportion to this as compared with
other new countries than under non-protective duties, then it must
be frankly admitted that the condition of the laborer on the whole
has been improved by the system of protection. Does it not also
follow that, if the contrary is true, the condition of the laborer on the
whole has been improved by low duties and non-protective tariffs?

Realizing the logical necessity of meeting this test in some way,
Mr. Henry C. Carey has invented a way of his own. In language
not at all ambiguous, he says: "The effects of the protective tariff
of 1829 exhibited themselves in the arrival" of 359,000 persons in
the six years 1832–'7 inclusive, "against 140,000 for the ten British
free-trade and semi-protective years by which that tariff had been preceded." It is difficult to notice such language without doubting the
honesty of the writer. It is hard to suppose that Mr. Carey really
believes that the effect of the tariff of 1828 upon immigration did not
begin until the very year in which that tariff was repealed! One
would suppose that his high reputation must have restrained him from
the intentional misrepresentations so common in discussions of this
question. Yet it seems hardly possible that it was a mere oversight
in him to style the ten years, 1819–'28 inclusive, "British free-trade
and semi-protective years." The characteristics of the tariffs of 1816
and 1818 have been mentioned, and readers will find it not easy to
believe that this language was used except in the hope that people
would neither know nor take the trouble to ascertain what sort of
tariff was really then in force. In its purpose and its essential features, the tariff of 1816 was as strictly a protective measure as any
ever adopted; it was proposed, advocated, and carried by the then
friends of the protective policy; it was the first act in our history to
apply the minimum price to foreign goods—the very feature of all
others which has since been held by protectionists the most effective,
and by non-protectionists the most odious; it was shaped from beginning to end with intent to discriminate between industries, favoring some and not others. The minimum on cottons was in effect

absolutely prohibitory as to the coarser qualities. On rolled iron the duty was $1.50 per cwt., or $30 a ton, then "equal to 85 per cent. on its cost." (Bishop's "History of Manufactures," vol. ii., p. 228.) The duty on anchors and bolt iron was the same; on hammered iron 45 cents, and on sheet, rod, and hoop iron, $2.50 per cwt. Yet this is the lowest tariff which was in force in all those years which Henry C. Carey, a writer of reputation, ventures to call "British free-trade years"—for he elsewhere calls the tariff of 1824 "semi-protective." Can it be that he does not comprehend the difference between "British free trade" and a tariff absolutely prohibitory on coarse cottons, and of 85 per cent. on British iron? It is a habit of that gentleman to accuse others of intentional suppression or misrepresentation of facts. But he may well consider whether one who stands in such need of charitable judgment had not better set the example of ascribing errors of statement to ignorance. In 1818 still higher duties were desired by the iron-makers, and granted. The duty on pig-iron was fixed at 50 cents per cwt., or $10 per ton, actually higher than it is to-day. Yet this is what Mr. Carey, a writer of reputation, ventures to call "British free-trade !"

If we turn to the figures given by Mr. Carey, we are forced to remark that they correspond neither with the records of the State Department, with the statistics given in the census of 1860, nor with reports from newspaper authority, but seem to have been evolved from his inner consciousness. Thus for 1832 he gives 45,000 as the total immigration; the census volume says 53,179; the State Department returns, quoted by Tucker, say 34,970, and tables of actual arrivals published by the New-York *Times* show that 48,589 persons arrived at that port alone. For 1835 he gives 53,000; the census table says 45,374; the State Department returns, quoted by Tucker, say 45,444; but Mr. Carey was apparently under the necessity of fitting the figures to his theory that the tariff caused "an almost regular rise." Also, to preserve regularity, he gives for 1836 the figures 62,000, while the census table says 76,242, the State Department returns 76,923, and the *Times* table shows that there were 60,541 arrivals at New York alone. It would seem that "regularity" had been preserved at the expense of exactness. And, again, comfortably assuming that the tariff ceased to protect in 1837, carefully suppressing mention of the currency panic of that year, asserting, contrary to facts by himself accidentally recorded, that "British free-trade prevented increase of mills and furnaces" after that year, he says: "The movement (of immigration) was irregular, but the general result to and including 1844 showed a diminution, the average having been but 75,000." Now, "an average of 75,000" is not a diminution, but is larger than any of the previous years by him quoted except one. And the records, which he is careful not to give, show that there was an increase to 84,066 in 1840, and to 104,565 in 1842. It will astonish every reader to learn that this same Henry C. Carey, even while accusing Mr. Wells of suppressing facts, himself utterly suppresses mention of the failure of crops and the great famine in Europe in the years 1846 and 1847, and ascribes all the immigration which followed that famine to the tariff of 1842, which expired in 1846! Yet this is exactly what he does. That his language may be observed, we quote (Carey to Wells, page 46):

> Counter-news arriving in 1844, and men learning how great, under the protective system of 1842, had here become the demand for labor, and how liberal its reward, we find the arrivals now running up from the 74,000 of 1844 to 102,000 in 1845, to 147,000 in 1846, 240,000 in 1847, 229,000 in 1848, and 300,000 in 1849, giving a total of 1,018,000 in the five years which followed the commencement of the movement, against one of less than 400,000 by which that movement had been preceded, giving *a gain under protection* of more than 600,000.

The italics are our own, and it is only necessary to remark that this gain did not take place "under protection," but under the non-protective tariff of 1846. But far more astonishing is the audacity of one who, professing to state facts, utterly suppresses all mention of the European famine, and ascribes this movement to the protective system which had already expired! Had this been done by an obscure or possibly ill-informed writer, it would have been easy to suppose that he was ignorant of the truth. Readers must judge whether such a misrepresentation as this, coming from a writer who surely cannot have been ignorant of the truth, does not destroy all confidence in the correctness of his statements.

It is only necessary to add that, in discussing the movement since 1860, Mr. Carey ignores the effect of the civil war, first deterring immigration, and afterward, by creating a great scarcity of labor, increasing immigration.

Turning, now, from the figures presented by that writer, to the facts, we adopt as a basis the table given in the census report of 1860, which corresponds in the main with other reliable records, and extends further than any other to us accessible. Tucker, who appears to have discussed this subject with care and with excellent sources of information, maintains that the returns of the State De

RECEIPTS FROM SALES OF PUBLIC LANDS AND IMMIGRATION.

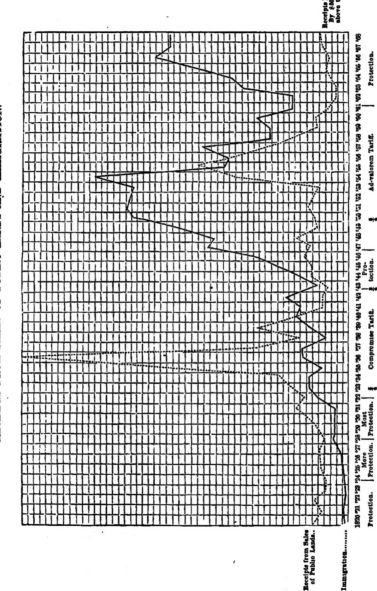

partment were incorrect for the years 1831 and 1832, and gives
107,104 as the true immigration for those years. At the same time
he points out the fact that a considerable proportion—not less than
10 per cent.—of the immigrants of that period merely passed through
this country on their way to Canada. This fact alone shows how
little benefit sixteen years of protection had conferred, since they
had not rendered this country so much more attractive than Canada
as to prevent immigrants going directly thither from New York.
But, in the main, the census table is as reliable and correct as any
that can now be obtained or constructed.

ALIEN PASSENGERS ARRIVING IN THE UNITED STATES FROM FOREIGN
COUNTRIES FROM 1820 TO 1860, INCLUSIVE.

From the Census Report of 1860.

Year ending Sept. 30, 1820..	8,385	Year ending Dec. 31, 1841..	80,289
1821..	9,127	1842..	104,565
1822..	6,911	Three-quarters ending Sept. 30, 1843..	52,496
1823..	6,354	Year ending Sept. 30, 1844..	78,615
1824..	7,912	1845..	114,371
1825..	10,199	1846..	154,416
1826..	10,837	1847..	234,968
1827..	18,875	1848..	226,527
1828..	27,382	1849..	297,024
1829..	22,520	1850..	310,004
1830..	23,322	Quarter ending Dec. 31, 1850..	59,976
1831..	22,633	Year ending Dec. 31, 1851..	379,466
1832..	53,179	1852..	371,603
Quarter ending Dec. 31, 1832..	7,303	1853..	368,645
Year ending Dec. 31, 1833..	58,640	1854..	427,833
1834..	65,365	1855..	200,877
1835..	45,374	1856..	200,436
1836..	76,242	1857..	251,306
1837..	79,340	1858..	123,126
1838..	38,914	1859..	121,282
1839..	68,069	1860..	153,640
1840..	84,066		

Examination of these statistics will satisfy every reader that any
change in the relative condition of the laboring class, on either side
of the ocean, affects immigration instantly, and not, as Mr. Carey
and his followers assert, only after the lapse of several years. The
first considerable change was caused by the general distress and
breaking of the banks in England, which occurred in 1825, and in
that very year—and not five years afterward—the immigration increased more than one-quarter, and rose to 10,199. In 1829 there
was general distress here, especially among those employed in
manufacturing, and in that very year—and not five years afterward
—the immigration decreased from 27,382 to 22,520. Just before
the close of the fiscal year 1837 the banks suspended, and the great
panic occurred. In the year 1838—within eighteen months, and
not some years afterward—immigration was reduced *more than one-
half*, from 79,340 in 1837 to 38,914 in 1838. Yet this was in spite

of the fact that the English crops of 1837 were not large, and those of 1838 decidedly bad. Again, the crops in England and Ireland were inferior in 1845, and in 1846, the price of wheat rising rapidly, and in 1847 the general failure of crops, and especially of the potato-crop, produced a famine. In 1845, in precise correspondence, immigration began to increase largely; in 1846 the number of immigrants was 154,416, and in 1847—the very year of the famine—the number was 234,968. This was more than double the immigration for any previous year except 1846. And, again, the panic of 1857 was instantly followed by a falling off of more than half in immigration, for the number for the year 1857 was 251,306, and the number for 1858 was 123,126. Finally, when the civil war interrupted business here, in 1861, the effect was instantaneous; immigration fell from 153,640 in 1860 to 91,920 in 1861. These facts are certainly conclusive. In view of them, the theory, that the change wrought by a tariff in the condition of labor does not affect the movement of immigration until after that tariff has ceased to exist, must be dismissed as adapted only to the needs of those who have to get around very inconvenient facts, and set themselves to make "the worse appear the better reason." If further proof were needed of the absurdity of Mr. Carey's statement, above quoted, it might be found in the fact that immigration from Great Britain to Canada and Australia, and other countries besides the United States, increased in the same years in which, he asserts, immigration was drawn this way by the protective tariff. For, in 1844, the emigration from Great Britain to other places besides the United States was 27,026; in 1845 it was 34,963; in 1846 it was 47,612, and in 1847 it was 116,116, and this increase was more rapid than that from Great Britain to this country, since, in 1844, about 62 per cent. of all emigrants from Great Britain came to the United States, while in 1847 only 55 per cent. of emigrants from Great Britain came to the United States. It is barely possible that a man may believe that a tariff in this country had some effect upon immigration hither after it had ceased to exist; but not even Mr. Carey will pretend that a tariff in the United States, after it had ceased to exist, attracted immigration from Great Britain to Canada and Australia !

The movement of immigration, it has been proved, is a faithful measure of the relative condition of labor in this as compared with other countries, which records instantly every material change on either side of the ocean, and is as sensitive as a barometer or steam-gauge. Whenever the demand for labor rises here or falls in Europe, immigration increases, and prostration of industry here checks it instantly. Famines or revolutions in the Old World have been the main cause of migration; men are moved to emigrate never so powerfully by rumors of prosperity elsewhere, as by the sight of the gaunt wolf of famine, or the grim demon of war, at their own doors. But it must also be observed that, under favoring circumstances, immigration causes increased immigration. People in the old country are induced to migrate hither, in a great degree, by the personal solicitation or direct aid of friends already here. Every immigrant becomes an active agent to induce his countrymen to follow him, and often remits the necessary funds, which the pinched laborer in Europe could obtain only after years of delay, if ever. Thus every great event which immediately produces a large immigration, causes also, after the lapse of a year or two, a second wave larger than the first. Sixty-eight thousand immigrants who arrived here, driven by English disaster, in 1827–'29, began by the years 1831–'32 to attract their friends in large numbers; the 234,968 immigrants who came here in 1847, the year of the Irish famine, attracted so many that the number amounted to 297,024 in 1849, and 310,004 in 1850. With these general principles in mind, let us see whether tariffs here have materially affected the movement.

The protective period of 1824–'28 witnessed the first considerable movement of immigration to this country, and there is no room to doubt that the rapid increase at that time was caused by the great industrial and financial disorders, to which McCulloch thus refers ("Commercial Dictionary," vol. i., p. 101) : "The destruction of the country banks has upon three different occasions, in 1792, 1814–'16, and in 1825 and 1826, produced an extent of bankruptcy and misery that has never perhaps been equalled, except by the breaking up of the Mississippi scheme in France." He shows that in 1825 thirty-seven banks broke, and forty-three in 1826. Just at this time the first strong current of immigration began to set toward this country, and immigration rose to 27,382 in 1828, but was then checked by the disaster here in the next year, and in 1830. Nor did it revive until 1832, the very year in which the protective tariff was repealed. The movement for these eight years of protection, ending September 30, 1832, was in the aggregate 188,947, or an average of 23,818 yearly. It is worthy of note that the large increase in 1832, the last year of this period, is partly due to the failure of revolutionary movements in Germany, and the persecution feared or.suffered, which drove not less than ten thousand Germans to this country.

The non-protective period which followed witnessed no considerable change in immigration caused by foreign events, though the exodus from Germany increased, in consequence of political oppression, to 23,035 in 1837. But the entire immigration increased much more largely, and though the table plainly shows the great reduction caused by the currency explosion in 1838, the aggregate for the eight years 1835–'42 under low duties was 576,859, or an average of 72,107 yearly, an increase of nearly 200 per cent. Yet these were the years of reduced duties, and non-protection, during which, it has been asserted, the condition of our laborers was exceedingly bad. The barometer indicates that it was at least 100 per cent. better than that of the protective period which preceded.

The protective tariff which went into effect with the year 1843 was coincident with a decided falling off of immigration—from 104,565 in 1842 to 52,496 for nine months of 1843, equal to about 70,000 for a year, and to 78,615 in the year 1844. The migration caused by disasters in England raised the aggregate for the whole period, 1843–'46, inclusive, to 399,898, or an average of 99,974 a year. But the aggregate for the four years preceding, 1839–1842, was 332,989, and the average 83,247 yearly; so that, with the English short crops to aid it, the protective tariff only attracted to this country an average of 16,727 more than had come hither during the four years of hard times, bank suspension, and commercial disorder. It is not strange that the advocates of that tariff seek to make it appear that its blessings were realized mainly after it had been repealed !

Contrasting, with this protective period of four years, the non-protective period 1847–'50 inclusive, we find that in the protective period the aggregate number of immigrants was 399,898, and in the non-protective period the aggregate was 1,188,499, and the yearly average 282,124, an increase of 282 per cent. If any opponent of protection could stoop to imitate Mr. Carey, in suppressing all mention of the Irish famine, he might make an argument at least as effective as the one already quoted. But, in fairness, the greater part of this immigration must be ascribed to causes in Europe. Following the Irish famine, came the great migration caused by the failure of revolutionary movements in Germany, in 1849 and 1850. But, with full allowance for these causes of increase, there is still evidence that the condition of laborers here was such as to offer greater inducements to immigrants than had been offered during the four years preceding.

It has been observed that the proportion of immigrants from Great Britain who came to this country was 62 per cent. in 1844, and only 55 per cent. in 1847. But in the next year, 1848, it rose to 75 per cent.; in 1849 it was 73 per cent.; and in 1850 and 1851 it was 80 per cent. These facts surely have great significance. Of persons driven from that country to seek homes in a new world, it appears that 50 per cent. chose this country in 1843, and 62 per cent. in 1844 and 1845, 63 per cent. in 1846, and only 55 per cent. in 1847. These years mark the relative condition of labor in this country during a period of protection—for the migration of 1847 was, of course, mainly influenced in selection by what was known prior to that year. But, in 1848–'51, the proportion of those who chose this country suddenly rose to 80 per cent. Of British emigrants to North America during the years 1843–'46, under protection, 121,684 went to Canada, and 212,772 to this country, the proportion being 60 to 100. But in 1848–'51 that proportion fell to 16 to 100. It may naturally be supposed that this difference was due to the discovery of gold in California, and a part of it doubtless was. But it must be remembered that a very small portion of British immigrants went to the mines; the great body of them came to find labor, either on farms, or in cities, or in mechanical employments, and they found it readily. Nor can it be supposed that the same cause continued to affect immigration after the mining excitement died out, but the immigration to Canada did not recover its proportion to that which chose this country during the whole of the period of low duties which followed, and was only 16 to 100 in 1848, 17 to 100 in 1855, 15 to 100 in 1856, and 11 to 100 in 1860. Thus, during this long period of non-interference with natural laws, the proportion of emigrants from Great Britain who chose this country as their home rather than Canada steadily increased, so that, where 60 had chosen Canada under the protective tariff, only 11 chose that country in 1860. It is not possible to ascribe the whole of this change to the discovery of gold in 1848. It simply corresponds with the fact, already well established, that, during the decade 1850–'60, labor of all kinds in this country was improving in condition, and the demand for it was increasing.

It only remains to show that the great decrease in immigration in 1855 was not owing to any unfavorable change in this country, but to improvement elsewhere. The immigration to this country fell from 427,000 to 200,000 in a single year; but, in the same year, the British immigration to Canada also fell from 43,000 to 18,000; and the migration to Australia from 83,000 to 52,000. The cause, whether it was the increased demand for labor arising from the Crimean War, or some other, was evidently not a change in this country, and, as has been shown, it did not prevent a still larger share of immigrants choosing this country in preference to Canada.

Since 1860, the movement has been retarded and afterward accelerated by the war, which created an enormous demand for labor in the years 1863, 1864, and 1865, and it has since been greatly increased by changes abroad. The crops in England have repeatedly proved insufficient. Political disturbances in Ireland have driven a throng of refugees to this country. The general prostration of manufactures in England has had a material effect. At the same time, the war involving Prussia, Austria, and Italy, and the great apprehension of a general strife, have led thousands to leave Europe; the annexation of new provinces to Prussia in 1866, with the consequent prospect of military service, drove away great numbers, and the opening of States formerly held by slave labor, and yet peculiarly rich in natural resources, like Virginia, Tennessee, and Missouri, has given an additional attraction to foreign labor. Nor must it be forgotten that our depreciated currency carries with its many evils one blessing—it gives our laborers wages nominally higher than are paid anywhere else, and in Europe, where the coin value of our dollar is known, while its depreciation is not fully understood, these high wages seem peculiarly attractive. Nevertheless, with all these potent causes working together to increase immigration, the number of arrivals during the four years 1865–'68 was only 1,162,247, against 1,128,499 in the four years 1847–'50, and 1,546,547 in the four years 1851–'54. With a combination of causes never existing before to drive or attract migration to this country, we are receiving less accessions than we did fifteen years ago under low duties, and scarcely more than we did nineteen years ago under the same non-protective tariff.

Any inference from this fact alone must be conjectural. For the weight of the influences mentioned, other than the present condition of labor here, cannot be measured, except in conjecture. But this, at least, is certain, that the present immigration does not contradict the teaching of the whole history prior to the war. And so fatal is that record to the theories of protectionists, that they have been forced to the theory that the magical prosperity of the laborer here, under protective tariffs, begins to have its effect upon immigration when those tariffs are repealed, while the exceedingly wretched condition of labor here, in times of low duties, does not begin to have its effect upon immigration until protection has been restored! "Who so excuses, accuses."

———————•••———————

CHAPTER XXV.

CONSUMPTION.

It doubtless has not escaped observation that certain articles, known to bear heavy duty, have not been at all times or correspondingly enhanced in price. Tea, coffee, and sugar, are the most important of these, and it has been noticed, in England as well as here, that the prices of these articles have been comparatively little affected by changes of duty. Giving the statistics which prove that tea in England has risen in price as duties have been removed, Mr. Wells remarks, "There is practically but one producing country, and the trade, therefore, partakes of the features of a monopoly." Perhaps the phenomenon may be more fully explained if we also consider that countries which produce a large surplus of any article, and are compelled to rely mainly upon the export of that for their foreign exchanges, are placed in an unnatural dependence upon their chief consumers. Any refusal by such a consumer to purchase their products, or to purchase of them except at a lower price, throws so large a surplus of the product upon the markets that the price is reduced. We were so situated with regard to cotton before the war, and China is in the same way dependent upon the chief consumers of her tea, Brazil of her coffee, and the West Indies of sugar. If England declined to buy freely of our cotton, it fell rapidly in price. In like manner, either England or the United States consumes so largely of sugar, coffee, and tea, that either can to some extent force the producer to pay any duty which threatens to check their consumption. Whatever cause we may assign, it is the fact that the prices of these three articles are not affected to the full amount of duties, but not infrequently fall in spite of an increased, or rise in spite of a decreased duty. Thus, in spite of the reduction of the duty on sugar from 3 to 2½ cents in 1832, the price, which had been 6 cents in 1831, and 6¼ in 1832, rose to 7¼ in 1833, and to 7 in 1834. But, under the same duty, the price fell to 4¾ in 1842, and rose to

6¾ again in 1846; and, though the change of duty to 30 per cent.
brought down the price at first to 4 cents, it rose again, and, in spite
of a still further reduction of duty to 24 per cent., stood steadily at
6 cents in 1858 and 1859, and at 5½ in 1860.   Similar facts may be
observed in the table of the price of coffee.   The removal of a duty
of 5 cents a pound in 1830–'32 only increased the price from 11¼ to
12½ cents.   The price of tea was more affected, yet it is observed
by economists that this article is usually less affected in price than
almost any other by changes of duty.

It happens that coffee and tea, two articles which are almost uni-
versally consumed, were absolutely free of duty if imported in
American ships from 1832 to 1862, a period of thirty years.   Nor
can it be said that the duties prior to 1832 had affected the price of
these articles nearly as much as other duties had affected the prices
of other articles of general use.   Of all articles, therefore, these are
the very best to test the general condition of the people at different
periods.   To these we may add sugar, for the duty on that article
has been very slightly changed.   In 1816, the duty on the quality
most largely imported was fixed at 3 cents a pound; in 1832 it was
changed to 2½ cents, and the same rate was preserved by the tariff
of 1842; in 1846 it was changed to 30 per cent.—a reduction of
less than one cent—and in 1857 to 24 per cent.; a change very slight
indeed.   These three articles are consumed, in different quantities,
indeed, by different classes and persons, but so generally that the
consumption affords, perhaps, the best test attainable of the progress
of the people as a whole toward comfort and prosperity.   In proportion as the country has thriven, the increase of consumption of
these articles has been accelerated, and, when the country has suffered, the consumption has either increased more slowly, or has been
temporarily reduced.   Thus the panic of 1837 reduced the consumption of tea from .915 thousandths of a pound per capita to .467; the
consumption of coffee from 6.1 pounds in 1835, and 5 pounds in 1836,
to 4.8 in 1837; and the "hard times" of 1843 again reduced it to
4.6 per capita.   In the same year the consumption of sugar fell to
11.29 pounds, though it had averaged over 13 pounds.   In like
manner the panic of 1857 cut down the consumption of sugar from
30.62 pounds to 26.10 pounds, and of coffee from about 8 pounds to
6 pounds; and the prostration of 1861 reduced the consumption of
sugar from 35.51 pounds to 28.45 pounds; of coffee from 7.3 pounds
to 5.8 pounds, and of tea from over one pound per capita to .79
hundredths of a pound.

Attention has been called to these details, because in England, and in other countries where extreme poverty and suffering exist, it has been found that the poor consume tea largely in place of more solid food. But no considerable class of persons in this country have ever been reduced to that point, nor is there reason to believe that the actual lack of bread and meat has at any time driven any appreciable proportion of the population to seek a substitute in the articles named. These articles have therefore been, in this country and in all times, not absolute necessities, but comforts, if not in some sense luxuries, and accordingly we find that in years of general prostration the consumption of them is suddenly diminished, while in times of great prosperity the consumption of these articles is very rapidly increased. No man of either party will deny that the years 1853–'54 were years of extraordinary prosperity. The consumption of sugar, only 23.90 pounds per capita in 1851, increased to over 33 pounds per capita in the years 1853 and 1854. It cannot, indeed, be supposed that the exact consumption for any year is known; in fact, it is stated, by men most familiar with the tea-trade, that not less than thirty million pounds were at one time on hand in this country, and any estimate based upon imports and exports only will be unreliable as to single years. But, for periods embracing several years, the consumption cannot vary materially from estimates based upon the imports, exports, known stock on hand as reported by the most competent authorities, and the domestic product in the case of sugar. From these data the following tables have been prepared, which show the amount of coffee, tea, and sugar, placed upon the market for consumption each year, the average prices each year in New York, and the rates of duty. Opposite the quantity entered as "consumed" each year is also entered the proportion of that quantity to the population in that year, but it must not be supposed that these figures represent with exactness the actual consumption in different years taken singly, for the reason just stated. Thus it will be observed, in tea and coffee especially, that unusually large imports in any year are often followed by imports unusually small, when the actual consumption was an average between the two. From 1850 onward, as the commissioner of the revenue has observed upon authority of the leading tea-dealers in this country, the amount imported was largely in excess of the actual consumption, so that the stock on hand was swollen to about thirty million pounds, and afterward, for several years, ending in 1860 and 1861, the stock was steadily reduced, the imports being less than the consumption. The average yearly con-

24

sumption for the whole decade, 1851 to 1860 inclusive, is therefore given, with the rate per capita. In other columns are presented the results for periods of several years each, during which, it is believed, the actual consumption cannot have varied to any appreciable extent from the statements thus prepared.

CONSUMPTION OF SUGAR.

YEAR.	Duty.	Taken for Consumption.	Per. Cap.	Consumption per Cap. In Periods of Years.	Average Price.
1821......	3 cents ℔ lb.	59,512,835	6.	4 years. 7.24	11½
1822......	"	88,305,670	8.57		9¼
1823......	"	60,789,210	5.73		9⅛
1824......	"	94,379,764	8.66		11⅝
1825......	"	71,771,479	6.52	4 years. 6.25	9¼
1826......	"	84,902,955	7.38		8¼
1827......	"	76,701,629	6.44		8½
1828......	"	56,985,951	4.67		8½
1829......	"	63,307,294	5.05	4 years. 6.22	7½
1830......	"	86,483,046	6.75		7
1831......	"	109,014,654	8.19		6
1832......	"	66,451,288	4.88		6½
1833......	2½ cents ℔ lb.	97,688,132	6.92	5 years. 9.21	7¼
1834......	"	115,389,855	7.95		7
1835......	"	126,036,230	8.56		7¾
1836......	"	191,426,115	12.42		9
1837......	"	161,092,811	10.19		6¾
1838......	"	201,624,719	12.44	5 years. 13.03	6¾
1839......	"	241,262,173	14.49		6¾
1840	"	194,764,937	11.45		5¾
1841......	"	232,103,397	13.26		6
1842......	"	243,274,422	13.51		4¾
1843......	"	209,056,749	11.29	4 years. 13.34	5¾
1844......	"	278,264,053	14.64		6¼
1845......	"	298,728,920	15.30		5¾
1846......	"	287,059,764	14.35		6¾
1847......	30 ℔ cent.	376,655,814	18.32	4 years. 19.47	6¼
1848......	"	474,637,773	21.65		4
1849......	"	453,456,333	20.60		4½
1850......	"	445,474,361	19.33		5
1851......	"	568,406,575	23.90	4 years. 29.66	5
1852......	"	706,086,000	28.70		4¾
1853......	"	835,495,360	33.02		4¾
1854......	"	863,067,520	33.02		4¾
1855......	"	846,164,480	31.45	4 years. 30.25	5¾
1856......	"	848,422,400	30.62		7¾
1857......	24 ℔ cent.	743,825,600	26.10		8½
1858......	"	965,780,480	32.85		6
1859......	"	1,072,370,880	35.51	2 years. 34.54	6
1860......	"	1,040,867,520	33.58		5½
1861......	"	922,096,000	28.45	5 years. 31.95	7
1862......	2 cents ℔ lb.	1,082,379,200	46.03		
1863......	3 cents ℔ lb.	762,720,000	31.25		
1864......	"	628,320,000	23.23		
1865......	"	922,880,000	30.76		
1866......	"	990,110,209	27.89	3 years. 27.47	
1867......	"	875,362,142	23.98		
1868......	"	1,145,444,163	30.54		

CONSUMPTION OF COFFEE.

YEAR.	Duty.	Consumed (lbs.).	Per Capita.	Consumption per Cap., yearly, in Periods.	Price (Rio).
1821.......	5 cents ℔ lb.	11,886,063	1.2		27½
1822.......	"	18,515,271	1.8	1.60	25¾
1823.......	"	16,437,045	1.5		23¼
1824.......	"	20,797,069	1.9		18¾
1825.......	"	20,678,062	1.8		17
1826.......	"	25,734,784	2.2	2.40	15
1827.......	"	28,354,197	2.4		14¼
1828.......	"	39,156,733	3.2		12¾
1829.......	"	33,049,695	2.6		12⅜
1830.......	"	38,363,687	2.9	3.45	11¼
1831.......	Free.	75,700,757	5.7		11¼
1832.......	"	36,471,241	2.6		12½
1833.......	"	75,057,906	5.3		12⅜
1834.......	"	44,346,505	3.0		11½
1835.......	"	91,753,002	6.1	4.84	11¾
1836.......	"	77,647,300	5.		11½
1837.......	"	76,044,071	4.8		10¾
1838.......	"	82,872,633	5.1		10¼
1839.......	"	99,872,517	6.		11
1840.......	"	86,297,761	5.1	5.66	10
1841.......	"	109,200,247	6.2		10
1842.......	"	107,383,567	5.9		8⅜
1843.......	"	85,916,666	4.6		7¼
1844.......	"	149,711,820	7.8	5.80	6½
1845.......	"	94,358,939	4.8		6¾
1846.......	"	124,336,054	6.		7
1847.......	"	150,332,992	7.3		7
1848.......	"	143,561,050	6.7	6.62	6
1849.......	"	150,954,271	6.9		6¾
1850.......	"	129,699,396	5.6		10½
1851.......	"	148,920,491	6.2		9
1852.......	"	204,991,595	8.3	7.05	8½
1853.......	"	175,687,790	6.9		8¾
1854.......	"	179,481,083	6.8		10⅛
1855.......	"	210,378,287	7.8		10⅛
1856.......	"	218,225,490	7.9	7.55	10¾
1857.......	"	172,565,934	6.		11
1858.......	"	251,255,099	8.5		10⅜
1859.......	"	222,610,300	7.3	6.45	11¼
1860.......	"	177,111,923	5.6		13½
1861.......	"	187,045,786	5.8		13¾
1862.......	5 cents ℔ lb.	88,989,911	3.8		22
1863.......	"	79,719,641	3.2	4.20	
1864.......	"	109,086,703	4.		
1865.......	"	128,146,356	4.2		
1866.......	"	159,918,881	4.5		
1867.......	"	203,506,671	5.6	5.33	
1868.......	"	223,200,937	5.9		

TEA.

Fiscal Years.	Quantity consumed.	Consumption, per Capita.	Price, Average, Y. Hyson.	Per Capita, yearly, by Periods.	Av. Price.
1821..........	4,586,223	.463	.93		
1822..........	5,305,588	.515	.90	.575	.94
1823..........	6,474,934	.610	.92		
1824..........	7,771,619	.713	1.02		
1825..........	7,173,740	.640	1.00		
1826..........	8,482,483	.737	.87	.538	.94
1827..........	3,070,885	.258	.96½		
1828..........	6,289,581	.516	.93½		
1829..........	5,602,795	.448	.92		
1830..........	6,873,091	.536	.88½	.491	.91
1831..........	4,656,681	.350	.98		
1832..........	8,627,144	.630	.88		
1833..........	12,927,043	.916	.75		
1834..........	13,193,553	.910	.61		
1835..........	12,331,638	.827	.58	.901	.64
1836..........	14,484,784	.940	.63½		
1837..........	14,465,722	.915	.61½		
1838..........	11,978,744	.740	.58		
1839..........	7,748,028	.467	.63		
1840..........	16,860,784	.990	.68	.712	65
1841..........	10,772,087	.615	.74		
1842..........	13,482,645	.749	.64		
1843..........	12,785,748	.691	.60		
1844..........	13,054,327	.686	.60	.759	.59
1845..........	17,162,550	.858	.60		
1846..........	16,891,020	.804	.58		
1847..........	14,221,910	.711	.52		
1848..........	20,876,861 est.	.975	.48½	.969	.49
1849..........	20,876,861	.952	.47½		
1850..........	28,752,817	1.239	.49½		
1851..........			.51		
1852..........	Average for		.49½		
1853..........	these years,		.45		
1854..........			.42½		
1855..........	27,363,965	1.019	.37	1.019	.38
1856..........			.37½		
1857..........			.42		
1858..........			.35½		
1859..........			.23		
1860..........	26,331,193	....	.25		
1861..........	25,520,000	.79	.43		
1862..........	27,468,600	1.17	.61½		
1863..........	26,906,365	1.10	.56½	.981	
1864..........	23,137,546	.85			
1865..........	29,853,433	.995			
1866..........	41,517,286	1.169			
1867..........	39,379,574	1.079	...	1.066	
1868..........	35,634,966	.950			

From 1821 to 1824 inclusive, when the duty on sugar was 3 cents for the quality usually imported, the yearly consumption averaged 7.24 pounds per capita. On tea the duty was 40 cents a pound for young hyson, and averaged from 30 to 34 cents on all teas, and the consumption, for the years 1821 to 1824 inclusive, was .575 thousandths of a pound per capita. On coffee the duty was 5 cents a pound, and the consumption was 1.60 pounds per capita. These duties remained absolutely unchanged until 1831, when the rate on coffee was reduced to 2 cents. With the exception of the last year, 1832, the duties on these three articles were not altered during the three periods of increased protection. If the general prosperity was great, if the condition of the laboring classes was really and materially improved, it is reasonable to infer that the consumption of these articles must have rapidly increased. Yet, excepting coffee, the consumption actually diminished! In the second protective period, 1825–'28 inclusive, the consumption of tea was .538 per capita, and the consumption of sugar only 6.25 per capita. In the third protective period, that of the highest duties, 1829–'32 inclusive, the consumption of tea was reduced to .491 per capita, notwithstanding a reduction of the price; and the consumption of sugar fell 6.22 per capita, notwithstanding a reduction in the price. Can it be believed that the great mass of the people were enjoying an increasing prosperity, at a time when the consumption of these articles was thus reduced?

That the reduction of price of tea and sugar would naturally have caused an increased consumption of those articles, it is fair to infer. If the condition of the laboring people had remained the same, it is surely reasonable to suppose that those who were able to spend in a given time one dollar for sugar or tea in the first period would have been disposed to spend at least an equal sum in the second and third, and an equal sum would have bought a larger quantity. But the fact is, that the average amount expended per capita was reduced. The price of sugar in the first period, 1821–'24, averaged 10 cents;* in the second, 1825–'28, only 8¼ cents; and in the third, 1829–'32, only 6¾ cents. The sum actually expended for sugar per capita in the first period was 72.4 cents yearly; in the second period it was 53.12 cents yearly; and in the third 41.98 cents yearly, so that the sum of money expended on the average yearly per capita for sugar was reduced from 72 cents in the first period, of low duties, to 42 cents in the third period, of extreme protection!

* Wholesale New-York prices are used for comparison in all these estimates.

Again, the average price of tea, taking young hyson, the most largely-imported variety, as the standard, in the first period, was 94 cents; in the second, 94 cents; and in the third, 91 cents. For tea, therefore, the average yearly expenditure per capita in the first period, of moderate duties, was 54.05 cents; in the second, of increased duties, it was 50.57 cents; and in the third, of highest duties, it was only 44.68 cents.

It must be remembered that no change of duty on these articles affected either their price or the consumption. Nor did a change of duty cause the great fall in the price of coffee, which was reduced from an average of 23¾ cents in the first period, to 14¼ cents in the second, and 12 cents in the third. This very large reduction in the price caused an increase of consumption. The consumption in the first period, of moderate duties, was 1.60 pounds per capita; in the second, of higher duties, 2.40 per capita; and in the third, of highest duties, 3.45 pounds per capita. Thus the sum actually expended yearly per capita in the first period was 37.98 cents; in the second, 35.40 cents; and in the third, 41.40 cents. In view of the enormous increase of consumption which immediately followed the removal of protection, this increase in the consumption of coffee, without any material increase in the sum of money expended per capita under protection, does not indicate an improved condition of the laboring classes.

It cannot be claimed that the use of any other articles superseded these three. Nor can it be claimed that their increased cost checked consumption. There was no change in the duty on these articles from 1821 to 1831, and during the last year, 1832, the duty on coffee only was changed. Yet the sum yearly expended per capita for these three articles of comfort and almost universal use was in the first period, 1821–'24, about $1.64; in the second period, 1825–'28, it was $1.39; and in the third period, of extreme protection, it was only $1.28. Is it possible to avoid the conclusion that a large share of the people restricted their use of these articles because their condition was such as to induce greater economy?

From 1832 onward, coffee and tea imported in American vessels were absolutely free until the year 1862. At the same time, as has been stated, the duty on sugar was but slightly changed, and its price but very slightly varied. The circumstances, therefore, render the consumption of these articles, separately and in the aggregate, a fair test of the general condition of the people at different periods. For convenience we may divide the thirty years into certain periods:

first, 1833–'37 inclusive, under reduced duties, period of currency expansion; second, 1838–'42 inclusive, under very low duties, period of currency contraction; third, 1843–'46 inclusive, period of protection; fourth, 1847–'50 inclusive, non-protection; and, finally, 1851–'60 inclusive, a decade of non-interference with the natural laws of industry and of growth. The contrast between these periods will be found decidedly instructive.

In the first of these periods the consumption of sugar suddenly jumped to 9.21 pounds per capita, of coffee to 4.84 per capita, and of tea to .901 per capita. A comparison of the prices shows that the increased consumption cannot be ascribed to a lower cost. Sugar averaged 7.55 cents; coffee, 11½ cents; and tea only 64 cents. The sum expended yearly per capita in sugar was 69.53 cents—an increase of 27 cents; in coffee, 55.66 cents—an increase of 14 cents; and in tea, 57.66 cents—an increase of 13 cents per capita. And the whole amount spent yearly per capita for these three articles was $1.82 against only $1.28 in the preceding period.

Can the conclusion be avoided that this largely-increased consumption indicates a rapid improvement in the condition of the laboring classes?

In the second period of contraction and panic, we find an increased consumption, except of tea, though the rapidity of increase is checked. Of sugar there were consumed 13.03 pounds, average price, 5.9 cents; cost per capita, 76.87 cents; of coffee there were consumed 5.66 pounds, price, 9.9 cents; cost per capita, 56.25 cents; and of tea .712 per capita, cost .65 cents; expense per capita, 46.28 cents. The aggregate yearly expenditure per capita for these articles was therefore $1.79 against $1.82 in the preceding period: Here can be seen, traced with unerring hand, the record of general depression, retarded progress in wealth, and increased economy, which it is known were the characteristics of that period.

But if the panic and prostration of 1838–'42 quite plainly checked consumption, the tariff of 1842–'46, with its extreme protection, operated still more powerfully in the same direction. It is exceedingly curious to observe how plainly the averages for this period disclose that embarrassment of the working-classes, and particularly of the farmers, the great body of consumers, which we have already inferred from other records. The consumption of sugar yearly per capita was 13.34 pounds, not a third of a pound more than the consumption in the period of panic. The consumption of coffee was 5.80 per capita, only fourteen-hundredths of a pound more than in the period of prostration, although the average price had fallen 3 cents. And the consumption of tea rose to .759 per capita, an increase of only forty-seven thousandths of a pound, though the price had fallen on the average 6 cents a pound. Thus the aggregate yearly expenditure per capita for these articles was only $1.67 under the tariff of 1842–'46, though it had been $1.79 in the "hard times" which preceded it. Is it possible to make more conclusive the demonstration that to the laboring people of the country the protective tariff of 1842 gave times harder than "the hard times," even though to capital employed in manufacturing it gave enormous profits?

The removal of the tariff in 1846 enables us to contrast the four years under its operation with the four years that followed under low duties, ending with 1850. In that period, as in every other when high duties have been withdrawn, consumption started forward, as well as the production of wealth, as a powerful spring will bound upward when the weight is removed which has held it down. The consumption of sugar was 19.47 pounds per capita, an increase of nearly 50 per cent.; of coffee 6.62 pounds per capita, an increase of nearly one pound; and of tea .969, an increase of two-tenths of a pound. Thus the aggregate yearly expenditure per capita for these three articles, which under protection had been $1.67, was increased to $1.94.

The increase in the consumption of sugar and coffee in the four years 1851–'54 inclusive, is still more remarkable. The quantity of sugar consumed yearly per capita rose more than ten pounds, to 29.66, the price having changed only a fraction of a cent. The quantity of coffee increased nearly half a pound, the price having nevertheless risen more than $1\frac{1}{2}$ cent. Supposing the consumption of tea to have been the same during these years as during the whole decade—it was doubtless less, but how much less it is not possible to determine—the aggregate value of these articles consumed yearly was $2.36. Again, in the next period of four years, though the price of sugar rose to 7 cents, the consumption increased in quantity; and, though the price of coffee increased to $10\frac{1}{4}$ cents, the consumption increased half a pound. Adding the decennial average for tea, as before, the aggregate value consumed was $3.28 per capita. The panic of 1857 and an increase of price checked consumption of coffee in 1858–'60, so that the average quantity consumed for the two years 1859–'60 is slightly smaller, though the value is higher. Sugar rose rapidly in quantity, but the price was so much reduced,

CONSUMPTION OF TEA, COFFEE, AND SUGAR, AS A TEST OF GENERAL PROSPERITY.

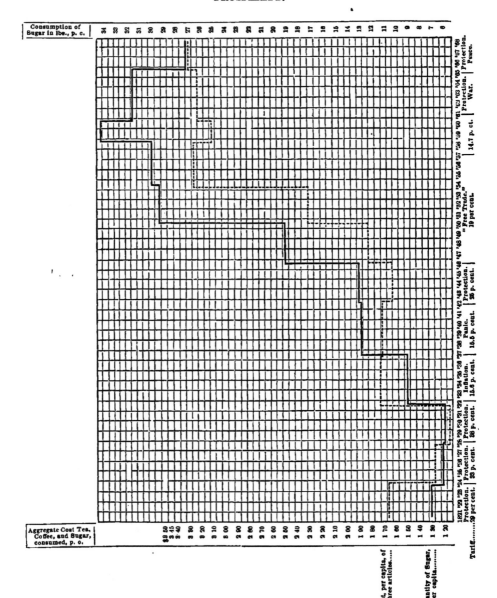

that the aggregate value is only $3.17 yearly. These statistics may be more readily understood by aid of the diagram, which shows the average cost of the three articles, tea, coffee, and sugar, consumed in each period, with the average quantity of sugar, and it will be observed that the reduced price of sugar in 1859–'60 causes more than the whole apparent decrease of consumption by value. The contrast between every period of protection and the nearest period of lower duties or non-protection will strike the eye at once. These figures and facts are not needed to prove that the country has advanced more rapidly in production of wealth during each period of low duties, and especially during the decade of non-interference, 1850–'60, than under any protective tariff. But they are of value because they show that, while the aggregate wealth of the country was increasing, it was so fairly distributed that the working-people, the farmers and mechanics who form the great body of consumers, were able to increase more rapidly than ever before their expenditure for articles of comfort, and their consumption of such articles. Tried by this test, every protective tariff since 1821 has either actually decreased the consumption of these articles, or has checked the natural increase, and, we infer, has unfavorably affected the condition of the laboring classes as a whole. Tried by this test, every non-protective tariff since 1821 has greatly increased the consumption of these articles, and, we infer, has improved the condition of the laboring classes on the whole.

The tariff period of 1861–'69 is no exception to the rule, although it has been purposely omitted from the examination thus far, because it may be said that the war, the inflation of currency, or the high prices, have affected the consumption. The prices of coffee, sugar, and tea, however, have not been higher in proportion than those of other articles generally, and the use of coffee and sugar for the army largely added to the consumption. Whatever causes may be assigned, the fact remains that in this period, both during and since the war, the consumption of these articles has been reduced or its natural increase checked. For the war period, 1861–'65, the consumption of sugar was 31.95 pounds per capita, estimating only by the population within our military lines, and since the war, 1866–'68 inclusive, the consumption has been only 27.47 pounds per capita— more than three pounds less than the consumption before the war. The consumption of coffee was, during the war, only 4.20 pounds, and since the war only 5.33 pounds per capita—less by nearly two pounds than the consumption before the war. And the consumption of tea during the war was only .981, and since the war 1.066 pounds per capita—a very slight increase as compared with the consumption of 1.019 before the war. Taking the average of the whole protective period, the consumption of sugar was 30.28 pounds, of coffee 4.6 pounds, and of tea 1.012 pounds, per capita—a decrease in the quantity of each article, as compared with the decade before the war. The prices, stated in currency or in gold, would, however, show an increase, but it must be remembered that the general average of prices and of wages has been at least correspondingly increased.

The principle holds good, therefore, that high duties have in every case reduced or checked the increase of the consumption of tea, coffee, and sugar, and the sum of money which the laboring classes have been disposed to expend on these three comforts. On the other hand, low duties have in every case rapidly increased the consumption, both in quantity and in the sum of money which the laboring classes have thus expended. Students of political economy will, we think, at once agree that the three articles chosen, as they are those of general use, the consumption of which can be most accurately ascertained, so they form, taken in connection with the prices, the most reliable test which can be found of the general condition of the working-people. Salt is an article of absolute necessity rather than of comfort or luxury. The consumption of soap— which some profound economists have regarded as the best test of progress in civilization—cannot be accurately ascertained. Neither can the quantity of meat consumed, nor of clothing used, be reliably ascertained. Tried by the best obtainable test, then, the protection of American industry proves an embarrassment and a burden to American labor.

CONSUMPTION OF TEA, COFFEE, AND SUGAR, AT DIFFERENT PERIODS, PER CAPITA, WITH PRICE AND COST.

CHARACTER OF TARIFF.	Periods.	SUGAR.			COFFEE.			TEA.			Total Cost.
		Consumption P. C.	Price.	Cost.	Consumption P. C.	Price.	Cost.	Cons. P. C.	Price.	Cost.	
Protection, 29 p. c.......	1821-1824	7.24	10.	72.40	1.60	23.75	37.98	.575	.94	54.05	164.43
Protection, 33 p. c.......	1825-1828	6.25	8.5	53.12	2.40	14.75	35.40	.538	.94	50.57	139.09
Protection, 38 p. c.......	1829-1832	6.22	6.75	41.98	3.45	12.	41.40	.491	.91	44.68	128.06
Non-protection, 15½ p. c.	1833-1837	9.21	7.55	69.53	4.84	11.50	55.66	.901	.64	57.66	182.85
Non-protection, 15½ p. c.	1838-1842	13.03	5.9	76.87	5.66	9.9	56.25	.712	.65	46.28	179.40
Protection, 25 p. c.	1843-1846	13.34	6.25	83.37	5.80	6.9	40.02	.759	.59	44.78	167.40
Non-protection, 19 p. c..	1847-1850	19.47	5.	97.35	6.62	7.5	49.65	.969	.49	47.48	194.48
Non-protection, 19 p. c..	1851-1854	29.66	4.78	131.77	7.05	9.19	64.78	} 1.019	38.7	39.43	235.98
Non-protection, 19 p. c..	1855-1858	30.25	7.	211.75	7.55	10.28	77.61				328.79
Non-protection, 14.7 p. c.	1859-1860	34.54	5.75	198.60	6.45	12.37	79.78	..	..	..	317.81
Protection (war)........	1861-1865	31.95	..	..	4.20	..	..	.981	..	..	..
Protection (peace)......	1866-1868	27.47	..	..	5.33	..	..	1.066	..	..	..

CHAPTER XXVI.

CONCLUSION.

No candid inquirer can attempt the investigation of this question without a constant sense of the imperfectness of his information, and the liability to error in the details of his work. But I have honestly tried to present the facts, as far as I could ascertain them, without distortion or unfairness, that every reader may judge for himself whether they sustain the conclusions to which I have been led.

It appears to me that protection does not stop excessive importations, nor turn the balance of trade in our favor; that it checks importations only for a short time, until its effect is felt in the arrest of improvement or the increased cost of production; and that it retards exports more than imports, and thus enlarges the balance of trade against us. The fact that in every period of high duties the proportion of manufactured products exported has decreased, while in every period of low duties it has increased, seems to prove that the protective system puts our manufacturing industry, as a whole, at a disadvantage in competition with that of other countries. Nor can the prostration of shipping and ship-building be regarded as a matter of small moment.

It seems to me that the natural progress of this country in the production of wealth has been retarded by the protective system. From agriculture we derive about three-fourths of that production, and the progress of that great industry has certainly been greater in non-protective than in protective periods. I cannot find any evidence that the loss by retarding the progress of this industry has been compensated—that the natural growth of other industries, producing in the aggregate only one-fourth as much, has been so greatly accelerated by protection as to pay for any loss through agriculture. On the contrary, it seems to me that more than two-thirds of the production of wealth by mechanic arts and manufactures is by branches of industry which are of necessity, and, in point of fact, ever have been, retarded in their natural growth by the protective system.

Neither do the records show that those great industries which have been especially protected have been hastened in any healthy growth by legislative favor. All of them throve before they were protected; all of them made remarkable progress during the long period of low duties, from 1846 to 1861, and each one of them achieved the greatest triumph in solid and healthy improvement, when pressed by natural competition and unchecked by artificial burdens. But, under high tariffs, certain pet interests have been invested with the tape-worm's faculty of feeding upon the vitals of all other manufactures; and while, under this infliction, our industry, as a whole, has suffered, these favored interests have grown, like the tape-worm, not in self-sustaining vigor, but only in useless length and destructive voracity.

The aggregate ability of any country to employ labor must depend upon its production of wealth; and, if the production of wealth in the aggregate has been retarded in its natural growth, the demand for labor, and the remuneration of labor, in the aggregate, must likewise have been retarded in their natural increase. I think the facts prove that the wages of labor, in the aggregate, have been lower, measured by their purchasing power, in times of protection than in times of non-protection; that the rewards of agriculture have been diminished by high tariffs, its expenses increased, and yet, through increased friction in exchanges, the cost of agricultural products has not been in like degree lessened to the consumer; and that even the manufacturing laborers have not, under protective tariffs, enjoyed any increase of wages sufficient to compensate them for the increased cost of living.

These conclusions as to the condition of labor in different periods have been confirmed, at every point: first, by the record of the movement of immigration to this country as compared with others; and, second, by the record of the consumption of articles of comfort and general use. These facts seem to me to prove, with regard to protective tariffs generally, that which Mr. Wells so convincingly proved with regard to the system now in force—that it does not benefit but injures the laboring classes.

Unless these conclusions are erroneous, it must be conceded that American labor cannot be helped by loading and taxing it; that a system which injures a country in its foreign exchanges, which retards its natural growth in the production of wealth, and which leads to such a distribution of wealth that the rich grow richer and the poor poorer, can in no wise benefit a nation; in a word, that protection does not protect.

What is the attempt to protect but a confession of weakness? How often we hear it, "American industry, because it is free, needs protection." Does freedom, then, put an industry at a disadvantage in comparison with others? Is freedom a source of weakness? Surely, history proves that freedom is strength. For freedom means intelligence, hope, activity of mind, the highest stimulus to all the faculties; it means industry, child of unbounded aspiration, married to inventive genius. Brains are better than tariffs. The mechanic who fears pauper-labor or prison-labor ranks himself below its level.

Yet " we must build up a home market." Statistics prove that manufactures in the aggregate have not increased as rapidly with protection as without it. Protection does not build up a home market; it only retards the natural progress of the country toward diversification of industry. Not only this, but it retards the increase of those facilities of transportation which bring all the markets of the world to the door of every farmer, and double the value of his farm.

It will be said, with truth, that the evils which have been traced as resulting from protective tariffs have been partly caused by an attempt to protect too many interests at once. It is a common mistake to suppose that, if protection is good for one industry, it must be good for all. High duties on one article may secure the market to the American producer; therefore, men mistakenly reason, high duties on all articles will protect everybody at once. A duty on one article may not affect at all the cost of producing others. But duties on three thousand articles, each duty being diffused in its effect through a whole community, must have some power to increase the cost of producing every thing, and thus must not only tend to neutralize every benefit contemplated, but to put even our most natural industries at a disadvantage. In proportion as protective tariffs are *broad*, or cover many industries, they defeat themselves. In a despotism, single interests can be persistently favored by law—possibly to some effect. But no republic will tolerate such exclusive favoritism. No tariff can be passed for protection that does not promise benefit to a great number of interests. And, therefore, in republics, where labor is free and intelligent, and needs less protection than other labor, precisely there protection most surely defeats itself. In this country, at least, it is a necessary feature of any protective system that it shall cover a great many interests, and so greatly increase the cost of production.

Again, it will be said, with truth, that the evils which have been traced are largely due to the frequent changes of the tariff. But this, also, is an inevitable consequence of protection by a republican government. A despotism, deaf to all popular clamor, can cling to a fixed policy for a century. A free government, doing the same, would cease to be a free government. If the taxation designed for protection could be distributed with exact equality, and the benefits derived could also be distributed with exact equality, every man who should receive ten dollars in the increased price of his products, would be taxed just ten dollars in the increased cost of articles purchased. To protect everybody equally is to protect nobody at all. The only possible effect, for good or evil, must arise from such unequal distribution of burdens and benefits as may help some at the expense of others. In proportion as a protective tariff is just to all interests, it benefits none. It can only have effect in proportion as it helps certain classes at the expense of other classes; the monopoly· feature of protection alone prevents it being a nullity. But, in a free government, any monopoly, whether absolute or qualified, is unpopular, and must be short-lived. The strife of interests for a greater share of benefits, or for release of burdens, must be constant, and, as long as the people are free, there must result, from every attempt to protect, frequent changes, and constant fear of change. Fear of change neutralizes the stimulus which peculiar favors give. Frequent change prostrates all industry. Hence, in proportion as tariffs are protective, they tend to defeat themselves, and to expose all industry to fluctuations.

Once more, it will be said that the evils which have been traced result, in part, from defective adjustment of duties between different interests. This is also true. It is a misfortune that even our wisest Congressmen are not wiser than the Creator. The laws of the universe which He has devised do not suit the advocates of protection, who desire to mend them. It is to be regretted that finite wisdom is not yet quite equal to the task; but the historian, upon a candid review of its performances, must sadly confess that it is not. The attempt to make an artificial world, instead of the one in which we live, can hardly be expected to meet with complete success, until men become able to mend those natural laws of trade which the Creator devised as the most beneficial stimulus for human industry. If protection could accomplish what its honest advocates desire; if it could build up some industries without injuring others more important; if it could enhance the price at which three thousand domestic products may be sold, and, at the same time, not enhance the cost of production; if it could get revenue, and yet exclude imports, and force a natural borrower to cease asking for money; if it could rid manufacture of competition without depriving it of the main stimulus to improvement; if it could contrive to so please everybody as to be permanent, and yet give benefits to some at the expense of others; if it could tax the whole country for the benefit of capitalists, and yet contrive to secure to all labor a larger share in the distribution of wealth; if, in short, it could take these United States and put them off on a planet by themselves, with artificial sun and moon, artificial air and water, and create for us a world better than that which God has made—then, protection would be a good thing! But the atttempt has not, thus far, been entirely successful.

We are here, in a world of labor and progress, linked, by ties which we cannot break, to our fellow-men in other lands. Whether we like it or not, we are forced to share something of their burdens, and to partake with them of the blessings which the progress of humanity secures. Science and invention have marvellously reduced the cost of supplying the necessities of life, and this nation cannot be altogether deprived of a share in the blessing. Our manufactures must either keep pace with the progress of improvement, or they must give room to industries more thrifty and profitable. With every year, increased facilities for communication bring distant nations closer to each other, and weld together into a more compact body all races of men. France orders by telegraph thousands of silk-cocoons from China, and ships them from Canton, by railway across this continent, to Lyons. Orders from New York are delivered at Liverpool within an hour; German bankers receive instructions at two o'clock, sell our bonds before three, transfer the gold by telegraph to New York, and sell that for currency before it is three o'clock in Wall Street. No longer can the Atlantic or the Pacific shut out a people from the influence of foreign trade and foreign industry. With every step of progress it becomes more clearly impossible to fence up a nation against competition; and high tariffs, never efficacious for protection, are constantly losing their power for good, and gaining only in power for evil. As the system of exchange becomes more perfect, the operations of commerce more rapid, the means of intercommunication more complete, the burdens imposed by any interference with natural laws are diffused the more quickly and thoroughly through the whole community; and thus, with every year, protective tariffs more speedily defeat themselves. It is time for the people of this country to seriously consider the truth that high duties cannot overturn the natural laws of exchange, nor wall up any nation against foreign competition. If the system

25

of protection was ever necessary, it is not now. Its burdens are real—its benefits unsubstantial. The manufacturer gets higher prices, but his goods cost him more. The laborer gets higher wages, but living costs him more. A short season of large profits and unhealthy growth in any industry—unhealthy, because not based upon solid improvement in comparison with like industry elsewhere—is followed by prostration, ruinous alike to the most useful and the most useless workers, and, more quickly than ever before, each protective tariff is followed by a pitiful appeal for more protection. How long shall it take us to discover that children who are always carried will never learn to walk?

When I began this inquiry, I still believed, as in earlier days I had been taught,-that, while the tariff was confessedly defective, permanent protection in some form and degree must be beneficial. The inquiry has led me to the conviction that protection, as a permanent policy, if ever useful, no longer benefits American labor as a whole; that its supposed benefits are mainly unreal, and, when they are real, fall to the share of capital, and do not improve the condition or stimulate the energy and inventive genius of labor; and that this country, realizing its natural superiority of resources, and its vast advantages in political freedom and intelligence of labor, should henceforth seek prosperity through the only efficient and enduring protection which can be given to industry—the removal of all unnecessary burdens. That inquiry has convinced at least one person that we need nothing else so much as to stimulate the native vigor and inventive power of our industry, by competition with the labor and skill of other countries. The best protection for industry is to let it alone. Human wisdom cannot better, by artificial laws, the conditions under which the Creator has placed human labor by the natural laws of exchange. The world which He has given us is, in those provisions, the work of a higher intelligence than legislators have at their command; they may mar, but can never mend it, by interfering with its fundamental laws.

INDEX OF TABLES.

THE END.

"Unquestionably the best living writer on Political Economy."—
PROF. BOWEN.

D. APPLETON & CO., 90, 92 & 94 GRAND STREET,

HAVE JUST PUBLISHED

Principles of Political Economy,

WITH SOME OF THEIR APPLICATIONS OF

SOCIAL PHILOSOPHY.

BY JOHN STUART MILL.

2 Vols., 8vo. *Printed on Tinted Paper.* *Cloth,* $6.

That there has heretofore been no American edition of a work held in such high estimation, may, perhaps, be owing in part to the fact that since its publication our politics have hinged on an engrossing question, which belongs rather to the domain of humanitarian philosophy than to that of political economy, and partly to the facility with which a European work not requiring translation can be supplied to American readers from the original publishers. The present state of our currency goes far to remove both of these obstacles to the success of an American edition. The most important economic discussions which have ever taken place in Great Britain grew out of the condition into which that country was brought by its protracted struggle against Napoleon. Our politics are likely to pass through a similar phase, in which we shall need all the light shed upon economic questions by the most advanced science.

In the whole range of extant authorship on political economy, there is no writer except Adam Smith with whom John Stuart Mill can, without injustice, be compared. In originality, Adam Smith, as being the acknowledged father of the science, takes the precedence, as he does also in exuberance of apt illustration. But in rectitude of understanding, clearness, and sagacity, Mill is fully his peer; in precision of method, range of topics, and adaptation to the present state of society, he is altogether his superior. The "Wealth of Nations" now belongs, indeed, rather to the history of the science than to its exposition. But the "Principles of Political Economy" is an orderly, symmetrical, and lucid exposition of the science in its present advanced state. In extent of information, breadth of treatment, pertinence of fresh illustration, and accommodation to the present wants of the statesman, the merchant, and the social philosopher, this work is unrivalled. It is written in a luminous and smooth, yet clear cut style; and there is diffused over it a soft atmosphere of feeling, derived from the author's unaffected humanity and enlightened interest in the welfare of the masses.